Sustainable Development Goals Series

The **Sustainable Development Goals Series** is Springer Nature's inaugural cross-imprint book series that addresses and supports the United Nations' seventeen Sustainable Development Goals. The series fosters comprehensive research focused on these global targets and endeavours to address some of society's greatest grand challenges. The SDGs are inherently multidisciplinary, and they bring people working across different fields together and working towards a common goal. In this spirit, the Sustainable Development Goals series is the first at Springer Nature to publish books under both the Springer and Palgrave Macmillan imprints, bringing the strengths of our imprints together.

The Sustainable Development Goals Series is organized into eighteen subseries: one subseries based around each of the seventeen respective Sustainable Development Goals, and an eighteenth subseries, "Connecting the Goals," which serves as a home for volumes addressing multiple goals or studying the SDGs as a whole. Each subseries is guided by an expert Subseries Advisor with years or decades of experience studying and addressing core components of their respective Goal.

The SDG Series has a remit as broad as the SDGs themselves, and contributions are welcome from scientists, academics, policymakers, and researchers working in fields related to any of the seventeen goals. If you are interested in contributing a monograph or curated volume to the series, please contact the Publishers: Zachary Romano [Springer; zachary.romano@springer.com] and Rachael Ballard [Palgrave Macmillan; rachael.ballard@palgrave.com].

More information about this series at
https://link.springer.com/bookseries/15486

Paul J.J. Welfens

Global Climate Change Policy

Analysis, Economic Efficiency Issues
and International Cooperation

Paul J.J. Welfens
European Institute for International Economic Relations
University of Wuppertal
Wuppertal, Germany

ISSN 2523-3084	ISSN 2523-3092 (electronic)
Sustainable Development Goals Series
ISBN 978-3-030-94593-0	ISBN 978-3-030-94594-7 (eBook)
https://doi.org/10.1007/978-3-030-94594-7

© The Editor(s) (if applicable) and The Author(s), under exclusive licence to Springer Nature Switzerland AG 2022

Translation from the English language edition: Klimaschutzpolitik - Das Ende der Komfortzone by Paul J.J. Welfens, © Springer Fachmedien Wiesbaden GmbH 2019. Published by Springer. All Rights Reserved.

Color wheel and icons: From https://www.un.org/sustainabledevelopment/, Copyright © 2020 United Nations. Used with the permission of the United Nations.

The content of this publication has not been approved by the United Nations and does not reflect the views of the United Nations or its officials or Member States.

This work is subject to copyright. All rights are solely and exclusively licensed by the Publisher, whether the whole or part of the material is concerned, specifically the rights of reprinting, reuse of illustrations, recitation, broadcasting, reproduction on microfilms or in any other physical way, and transmission or information storage and retrieval, electronic adaptation, computer software, or by similar or dissimilar methodology now known or hereafter developed.

The use of general descriptive names, registered names, trademarks, service marks, etc. in this publication does not imply, even in the absence of a specific statement, that such names are exempt from the relevant protective laws and regulations and therefore free for general use.

The publisher, the authors and the editors are safe to assume that the advice and information in this book are believed to be true and accurate at the date of publication. Neither the publisher nor the authors or the editors give a warranty, expressed or implied, with respect to the material contained herein or for any errors or omissions that may have been made. The publisher remains neutral with regard to jurisdictional claims in published maps and institutional affiliations.

This Palgrave Macmillan imprint is published by the registered company Springer Nature Switzerland AG.
The registered company address is: Gewerbestrasse 11, 6330 Cham, Switzerland

Preface

Since 2016, the challenge presented by long-term global warming and the topic of climate protection have increasingly become key issues in society, for the political sphere and for the business community worldwide. The expectations of the younger generation (and indeed also of the older generations) in many countries have risen noticeably. The digital, Internet-connected world ensures that the pros and cons of more climate protection policy or even the risks of political inaction are discussed on a much more international basis than was the case before the year 2000. This development may also be due to the fact that climate instability is indeed a global problem; in other words, it rightly concerns people in around 200 countries. In many OECD countries, climate policy has become a major topic on the political agenda – under the government of Prime Minister Boris Johnson in the UK, under the Biden administration in the US and in Germany in 2021 under the impact of a massive increase in the political popularity of the German Green Party. The British government's goal of cutting greenhouse gases by 68 percent by 2030 makes the UK a European leader in climate policy. However, British pragmatism which combines nuclear power with strong renewable energy investment, electrical mobility expansion and carbon capture and storage (CCS) approaches might deliver progress in climate policy which in turn seems to be a new strategic policy field for British post-Brexit ambitions in terms of an international leadership role. To the extent that UK climate policy initiatives could be combined with a renewed US green modernization policy under the Biden administration in the US, British sustainability and climate policy initiatives could achieve considerable progress. As financial services are a key sector in the British economy, the many new pro-climate protection approaches in the financial sector of OECD countries could allow British financial services providers to become pioneers in sustainable financing of private investment and the placement of green government bonds from many countries.

The Corona shock of 2020, the global pandemic challenge, has displaced the climate policy priorities on many agendas for more than a year. However, economic recovery plans in Germany, France, Italy, Spain and the whole EU include extra spending for climate policy modernization. Moreover, the European Commission strengthened the CO_2 reduction goal for 2030: 55 percent relative to the benchmark year 1990 is a major challenge for all EU countries. This will be, above all, a new field of innovation for industrialized countries and indeed for other country groups in the future, not least because prudential supervision has started to focus on climate change risk in banks and insurance companies in OECD countries since 2020—with the first climate change risk-related banking stress tests in the UK and the Eurozone in 2021.

The global warming problem ranges from the inhabitants of Fiji, who fear losing their residential and commercial areas as well as agricultural space to rising sea levels, to the better-positioned, from an information and educational perspective, populations of Western countries plus Russia, Japan, China, Indonesia, Brazil, Mexico, South Africa and India, which are active as a group together in the Group of Twenty (G20) with other countries. In contrast to the leading and largest economies, Fiji has a different approach. There, the government hopes for support from the United Nations (UN). The great contradiction that is visible in many countries between hesitant climate protection and economic policies on the one hand, and the reports of the Intergovernmental Panel on Climate Change (IPCC), an international expert group which are increasingly calling for quicker and more energetic policy action with regard to climate protection, on the other hand, is giving rise to concerns about a secure future for millions of people worldwide. With the new Biden administration, the US has returned to the UN Paris Climate Agreement, and a new start in the field of climate policy cooperation between the US and China has become visible in 2021.

The creation of emissions trading systems (ETS) went along with the government distributing many emission certificates for free to several sectors and many firms, particularly in the tradables sector. It is little known to the general public that a decade of analysis of economists has shown that a free certificate allocation of more than 20 percent of CO_2 emissions (more strictly, greenhouse gas emission certificates) brings major redistribution effects in favor of capital and investors, respectively. While so many parties and politicians in Europe—and in some US states—complain about excessive and growing economic inequality, dozens of governments have been active in reinforcing inequality by broad generous free allocations of CO_2 emission certificates to many companies. This is a strange paradox. Moreover, many governments in OECD countries have introduced new CO_2 taxes in certain sectors, despite the fact that bringing those sectors into an emissions trading system would be so much more efficient—cheaper for the taxpayer, but just as effective for climate protection progress. There are yet more contradictions at the national and international level.

As regards the introduction of ETS in the EU in 2005, and of some cooperation of California's ETS with an ETS in Canada (if temporary in the case of Ontario), one can see that institutional innovations helping to sort CO_2 emission problems can prosper for some time. Ontario's repealing of its ETS after just six months also suggests that there might be lack of stable political support for ETS. In the EU, most people in 2020 had no real idea what the pioneering emissions trading system actually does or means: there is an apparent contradiction between successful climate policy of government on the one hand and the lack of governments' seeming willingness to explain new policy concepts to the broader public on the other—a strange and unnecessary policy pitfall in the digital age in which more information for everybody should be expected from government authorities. In Asia, China's launching of a new, national ETS (with an exclusive focus on the energy sector) in 2021 has been a visible sign that institutional innovations are relatively quickly picked up by the West's new big rival in Asia.

Meanwhile in Europe, an increasingly concerned young generation has turned its attention to the challenges of climate policy. Fridays for Future is the new international movement which enjoys considerable support among many scientists. However, it is not true that all scientists with strong research backgrounds in sustainability and climate protection hold the same view. The argumentation of Fridays for Future that "science" is behind them and that there is little to discuss when it comes to alternative means and strategies for achieving climate neutrality is misleading. Non-government institutions—often with many more members than even leading political parties—have become crucial drivers of climate policy in many countries, but not always with solid analytical background. In a publication in April 2021, the World Wildlife Fund (WWF) was calling for an increase in the annual minimum reduction of greenhouse gases in the EU beyond the existing requirements in the 2020s—a step for which good arguments exist, not least since the EU has raised its goal for CO_2 reduction by 2030 calling (WWF: Raising the Climate Policy Ambition of the European Union). However, one can raise doubts about the WWF calls for measures that would largely increase the burden of greater CO_2 emission reductions in the EU on the sectors already subject to the current EU ETS (read: energy and industry); rather one should consider extending the coverage of the existing ETS to a larger number of sectors—as a share of national income, energy and industry stand for around 40 percent in the EU; with a coverage of 80 percent of CO_2 emissions via a modernized ETS, the minimum annual CO_2 reduction requirement could be achieved in a far less dramatic way than what the WWF is calling for. Very rapid structural change would be extremely costly in terms of stranded assets (whose market value is moving toward 0) and jobs lost. Without an adequate economic analysis and modeling of climate change policy—or a mix of fiscal policy, monetary policy and climate policy—there are bleak prospects for fast global progress in climate protection. In this context, the modeling of foreign direct investment and multinationals in DSGE macro models has just started as a new research paper by Werner Roeger and myself (see Chap. 1) has shown, and there are still several steps to take in order to include an ETS for CO_2 emissions in such a macro model plus endogenous innovation and growth.

Since 2018, the Fridays for Future movement in particular has been active among young people with regular demonstrations every Friday to express climate concerns. The traditional environmental and climate protection policy, which in the past has delivered partial results very slowly over many years, is increasingly being criticized. The end of the political comfort zone is foreseeable for many politicians, and many people are now asking whether the politicians will reach the climate protection targets, which have previously been announced to much acclaim and fanfare, in 2030, 2040 or 2050. Here, new long-term voter interests have emerged that stand in the way of the traditionally rather short-term political horizons. The contradictions are obvious.

A particular contradiction is the case of the US, where President Trump distanced his country from the Paris UN Climate Agreement of 2015. Trump argued that global warming is not a serious problem and certainly not influenced by human beings and anthropocentric influences; it is unclear why Trump ignored the consensus view of all leading climate research institutes, including those in the US. He clearly does not like the idea that global warming has been significantly influenced by industrialized Western countries. At the same time, he considers that there is a trade-off between economic growth and environmental protection/stopping global warming (which is strongly related to CO_2 emissions). This, however, completely overlooks some basic advantages of CO_2 pricing through CO_2 taxes or CO_2 certificate markets: CO_2 taxes/certificates clearly help achieving a better long-run global climate situation, that is, less global warming, which thus is a first benefit of CO_2 pricing. A second benefit can be obtained from fiscal recycling, namely that the additional government revenues will largely be used to lower income taxes, income tax-related distortions and income dampening effects on the one hand and, third, to provide higher subsidies for more research and development—ideally with a climate-friendly focus—on the other; and thusly to achieve a higher innovation intensity which will go along with positive national or international spillovers. A triple dividend from CO_2 taxation or CO_2 emission certificate selling by government is possible.

The role of the US is crucial. As regards the new Biden administration, it is noteworthy how quickly the new US president has adopted a policy agenda in favor of climate protection; however, the broad concept of Spring 2021, which entails many elements in favor of green innovation and electrical mobility, has not included support for a national initiative to move toward introducing an emissions trading system. It is unclear whether or not the Biden administration will emphasize the crucial role of ETS going forward. At least California—with an economy that will be close to Germany's GDP within a decade—has introduced an emissions trading system (ETS) for 85 percent of its CO_2 emissions already in 2015 (the certificate scheme started in that US state in 2012 and thus seven years later than in the European Union (EU), which, however, maintained its original 45 percent coverage of CO_2 emissions, namely for energy and industry). The US thus stands for considerable contradictions, while the EU has been hesitant to expand its innovative CO_2 emissions trading system. At least several other countries have also introduced an emissions trading system while some countries also rely on complementary CO_2 taxation as is the case, for example, in Switzerland and Sweden. In 2018/2019 more and more countries promised to adopt stricter climate change policies, but it is quite unclear what the cost of the adopted policies will be or what alternatives could be considered.

In April 2019, I stayed at Princeton University for a lecture, and the following day I visited the university's art museum with my wife. The exhibition featured a painting from 1748 by a French painter, Francois Boucher, which shows a section of a sinking ship and the shipwrecked crew and passengers in a desperate pose in the stormy sea: the image of the hero, Arion, and his companions in the sea being rescued by a dolphin, is by no means solely reminiscent of religious and historical references. My own initial and involuntary thought was that this was a painting depicting the problem of global warming and the threat of climate catastrophe. When one sees the NASA images of the melting of Greenland ice between 1982 and 2012, one immediately sees a serious structural problem with the inland ice of the southern polar regions melting visibly in decades: rising sea levels and flooding hazards. Part I shows the pictorial result of the synopsis of such a NASA photo and the Boucher painting.

However, a third mental element is missing, since NASA's North Pole photograph is a scientific document, while the Boucher painting may be classed at its core as representing the emotions of despair and love in the pose of human beings: human reason is lacking, namely the contribution of thought to solving the problem of global warming. This book presents this third element in selected fields, and, of course, the analysis also takes a critical look at Trump's America, for which further melting of the polar ice caps in the event of a sustained rise in sea level could cause dramatic problems in the long term.

A private visit to Ciudad Guayana in Venezuela about three decades ago showed me just how impressive the natural dimensions in parts of Latin America are. People in some countries of the region are apparently proud of the great variety of native flora and fauna, as every visitor to Brazil learns in the first few days when paying with Brazilian banknotes—the 50 Real banknote shows a jaguar. Not only are the regions of Amazonia and the Orinoco River basin in Brazil and Venezuela, respectively, incredibly densely wooded and, with their large watercourses, important for the regional climate, but the huge forests of Brazil and other countries in Latin America form what are known as the "lungs of the planet".

Climate protection policy can lead to climate neutrality in 2050 if national policy approaches in the G20+ countries are well thought out, if the major international cooperation requirements are considered, if green innovation promotion is intensified and if distribution policy supporting requirements are sensibly addressed.

Whether poorer households should be helped with more transfer payments, more training vouchers or more sustainable social housing in the adaptation process will be for each country to decide for itself. While the book focuses strongly on CO_2 reduction issues, questions of forest protection and the role of reforestation programs are only marginally considered. To the extent that emission reductions through emission certificate trading are linked here with the dynamics of other markets, such as the stock markets, important interrelationships are also pointed out, but they have not yet been the focus of much research.

In the context of this study I would like to express my special thanks for discussions I had in Washington, DC, in 2017–2019 with various representatives from the worlds of politics, business and research. I would like to point out that my analysis of US populism can largely be traced back to insights I gained during my participation in the UN Conference "New research on inequality and its impacts" of the UN Department of Economic and Social Affairs (DESA) 2018 in New York—to be read in detail in my book *The Global Trump* (Palgrave Macmillan, London, 2019). I am especially thankful for discussions with Nan Yu, Vladimir Udalov and Evgeniya Yushkova (EIIW) as well as my colleagues Raimund Bleischwitz and Paul Ekins, UCL, London, and other participants in two DFG projects in China supported by me and my research team. Some of the innovative proposals presented here, particularly in the fields of housing, transport and tax policy, are based on impulses from international EIIW research. For Germany, the EU and the global economy, this is an important stimulus—it should also act as a national and international stimulus in the political sphere. There are certainly controversial points in this book, and responsibility for all statements lies with me alone.

I would like to thank numerous EIIW employees for their many years of support in the area of sustainability research. At the EIIW, my special thanks for technical support go to Christina Wiens and Kennet Stave, for the scientific exchange of ideas not least Tian Xiong, Julia Bahlmann, Christina Peußner, David Hanrahan, Oliver Ebbers, Fabian Baier as well as Tobias Zander.

My sincere thanks go to my wife Jola Welfens for her great patience and our lively exchange of ideas on environmental and climate issues over many years. Finally, I am grateful that this book can be published almost simultaneously in English, German, French and Chinese.

Wuppertal, Germany Paul J.J. Welfens
Fall 2021

Contents

Part I	Background to the Climate Problem	1
1	Introduction	3
2	The Climate Challenge and Its Consequences	69
3	Climate Protection Problems and Options for Action	113
4	Global Warming Perspectives	143
5	Perspectives on the Climate Debate and International Economic Aspects	161
6	The Wrong Climate Debate?	189
Part II	What Could Policymakers, Business and Consumers Achieve?	197
7	Climate Protection in the EU: Instruments and International Cooperation Aspects	199
8	Reservations About Climate Protection Issues	205

9	Modernization of the Energy Industry and National Interests	223
10	Climate Protection Policy: 2019 Special Report of the German Council of Economic Experts	241
11	Failures in Carbon Certificates and Emissions Trading Systems?	249
12	Macroeconomic Aspects of CO_2 Pricing	257
13	Financial Market Aspects of CO_2 Certificate Trading in the European Union	267
14	The Housing and Transport Sectors	271
15	A CO_2 Tax as a Sensible Climate Policy Instrument	279

Part III	Multilateralism as a Solution to the Climate Problem	289
16	International Perspectives	291
17	G20 Problems in Climate Protection Policy	305
18	Global EIIW-Vita Sustainability Indicator and Green Bonds: Opportunities and Problems	311
19	Weaknesses of the EU Emissions Trading System and Prospects of Linking Emissions Trading Systems and Further Development of the WTO	333

Part IV	Concepts and Practical Fields for More Sustainability	339
20	Climate Policy Problems: The Concept of a Sustainable Social Market Economy	341

21	Economic Policy Consequences: Innovation, Mobility Policy and Global Cooperation	349
22	Mobility Policy	359
23	Conclusion: International Cooperation and the Climate Protection Concept	371

Appendix 1: Climate Policy Information on California — 423

Appendix 2: CO_2 Emissions in a Macro Model of the Closed Economy: World Economy — 433

Appendix 3: World Heat Map, July 2019 (University of California at Berkeley) — 437

Appendix 4: Sustainable Development Goals — 439

Appendix 5: Composition of the "German Coal Commission" (Chairpersons and Other Members of the Commission for Growth, Structural Change and Jobs) — 441

Appendix 6: Members of the Ethics Commission for a Safe Energy Supply — 445

Appendix 7: The G20+ in 2019 — 449

Appendix 8: An Optimum Emission Reduction — 453

Appendix 9: Greenhouse Gas Emission Statistics: Emissions Register — 455

Appendix 10: Germany—A Model for Climate Change Policy? — 459

Bibliography — 463

Index — 477

About the Author

Paul J.J. Welfens President of the European Institute for International Economic Relations, Jean Monnet Professor for European Economic Integration and Chair for Macroeconomics, at the University of Wuppertal, Wuppertal, Germany; Alfred Grosser Professorship 2007/2008, Sciences Po, Paris; Research Fellow, IZA, Bonn; Non-Resident Senior Fellow at AICGS/Johns Hopkins University, Washington DC. Welfens has testified before the US Senate, the German Parliament, the European Parliament, the European Central Bank, the ECB, the IMF, the UN. Welfens is one of Europe's leading economists and the author of *An Accidental Brexit*, London: Palgrave, September 2017; and *the Global Trump*, London: Palgrave, 2019.

LIST OF FIGURES

Fig. 1.1	CO_2 emission figures in a trade-related perspective, 2018. (Source: Own representation of data available from Our World In Data; https://ourworldindata.org/co2-and-other-greenhouse-gas-emissions)	23
Fig. 1.2	CO_2 emissions per unit of consumption and production for selected countries, 2018. (Source: Own calculations and data based on emissions: kg CO_2 per unit of GDP (OurWorldInData.org) and gross domestic product (GDP, PPP Constant 2017 International \$) from World Bank. Per unit consumption = Per unit production × CO_2 emissions embedded in trade (see Fig. 1.1))	24
Fig. 2.1	The long-term increase in global average surface temperatures, 1880–2020 (the blue line stands for annual average temperature). (Source: Own representation of data from NASA's Goddard Institute for Space Studies. https://data.giss.nasa.gov/gistemp/graphs/)	79
Fig. 2.2	The emissions trading sectors and non-emissions trading sectors. (Source: Own representation)	93
Fig. 2.3	Structure of climate protection policy in the European Union. (Source: Own representation)	100
Fig. 2.4	EU certificate trading (ETS = emissions trading system): maximum emission quantities and planned reduction path (blue). (Source: Weimann (2019, p. 19))	105
Fig. 3.1	Three approaches to climate protection policy. (Source: Own representation)	128

Fig. 3.2	Smoke development in Brazil on 19 August 2019 (with influences from fires in Bolivia). Note: The author would like to thank EDEO GmbH, Roding, Germany, for kindly providing this graphic which was created using Copernicus CAMS data 2019. (Source: EDEO GmbH (with project funding from StmWi Bayern)	135
Fig. 3.3	Regional distribution of particulate matter in South America on 19 August 2019. Note: The author would like to thank EDEO GmbH, Roding, Germany, for kindly providing this graphic which was created using Copernicus CAMS data 2019. (Source: EDEO GmbH (with project funding from StmWi Bayern)	136
Fig. 3.4	Afforestation possibilities worldwide (bright areas = afforestation reserve or desert). (Source: ETH ZURICH/CROWTHER LAB (2019) and Bastin et al. (2019), https://ethz.ch/en/news-and-events/eth-news/news/2019/07/how-trees-could-save-the-climate.html)	137
Fig. 4.1	Extent of the Arctic ice field in 2012 (the yellow line stands for the average of the 30 previous years). (Source: NASA/Goddard Scientific Visualization Studio. https://www.nasa.gov/topics/earth/features/2012-seaicemin.html)	153
Fig. 4.2	Arion on the dolphin (1748), painting by François Boucher. (Source: Arion on the Dolphin, 1748, François Boucher, Oil on canvas. Princeton University Art Museum purchase, Fowler McCormick, Class of 1921, Fund)	154
Fig. 4.3	Greenhouse gas emissions in 2000 by source. (Source: Created by Stern Review using data obtained from the World Resources Institute Climate Analysis Indicators Tool (CAIT), online database version 3.0)	158
Fig. 5.1	UN world population forecast up to 2100 (medium variant). (Source: Own presentation of UN data; United Nations, DESA/Population Division, World Population Prospects 2019 https://population.un.org/wpp/)	167
Fig. 5.2	Nominal CO_2 certificate price in the EU ETS from April 2008 to April 2021, weekly data points, price in €. (Source: Own presentation of data from Sandbag Smarter Climate Policy, https://sandbag.be/index.php/carbon-price-viewer/ (last accessed 01.06.21))	173
Fig. 5.3	Real CO_2 certificate price in the EU ETS from Q2 2008 to Q1 2021; quarterly data points, price in €. (Source: Own	

	calculations and presentation; data from Sandbag Smarter Climate Policy, https://sandbag.be/index.php/carbon-price-viewer/ (last accessed 01.06.21) and Eurostat; relative price—nominal certificate price divided by national product deflator)	174
Fig. 5.4	China's patent dynamics in renewable energies: shares of patents by technology based on Office of First Filing. (Source: Own representation based on Figs. 7, 11, 14 and 17 in Helm, S.; Tannock, Q.; I. Iliev, I. (2014), Renewable Energy Technology: Evolution and Policy Implications—Evidence from Patent Literature, Global Challenges Report, WIPO: Geneva https://www.wipo.int/edocs/pubdocs/en/wipo_pub_gc_3.pdf)	180
Fig. 5.5	Action approaches to the climate problem. (Source: Own representation)	184
Fig. 5.6	Strategic approaches to modern integrated climate policy. (Source: Own representation)	186
Fig. 6.1	Percentage of under-qualified workers (low literacy or numeracy skills, or both) in selected OECD countries. *Note: The term working-age adults refers to all adults aged 16–65. Data are from the year 2012. Low skilled are defined as those who are below level 2 on either literacy or numeracy according to the Survey of Adult Skills of the OECD Programme for the International Assessment of Adult Competencies (PIAAC). Low-skilled adults struggle with basic quantitative reasoning or have difficulty with simple written information. Data for Belgium refers to Flanders only. Data for the UK are calculated as the population-weighted average of England and Northern Ireland. The OECD aggregate is calculated as an unweighted average of 22 OECD countries (with the data for England and Northern Ireland combined by population weights) that participated in the first round of the Survey of Adult Skills.* (Source: Own representation of data from OECD (2017), Fig. 38, p. 51)	195
Fig. 7.1	Starting points for a national climate policy and complementary policy approaches. (Source: Own representation)	200
Fig. 9.1	Power supply from renewable energies, 2018 (GWh). (Source: Own representation of data available from IRENA (2021), Renewable Energy Capacity Statistics 2021, International Renewable Energy Agency (IRENA), Abu Dhabi)	228

Fig. 9.2	Electricity generated from renewable energy sources (by type in percent), 2018. (Source: Own presentation of data available from IRENA Renewable Energy Statistics 2020, International Renewable Energy Agency (IRENA), Abu Dhabi)	229
Fig. 9.3	Electricity capacities from renewable energy sources (by type in percent), 2020. (Source: Own presentation of data available from IRENA Renewable Capacity Statistics 2021, International Renewable Energy Agency (IRENA), Abu Dhabi)	229
Fig. 9.4	The global distribution of wind energy intensity. (Source: NASA (2004), NASA Surface Meteorology and Solar Energy: Methodology, 12/16/04, p. 47)	230
Fig. 10.1	Equity (subscribed capital) of multilateral development banks and the World Bank (in billions of US$, 2017). (Source: Own calculations and presentation according to published, publicly available data from the relevant banks for 2017)	245
Fig. 11.1	EU Emissions Trading System (EU ETS). (Source: German Council of Economic Experts (2019), Setting out for a new climate policy, Special Report 2019, Chart 7, p. 36)	250
Fig. 18.1	Top 10 countries ranked by RCA indicator, 2015. (Source: Own representation)	317
Fig. 18.2	RCA indicator for environmentally friendly products, G20 countries in 2015. (Source: Own representation)	318
Fig. 18.3	World sustainability indicator positions, 2000 (green = leading). (Source: Welfens et al. (2015), toward global sustainability. Issues, new indicators and economic policy, p. 131)	320
Fig. 18.4	EIIW-vita indicator 2000–2015 world, China and Germany. (Source: Based on Welfens and Debes (2018), Fig. 4, p. 8)	322
Fig. 18.5	Development of the yield in ten-year government bonds (for the top 10 and top 9 sustainable countries according to the RCA indicator). (Source: Based on Welfens and Debes (2018), Fig. 5, p. 14)	323
Fig. 20.1	Environmental tax revenues as a percentage of gross domestic product, 2019. (Source: Own presentation; OECDStat "Environmentally-related tax revenue", annual revenue 2019 or latest available, https://stats.oecd.org/Index.aspx?DataSetCode=ENV_ENVPOLICY)	347
Fig. 23.1	The monthly fluctuation intensity (based on daily data) of the EU CO_2 allowance trading price between September 2005 and May 2021. (Source: Own representation of EIIW calculations based on data from Ice Futures Europe. Note: this graphic shows the monthly standard deviation of the EU ETS CO_2 price in euro (first beginning future nearby settlement price) calculated using daily data)	373

Fig. 23.2	California cap-and-trade current carbon auction settlement price in US dollars per metric ton, November 2012–February 2021. (Source: California air resources board, California Cap & Trade https://ww2.arb.ca.gov/our-work/programs/cap-and-trade-program/auction-information accessed 10.05.21)	376
Fig. 23.3	EU CO_2 allowance price (forward price) in euro (€) per metric ton. (Source: Own representation of data available from ICE Futures Europe, IHS Markit)	377
Fig. 23.4	EU CO_2 allowance prices: forward price at the year end (in euro [€] per metric ton). (Source: Own representation of data available from investing.com)	377
Fig. 23.5	Challenges: climate protection policy options. (Source: Own representation)	397
Fig. 23.6	The contradiction of EU plans on climate protection policy. (Source: Own representation)	402
Fig. 23.7	Steps toward an integrated G20+ certificate system. (Source: Own representation)	408
Fig. A1.1	California emissions by sector in 2015. (Source: Greenhouse Gas Inventory Data (CARB, 2015); Courtesy: Center for Climate and Energy Solutions www.C2ES.org)	425
Fig. A1.2	California emission cap and business-as-usual forecasts. (Source: 2020 Business-as-Usual (BAU) Emissions Projection 2014 Edition (CARB, 2017); Courtesy: Center for Climate and Energy Solutions www.C2ES.org)	429
Fig. A1.3	Projected reductions (in MMT CO_2e) caused by AB 32 measures by 2020 and share of total. (Source: California Greenhouse Gas Emission Inventory Program (CARB, 2017); Courtesy, Center for Climate and Energy Solutions www.C2ES.org)	430
Fig. A3.1	World Heat Map, July 2019 (University of California at Berkeley). (Source: Rohde (2019). World Heat Map, July 2019. Retrieved from https://twitter.com/RARohde/status/1162011232095920128. Robert Rohde, Lead Scientist at BerkeleyEarth.org)	437
Fig. A4.1	Overview of the UN Sustainable Development Goals. *Note: The content of this publication has not been approved by the United Nations and does not reflect the views of the United Nations or its officials or member states.* (Source: United Nations Sustainable Development Goals. Communication Materials. Retrieved 01/11/2021 from the website of the United Nations Sustainable Development Goals https://www.un.org/sustainabledevelopment/)	440

Fig. A8.1	Optimum emission reduction. (Source: Own representation)	453
Fig. A9.1	Total greenhouse gas emissions (including international aviation and indirect CO_2, excluding LULUCF) trend, EU-28, 1990–2019 (Index 1990 = 100). (Source: Own representation based on data from https://ec.europa.eu/eurostat/web/environment/data/database	455
Fig. A9.2	Total greenhouse gas emissions (including international aviation and indirect CO_2, excluding LULUCF), by country, 2019 (index 1990 = 100). (Source: Own representation based on data from https://ec.europa.eu/eurostat/web/environment/data/database)	457
Fig. A9.3	Greenhouse gas emissions by sector, EU28, 1990 and 2019 (percentage of total emissions). (Source: Own representation based on data from https://ec.europa.eu/eurostat/web/environment/data/database)	457

List of Tables

Table 9.1	The main natural gas-producing countries in the world, on the basis of proven reserves	225
Table 9.2	The main oil-producing countries in the world	226
Table 9.3	The main coal- and lignite-producing countries in the world	227
Table 15.1	CO_2 pricing in selected countries, 2018	282
Table 15.2	Key figures in international comparison, 2019 (ranked by gross domestic product)	283
Table 17.1	G20 countries: gross domestic product (in purchasing power parity (PPP)), 2019	306
Table 18.1	Top and bottom 10 RCA ranking countries (leading countries 2015: green field; comparison with results from 2000)	316
Table 18.2	Long-term changes in ranking in the top and bottom groupings	321
Table 18.3	Comparison of "savings indicator", "renewables indicator" and "RCA indicator/green international competitiveness" (rankings in color)	323
Table 18.4	EIIW-Vita Global Sustainability Indicator-based sample government bond portfolio 2000–2015 (SABIS strategy; EIIW calculations), ten-year government bonds of the most successful ten countries of the RCA indicator	327
Table A1.1	Comparison of ETS: EU and California	423
Table A1.2	California cap-and-trade details	427

Table A7.1	The G20+ in numbers, 2019 (Mt = megatons)	450
Table A9.1	Total greenhouse gas emissions (including international aviation and indirect CO_2, excluding LULUCF), by country, 1990–2017 (million tons CO_2 equivalents)	456
Table A10.1	An evaluation of different carbon pricing options	460

PART I

Background to the Climate Problem

CHAPTER 1

Introduction

The basic view developed in this study is to argue that climate change policy is necessary—taking natural scientists research findings seriously—but that one also has to consider the income distribution consequences of climate change policy and the necessary enhanced innovation dynamics needed to achieve climate neutrality, plus the need to organize broader CO_2 emissions trading in all "Group of Twenty" or G20 countries (often this would at first require the introduction of a national Emissions Trading System (or ETS)), which together represent circa 80 percent of global CO_2 emissions. This group is much easier to organize than the 195 or so signatory countries of the Paris Climate Agreement of 2015. It is surprising that inequality aspects of climate change policy have thus far been largely overlooked in part of climate policy debate: for example, giving more than 20 percent of emissions as free emissions allowances is effectively a program to generate capital gains in favor of capital so that inequality is reinforced in Organisation for Economic Co-operation and Development (OECD) countries. At the same time, it is also surprising that economists in many countries have argued that CO_2 taxes and CO_2 allowance prices are totally equivalent which indeed are certainly not. Moreover, it is noteworthy that national CO_2 emission certificate trading programs should be integrated internationally since this generates large gains from international trade as will be shown extensively in this book.

© The Author(s), under exclusive license to Springer Nature Switzerland AG 2022
P. J.J. Welfens, *Global Climate Change Policy*, Sustainable Development Goals Series,
https://doi.org/10.1007/978-3-030-94594-7_1

While Fridays for Future protests often center around complaints that governments are not delivering on promised progress in terms of climate change policy, one could also raise the question as to the costs at which certain policies are realized. The economist's natural question is to ask what efficient trajectories to climate neutrality in 2050 are possible, and thus how one could minimize the costs of the adjustment process. As Pew opinion surveys in many countries in 2013 have shown, there are many countries in which a large share of the population is concerned about global warming; at the same time there is a large number of countries where such concern does not translate into more efforts by individuals to cut back on fossil fuel consumption or to invest in climate-friendly innovations.

This is the medium- and long-term background for this book, which combines climate policy issues and economic aspects with issues of international policy cooperation, especially at the G20, but also at the European Union (EU), United Nations (UN) and other institutions. Of course, the question of whether a single EU country—such as the large EU countries Germany, France, UK (still a member as of mid-2019) and Italy—can make a meaningful independent contribution to global climate protection policy will also be addressed: after all, each individual country represents only 1 to 2 percent of global CO_2 emissions, which are regarded as critical for global warming. The latter refers to the average global warming across both land and sea surfaces. Of course, it can be shown that individually EU countries can contribute only relatively little to global climate protection and to the goal of global climate neutrality set by many countries for 2050. But the sum of all EU countries or even the G20, the 20 participating countries which accounted for 81 percent of CO_2 emissions in 2018, can very well provide clear impetus for significantly improved climate protection worldwide. At its core, this is about innovation dynamics and political cooperation.

Developing climate protection policy faster, more effectively, with less contradictions and more comprehensibly than before can be seen as a very important task for policy in the period 2020–2050.

This means that climate change policy cannot be a small policy field on the sidelines for the EU, individual EU member states, the United States US(or California, Texas, Massachusetts, etc.), China, Japan, India, Russia, Turkey, Indonesia, Mexico, Brazil and other countries. Climate protection policy must move into the center of politics, including economic policy. Because climate protection policy is so important and internationally effective, a limited national perspective cannot be appropriate. A broader international perspective is needed. It can also be shown that climate protection policy is often linked to issues such as distribution policy, foreign trade policy and the policies of international organizations. The climate protection policies of most Western countries, which have so far been pursued in a rather isolated manner, are not effective, and there are astonishing technical errors with regard to some economic policies in this context, which mean very high costs for traditional environmental and climate policies. The mobilization and politicization of young people on climate issues should therefore lead to a broader political interest in the medium term. If one looks at the considerable global climate risks—which have increased since 2010 according to the Intergovernmental Panel on Climate Change (IPCC)—one could expect that from the point of view of most firms, individuals and politicians, the role of risks will increasingly come to the fore. But this is not the case if you look at an evaluation of Google Trend results for the period from 2014 to mid-2019.

There appears to be a partial lack of adequate climate policy risk awareness in large sections of society and the economy. Without such an increasing risk awareness, however, the motivation of institutions, companies and politicians to face the new challenges with extra effort and vigor is lacking. This appears to be problematic—from the point of view of economics, therefore, there is a need to work harder toward fueling a public debate. It is a matter of assessing the risks, policies and individual alternatives, and the costs of alternative measures worldwide.

The analysis may be shortened to the G20 countries in an initial analytical step for the purposes of simplification, but this in itself is demanding. If, for example, Germany, or the UK, or France or Japan or China or India or Russia or Brazil or the US was to present a national climate protection policy without at the same time developing the prospects for a connection to the G20, this would be a flawed approach considering the global nature of the issue of climate protection. After all, there are technological advances that facilitate global climate protection monitoring—a review of the political progress of all countries and regions. One might think, for example, of modern satellite and sensor technology which, in conjunction with the Internet, can provide every citizen of the earth with timely climate-critical information, for example, on water quality and air quality. If billions of people actually look at and discuss such developments with real interest in relation to their own and other regions, climate protection policy will indeed become part of a new "global domestic" policy. This will trigger a transformation of institutions in many ways. If reasonable measures are undertaken and coordinated internationally, the desired goal of achieving climate neutrality by 2050 is possible. However, here the old political recipes are of little use, to this end new initiatives and innovative concepts are urgently required!

There is a European and global debate on the challenges of climate change and the possibilities of meaningful climate policy. With this book, a new contribution is available that for the first time combines ecological and economic aspects with the necessary perspectives for international policy cooperation. The goal of climate neutrality by 2050 cannot be achieved without a completely new and binding climate protection organization for the G20 countries. Climate neutrality is understood here as a global emissions level in 2050 of 10 percent of the 1990 level. It is foreseeable that this will be a major change accompanied by enormous structural changes in the world economy. It will not be possible to achieve climate neutrality without wise economic policy decisions, massive innovation efforts for a CO_2- and resource-light economy, and the mobilization of the creativity of billions of people around the world for the next several decades.

It is good that millions of companies around the world use innovation as an established basis for business success. How the global innovation dynamics of companies and individuals in the twenty-first century can be best strengthened and linked in a climate-friendly way must be decided upon. Global warming and climate destabilization, while global problems, are not insurmountable. Efficient solutions are required here, whereby policy alternatives for CO_2 reduction are fundamental: prohibition of CO_2-intensive activities, CO_2 taxes or CO_2 certificate trading, where companies have to buy emission rights (or indeed can sell surplus emission rights). A global trade in CO_2 certificates can be an efficient main impulse for a global solution to a global problem, as can be shown. This presupposes that internationally coherent and reliable new framework conditions are created politically, that complementary policy measures are meaningfully included and that international coordination of policy actors is reliably organized. It can also be shown that CO_2 taxes and CO_2 certificate prices are by no means equivalent instruments. As a rule, CO_2 certificate trading approaches bring enormous international efficiency gains; they make the desired limitation of global warming more cost-effective for the participating countries.

Global population growth by 2050 is an additional challenge. But with more educated minds, the creativity available worldwide can also gain critical mass in terms of green, climate-friendly innovations. The current young generation is the best educated in recent history, and certainly also the best networked group internationally. Through the Fridays for Future demonstrations of young people—and adults—in many countries of the world, there is more pressure for politicians to act on climate policy. That can be useful.

However, if political responses are not properly conceived, there is also a risk of disorderly climate policy whereby the fundamental building blocks do not fit together nationally or internationally: a stable Earth with global climate neutrality cannot be built arbitrarily. Cost minimization in the climate neutrality project, that is, an economically efficient solution, is important, as otherwise enormous—and unnecessary—distribution conflicts will arise (see, e.g., the yellow-vest protests in France in 2018, when the government raised petrol prices for environmental reasons, but parliament canceled the compensation payments to poorer households, originally provided for in the law, for unclear reasons), and the target of climate neutrality will not be achieved by 2050 or 2055. Cost minimization means minimum use of resources to achieve a given goal. Minimizing the use of resources—and recycling—was already an important topic in the sustainability debate.

Regarding how to achieve climate neutrality by 2050, the analysis contained herein looks at the role of innovation, regulation, CO_2 taxes and emissions trading, as well as distribution and financial market effects. In some Internet discussions, CO_2 certificate trading is classified as a kind of questionable indulgence trade. In reality, trading CO_2 emission rights is usually the cheapest method of achieving the goal of climate neutrality efficiently and effectively. Especially since the annual reduction in the volume of emissions in the EU, for example, can be set by politicians simply and over several years at a certain percentage—that is, percentage reduction can be expected.

Over time, the state, acting alone or in cooperation with other countries, can set the adjustment path for the quantity of CO_2 emitted. The resulting CO_2 market price makes CO_2-intensive production more expensive, providing incentives for innovation and structural change. There is certainly a need for an ethic of responsibility that asks how the goal of reducing global CO_2 emissions can be achieved efficiently and meaningfully. Clear market signals, for example, in CO_2 certificate trading systems, are a conceivable starting point for a modern climate policy. If companies have to buy additional polluting rights or can sell surplus rights, a market emerges which, under certain conditions, can efficiently lead to emission reductions locally, regionally, nationally and indeed globally, depending on the geographical definition of the allowance trading area. This could be done by restricting certificate trading to transactions between emitting companies (CO_2 is generated in the course of production of goods or services) and excluding longer-term transactions (e.g., on a certificate futures market or a certificate derivatives market). On the other hand, a larger transaction framework may be more attractive, which may also include non-issuers, such as banks, engaging in trading emission certificates. However, this will then require that certificate trading be included within the framework of existing international financial market regulations; this is not yet the case. These important questions need to be taken into account when looking at the future prospects for certificate trading.

The focus here is not only on existing CO_2 certificate trading systems, such as those in the EU, California, Japan, China and the Republic of Korea. Rather, it is also about the possibility of implementing globally an inexpensive and effective climate protection policy by extending such trading systems to the G20+ states (G20 plus Nigeria) and gradually integrating these systems. It goes without saying that the activities of the US, but also of India, South Africa, Indonesia, Russia, Mexico, Brazil, Turkey and other countries—including those from the EU—are important in terms of climate protection. But how to make a coherent whole out of the G20 or the 196 signatories of the UN's Paris Climate Agreement is a pressing, but interesting, question. Once Russia has also ratified the Climate Agreement, one of the few missing G20 countries will be on board for the Paris Agreement. The faster certificate trading is activated and integrated internationally in the G20 countries, the more efficient global cooperation in CO_2 mitigation should be. The annual reduction requirement in terms of the CO_2 cap in the EU's Emissions Trading System is, however, inadequate to achieve—by way of a smooth, gradual transition process—climate neutrality by 2050: an annual reduction of 2.2 percent is much too slow since such a low pace over the next decade would require unrealistically large reductions in the emissions cap between 2030 and 2050. At the same time, the EU approach—with a focus only on energy and industry (covering circa 45 percent of all CO_2 emissions)—is surprisingly narrow when one considers California's coverage in 2020 of more than 80 percent of emissions and since the experience from two Japanese regions clearly suggests that integrating office buildings in a regional ETS system can be a very useful approach.

Of course, there are important national issues for individual countries, but it is nevertheless essential to consider an efficient, international interaction of measures and adaptation processes in any serious analysis: every G20 country—ultimately every country on earth—can make a significant contribution on the road to climate neutrality by 2050. There are few knowledge gaps in the main fields of action in this area, but what the optimal combination of the many individual steps, which are both desirable and capable of winning a majority in democracies or the G20, looks like is less clear. It is obvious that the innovation dynamics of millions of companies in the global economy will have to be increasingly mobilized in order to achieve climate neutrality (at a bearable cost) by 2050. On the way to climate neutrality, national and international compromises will also have to be made at certain times. This is reflective of a world of diversity and of the mutual respect which is required between states in the process of adaptation. In addition, there is not only the goal of climate stabilization, but the process should also be about achieving income, employment and distribution goals at the same time. It would be of little use to achieve climate stabilization but end up in a world characterized by greater economic and political instability at the same time.

The necessary economic analysis here goes well beyond the usual approaches and shows that climate protection policy in Germany, Europe and worldwide is also associated with new problems of income inequality. A redistributive effect in favor of both capital and qualified workers can be expected. How climate protection policy could be combined with an accompanying policy of redistribution and further (re-)training therefore appears to be a parallel challenge to tackling climate change. Preventing critical global warming requires a transformation of the energy industry, manufacturing industry and other sectors of the economy. Achieving meaningful and consequential international cooperation between industrialized countries and the G20 countries in the field of climate policy is an additional challenge. Such cooperation must be forthcoming if we are to reach the goal of climate neutrality and to prevent an excessive burden on the export economy of individual countries.

It is not difficult to understand that there would have to be enormous changes in the energy and heating sectors of the economy in order to achieve climate neutrality. After all, the topic of higher energy prices and energy-saving innovations is not really new, since the OPEC oil price shocks of the 1970s already mobilized industrialized countries on these points. However, the challenge of climate neutrality requires a different focus, namely on the G20 countries (plus Nigeria, as can be shown).

This group of 20 countries meets once a year and considered a topic with climate relevance for the first time in the 2009 official summit press release with the topic of fossil energy subsidies. However, since then an entire decade has passed without any real progress. Subsidies for tradition, fossil fuel energies—thus for CO_2 emissions—still equated to more than 6 percent of global income in 2017. That is like two dozen or so countries supporting climate euthanasia. This is an unacceptable contradiction in a century that needs to witness a significant reduction of CO_2 emissions and a long-term transformation of mobility and energy systems for reasons of climate protection.

The fact that an increased level of renewable energies in electricity generation may increase the risk of grid stability must also be taken into account in all countries. This risk must be countered by optimizing network management, including network expansion. The current set-up regarding electricity supply comes with its own risks, especially with regard to nuclear power generation, where in no country in the world does the liability insurance of nuclear power plants cover even 1/1000th of the risks of a serious nuclear accident—this situation amounts to a massive but hidden subsidy for nuclear power (for comparison: imagine that you would have to have car insurance which provides coverage only for small accidents involving fender benders or scratches to the paintwork while parking, while the major accident damage is paid for by the taxpayer).

Many climate researchers and economists, as well as political scientists and lawyers, have already highlighted the important interrelations which must be taken into account if the global collective good of climate protection—understood as climate neutrality—is to be achieved. The contributions and discussions are, however, not always goal oriented. The easiest way to see this is to look at how modest the results of the first G20 environmental summit in Japan in 2019 were. Some of the policy papers provided by experts in the background are not very convincing. Overall, there is a lack of proposals for a general, holistic concept that will actually achieve climate neutrality by 2050. However, many interesting contributions can be found on sub-points in many areas.

Long-standing points of reference in terms of environmental policy result from the sustainability debate. Since the 1970s, researchers, voters, companies and politicians have been interested in how economic and environmental policy can be designed in such a way that future generations could expect a similarly high standard of living as the current generation. The current issue of global warming is about the risks to future prosperity: if climate protection policies are inadequate, the risks to consumption, wealth and indeed life for future generations will be considerable.

It is also not easy to see how sufficient political mobilization for a better climate protection policy can be achieved in a suitable forum, nationally or internationally. A high degree of competence is required in environmental and climate protection policy; this is not always to be found in the environment ministries of industrialized countries.

However, the issue also requires effective cooperation between the various ministries, which, however, is rarely seen: climate policy has economic, transport and agricultural effects plus government revenue effects, which requires the respective ministry of finance to be included. Since international cooperation is so important, we similarly cannot do without the foreign ministry. In a democracy, therefore, climate policy is sometimes complicated. The aim is to find an electoral majority for a new, well-considered policy that should also be internationally compatible. Democracy, in turn, demands transparency as well as clear and timely communication. Thus, a policy area that is, at times and in parts, quite complex, such as climate policy, should be refined and pared back to simple structures and important points and thus explained to the citizens, also, by the scientific community.

The role of the Fridays for Future movement, which criticizes the indecisiveness and contradiction of many countries' climate change policies, is a positive impulse for better economic and climate policies. The Fridays for Future demonstrations express both a concern for the environment and protest voice against the response of policymakers. Within a year, the movement has contributed to a wide-ranging public debate on climate change policy in many countries around the world. As a large share of those involved come from the younger generations, that is, those who see their own futures darkly threatened, the protest for more climate protection policy will probably not fade away so quickly. This puts politics under more pressure to explain, act and justify. If these impulses and the work of the scientific community were to lead politicians to a better climate protection policy, the Fridays for Future movement would have made a meritorious contribution, and Greta Thunberg, as a prominent representative, has apparently set things in motion—her voice now stands for the demands of many, many young people across the globe.

On the other hand, one side effect is that Thunberg, with her publicly declared climate concerns, is also leading quite a few young people into a state of exaggerated anxiety. Thunberg argues that the politicians of Western countries have kept too few promises in climate protection policy and that the policies of many countries are insufficient to stop global warming by 2050. It can certainly be shown that the approaches and means chosen are indeed inefficient to some extent. There is, however, no reason for pessimism in climate protection policy, especially since the instrument of certificate trading has been tried and tested and can be expanded worldwide. Overall, it is important to organize a public and understandable dialogue on global warming and climate policy: so that critical questions about the present can be turned into a sensible economic policy answer for a bright future.

Incidentally, even the policies of leading EU countries are somewhat surprisingly not really geared toward achieving more global cooperation in CO_2 certificate trading: this important field of success for the EU, as a pioneer of CO_2 certificate trading, has not yet been sensibly communicated and exported by the EU Commission and the European Parliament. The EU will reach its climate targets in 2020, mainly through certificate trading—supported by many scientists in the field of economics.

Scientists4Future is a broad group of climate and environmental researchers and economists who support Fridays for Future demands. At Fridays for Future, it is to be hoped that the protests will remain within reasonable bounds, follow rational arguments and effectively promote changing behavior on the part of individuals and companies. Since 2018, many companies and service providers have been making greater efforts to achieve a positive sustainability profile—for marketing and image reasons alone. You will see how much substance there really is. Of course, there are also scientists outside the framework of the international Scientists4Future group who call for more climate protection policy. Incidentally, it is indeed the case that there are some topics which are discussed controversially within the scientific community. However, that there is a man-made element in terms of climate change appears to be a common finding among all leading research institutes—from very different countries. If the political system did not want to react vigorously to these findings and analyses, it would be strange and irresponsible. It remains to be seen whether politicians in many countries will be able to develop sensible climate protection approaches at the same time and find the necessary political majorities. In any case, there is no point in just looking at the climate protection policy of a single country or a handful of countries. The internationality of climate protection is a particular challenge, due to the fact that there is ultimately only one climate for the whole world (economy).

On the other hand, there are also many populist leaders who obviously do not think much of empirical findings and comprehensive simulation analyses and do not see the problem of global warming as a real challenge. However, nobody wants to get on a plane or a high-speed train which has not been the subject of thousands of computer simulations in order to ensure safe systems. When it comes to climate protection policy, there is also a dispute in the background between a very influential, successful direction in science and a political counter-position that sometimes seems to be little more than wishful thinking. Qualitative and empirical analyses as well as simulation analyses and experimental findings form the basis of successful economic policy.

Due to the conceivable connection between a high number of climate refugees and further global warming, climate change is a favorite irritant topic for many populists whose core brand is based around nationalism, protectionism and anti-immigration policy (in the broad sense of the word), strangely enough, however, also the rejection of the scientific findings on man-made climate problem. Thus, it can be argued that populists are reverting to the time before Copernicus (1473–1543), one of the last scientists to experience that his telescope-based observations, which led to the geocentric world view, were rejected by the top echelons of the Catholic Church—carried more by wishful thinking and dogma. This kind of wishful thinking and a recognizable reluctance to deal with scientific findings or logic can also be found among quite a few populists.

Inevitably, a global issue such as climate protection attracts big names and many research institutes, but also particularly loud—sometimes extreme—voices. In the Internet society, the diversity of perspectives on international issues is greater than ever before. It is the task of the scientific community to illuminate the complexity and intricacies of climate change and possible climate protection policy, to present the main results of the debate to the public in an understandable way. Unfortunately, that does not happen enough. Sometimes politicians try to suppress inconvenient scientific results. In the case of the US, this development has emerged for the first time in two centuries: President Trump's administration played a strangely inglorious role—even more so when one considers that it lacked around 1000 experts compared to the Obama administration, with probably about 100 crucial positions unfilled in the key departments of energy, trade and finance.

In the G20, however, at least in 2019, there was still an understanding that they wanted to proceed with climate protection cooperation even without the US. Among the most ambitious countries in terms of green economic growth are the Republic of Korea, but also some countries in Europe and presumably Japan and China as well. The EU, China, Korea, Switzerland and New Zealand as well as California (and some other US regions) plus two Canadian provinces and two prefectures in Japan use CO_2 emission allowance trading schemes for parts of the economy, in particular the energy sector, to provide incentives for climate-friendly structural change: companies receive an initial supply of CO_2 certificates from the state or buy such certificates from other companies, thus creating a CO_2 certificate market, in one country or in several countries in one world region or, as proposed here, at G20 level. Alternatively, one can try CO_2 pricing via CO_2 taxation, whereby here too the idea is to provide incentives through pricing so that companies steer investment and technical progress toward CO_2-light technologies.

However, CO_2 taxes are not very precise, and there are hardly any cross-border taxes (conceivable in the form of certain customs duties). The prospect of one day giving up taxes once they have been introduced is also vague in the political system of Western democracies—with the exception of Switzerland. The negative side effects of taxes can be very considerable, so that CO_2 taxes should tend to play a complementary role to certificate trading. Certificate prices may fluctuate and could rise sharply under certain circumstances. If necessary, the state can counteract this by issuing new certificates, and a new (international) stabilization institution may also be conceivable. A kind of international certificate bank, the operational rules for which would have to be laid down when the institution is founded.

If a large number of countries want to turn away from the use of fossil fuels on a broad basis, then obviously energy savings must be made, and the expansion of renewable energies must be pursued. The latter is happening in all G20 countries, but there are many problems. Can climate neutrality be achieved in time by 2050? When one billion people still have no electricity at all? When politics in many countries is hesitant, sometimes even unprofessional?

It must be assumed for almost all countries that the necessary steps will not be easy to implement. In the EU, moreover, where probably more than 80 percent of the population of EU member countries is unaware of the trade in emission certificates in the EU—a system which has been active since 2005 and is valuable as a means of reducing emissions. It is strange that the European Union has developed a pioneering economic innovation here, but hardly talks about it, and it has not really had the necessary political backing from the citizenry so far.

It is easy to imagine that the public and political discussions, as well as some protests, are sometimes problematic and misleading in an environment where knowledge is lacking. Why exactly national governments and the EU Commission seem hesitant to explain this advantageous system remains a mystery. But at least other regions and countries have adopted the EU certificate trading system.

Existing certificate trading systems, whose upper limit for carbon dioxide emissions is lowered annually, are on the one hand unerring, since it is easy to calculate what an annual reduction of the accepted maximum amount of emissions by 3 percent per year will lead to. On the other hand, existing certificate trading systems in some countries are surprisingly flawed with regard to some important points. It cannot stay that way. The link between financial market dynamics and price developments in certificate markets, for example, has also been little investigated.

Particularly in Germany there is the problem that the government repeatedly enforces historical decisions in a kind of substitute parliament via mega-commissions, which somewhat goes against democratic principles. The "Coal Commission" (active in 2018/2019, to name one example) may be well intentioned, according to the motto that the big political parties intended to include many influential groups and stakeholders in one commission. However, the august composition of the body, supplemented by members of the Bundestag, means that there is a problem: a broad public discussion on the subject can never take place in this way. One may opt for certain solutions in a society, in a country, but without a sensible debate on the matter in parliament it will not work. If the government can avoid contentious public debates via the establishment of mega-commissions, it may be comfortable for it to do so. But to really take the people in society with you when making difficult decisions means the debate cannot proceed in this way. A critical parliamentary control of government policy that implements the recommendation of the mega-commission is unlikely to be possible in practice. After all, parts of EU climate policy can be regarded as being quite good.

The fact that the EU must expand its own certificate system for the period 2020–2040 in order to have a chance of making a reasonable EU contribution to climate neutrality by 2050 has not yet been discussed. Moreover, the annual reduction of the CO_2 emission cap of 2.2 percent from 2021 is simply insufficient. For the next two decades after 2030, there is the risk of a quasi-oil price shock if the system is not adapted in a sensible and steady manner without major leaps and bounds. Until now, the following has been true: for 2030–2050, one would have to enforce an annual emission reduction of over 8 percent in order to achieve climate neutrality in 2050. But then the CO_2 certificate price will rise to several times the level of 2019 (€27) and since practically all forms of production and consumption are linked to energy and therefore CO_2 consumption, stagnation and recession in the EU economy and beyond would be conceivable. The reduction in the upper CO_2 limit planned by politicians would have to be higher in 2021–2030 than previously planned in order to make do with 6–7 percent annual reduction in the amount of CO_2 in the two decades starting in 2030. An international integration of certificate trading systems can significantly curb the upward price trend for CO_2 certificates.

It is doubtful whether politicians have thought much about the adjustment path beyond 2030 so far. With a 2050 target chosen by EU, US and G20 policymakers themselves, it cannot be the case that a relatively harmless, easy looking adjustment process is planned for 2020–2030, which at the same time means that 2031–2050 would require a hell of a ride for the economy toward climate neutrality. This cannot function economically, socially or politically. What also cannot work is an EU model where just 45 percent of emissions—from the energy sector and industrial production—is subject to certificate trading and where annually decreasing CO_2 emission quantities are actually achieved. At the same time, there is hardly any reasonable incentive to reduce emissions in other sectors, and CO_2 emissions will even increase for those in the 55 percent of emissions not covered by the EU system. California is better than the EU with 85 percent coverage of emissions from CO_2 certificate trading and a programmed -3 percent reduction in emissions per year.

The analysis shows that climate neutrality can be achieved globally by 2050. However, the tasks and challenges—presented here—are very considerable. If a sensible concept is developed and digital and traditional information on climate protection policy is implemented, nationally and internationally, the goal can be achieved. There is no reason for climate hysteria, but there is no reason for complacency and a continuation of the current climate policies of Germany and other G20 countries either.

The G20 countries are of great importance for global climate protection policy as they account for 80 percent of global emissions. The G20 as an organization clearly lacks a serious role in climate protection policy in particular areas. At the 2009 G20 summit in Seattle, it was stressed that global subsidies for fossil fuels were far too high and should be reduced. The strange thing is that the amount of these subsidies relative to world income in 2017 was still a good 6 percent—there is no clear visible reduction of this catastrophically high subsidy ratio. How is a CO_2-minimum global economy to be achieved by 2050 if huge subsidies are paid by the G20 countries for CO_2 emissions at their taxpayers' expense? At the same time, CO_2 pricing has been or is being introduced in many countries, via CO_2 emission certificates that have a market price, or via a CO_2 tax in certain sectors. The global challenge in the energy sector is enormous because of these contradictions in many countries' climate protection policies.

How a sensible G20+ climate protection policy should be drawn up is examined here. In addition, many findings from the sciences are combined in new ways. Setting up national CO_2 certificate trading schemes is very useful, but the market prices of national CO_2 certificates will be relatively high in Europe (the EU plus Switzerland), the US and China; the prices in these countries will be different, as of course will those in India, Russia and so on, provided these countries introduce also certificate trading schemes. Only the integration of the certificate systems of all G20 countries would result in a lower—and G20-wide—uniform CO_2 certificate price, which is important for the preservation of jobs and for efficient climate protection.

A new problem with the perspective of more necessary cooperation between the G20 countries is that the US has developed a kind of maverick and individualist (from a national perspective) position under the Trump administration. Even if the US were to be maintained a populist approach in the medium to long term, it would be worthwhile for the remaining G19 countries to take the lead in new cooperation in certificate trading. So far, there is no convincing approach for more sustainability cooperation in the G20. A kind of global Dutch polder model of cooperation at the international level would be desirable; for the time being it is unclear how such enhanced cooperation can be achieved. Cooperation between the dike-building protectors of neighboring municipalities and towns in the medieval Netherlands was the key to securing the Dutch mainland. The common motivation of local leaders to cooperate not only in each building their own section of the dikes but also in connecting the dikes of neighboring sections was obvious—one missing section of seawall could have resulted in the flooding of all low-lying regions including those which had invested in a dike of their own. Nowadays, intensifying cooperation at the G20 is more complicated.

More rationality in climate protection policy is necessary and possible. From a scientific point of view, the idea that global warming is a real problem, and also due in part to human activity, is not seriously denied by anyone after almost 50 years of research on the topic of global warming—apart from the experts in wishful thinking, that is, the populists. The fact that former US President, Donald Trump, was a major proponent of this approach may be somewhat surprising, since the US has owed its global rise since 1850 largely to the combination of a functioning market economy—with the exception of the 1930s and the years 2008/2009—on the one hand, and being a leading scientific power throughout the twentieth century on the other. If Trump had achieved somewhat more economic growth through a renewed expansion of coal and oil production and the dismantling of environmental regulations, it would have been detrimental to the welfare economy of the US in the longer term. The quality of growth is declining and the necessary adjustment costs which will need to be incurred later will be all the higher. From the perspective of a melting of the icecaps in the polar regions, including Greenland, alone—the US is a country where almost 40 percent of its inhabitants live near the coast. New York is not located in the mountains; a long-term rise in sea level would not only affect this major city but also other important parts of the country.

Moreover, there is also a need for further research in the area of climate protection, which affects important areas of the economy, such as the interplay between stock market developments and the price of CO_2 certificates. The EU is called upon to continue its pioneering steps toward certificate trading at the beginning of the twenty-first century and to export this functioning and excellent system, to make use of its numerous opportunities to exert a meaningful influence on more than half of the world economy in terms of climate protection policy and—if desired—to also provide technical assistance to partner countries. How CO_2 reduction policy, innovation policy for CO_2-light technologies and products as well as CO_2 taxation and regulation (also of financial markets) can be optimally combined and anchored within the framework of multilateralism remains to be examined in more detail. Multilateralism means developing a meaningful role for international organizations in terms of facing up to international or even global challenges: *to make the small big and the big civilized*, to put it in the words of Roberto Azevêdo, the Director General of the World Trade Organization (WTO) in 2017.

Climate protection policy ultimately needs to do its homework nationally and internationally and, with a view to the goal of climate neutrality, also to consider exotic options for action such as so-called geoengineering (undertaking climate cooling measures by intervening in and altering the atmospheric conditions). In the end, it is amazing and a source of optimism that each individual can also make an important contribution himself or herself so that the world economy does not become unbalanced in the long term due to more and more extreme weather events, floods and climate-related economic disturbances. Of course, climate protection also generates costs, and minimizing them is the task of intelligent economic policy—being also the subject of this book, which aims to make a contribution to the global debate.

Transitioning on from the age of fossil fuels and traditional sources of energy will have many opponents, such as large oil companies that derive their profits from the sale of oil and gas. On the other hand, innovative companies could also develop new synthetic CO_2-neutral fuels. It can, however, be assumed that the leading export countries of coal and oil will not be the natural initiators of modern climate protection policy. Large gas-producing countries are, however, more interested in climate protection policy, as this is changing the demand away from coal and oil and more toward gas—at least temporarily. If you look at the list of the leading oil- and gas-producing countries globally, you will also find some of the G20 countries. Who are the largest producers of solar energy systems? China, the US, Canada, India and the EU, as well as the United Arab Emirates in mid-table were the leaders in this area in 2018. Who is the world's largest user of wind turbines? The UK. Who are the largest suppliers of offshore wind turbines? Denmark, Germany, the US, China and India, if you look at the headquarters of the relevant corresponding large companies. There is an interesting mix of countries for renewable production capacities for solar and wind, with Japan, Russia and France not really featuring. This can only mean that great potential still needs to be realized here. Canada, Brazil and Norway are leading countries in hydropower. Here, too, there is great further potential globally, with the leading companies producing in many countries.

The political economy of climate protection means that producer interests can be organized relatively easily and therefore the resistance on the part of the energy and other industries against an intensified climate protection policy could be considerable. From the point of view of leading industrialized countries, better global climate protection also offers the opportunity to export more modern capital and consumer goods.

Among the new major players—often with comprehensive rights of action—are the key environmental associations in the EU and the US as well as Canada. These are likely to have a rather low tendency to allow narrow economic interests to have an undue effect on climate protection, as here the profiteers would be players in the market. Some environmental associations or law firms see the starting point to helping climate protection in rather in large lawsuits—against cities, governments and companies, occasionally recognizable also from their own interests. Because of their large number and their diversity, consumers are a very difficult group to organize both nationally and internationally—some new environmental regulations on the part of politicians are likely to be directed against them: sometimes an act of symbolic dirigisme against which individuals are hardly able to defend themselves. The corresponding displeasure of millions of voters feeling burdened or victimized will then be exploited by populists in many countries.

Climate change policy, with good choices at the G20+ level, could bring the people of the world closer together as there is a common goal to be achieved. If this is achieved in time in terms of climate neutrality, there will be additional global economic cooperation gains outside climate protection that could even exceed the cost of climate protection measures. The move to a climate-neutral planet Earth is a challenge for all mankind; if it is successfully organized on an international basis, we can breathe new life into the famous words of Neil Armstrong upon stepping onto the surface of the moon.

Without more innovation dynamics and changed financial markets, which put a greater focus on financing sustainable investment projects, this earthly lunar landing cannot succeed. This book also emphasizes the link between financial market dynamics and CO_2 emissions developments. A new empirical analysis by De Haas and Popov (2019) shows that countries with well-developed stock markets—with otherwise identical economic indicators—have lower per capita emissions. Financial market modernization in Europe and other regions of the world can therefore be important for more growth and better emission development.

The member countries of the International Monetary Fund will also have to rethink which indicators should be the focus of economic policy monitoring in member countries; can expansionary fiscal policy be accepted if economically sensible climate protection projects are not also part of a (new) standard package of measures? It would make sense not only to use conventional macroeconomic indicators, but also to consider the World Bank's "real savings rate", which adds investment in education to the normal savings rate and subtracts the extraction of natural resources. Climate protection policy naturally leads to more interest in the topics of innovation dynamics, structural change, economic growth and social policy than was previously the case. The scientific analyses of leading universities and institutes will be very useful in capitalizing on this new interest.

The climate protection debates in Germany, Europe and worldwide are likely to intensify further in the second and third decades of the twenty-first century. The year 2017 was the warmest on Earth in terms of surface temperature since records began in 1880. The previous two years were similarly record-breaking, albeit distorted by the regional El Niño phenomenon in Latin America. Short-term weather patterns are not the same as climate, but the trend of global warming and more extreme localized weather events go hand in hand. It is not for nothing that some of the largest insurance companies are now very active in the field of climate research. This is because conclusions can be drawn, for example, for expected loss events or flood risks worldwide.

Comprehensive data are available indicating a historically high regional, and probably also global, concentration of carbon dioxide. Rising emissions of CO_2 are a critical driver of global warming. Since 1957, the concentration of CO_2 has been continuously measured at a summit in Hawaii. From ice core drillings, one can see even further back into the history of the earth. Measurement results from such wells suggest that the CO_2 concentration in 2018 was higher than has been identified over the course of the last 800,000 years. The World Meteorological Organization also reports that the increase in CO_2 concentrations is worryingly high, comparable to a CO_2 concentration a good two million years ago. The global temperature at that time was two to three degrees higher than today, and the sea level 10 to 20 meters higher. More recent global warming and the increase in CO_2 concentrations since 1850, that is, since the Industrial

Revolution, are reflective of a modern global economy of currently around 7.5 billion people. For them, global warming poses a major challenge—from people on low-lying islands, who lose the very ground beneath their feet due to the rising oceans, to the warmest regions in the world which will see massive crop failures.

Consumption and Production-Based Greenhouse Gas Emissions

Climate neutrality at a global scale can only be achieved if the emission of greenhouse gases can be reduced—on the one hand, emissions should fall and, on the other hand, new absorption technologies be deployed and utilized. The incentives in all countries of the world to engage in the reduction of greenhouse gas emissions differ as relative prices for CO_2 also differ strongly: emission certificate trading plays a role in the Emissions Trading Systems (ETS) of the EU, China, Korea, Switzerland, Japan (two prefectures), and in the US (e.g., California or the Regional Greenhouse Gas Initiative (RGGI) in the northeastern states) and some other countries, but there has been little progress toward an international integration of national ETS thus far. However, as long as certain major countries continue not to implement an ETS and as long as not all countries' emissions trading systems are integrated—which would lead to the emergence of a uniform global CO_2 price—there are inefficiencies in the field of greenhouse gas reduction and the internalization of negative external greenhouse gas effects, respectively. Furthermore, there are inefficiencies related to a lack of internalizing positive external effects from research and development (R&D) and innovations, broadly speaking, and green innovations in particular, respectively.

One important aspect of CO_2 emissions (with CO_2 here standing for greenhouse gas emissions generally) is that international trade leads to differences between production-based CO_2 emissions and consumption-based CO_2 emissions. Countries around the world export and import goods and services, and both exports and imports stand for a certain CO_2 emission intensity. For example, as the US has high imports from China—and a large bilateral trade balance deficit—while China's exports are rather highly CO_2-intensive—then the US CO_2 emissions associated with consumption are larger than US CO_2 emissions from domestic production. This indeed holds because the net import position of the US stands for net imports of CO_2 from the rest of the world as an input-output analysis shows. Thus, the phenomenon that CO_2 is embedded in exports and imports is crucial and has to be considered if global progress toward CO_2 neutrality by 2050 is to be achieved.

A considerable difference can be identified for many countries when one compares production-based CO_2 emissions on the one hand and consumption-based CO_2 emissions on the other. The latter is a figure which can be obtained from trade-embedded CO_2 emissions; including both exports of goods and services and imports of goods and services—each with different CO_2 emission intensities—matters here. Switzerland, Sweden, the UK, Italy, France, Japan, Germany and the US represent countries with large net import embedded CO_2 emissions (see Fig. 1.1). The per capita consumption-based CO_2 emissions in Switzerland were more than twice as high as the per capita production-based CO_2 emissions

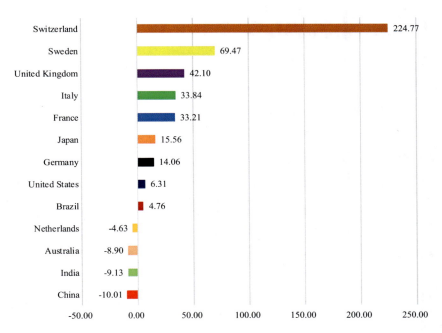

Fig. 1.1 CO_2 emission figures in a trade-related perspective, 2018. (Source: Own representation of data available from Our World In Data; https://ourworldindata.org/co2-and-other-greenhouse-gas-emissions)

in 2018; Sweden's per capita consumption-based CO_2 emissions were 69.5 percent higher than the per capita production-based CO_2 emissions, and in the case of the UK, per capita consumption-based emissions were 42.1 percent higher than the per capita production-based CO_2 emissions (see Fig. 1.2). Thus, the claim of the government of Prime Minister Boris Johnson that the UK is a global leader in CO_2 mitigation is not really adequate. The Netherlands, Australia, India and China were net exporters of CO_2 in 2018. Chinese net exports of CO_2 were 10 percent of China's

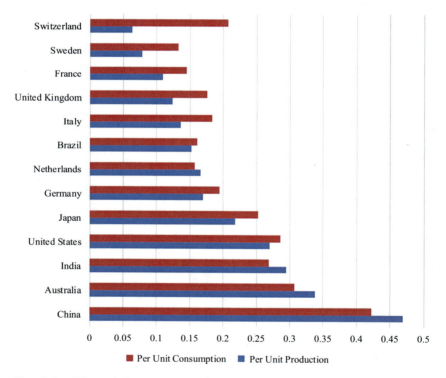

Fig. 1.2 CO_2 emissions per unit of consumption and production for selected countries, 2018. (Source: Own calculations and data based on emissions: kg CO_2 per unit of GDP (OurWorldInData.org) and gross domestic product (GDP, PPP Constant 2017 International $) from World Bank. Per unit consumption = Per unit production × CO_2 emissions embedded in trade (see Fig. 1.1))

GDP-related CO_2, which means that consumption-related CO_2 emissions in China were significantly smaller than Chinese production-related emissions.

It is not generally a problem that consumption-related CO_2 emissions differ from production-related CO_2 emissions, namely to the extent that in all countries positive and negative externalities are internalized. However, large discrepancies between consumption-related CO_2 intensities and GDP-related CO_2 intensities suggest that one should take a closer look at national taxation and subsidy regimes in key countries.

If government wants to maximize per capita consumption while related CO_2 emissions are to a considerable extent embedded in net imports of goods and services, the maximization of policymakers is distorted. A recent important finding for the foreign direct investment (FDI) of OECD countries is that multinationals have a tendency to relocate investment in favor of countries with a relatively weaker performance related to an environmental stringency indicator (Welfens & Bahlmann, 2021), so that there is clear evidence for the pollution haven hypothesis as will be discussed subsequently. These findings are also of interest when one considers global efficiency gains. FDI-diverting effects could be minimized in the EU and the OECD countries if there would be more cooperation in corporate income taxation. However, new conflicts could be anticipated if the result of such cooperation would be in favor of very low corporate income tax rates for which one could make some arguments.

The above findings raise several crucial policy questions. From this perspective, there are several challenges and policy options: FDI outflows could be taxed to some extent, namely to the extent that there are international emission spillovers—either directly or through trade. A general FDI outflow taxation would, however, be a problem for those sectors and countries, respectively, where asset-seeking FDI would be negatively affected so that technology transfers are impaired. This makes an FDI outflow tax a doubtful policy option since (green) innovation dynamics—which to a large extent are related to multinational companies—should not be impaired. One should also not ignore that inward FDI and outward FDI seem to stimulate world output growth in the long run in a macro model with cumulated foreign direct investment, trade and product innovations as well as process innovations (Roeger & Welfens, 2021).

A second policy option is to raise consumption taxation on the basis of effective CO_2 intensities which must include trade-related CO_2 emissions. Such a tax regime could be designed in such a way that the relative prices of consumption goods reflect the negative externality of net imports of intermediate products or final consumption products. Such an internalization approach is feasible at modest cost related to research (input-output analysis for open economies) and to tax collection. A truly efficient system of internalizing negative external effects from greenhouse gas emissions would be the creation of national ETS in all G20 countries and a global integration of these national ETS—assuming that the respective national coverage of CO_2 sources is roughly equal; note that even the EU with a 45 percent coverage of emissions and California with more than 80 percent coverage in 2020 have rather dissimilar coverage rates while it is also noteworthy that the respective CO_2 certificate prices in the EU and California also showed considerable difference in 2018/2019/2020, namely of about €10 per metric ton, which suggests large gains could be realized from an integrated EU-California system (as a small blueprint for a powerful G20 ETS integration).

An additional and useful policy option would be an international CO_2-innovation fund to which net importer countries of CO_2 will have to contribute, and these funds would be used to subsidize CO_2-mitigating product innovations and process innovations. The G20 could organize such a CO_2-innovation fund, and firms from CO_2-exporting countries could then compete for R&D subsidies; the minimal subsidization of research and development would be the guiding principle of the green R&D fund. At the bottom line, a combination of ETS integration in the G20 and green R&D promotion can be recommended in a policy perspective. The necessary modeling could be made within an augmented DSGE (Dynamic Stochastic General Equilibrium) model which should include trade, FDI and innovation dynamics.

Multinationals and Environmental Policy Stringency

For about the last two decades, there has been an increasingly stronger climate protection policy approach in industrialized countries (i.e., the OECD group of countries). The problem, however, is that although the CO_2 emissions of OECD countries are gradually declining, CO_2 emissions are rising in China, India, South Africa and many other countries. On a closer inspection, one finds that even among the OECD countries there is some heterogeneity—whereby there are still a number of countries with weak climate policy and environmental policy stringency, respectively.

In the field of innovation, investment and trade, there is a powerful influence in the world economy—namely, multinational companies. They are key drivers of global innovation dynamics, and the output of affiliates was about 12 percent of source countries' gross domestic product in OECD countries in 2018. How will the response of MNCs be if certain countries adopt a more pro-climate environmental policy: the gravity equation of Welfens and Bahlmann (2021) has shown that a rise of the environmental policy stringency index in OECD countries reduces foreign direct investment inflows—providing evidence which suggests that the pollution haven thesis seems to be a realistic perspective. This, however, could make a more ambitious climate policy in OECD (and elsewhere) a rather difficult challenge, unless international cooperation in sustainability policy is reinforced among OECD countries and G20 countries. This, however, could be rather difficult for the G20 country group, where per capita differentials are rather high so that the similarity and alignment of interests is rather weak and hence political consensus is more difficult to achieve. Moreover, the economic rivalry between the US and China could make G20 cooperation even more difficult.

There could also be opportunities for the European Commission to push for more green innovations in multinational companies and to support more green techno-globalization: that is, joint research projects of multinationals from different countries as well as more green R&D in affiliates abroad. One should not underestimate the positive macroeconomic impact of both process innovations and product innovations which go along with international—sectoral—technology transfer (Roeger & Welfens, 2021).

New Analytical Perspectives

The adaptation processes of economic policy and the new course set for climate protection policy have national and international consequences. At the end of the day, there will be considerable economic and social changes; at least another three decades of accelerated structural change will be necessary worldwide to tackle the challenge, which will represent a historical, and at times difficult, period of upheaval. Prices, economic structures and technologies will change, but this will also involve other key variables in the economic systems of both the industrialized and emerging economies, including naturally the G20 countries, regarded as the "leading countries of the world economy", which meet annually for a global economic summit. The G20 represents a good 60 percent of the world's population. Leading UN climate researchers have argued that "climate neutrality" must be achieved by 2050: compared to 1990—the standard year of comparison—CO_2 emissions must by then be reduced by around 90 percent. Thus, if you set 1990 = 100, the EU will be at about 65 in 2022; it will take until 2050 to reach the level of 10. In China, India, Indonesia and other countries, CO_2 emissions have risen since 1990 and will continue to rise for the time being. How can a sensible and meaningful cooperation take place between the Global North and South? Here, one can acknowledge that finding common ground has been a difficult task. At the 2007 G8 summit in Heiligendamm, Germany, the leading industrialized economies formalized a forum for discussions on topics of joint interest with the largest emerging economies or the so-called outreach countries, namely Brazil, China, India, Mexico and South Africa. In 2007, leaders of these countries took part in discussions with the G8 including on issues concerning emissions. Here the divergence of interests became clear with then Prime Minister of India Manmohan Singh calling on industrialized countries to bear the brunt of cutting emissions (Federal Government of Germany, 2007; Kade, 2008). Highlighting the fact that industrialized countries had "enjoyed" centuries of carbon emissions, whereas emerging economies such as India or China were still catching up in terms of development, Singh noted that India and China, for example, could still emit carbon while using their "fair share" of the global atmosphere (Antholis, 2009). For Singh, who became a leading voice for an "equitable" distribution of the burden of cutting emissions, carbon reduction is inextricably linked to facilitation of financial and capital flows as well as technology transfer from the leading economies to the emerging economies. There are issues picked up later in this book. However, one can note that in the intervening years, the threat of climate change has focused attention, with India and China—with its new national emissions trading system—playing key roles in the field. Thus, finding agreement and consensus between developed and developing countries may no longer be as difficult a task as it once appeared to be.

What are the longer-term impacts of climate protection policy on the economies of individual countries and on the global economy as a whole? What does climate neutrality cost, and what adaptation paths are reasonable?

This book is the first study that does not consider climate change issues in isolation but that also integrates related issues of income inequality and innovation dynamics, as well as opportunities for G20+ cooperation (G20+ = G20 plus Nigeria, which according to UN projections will have about 400 million inhabitants by 2050), which is seen as a crucial prerequisite for achieving climate neutrality by 2050. G20+ represents circa 80 percent of global carbon dioxide emissions.

While a great deal of specialist literature can be found on climate protection, there is a lack of analysis on how the cooperation between countries and global regions that is necessary for the goal of climate neutrality to be reached. At the same time, national climate protection policy in many countries is a key element of the steps necessary on the journey toward climate sustainability that will also enable future generations to enjoy similar opportunities and prosperity as current generations. Since, according to the International Carbon Action Partnership Status Report (ICAP, 2018), only 15 percent of global CO_2 emissions were covered by an emissions trading system in 2017—such systems initiated by the EU in 2005 (5 percent of global emissions comprehensively covered) —the road is a long and difficult one: increasing coverage to at least 80 percent or so of global emissions which is considered a must taking the G20+ bloc into consideration. In mid-2019, the World Bank, on its website, reports on its website that 38 countries either used or were planning to introduce a certificate trading system (https://carbonpricingdashboard.worldbank.org/map_data). But many of the key G20 countries are missing, even though such trading systems are efficient.

There are no discernible approaches at a G20 level to rapidly introduce more CO_2 emissions trading systems in those G20 countries which are not yet participating. Mexico is an exception, but the impetus here does not come from the G20. The strong focus of official policy in many regions of the world on the Paris Agreement, with over 190 signatory countries, makes sense in some cases, but due to the huge number of countries involved it is also an unnecessary overtaxing of oneself.

So how can national climate protection policy be coordinated meaningfully, and what are the prerequisites for effective international cooperation in economic policy? What combination of policy elements is necessary to deliver, with a high degree of certainty, climate neutrality by 2050 without destabilizing the economy? It is shown that the existing EU pre-planned annual reduction of the emissions cap for 2020–2030, namely of -2.2 percent, will lead exactly to such a destabilization effect, since during the period 2030–2050, the cap of CO_2 emissions would have to be reduced by 8 percent annually if the climate-neutral target is to be met. This would bring a kind of oil price shock at the end of the 2020s, here through certificate prices of probably over €100 (about $110) per metric ton of CO_2. This is an economically risky, indeed nonsensical path, about which no major concerns appear to have been raised so far. It is an urgent issue that as early as the decade 2020–2030, the annual percentage decline in the EU's upper limit would have to be gradually reduced to around 5 percent. The great contradictions in parts of the political sphere show that the task of meeting the climate neutrality goal by 2050 has not really been taken seriously thus far. However, if the necessary adaptation steps in EU and the other G20+ countries are taken in time, climate neutrality can indeed be achieved by 2050.

New answers to the above questions are developed in this book. In addition, alternative regulation, emission certificate trading systems and CO_2 taxes plus other policy options will be discussed, and existing contradictions on important policy-relevant issues—such as the level of CO_2 damage per ton of CO_2 emissions—will be highlighted. The question of the best strategy for achieving global climate neutrality by 2050 is also raised. This broader approach will develop a necessary global economic perspective and provide a comprehensible insight into the national and international climate protection debate. The new analysis and policy perspectives presented here in part extend existing approaches, but they also differ significantly in part from current approaches in Germany, the EU and the UN.

The Fridays for Future protest movement of students in many countries of Europe, indeed in many countries across the world, stands for the great concern among the younger generations that sufficient climate protection policies will not be implemented in time in industrialized and emerging countries. Millions of youths are wondering whether their future is in existential danger, and why national and international policymakers may not want to or are not able to set a clear course for a more energetic climate protection policy at an early stage—at least in good time to be truly effective.

This is a very justified question, and older people, with a view to the generations of their children and/or grandchild, are also partly taking this concern on board. The Fridays for Future movement creates more pressure for action in politics, but it is unclear whether it will then carefully consider rational policy alternatives with sufficient knowledge base. Will the activists of the Fridays for Future movement engage in controversial discussions and inspire progress in the field of climate research? Fridays for

Future is certainly evidence of the great potential for international action and cooperation. The commitment of young people to climate protection can actually be a reason for optimism—with politicians in many countries simultaneously coming under pressure to act on climate protection policy.

The fact that Greta Thunberg sat on the street in front of the Swedish parliament buildings in her first protest may at first seem surprising, as Sweden in particular has achieved an exemplary reduction in CO_2 emissions on the European continent compared to 1990 due to the early introduction of a carbon dioxide tax in combination with applying the EU CO_2 certificate trade approach in other sectors. Greta Thunberg, however, is clearly concerned not just with Sweden, but with instigating a European or global climate protest movement. In Europe as a whole, student protests are an impulse for an otherwise lethargic climate policy to develop more rapidly. Is strengthened European and global climate protection policy now moving in the right direction? With sufficient speed? It is important to find answers to these important questions. How can climate protection policy be meaningfully linked with other fields of economic policy? Taking a broader view of the problem could initially be seen as an irrelevant nuisance, but in fact it is crucial if climate protection policy is to be successful.

From an economic-ecological-social point of view, of course, one must also ask the question of how the desired national and ultimately global climate protection can be achieved at minimum cost—is there currently a mismanagement of climate protection? What could be done better? What is the most effective sequence of reform steps, how much international cooperation is necessary and how can meaningful reforms of citizenship be explained in an understandable way? How do you avoid turning climate policy into a series of expensive headline-grabbing but ineffective reforms or knee-jerk actions? Rather, it should be considered how best to mobilize people's creative energies to meet the challenge of climate protection in a positive, well-thought-out and internationally networked way?

The present study examines these plus other important questions and matters of concern from a fundamental economic-political perspective. The answer to the youth of today is that one can be justifiably worried, but that at least for the time being there are still good opportunities to reach the two-degree target set down in the UN Paris Agreement in time via a sequence of comprehensive reforms in Europe, North America and Asia. Compared to 1850, and the beginnings of industrialization, the average global surface temperature is to rise by a maximum of 2 degrees Celsius in the twenty-first century, if possible by only 1.5 degrees. However, as the IPCC (2021) suggests in their report—discussing the natural science base findings which further underline and support previous IPCC research—breaching the 1.5-degree "upper limit" for global warming might already become a reality by 2030, earlier than was anticipated in previous reports. This means that we are talking about a major goal in three respects: a goal for the whole world, a goal for the first half of the twenty-first century (hopefully already achievable in the 2040s) and a goal the achievement of which will be the basis for prosperity and stability on earth for many decades to come.

The Influence of Populism on Climate Protection Policy

Populism in the US under President Trump undermined the EU by eliminating traditional US support for European integration, in addition to Trump's support of the Brexit project in the UK. Trump presided over an end to more than 60 years of solid US support for EU integration. Brexit not only represents the withdrawal of the UK from the European Union, but also represents in a way the voiding of 45 years of British participation in the EU. If political lines of cooperation within the EU should break after such a long time, then one will have to ask oneself which supposedly long-term cooperation projects in the West one should still trust.

The domestic polarization of British and American politics is a phenomenon that can in part be traced back to the Internet: national consensus-building becomes more difficult and protracted in a digitalized world. This will also slow down international climate protection cooperation alarmingly. In any case, these dynamics do not correspond to the prerequisites for more long-term international cooperation projects. Climate protection in particular is a global cooperation project as there is only one climate for the earth.

With the Biden administration, the US is moving back to international cooperation in climate protection policy—this is welcome, but it is not clear that the US has overcome populism. At the same time, it is remarkable that the US and China have restarted cooperation in the field of climate protection as became visible in the international digital climate conference in April 2021; China has indicated some willingness to accelerate climate-friendly technological progress and for the first time has no longer claimed for itself to be a developing economy (for which softer adjustment paths can be expected compared to OECD countries and newly industrialized countries). Biden has announced that the US will cut greenhouse gas emissions by 50 percent—compared to 2005—within a decade, and part of the massive fiscal expansion plans of the Biden administration for the post-Corona recovery indeed has put the focus on infrastructure modernization and green technological progress. This is an interesting signal, but one should not exclude that strongly enhanced digital growth after the Corona epidemic will raise the demand for electricity strongly, and it is not clear that the share of renewable energy will rise massively in the medium term. Many countries, including the US, the UK, France, Russia, Japan, China and a few other countries, have emphasized that nuclear power plant is associated with roughly zero CO_2 emissions so that nuclear energy seems to be part of the solution for achieving climate neutrality by 2050. However, from an economic argument the pro-nuclear power argument is rather strange—unless one could consider inherently safe new nuclear energy plants (existing in research labs only). The key problem of nuclear energy generation is that it represents large potential negative external effects, namely the risk of a major nuclear accident, and liability insurance of nuclear energy is quite low so that the implicit liability insurance effectively is the government—this in turn means that there is a massive implicit subsidy in many countries for nuclear power generation. There is no level playing field in the energy sector. Whether or not countries support nuclear energy generation is largely a political decision, not one without international distortions since nuclear electricity is traded across countries in Europe and in other regions of the world.

The rise of populism is an indication that a considerable section of the population in various countries see a problem surrounding the concept of identity in the wake of many years of high immigration. Possibly also because in a world of digital media the integration of immigrants is slower with regard to learning the language of the host country than before. Once in New York, on a trip to a meeting at the UN, I had a taxi driver who spoke only Spanish, a situation which I did not find particularly easy or pleasant, especially since my Spanish is not very good. At least a basic knowledge of a common language facilitating the communication of all in a country seems to be important for a perception and feeling of a common identity; of course, it is also crucial for a meaningful public and professional debate. Not over-emphasizing and going too far with respect to diversity can be seen as an important policy concern; otherwise the idea of national solidarity as a fundamental principle of social coexistence will be insufficiently accepted by the general public. If the concept of solidarity is politically weakened in many countries, then the concept of solidarity and cooperation can hardly be strong internationally either. But this sense of global togetherness and common purpose is a prerequisite for global climate policy.

Moreover, if in many countries the forces of globalization and digitization are perceived as confusing, unfair and at times chaotic (sometimes caused by too rapid liberalization in some fields), the search for new and seemingly simple political answers will intensify in parts of the population: populist authoritarian structures will spread, and democratic governments may show a diminished propensity to promote public debates on big and divisive issues. But climate protection and democracy should go hand in hand.

Populism, protectionism and nationalism mean that international cooperation in an era of anti-multilateralism—that is, the rejection of the role of international organizations by the Trump administration, among others—will become more difficult, and the efficiency of environmental and climate protection policy will deteriorate significantly. Thus, the costs of climate protection will increase significantly. Under unfavorable circumstances, a globally rational climate protection policy can become impossible, which in the long term could lead to massive new international conflicts—for example, via a massively increased number of climate refugees destabilizing the world economy, immigration pressure on the North due to the sharp increase in the frequency of extreme heat waves in the South of the world economy.

More immigration pressure means more opportunities for the populists to expand their base. There's a dangerous inequality looming. Populists also doubt that man-made climate change exists. It is often claimed that much of the scientific climate research shows doubts about the extent of human influence on climate change; NASA wrote as early as 2015, however, that 97 percent of studies show such an influence, and leading scientific institutes now assume such an influence as a consensus position (https://climate.nasa.gov/scientific-consensus/). It would be reasonable not to focus too strongly on the 97 percent figure, as not all studies are methodologically convincing; rather one should reflect on the fact that the leading research institutes in the field of climate research worldwide have presented largely similar findings and conclusions in matters of man-made global warming (however, especially in Germany, there are some economists who, with a strange reference to Friedrich von Hayek and a misjudgment of the importance of empirical economic and climate research, think that it is impossible to make well-founded statements on global warming; these economists apparently do not understand the arguments of the well-known science theorist Karl Popper).

According to populists, man-made climate change does not exist in the West, which could be seen as a kind of return to the time before Copernicus. Critical doubts about the "elites" are used to instill a general doubt about every expert insight and practically every institution, which is a risky approach. A certain anti-scientific attitude is a characteristic of populists who are often experts in wishful thinking and simple—then often popular—sham solutions. Brexit is also based upon such tactics (Iain Duncan Smith as a former leader of the British Conservative Party showed in a Hard Talk BBC Interview in 2019 that he understands nothing about scientific analysis: the banking crisis of 2008/2009 had not been predicted by numerous research institutions, and therefore one could not expect a reasonable forecast for Brexit from them—the welfare effects of British EU membership from more than four decades have been confirmed in relevant empirical research). One-time Secretary of State for Justice under Prime Minister Cameron, Michael Gove, said on TV before the 2016 EU referendum that the British public had "had enough of experts". In the UK, some Conservatives are strangely positioned against Britain's long and proud scientific tradition.

Many industrialized and emerging countries have been committed to climate protection for years; this includes Germany, which participates in the EU Emissions Trading System (ETS) and can certainly demonstrate success in reducing emissions. Beyond the scope of the ETS, which includes energy and industry, there is an obligation to reduce emissions under other EU agreements (e.g., EU Climate Action Regulation): by 2020, emissions in sectors outside the EU ETS must be reduced by 14 percent, and by 2030 by 38 percent compared to 2005. This concerns agriculture, transport and buildings, with an upper limit on the volume of emissions set for 2013–2030. Germany would have failed to meet the 2020 targets in this area in normal circumstances—due to the Corona pandemic and associated economic downturn (Welfens, 2020a, b) reduced production, consumption and transport emissions mean Germany will meet its target for 2020, but with levels returning to normal it is likely to face serious problems again in 2030. Germany will then have to make up for its shortcomings by buying emission rights from other EU countries, which could cost several billion euros.

Climate protection policy should be carefully analyzed, the pros and cons should be publicly discussed, and efficient climate protection policy should then be implemented. This book takes a critical view of the new tendency in German federal politics over many years to barely discuss the major issues of the future publicly in parliament, but to make politically sensitive decisions in mega-commissions—as in the case of the phase-out of coal and nuclear energy production—as a kind of substitute parliament. Not only questions of climate protection policy, but all major issues of economy, society, politics and security need to be discussed transparently and audibly in a representative democracy, society and parliament. In the long run, democracy cannot tolerate the remoteness (from the public's point of view) of grandiose mega-commissions. It will not work to implement majority votes in parliament without first having publicly discussed the important arguments, facts and decision options, and thus wanting to steer the behaviors of consumers or firms. Especially major changes such as climate protection policy need legitimacy, in full consideration of those ultimately affected. Achieving climate neutrality is not the same as the moon landing but could have the same impact on Earth. Successful global climate protection policy could give ten billion people (in 2050) a new confidence in humanity's ability to shape the future viability of the planet jointly and peacefully on an international scale. A lot is at stake.

Some climate questions tend to have complicated answers. However, there are still some simple answers to the topic of climate change for three quarters of the world. For example, an uptake of cycling as a means of transport, which is not expensive in terms of bicycles, but which does require considerable investment in a city—see, for example, the model cities of Copenhagen, Amsterdam or Hamburg. Safe new turning systems for the fleet of heavy goods vehicles are also long overdue, as trucks are all too often involved in (often fatal) collisions with cyclists during turning maneuvers due to a lack of good driver visibility. Many other measures are also conceivable by individuals making smarter climate-considerate decisions. But without national and international policy measures—without more cooperation—the necessary level of climate protection will not be achieved.

Leading OECD countries and emerging economies are called upon to provide an independent impetus for climate protection through more climate-friendly innovation dynamics and to encourage climate-friendly investments in infrastructure and building construction. Austria is a global leader in the area of emission-neutral houses, but to date the EU is facilitating such Austrian-designed and built houses being constructed in the other EU27 countries, despite the internal market. This is absurd—there are real solutions to many problems, but their application is prevented by national, protectionist and climate-damaging regulations. In addition to progress in the EU, steps toward cooperation on climate protection at the international level between the G20 countries are necessary. Some things are happening at UN conferences, but the work is not focused enough. Influential EU countries and the EU itself have no discernible strategy for making serious progress at G20 level. There are old G20 press releases calling for the huge subsidies for fossil fuels to be reduced—but practically nothing has happened on this. Many *non-binding* announcements are also made to great acclaim, but there is no website where you can easily see the aspirational goals and the progress of individual countries in achieving them. That is no way to achieve climate neutrality.

The climate problem with CO_2 emissions is, like the Internet, really limitless. Economic policy of the traditional kind is not good at providing international public goods: a secure Internet, for example, or sufficient climate protection, which amounts to limiting CO_2 emissions (and similar gases) worldwide. In view of the heating of the earth and the increase in the mean surface temperature, the climate does not care where the respective CO_2 emissions come from. If it is possible to make progress on climate protection, this will not remain without side effects—for example, in the area of economic inequality in the countries of the world. Here there are sociopolitical compatibility limits that must be observed. Otherwise, climate protection will be a thing of the past in the long run. Economic policy as a whole is challenged in a new way.

Due to the side effects of climate protection measures, a broad concept of economic policy should be developed, and of course costs should be taken into account in climate protection. Unnecessarily expensive climate protection measures should be urgently avoided. Achieving climate neutrality does not have to be popular above all other considerations (e.g., rapidly reducing coal-fired power generation capabilities), but rather securely affordable and organized at minimum cost, then more climate protection becomes feasible. A major global climate protection effort is needed from politicians, which must include a modification of the various tax systems. It is difficult to understand why Denmark, the Netherlands and some other EU countries have revenues from environmental taxes of

3.5 to 4 percent, while in Germany the corresponding figure is just over 2 percent. Higher eco-taxes and lower income and corporate tax rates could stand for a gain in environmental quality, growth and jobs in many EU countries. Outside the EU, this applies in a very similar way, while some countries are still pursuing anti-environmental and anti-climate protection policies.

Environmental and climate protection, as well as sustainability considerations will gain in importance in the long run within economic policy, where the framework conditions for more climate-friendly innovations and CO_2 reduction should be realigned. Those who credibly stand behind feasible climate protection goals could distinguish themselves in politics by being able to garner the support of large sections of the population and to reliably develop the necessary comprehensive international cooperation.

CO_2 emissions are a global phenomenon and therefore neither Germany nor even the EU alone—which stand for 2.2 percent and 10 percent of global greenhouse gas emissions respectively—can solve the global climate problem. There is already a need for a wider international approach. There are impulses for this from some sides, including Europe, but here the measures are still clearly inadequate by 2020. It is important to understand the interdependencies in the US-Asia (i.e., China, Japan, India, etc.)-EU tripolar world as well as Russia: if a major actor, such as the EU, develops efficient climate protection policies, this will have positive effects on Asia and North America; and from there, there will be positive economic repercussion effects on the EU, that is, Germany, France, Italy, the UK, the Netherlands, etc. (and it is conceivable that other countries will also adopt EU climate policy approaches, which would then facilitate international cooperation). This is certainly also true if one considers China as a major actor in climate policy at the starting point and then analyzes the impulses that emanate from there to the rest of Asia (excluding China), the EU and North America, and the feedback effects from there which flow back to China. Those who consider the mutual dependencies at an international level can achieve efficient cooperation solutions. If you look at the problem from the perspective of a single country such as Germany or the Netherlands, you will not get very far. Then one might think that Germany alone cannot achieve anything with a well-thought-out climate policy. This way of thinking, however, is inadequate, and a European—including Russia—and global view is often more meaningful.

On the other hand, the potential reach of EU countries and the EU should not be underestimated. This is because it is possible to exert influence through international organizations (with a multiplier effect on climate protection) if green innovation impulses could be set worldwide, and this must also be addressed in the scientific analysis (this aspect was, however, hardly considered in Germany in the very readable July 2019 special report of the German Council of Economic Experts (2019)). However, Germany and the EU also have credibility problems, as they struggled to meet their own targets for 2020. Part of this loss of credibility is politically self-inflicted, as too many goals are set at the same time, some of which are even contradictory. Germany would have failed to meet its national target for reducing CO_2 emissions were it not for the Corona pandemic, but the EU as a whole is reaching its 2020 target at this point. The new EU Commission President will certainly also be called upon to provide more impetus for global climate policy from Brussels.

On top of that, there are efficiency problems: a reduction in CO_2 emissions cannot be achieved at the lowest possible cost. California covers 85 percent of CO_2 emissions through emissions trading, the EU only 45 percent. The EU is the political inventor of the trade in CO_2 certificates and has been active in this field since 2005. CO_2 certificate trading generates a market price for one ton of CO_2, and this price, and its development over time, exerts adjustment pressure on the economy, state and private households. If the G20 countries could all be quickly persuaded to use a comprehensive certificate system, the global economy could achieve climate neutrality by 2050—as can be seen herein. The price mechanism is important in certificate trading, whereby a very low certificate price does not, of course, lead companies to expect major innovations and other adjustments. It should also be considered how an unnecessarily large fluctuation margin (i.e., price volatility) of the certificate can be avoided over time.

In an open economy, the question is to what extent other countries can be won over in terms of cooperation. This is a difficult question for the EU countries in the time of Trumpian populism and Brexit, which as a project is also a populist phenomenon. Populism means nationalism and protectionism, that is, not an easy avenue for international cooperation, not in trade policy and not in climate policy. Yet trade policy is actually already part of climate policy. The more free trade there is worldwide, the greater the competitive pressure to minimize costs and resources in production.

The economic and political debate on the complex issue of climate protection is sometimes confusing, and even expert analyses sometimes contribute little to clarification and a sensible debate. This study aims to make a clear and in part new contribution. What is new is the analytical combination of climate protection, innovation, distribution and multilateralist policies. The latter means that international organizations are used specifically for innovation and climate protection policy; of course, a large number of countries are involved. What is also new, however, is that when relevant policy areas are thoughtfully linked, conclusions must ultimately be drawn that go further than discrete policy measures in the EU or California or China or Japan have done so far.

Within a few decades, we could be facing the threat of irreversible changes in the climate, related major welfare losses of 10 to 15 percent worldwide and possibly also regional and global economic and political instability. This will happen if we do not do enough to protect the climate. If, on the other hand, climate protection policy is implemented too late and inefficiently—that is, too expensively in terms of the selected strategies and measures—this will also have serious negative economic consequences and entail risks for international stability. Climate refugees from countries in the Global South moving to the Global North is just one of the conceivable new problems facing the EU.

The EU certificate trade for carbon dioxide certificates is largely exemplary: there are incentives for the energy sector and industry to reduce CO_2 emissions at minimum cost in accordance with a politically prescribed time path for reducing emissions. This certificate trade should be rapidly expanded from covering 45 percent of emissions to 85–90 percent, if possible, and the EU should win over trading partners on the benefits of certificate trading in a targeted manner. The systems can be interconnected in the medium term, which reduces the cost of reducing CO_2 emissions. China will have implemented a national certificate trading system by 2021, California stands for a sensible CO_2 certificate system in the US that indeed covers 85 percent of Californian emissions—California's system is inspired by the EU trading system. This creates the basis for EU-US-China cooperation.

Since 2010 at the latest, the issue of providing free certificates to companies in the export sector in the EU and in the energy sector in California has been flawed. Switzerland generously grants free certificates in sectors where there are fears that international carbon leakage will occur—that is, the increase in the cost of CO_2-intensive production resulting from emissions certificate trading could lead to production being shifted to countries without such certificate trading and without a carbon dioxide tax. Then there is the threat of job losses and ultimately little impact on the climate if a high proportion of free certificates is not generously distributed to companies in certain sectors when certificate trading is introduced. But this does not remain without consequence in the distribution of wealth.

In the EU, companies in some sectors have been allocated allowances free of charge by the state to a considerable extent: it is said that this is done in order not to impair international competitiveness. In some cases, too much is happening here. Analyses show that companies have to be allocated free certificates for only about 20 percent of their emission volume in order to leave the company profit unchanged. An additional free allocation of allowances is a state redistribution policy in favor of the production factor capital, leading to share price increases falling into the laps of investors—in quite a few cases into those of foreign investors. This scenario is unfair and politically unreasonable. Since 2010, there has been a visible shortfall of competence in the area of environmental policy, as this problem of the wealthy shareholders and the issue of free certificates to companies in Germany and many other countries has not been considered.

It also shows that certificate prices influence the share prices of companies in the energy sector and industry in the EU: if certificate prices fall, there is an impulse for falling share prices; if certificate prices rise, share prices rise. A certificate market will not have an adverse economic effect on investment and innovation dynamics and thus on the economic growth of the country concerned. Thus, it would be wise to increase emissions from 45 to 85 or even 90 percent in the EU and to rapidly expand allowance trading.

Public understanding of the functioning of the EU allowance market is surprisingly weak in Europe, or perhaps not so surprising, considering that allowance trading has been taking place in the EU since 2005, but governments have made no effort to explain the logic of the EU Emissions Trading System. Very many of the striking school pupils, and indeed teachers, are obviously unaware that the decommissioning of the coal-fired power plants in Germany proposed by the so-called Coal Commission by 2038 is about twice as expensive as actually necessary. The transition from a CO_2-emission world to a climate-neutral Earth is like moving from one planet to another. The move should be organized carefully and with minimum risk, and poorer households should be granted financial support from a special fund over two decades—a kind of relocation premium. For this you can easily set up a special fund, which is not difficult to finance in a period of historically low real interest rates. However, with nominal interest rates on government bonds and large corporate bonds still negative, the market economy will run into difficulties. The European Central Bank is obliged to push up the interest rate; a long phase of artificially ultra-low interest rates—even a negative real interest rate (market interest rate minus inflation rate)—undermines households' propensity to save and leads to bad investments.

Moreover, it is also true that at historically low interest rates the state should increasingly initiate well-thought-out infrastructure and climate projects, since future generations will also benefit considerably from them, so that credit financing makes double sense. A problematically low structural deficit limit of 0.35 percent of gross domestic product is anchored in Germany's constitution. This leads to a long-term debt ratio of 23.3 percent if this deficit ratio is realized and a real trend economic growth of 1.5 percent is assumed, which appears to be too low, especially as the average government bond rating in the Eurozone is pulled down as a result (Germany has an AAA rating, the rest of the Eurozone averaged around B in 2019), which will make private investment financing unnecessarily more expensive throughout the Eurozone, including in Germany. If Germany even wanted to keep the government deficit ratio below 0.35 percent in the longer term, this would be all the more problematic. It would be more expensive for the national economy to realize a deficit ratio of 0.1 percent—in the case of public underinvestment—than a deficit ratio of 0.35 percent with reasonable infrastructure and climate projects.

With the German Coal Commission—officially the Commission for Growth, Structural Change and Jobs—the federal government in Berlin has created a seemingly august body comprising leading academic, public and even religious figures of German civil society that unintentionally undermines democracy and appears authoritarian because it effectively ends the public debate (the Ethics Commission for Safe Energy Supply—which recommended Germany's complete withdrawal from nuclear as a source of energy—was knitted together according to the same pattern; this point is relevant regardless of the fact that there indeed are good arguments for an exit from nuclear power). If the public does not have a chance to thoroughly discuss the corresponding legislative measures taken after the Commission presents its report, this is anti-democratic; the commissions represent quasi-authoritarian structures which have emerged in the middle of a democracy, which are directed against an open society (in the sense of Karl Popper). This is regrettable from an economic and climate policy point of view as well as from a social and educational policy perspective. According to the Coal Commission, for the planned economic phase-out from coal-fired power generation and coal mining (which is unnecessarily overpriced with estimated costs of about €90 billion meaning a price twice as high for the phasing out of coal as would actually be required), one should reckon with a loss of about €500 per capita in Germany. An inflated figure which has been determined by a commission composed somewhat confusingly of members representing organizations from religious congregations, to the Red Cross to Greenpeace. Around €45 billion in overpricing stands for an enormous amount of money that is lacking in social and education policy, among other areas.

Even without a government-imposed coal phase-out in 2038, there would be great pressure over time to shut down coal-fired power plants due to a lack of profitability if the certificate trade were to take effect; with a conceivable certificate price of €30 per ton, the pressure would of course be greater than with a certificate price of €10 per ton. The idea of the Coal Commission to stop CO_2 emissions in a sector where they are relatively high is recognizable. This makes no economic sense, however, since CO_2 emissions should be reduced above all where the (marginal) costs of CO reduction are relatively low. That is exactly what the certificates market does, a coal commission cannot know this—many members follow an interest-driven or emotional compass. Those who ignore the logic of emissions and certificate markets in this way can probably exploit the popularity of symbolic policies, but that is not the way to make an efficient contribution to CO_2 reduction. If one organizes an unnecessarily expensive CO_2 reduction, this is primarily to the detriment of poorer households. Wealthy households could easily cope with unnecessarily high electricity prices, but poorer families certainly could not. Is it now the case that parties that want to represent the interests of poorer classes pay particular attention to efficiency arguments in climate policy?

A bureaucratically planned withdrawal from coal in Germany can result in income losses just as much as an under-regulated banking or market economy, for example, in the run-up to the 2008–2009 Transatlantic Banking Crisis. It ignores the impact of emissions trading as well as the important role of relative prices and companies in competition, to which the West owes much of its prosperity.

Since climate protection is a global problem, an isolated climate protection policy in Germany or the EU alone is of course of little use; a sensible, broader climate protection policy depends on a good model effect and positive network effects in Germany's (or the EU's) partner countries.

Even if the EU causes only 10 percent of global emissions, and Germany only 2.2 percent, it should not be overlooked that there are natural allies for the partly exemplary climate protection policy of the European Union. Since 2005, the EU's emission allowance system has covered 45 percent of emissions; it can be further expanded and combined with similar policies in California, parts of Canada, China as a whole, as well as Japan (Tokyo, Saitama plus all other regions) and the Republic of Korea. The more comprehensive certificate trading in the global economy becomes, the more favorable the transition to a CO_2-neutral global economy by 2050 will be, provided that certificate trading is also included in international financial regulation.

The compact G20+ group is classified here as a reasonably capable institution, namely the G20 countries, including all EU member states (especially as all EU countries participate in the EU certificates trading system), plus Nigeria, which is not yet a member of the G20. It would be strange not to want Nigeria, estimated to be the third largest country in the world in terms of population in 2050, to participate in a process aimed at climate neutrality by 2050. Incidentally, the G20 do not only consist of rich countries, but there are also medium- and low-income countries—without the participation of Russia, Brazil, India or Indonesia it will not work, nor without the very wealthy, but little industrialized, Saudi Arabia.

In the longer term, all G20 countries should have certificate systems; many countries in the world still want to be convinced of the advantages of such systems. In any case, renewable energies must also represent a growing share of the energy sector on the supply side in the longer term, with every G20 country fortunately having capabilities in terms of wind power generation, solar power generation, geothermal power generation or hydroelectric power plants. Spain and Brazil, as well as Italy and India, can rely on both solar power and wind power, although India has few locational advantages for wind power generation for geographical reasons. South Africa, the EU, the US and China have enormous potential for various types of renewable energies. In dozens of countries, energy and production systems need to be rebuilt; this is a complex challenge, where market signals are important.

A certain risk of emission certificate systems presumably lies in the sometimes considerable fluctuation intensity of CO_2 certificate prices: if this should make share prices less stable than they have been so far, there will be additional costs for the otherwise ideal certificate model, under which regions, states or cities will dictate decreasing emission quantities for the economy over time. In principle, certificate trading between companies can result in a market price for emissions that achieves the desired emission reduction at the lowest possible cost, provided that the policy only reduces the upper limit of the emission quantity year after year by announcing it in advance. Whether the stock markets themselves influence the prices of CO_2 certificates needs to be investigated.

However, the pace set for reducing emissions in Germany and Europe in 2005–2019 appears to be obviously too slow; the reduction of the CO_2 maximum quantity by -2.2 percent per year planned for 2021 is also too low, and the government knows this. Reductions of below -5 percent per year in the decade after 2020 will see the emissions reduction target of 90 percent required for climate neutrality in the EU by 2050 going unmet. On the other hand, these are not the only options to tackle emissions. According to the argumentation of scientists from the Swiss Federal Institute of Technology (ETH) in Zurich, global reforestation strategies can also reduce the pressure, since a world with more forests can also absorb more CO_2. In addition, the earth's atmosphere can also be artificially cooled by certain measures. However, these so-called geoengineering methods still need to be investigated further. Whether or not it is also possible, and viable, to extract CO_2 from the atmosphere using certain technologies is also not well established scientifically.

PERSPECTIVES ON INTERNATIONAL POLICY COOPERATION

In the longer term, global measures are important, whereby the 2015 UN Climate Convention in Paris seemed to show 195 countries a common path for climate protection on the basis of cooperation and shared reforms. Cooperation among the largest 20 or 30 CO_2-emitting countries is indispensable for successful medium-term climate protection worldwide. The G20 club could possibly play an important role in climate protection, especially since the G20 countries account for about 80 percent of the world economy. However, the G20 is not a homogeneous group of countries with very similar interests, but there are large and small, rich and poor countries. Strangely enough, since 2017, even the rich countries in particular no longer agree among themselves on climate protection, and the reason for this was Donald Trump's victory in the 2016 US presidential election.

Since the US withdrew from the Paris Agreement under the populist Trump and because he rejected multilateralism, the important role of international organizations, there has been a marked deterioration in the prospects of global political cooperation since 2017. This will make climate protection more expensive, and the US is also likely to have a greater impact on the climate than expected in 2015. After all, Germany and other EU countries have experienced considerable problems with their climate policy; the German interim climate protection target of a 40 percent CO_2 reduction—compared to 1990—by 2020 was clearly not going to be achieved but for the Corona pandemic and related fall in emissions due to lower levels of production, consumption and transport. It is therefore doubtful whether even a significantly improved policy by 2030 or 2040 will make it possible to limit the extent of global warming—emphasized by many scientists—by a maximum of 2 degrees Celsius by the end of the twenty-first century, or even better by 1.5 degrees. In any case, there is little to suggest that one can assume that those actors and approaches that are responsible for falling short of achieving the 2020 targets will easily and quickly achieve better levels of target achievement by 2030.

Those who, on the part of the government, pursue climate protection policy in a haphazard approach—for lack of knowledge or for lack of planning—promote dangerous populism that will ultimately prevent adequate climate protection. You need a clear, well-thought-out and feasible national and international roadmap toward climate neutrality. To achieve this, it will be necessary for the G20 to discuss cooperation on climate policy much more strongly than before. The worlds of science, business and politics are challenged, as are of course the citizens themselves, or international city networks based on partnership. In climate policy, it does not make sense to get bogged down in the headlines and create new points of disquiet, to repeatedly tackle individual sectors or economic activities with a reproachful wagging finger (against air travel today, sea travel tomorrow, driving cars the day after and coal-fired power stations every day). An overall approach is needed that allows all companies in the economy to contribute to climate neutrality through meaningful incentives. If the EU trading system is extended to 85 percent of emissions and a further 10 percent is subject to an emissions tax, a modernized social market economy can cope with all tasks. It would then be possible each year to measure the progress made in climate protection and try to predict whether, according to the latest computer model simulations, those actions will be sufficient or further long-term adaptation steps will be required to achieve meeting the target for planet Earth in 2050. One usual feature of such simulation results is that they have an uncertainty range. As a rule, long-term simulation results should have a somewhat lower uncertainty range than short-term analyses for considerable policy or innovation impulses will lead to a new market equilibrium in the long run rather than in the short run, and many computer models are easier to handle in terms of an equilibrium analysis than in the complex adjustment paths in the short run.

Since the Transatlantic Banking Crisis, there has been great uncertainty in the West as to whether the economic system is trustworthy and stable enough. If the public regards the democratic political system as no longer being capable of action or of being less than sufficiently comprehensible and successful, the proportion of votes cast for those political actors promising new security with simplistic slogans and measures will increase significantly along with approaches toward authoritarianism. Since climate protection policy is necessary internationally and is in part complicated, there is a serious need for competence in the fields of economics and climate protection; otherwise a wave of uncertainty and a new breeding ground for populism will emerge as a result of government blunders. Since populism is generally nationalist and protectionist, it endangers the international division of labor and the expansion of trade, that is, the efficiency gains necessary for successful climate protection through the economical use of scarce (natural) resources.

Within the framework of a possible integration of CO_2 certificate trading systems of different countries and regions, there are new possibilities for more democracy globally. One conceivable starting point would be to create a supranational quasi-parliament for the countries of the G20 group—partly based on ideas from Western democracies, but partly also incorporating ideas from Asia and other regions of the world. Such a parliament could also address other global issues such as the Internet and globalization, and a G20 commission could become a kind of executive as a counterpart to such a parliament.

While some countries may dream that global warming and climate change will bring them benefits, for the vast majority of humanity global warming represents a serious problem. In some areas, the very wealthy industrialized countries can also arm themselves against climate-induced problems with costly projects, such as constructing higher dams, better insulated and more stable homes, and more robust infrastructure. For many people in many poor countries, however, there will be few opportunities in 2040 or 2050, and perhaps there will also be increased emigration pressure from the hotter Global South to the still halfway cooler North of the world economy. It is unlikely that the EU could easily deal with millions of climate refugees after the experience of the wave of refugees from the Syrian civil war.

There are also contradictions in Western climate and economic policy. In Germany, an advisory body to the federal government delivers little in the way of sensible advice and even harms climate protection through ideological albeit science-based texts; the Scientific Advisory Council on Global Change, of all things, attracted a lot of attention in 2019. Certainly, some progress has been made in Europe in climate protection, but technical progress can also contribute to climate protection, especially in Germany and globally, if the incentives and diffusion mechanisms in many countries are coherent and powerful international organizations—such as the World Bank, regional development banks and the G7 and G20—act sensibly and in good time. From an EU perspective, there is a great deal of room to maneuver that still needs to be explored, although this could include more emissions trading and, at times, CO_2 taxes in Germany as well—as the German Council of Economic Experts pointed out in its Special Report of 2019 (German Council of Economic Experts, 2019). However, that same report does not address the issues of "green innovation dynamics" to any great extent and hardly develops a view on how a global climate protection policy could be developed beginning with Germany and the EU. There are, as will be shown, some starting points for this, although the distribution effects of climate-friendly economic development, which are not taken into account in the report, will also be addressed. These effects will show up as a relative wage rate increase for qualified employees in Germany and the EU countries.

If, however, citizens are to be taken along on the journey toward effective climate policy, if the democratic debate is to support climate protection, then communication policy cannot be limited to those over 30 years of age. Younger people in particular have little affinity with TV, and social networks represent a fragmented public, which makes national and international climate policy difficult to implement. On the Internet, however, there is also a tendency to grossly exaggerate certain problems and to radicalize positions in a way that jeopardizes political compromises.

At the European Institute for International Economic Relations (EIIW), research work on environmental, sustainability and climate issues has been developed over many years; numerous contributions have been submitted via the EIIW within the framework of research projects, in quite a few areas by myself—even though I have also been active in other fields of analysis. I have always tried to combine different analytical perspectives and policy fields in a meaningful way. Climate protection policy alone will not work; climate neutrality needs a broader perspective and view of the global economy. Occasionally, this makes analysis less easy but the policy outlook all the more promising.

One result of this approach is that it makes sense to work with different scenarios: (a) a global cooperation strategy, which should also be as efficient as possible in terms of climate protection; there are also some research questions which have been little clarified to date, so that the pros and cons should continue to be illuminated; (b) an international cooperation strategy without the US, which is likely to task the rest of the world with intensifying climate protection by more than 20 percent—whether the old Western alliance will then continue to function is unclear. For the time being, it seems unlikely that the EU will disintegrate as a political area of action and at the same time the US will stay away from the Paris Agreement. If this were to happen, the 2-degree target for the twenty-first century would not be achievable. Massive global warming and international chaos as well as slow growth and increased cyclical instability are likely to result. There are indeed long-term challenges presented by the problem of climate change, but here the economic-ecological analysis has at least some good modeling results to show (on the other hand, short-term predictions are fraught with great uncertainty in the forecast).

Climate change played an important role in the 2019 European Parliament elections, and the Fridays for Future movement, with Greta Thunberg, is creating new pressure for a reform of climate policy in Europe and other regions of the world; the Rezo critique on YouTube has had a similar effect in Germany in particular. Despite the dynamism of the Fridays for Future, the question arises as to whether the welcome commitment of young people and the orientation of economic policy are both going in the right direction. Too late, unnecessarily expensive and poorly communicated: three risk areas of climate protection for missing the goal of a climate-neutral world economy by 2050. This book conclusively shows what is needed in Europe, Asia, North America and other regions: networked, broader emissions trading systems of all G20 countries, limited free certificates and an understanding of the side effects—including distribution effects—of global climate protection policy; of course, the practical commitment of the individual is also required, which corresponds to a 5 percent CO_2 reduction in the case of the Albedo effect alone. The Albedo effect is about the color and texture of surfaces—for example, of homes, commercial buildings or street surfaces—having an influence on the reflection of sunlight; with bright, smooth surfaces more heat is reflected back into space than with rough, black or dark surfaces. So, for example, brighter roofing solutions can help the climate (see the concluding chapter). Each individual can contribute to climate stability—even free of charge—when moving from the emission age to a CO_2-neutral planet: for an innovative and sustainable social market economy.

The present study is based, among other things, on the EIIW's many years of research in the field of environmental and climate policy. The European Institute for International Economic Relations developed its own Global Sustainability Indicator[1] some years ago. In the standard version, the EIIW-vita indicator comprises three pillars: the share of renewable energies, the so-called real savings rate (according to the World Bank) and the international competitiveness position in environmentally friendly products—the latter is essentially based on previous position improvements in environmentally relevant innovations. New research results show that there have been improvements in sustainability-relevant fields in a number of countries, especially in China. However, the global pace of innovation in the area of sustainability is still too slow. The EIIW-vita indicator shows how the green innovation dynamics and sustainability position of more than 100 countries around the world have developed over more than a decade. The indicator is also a useful starting point for sustainability investments. Those countries which intensively mine non-renewable resources over a short period of time give up part of their natural capital stock and thus damage the foundations for securing sustainable prosperity for future generations. Important research publications include a special publication in the journal *International Economics and Economic Policy* and various books, including the book *Energiewende nach Fukushima* [translation: *The Energy Transition After Fukushima*] by myself and Peter Hennicke, a Japanese translation of which was published in 2019. In addition, there are publications within the framework of the DFG-funded SINCERE (Sino-European Circular Economy & Resource Efficiency) project, which was carried out with scientists from numerous EU countries and China.

---

[1] In this context, the EIIW is grateful to the vita Foundation, Oberursel, Germany, for its many years of financial and research support—and also for the lively exchange of ideas with Dr. Frank Müller.

This book is an offer of thought and knowledge for all those who deal with questions of climate protection. I have tried to write this study in a way that is easy to understand for all: at least to use language that neither is unnecessarily complicated to read or nor makes the text more difficult than necessary due to many abbreviations. It therefore concerns everyone with an interest in the future. The important insights from this book are new in various ways related to the public debate:

1. The world's climate presents serious stability problems that can bring global economic destabilization.
2. In essence, there is no contradiction between free trade and environmental protection, quite contrary to what is often claimed—restricting or making free trade more difficult directly contributes to more environmental problems worldwide.
3. There is a lack of a global climate-friendly innovation promotion policy, with the result that there are too few climate-friendly innovations.
4. An international economic policy that relies more strongly on emissions trading and emissions taxes can make a major contribution to climate protection.
5. If the state interferes in the emissions trading sector with extra intervention, this weakens and destabilizes the signaling power of the certificate trading system; this damages climate protection.
6. Investors and investment funds that focus on sound sustainability indicators are expected to generate long-term benefits for all: a longer average life expectancy of the world's population in a stabilized global climate.
7. Increased cooperation between regional integration areas and in particular between the EU, ASEAN and China plus Russia, Brazil and India could make a decisive contribution to climate stabilization, especially if the US were to remain politically populist for a long time. A return of the US to multilateralism is certainly desirable.
8. Ultimately, there is a need for further economic-ecological research, especially with a view to stronger EU-US-Asia cooperation; the existing scientific cooperation approaches in the field of natural sciences (CERN, ITER as examples) should therefore be expanded to include social science issues; Europe, China and the US should cooperate in the environmental and climate field but should also

jointly consider meaningful and necessary accompanying measures for the intensified structural change required by climate protection in the coming decades. One can certainly wish for many things, but whether the insight and interest to bring about a corresponding reality here remains to be seen.
9. The G20+ can become an effective policy area if the CO_2 emissions trading systems of these countries can be integrated.
10. The Fridays for Future movement has the potential to become a global driver for climate change policy; many activists will probably think in the medium term as many scientists do—international cooperation is important and conducive to gaining knowledge and solving problems. It is yet to be seen whether Fridays for Future will succeed in gaining a sustainable foothold in China, Russia, Brazil, the US and other influential countries.

The book is simply structured. Based on the background to the climate problem (Part I), Part II of the book is devoted to the question: what can private households, companies and policymakers actually do that makes sense when it comes to climate protection? Part III has a multilateralism perspective: here, the question concerns what role international organizations could and should play in climate protection policy—climate protection as a challenge for globally networked policies. Part IV shows perspectives for new approaches on the one hand and focuses on new practical conceptual options for action on the other. It is basically possible to achieve climate neutrality by 2050. However, this is an enormous global task; several years of uncomfortable adjustment steps are necessary, as well as a real economic policy focus in at least 20 countries at the same time. This is a task of the century that can be accomplished; for a number of years it means politicians, firms as well as private households accept a stark message: the end of comfort zone. This challenge must be met vigorously, prudently, intelligently and with risk management; every major step must be explained politically, economically and in terms of climate policy. Various scientific groups are called upon to cooperate; in this sense IPCC (Intergovernmental Panel on Climate Change, founded in 1988) is not enough as a UN group of climate protection experts. In addition, the Internet-based networking of other groups can also be helpful, for example, climate protection-friendly innovators within the framework of an "open innovation" approach.

Of course, politicians in many countries are making big announcements about climate protection policy, and often also energetic long-term measures based on well-thought-out concepts. But there may also be too much promise and too little "political delivery". In the UK, the Committee on Climate Change pointed out many inconsistencies and shortcomings in government policy in a 2019 report for parliament, with the May government setting a target of "net zero" emissions for 2050: in the national adaptation program there were 21 points missing on the 56 risks and opportunities mentioned in the Climate Change Risk Assessment report. Of the 25 main action policy elements identified by the Committee in mid-2018, the government had only fully implemented 1 a year later; in 10 areas of action there was not even partial implementation, so that the government's "clean growth strategy" showed many good intentions, but so far only modest real political progress.

The Committee on Climate Change wrote in 2019 that the CO_2 reduction performance to be achieved by the "net zero" target is 50 percent higher than the previous target of climate protection policy and 30 percent higher than the progress achieved in the period 1990–2018 (Committee on Climate Change, 2019). In addition, the UK is not prepared for possible negative global developments in climate protection policy, which could mean a temperature increase of three or even 4 degrees Celsius by 2100. Here you can see from the British example—even if the UK government had in 2018/2019 perhaps paid too little attention to climate policy because of Brexit—that in the leading Western countries there is the following danger: big announcements, too little real policy effort. There is apparently a lack of political and social awareness that national measures toward climate neutrality and international cooperation steps in climate protection policy require special effort. The need for politics, society and the economy to leave the familiar comfort zone and to tackle a major climate protection task globally in good time with extraordinary, well-thought-out concepts is seen far too little in the Western industrialized countries. This is made even more difficult by the fact that political populism in the US and Western Europe is likely to expand for several years, probably decades. In addition, the climate debate could contribute to political polarization, since the interests of influential groups in society are ignored and they are confronted with subjectively unreasonably high adaptation costs. Another part of society may constantly see a deficit in committed climate policy and consider it a threat to their very existence. Good communication policy by government and international organizations is therefore indispensable, as is sensible policy. Politicians will also need a feel for political psychology: it is much better for citizens in Switzerland to receive an annual CO_2 tax refund in one lump sum via their health insurance provider than for the state to organize a diffuse policy of refunding CO_2 tax revenues by lowering electricity prices (in Germany: the levy for renewable energy—to finance the feed-in tariffs for such energies) and slightly increasing transfers to households and, if necessary, selling certificates to private households.

This book brings with it a number of new insights, not least that a successful climate protection policy of the G20+ countries offers opportunities for new international cooperation gains. These could be much greater than the undeniably significant costs of the steps toward climate neutrality. The Fridays for Future movement should be a serious dialogue partner for the worlds of science and politics; this movement is creative and interesting because of its great internationality, albeit probably not easy to organize and lead in the medium term.

Climate protection policy requires the cooperation of several scientific disciplines, and a functioning international cooperation is indispensable, especially of the G20+ countries. The fact that Nigeria, with a population estimated to be around 400 million people in 2050, should be the 20th standalone country to be included in the G20 (currently comprising 19 individual countries plus the EU) should be understandable as a proposal. Without the third largest country in the world in terms of population, we cannot talk sensibly about climate protection policy with the goal of global climate neutrality by 2050. The presented analysis will hopefully be a helpful impulse—among many necessary impulses—to achieve this goal patiently, intelligently and energetically in an internationally networked novel policy project and to strengthen the sustainability of the social market economy globally.

The New US Climate Approach Under President Biden

As regards the approach of the new Biden administration, one may emphasize that President Biden obviously considers climate policy modernization as a necessary element of foreign policy, security policy as well as economic policy. This new approach indicates that the US will push for a more ambitious climate policy (certainly when compared to the Trump administration), and a strong focus will be on the expansion of renewable energy and the creation of new political institutions in favor of a broader climate policy (see Box 1.1).

Box 1.1: Biden Administration's Pro-climate Policy Focus (White House, 2021a)

"**President Biden Takes Executive Actions to Tackle the Climate Crisis at Home and Abroad, Create Jobs, and Restore Scientific Integrity Across Federal Government**

President Biden set ambitious goals that will ensure America and the world can meet the urgent demands of the climate crisis, while empowering American workers and businesses to lead a clean energy revolution that achieves a carbon pollution-free power sector by 2035 and puts the United States on an irreversible path to a net-zero economy by 2050. Today's actions advance those goals and ensure that we are tapping into the talent, grit, and innovation of American workers, revitalizing the U.S. energy sector, conserving our natural resources and leveraging them to help drive our nation toward a clean energy future, creating well-paying jobs with the opportunity to join a union, and delivering justice for communities who have been subjected to environmental harm.

President Biden will also sign an important Presidential Memorandum on scientific integrity to send a clear message that the Biden-Harris Administration will protect scientists from political interference and ensure they can think, research, and speak freely to provide valuable information and insights to the American people. Additionally, and in line with the scientific-integrity memorandum's charge to reestablish scientific advisory committees, President Biden will sign an Executive Order re-establishing the President's Council of Advisors on Science and Technology.

TACKLING THE CLIMATE CRISIS AT HOME AND ABROAD EXECUTIVE ORDER

Today's Executive Order takes bold steps to combat the climate crisis both at home and throughout the world…[…]…

Center the Climate Crisis in U.S. Foreign Policy and National Security Considerations

- The order affirms that, in implementing—and building on—the Paris Agreement's objectives, the United States will exercise its leadership to promote a significant increase in global ambition. It makes clear that both significant short-term global emission

(*continued*)

(continued)
   reductions and net zero global emissions by mid-century—or before—are required to avoid setting the world on a dangerous, potentially catastrophic, climate trajectory.
- The order reaffirms that the President will host a Leaders' Climate Summit on Earth Day, April 22, 2021; that the United States will reconvene the Major Economies Forum; that, to underscore the administration's commitment to elevating climate in U.S. foreign policy, the President has created a new position, the Special Presidential Envoy for Climate, which will have a seat on the National Security Council, and that it will be a U.S. priority to press for enhanced climate ambition and integration of climate considerations across a wide range of international fora.
- The order also kicks off the process of developing the United States' "nationally determined contribution"—our emission reduction target—under the Paris Agreement, as well as a climate finance plan.
- Among numerous other steps aimed at prioritizing climate in U.S. foreign policy and national security, the order directs the Director of National Intelligence to prepare a National Intelligence Estimate on the security implications of climate change, the State Department to prepare a transmittal package to the Senate for the Kigali Amendment to the Montreal Protocol, and all agencies to develop strategies for integrating climate considerations into their international work.

Take a Whole-of-Government Approach to the Climate Crisis
- The order formally establishes the White House Office of Domestic Climate Policy—led by the first-ever National Climate Advisor and Deputy National Climate Advisor—creating a central office in the White House that is charged with coordinating and implementing the President's domestic climate agenda.
- The order establishes the National Climate Task Force, assembling leaders from across 21 federal agencies and departments to enable a whole-of-government approach to combatting the climate crisis.

(*continued*)

(continued)

Leverage the Federal Government's Footprint and Buying Power to Lead by Example
- Consistent with the goals of the President's Build Back Better jobs and economic recovery plan, of which his clean energy jobs plan is a central pillar, the order directs the federal agencies to procure carbon pollution-free electricity and clean, zero-emission vehicles to create good-paying, union jobs and stimulate clean energy industries.
- In addition, the order requires those purchases be Made in America, following President Biden's Buy American executive order. The order also directs agencies to apply and strictly enforce the prevailing wage and benefit guidelines of the Davis Bacon and other acts and encourage Project Labor Agreements. These actions reaffirm that agencies should work to ensure that any jobs created with funds to address the climate crisis are good jobs with a choice to join a union.
- The order directs each federal agency to develop a plan to increase the resilience of its facilities and operations to the impacts of climate change and directs relevant agencies to report on ways to expand and improve climate forecast capabilities—helping facilitate public access to climate related information and assisting governments, communities, and businesses in preparing for and adapting to the impacts of climate change.
- The order directs the Secretary of the Interior to pause on entering into new oil and natural gas leases on public lands or offshore waters to the extent possible, launch a rigorous review of all existing leasing and permitting practices related to fossil fuel development on public lands and waters, and identify steps that can be taken to double renewable energy production from offshore wind by 2030. The order does not restrict energy activities on lands that the United States holds in trust for Tribes. The Secretary of the Interior will continue to consult with Tribes regarding the development and management of renewable and conventional energy resources, in conformance with the U.S. government's trust responsibilities.

(*continued*)

> (continued)
> - The order directs federal agencies to eliminate fossil fuel subsidies as consistent with applicable law and identify new opportunities to spur innovation, commercialization, and deployment of clean energy technologies and infrastructure.
> **Rebuild Our Infrastructure for a Sustainable Economy**
> - The order catalyzes the creation of jobs in construction, manufacturing, engineering and the skilled-trades by directing steps to ensure that every federal infrastructure investment reduces climate pollution and that steps are taken to accelerate clean energy and transmission projects under federal siting and permitting processes in an environmentally sustainable manner".

Despite the fact that Biden has announced that the US will cut greenhouse gas emissions by about 50 percent—compared to 2005—by around 2030 (White House, 2021b), the administration has made no particular effort to adopt a national emissions trading system or to encourage states other than California—which has an impressive ETS—to create a broad emissions trading system. As regards G20 cooperation, the lack of a clear US commitment to ETS will be a major problem for achieving global CO_2 neutrality by 2050.

Carbon Leakage and a Border Adjustment Tax

The carbon leakage problem occurs in the context of significant international differences in carbon pricing and high levels of international capital mobility. It primarily concerns investments being undertaken by multinational companies which relocate production, say from the EU—with its strict CO_2 pricing system—to certain Asian countries, to Russia or to Ukraine, where CO_2 pricing is close to zero, allowing production and the resulting carbon emissions to continue—while output is often exported back, for example, to the EU. The EU's proposed solution—to impose a border adjustment tax (or "border equalization tax") on imports from countries which have no CO_2 pricing framework—is likely to work only vis-à-vis small- and medium-sized countries since the largest economies such as China or India could impose countermeasures in the medium term. In 2020, major EU exporting countries such as Germany, France, Italy, Spain, Austria, Belgium and the Netherlands pushed for a border equalization tax; mainly because one considers a world economy with very asymmetric national CO_2 pricing to be the equivalent of a global system of biased trade in which free rider countries—here, in terms climate change policy—obtain unfair economic gains; and this often from multinational firms' relocation of production to "soft climate policy countries". The EU and the UK are afraid that they will face higher outward foreign direct investment flows, and this can have considerable macroeconomic effects; key macro aspects of FDI indeed were identified in the pioneering DSGE macro model of Roeger and Welfens (2021).

There are many practical problems with a border adjustment tax even if the European Commission would impose such a tax only on a rather limited range goods, that is, those which are energy-intensive—read: CO_2-intensive—in production. The globalization process means that it would often be difficult to identify the international production networks involved in the production of certain goods so that one will face serious challenges in calculating how large the CO_2 burden resulting from production by firms/countries outside the EU and the European Economic Area, respectively, actually is. Various EU partner countries could take a case against the EU before the World Trade Organization's appellate body, and this in turn would create new legal and economic risks for the world economy. As long as the EU fails to convince the US and the UK to also adopt a border adjustment tax which offsets the cost advantage of countries without CO_2 pricing, the approach of an international border equalization tax will hardly work.

The more countries the EU could convince to join an international CO_2 emissions trading system club, the lower the political pressure in the EU to come up with a border equalization tax will be. However, the European Commission has thus far not developed a G20-oriented approach for an ETS club, which is surprising for two reasons:

- The EU with its Emissions Trading System, launched in 2005, could indeed claim to be a pioneering actor in the world economy in the field of climate change policy.
- The G20 stands for a powerful and important institution—and a decisive group of countries in the world economy.

As will be highlighted at the end of the analysis presented herein, there is also a need to combine an innovative anti-Corona pandemic policy—with an international focus—with a clear strategy for establishing an internationally integrated G20 ETS system involving actors in the global North and South.

International Political Economy Aspects

One should, however, not overlook that the G20 group of countries is heterogeneous in broad economic terms, including in terms of per capita income in purchasing power parity figures. Thus, one could assume the idea of the countries involved agreeing to an integrated emissions trading system to be fanciful. However, as previously noted, the distance between the positions of, for example, India and the developed countries in terms of climate change policy has reduced over the last decade or so. To the extent that international economic convergence makes finding a political consensus easier, the "Corona shock" has to be taken into account here: the Corona shock is indeed global in nature, but to some extent it seems to be asymmetrical in economic terms—for example, the US and China seem to have experienced a stronger post-Corona economic recovery than certain other G20 countries.

As regards the West, there is a lack of leadership which is already visible at the forum of the G7/G8. The internal political polarization of the US has clearly undermined the US leadership—a development particularly visible since President Trump took office in 2017. To the extent that leadership in the Western world has been weakened, the challenge of G20 coordination and steps toward a consistent and efficient joint climate policy is considerable; here, a fresh opportunity might arise for the EU (plus the UK) to launch new initiatives. Coming up with extra funding for key partners in the South—for example, India, Indonesia and Brazil—could be only one aspect of a new Europe-led global climate policy approach. A new EU strategy to support the enhanced international diffusion of climate-friendly technologies should indeed also be part of an innovative Western climate policy approach; the study by Glachant et al. (2020) has indeed pointed out the critical relevance of both climate-focused innovation policy, with clear leadership among leading OECD countries, and a new accelerated North-South technology diffusion approach.

Low-carbon energy systems will be of particular importance in the transition toward climate neutrality within a few decades. While in most Western countries, plus Japan and the Republic of Korea, private companies—actually MNCs—are the leading actors on the supply side, in China, Russia and India it is state-owned companies which play a crucial role. As the example of China shows, the strong role of state-owned energy companies does not rule out that a national CO_2 emissions trading system would be adopted. Whether or not Western countries can really establish an internationally integrated emissions trading system together with other partners such as China, Russia and India could depend to some extent on the ability of the US, the EU plus the UK to accept that there are broad opportunities for unusual forms of cooperation with the three countries mentioned; for example, Russia could become a leader in sustainable fuel innovation and the country might also be rather innovative in combining gas exploration and CO_2 sequestration technologies—Canada, in turn, also seems to be a strong country in this field, with a sufficient motivation as a strongly resource-dependent country thus, in part, similar to Russia.

Rapidly rising global trade in solar energy and indeed wind farming plant and equipment should also be key elements for G20 and global climate neutrality progress. However, Japan and Europe are thus far only partly open to exports of solar technology and solar equipment from India and China. Free trade should be fully exploited as the basis of global ecological and economic efficiency gains in the early twenty-first century, and realizing comparative advantages in renewable energy should naturally be a key element in such an approach. A report by the WTO and the World Bank on opportunities to enhance global free trade in renewable energy is highly desirable, and it would be no surprise if such a report would identify many countries (in the G20 group and in other country groups as well) with hidden import barriers.

As regards climate change policy, there are different—and in some cases competing—interests in G20 countries which make cooperation somewhat difficult. Relative endowment differences in natural fossil energy fuels, income and the level of technological progress in various countries imply potential conflicts of interests in the field of climate change policy. There is a large literature on the political economy of policymakers proposing and developing environmentally and climate-friendly policies including considerations at an international level (see Oates & Portney, 2003; Fankhauser et al., 2015, 2016). Jakob et al. (2020) have developed an approach with a focus on countries, actors and institutions which form a combined basis to develop respective national low-carbon versus high-carbon energy systems. There could be other approaches which, for example, emphasize the ability of institutional innovativeness and the relative role of countries in various integration groups; Welfens (2020c) has pointed out that the economic and demographic dynamics as well as the growth of regional integration schemes seems to reinforce the role of Asia in a global context on the one hand; on the other hand regional integration groups such as the EU, ASEAN and Mercosur might try to cooperate more than in the past in both the economic and ecological spheres—so far with a visible lack of cooperation in sustainability policy and climate change policy. Whether or not in the post-Brexit setting a new rivalry between the UK and the EU in Asia could undermine prospects for cooperation between regional cooperation clubs still remains to be explored.

The financial markets have increasingly emphasized sustainable investment and climate-friendly investment projects. The fact that since 2018 more than 60 central banks around the world have cooperated in a joint analytical venture to focus more strongly on the physical and transitory risk of achieving climate neutrality—a challenge for banks plus insurance companies in general and for many firms in certain sectors in particular—has added to the international institutional pressure in favor of greening investment dynamics. Government regulations in new fields could be useful for competition and climate neutrality in the medium term: with stronger publication standards regarding the balance sheets of companies, at least those quoted on stock markets, there will be new opportunities for market-driven, climate-friendly innovations. Looking at Singapore, New York, London, Paris, Frankfurt, Tokyo and other financial centers—with a delay possibly also at Shanghai and Hong Kong—one might consider that financial investors could reinforce adjustment dynamics toward climate neutrality worldwide. Financial regulations should be modernized at the global level (involving the Bank for International Settlements (BIS), and the International Monetary Fund) and the national level in order to take into account climate neutrality aspects.

If one assumes that climate neutrality is to be achieved by 2050, one will have an implicit answer about countries as well as sectoral losers and winners within individual economies since a major element of achieving this goal is speed:

- Countries with strong competition dynamics are rather likely to develop sufficient adjustment and innovation dynamics to cope with the enormous challenges of climate neutrality.
- High-income countries—given their technological leadership—should have an advantage in developing new profitable but climate-neutral business models.

- Since ICT dynamics are critical for growth and climate neutrality and since it is not only the OECD countries but also India, China and Malaysia which are digital leaders in certain fields, one may anticipate that countries in Asia in particular could be economic winners in the period 2030–2050 and beyond.
- The highly innovative automotive industry—standing, for example, for about 50 percent of all national patents issued in Germany—which consists of globally networked firms could be a winner both because of high Schumpeterian dynamics, but also because its lobbying power in G20 countries is unrivaled. The ICT sector, with its high share of immaterial assets and its strong high-tech dynamics, may certainly be expected to be a winner on the journey toward climate neutrality, as will be the investment goods sector whose firms are expected to construct and deliver all the critical new equipment needed by industry and the services sector worldwide. As there is a significant demand for greater levels of clean investment, the financial industry can also be expected to be a winner of the global transition to climate neutrality.
- Since the three aforementioned sectors are skill-intensive, it seems obvious that skilled labor is the natural winner among workers and that governments and firms should invest more in education and retraining, respectively, than in previous decades.
- Aging societies—such as Japan and Germany, Italy and some other EU countries—might face special problems in a period of accelerated structural adjustment; this does not rule out that some of these countries will switch early enough to more digital training and retraining and thereby create new opportunities for rejuvenating the "effective human capital stock" and thus raise productivity growth to a similar extent to those OECD countries or Newly Industrialized Countries with a rather modest aging of the respective labor force.

Based on these reflections, one may in turn focus on the UN countries and try to identify relative winners and losers based on current and expected medium-term sectoral output shares. As a final remark here, the groups of winner and loser countries emerging in 2030–2050 could bring about more international economic inequality, but this is not necessarily the outcome of the global adjustment toward climate neutrality. If the European model of a social market economy should be able to combine an emissions trading system, higher innovation dynamics and a solid social policy of governments—with sustainable government finances—the long-run results of achieving climate neutrality might bring reduced global inequality. The economic model of the US is not as strong as many observers have believed for many decades now and certainly there is not—as often assumed—a clear lead of the US in terms of expected effective life per capital income as compared to leading EU countries as has been shown in Welfens (2019). However, Brexit has shown that—as an integration club—the EU has several weaknesses, and one cannot rule out that regional disintegration and excessive adjustment pressures, namely in favor of achieving climate neutrality in a hurried but rather inefficient way, will lead to sharper distribution conflicts and more international economic instability. If politicians, leading managers in industry and the general public would follow key suggestions in this study, the world economy could indeed achieve climate neutrality, broader prosperity *and* stability in the global system.

Long-Run Perspective on Global Climate Neutrality Is Crucial

Millions of people and managers—and firms—will have a natural tendency to emphasize the short- and medium-term costs and benefits relating to climate change policy. However, the really decisive issue, in a normative perspective, is to ask about the long-run global net gains from climate neutrality. If there are global net gains, one should raise the question as to the extent to which it could be possible to compensate the losing groups from the transition to global climate neutrality, and to develop approaches which indeed allow to compensate the losing groups so that the global picture would indeed be a win-win perspective. If such a perspective can be developed and communicated effectively worldwide, this could be a powerful impulse for enhanced climate change policy in the coming decades.

One should not overlook a double long-run gain from climate neutrality which should be emphasized by the political systems around the world to their respective electorates in a clear and understandable way:

- Climate neutrality will bring a reduction in the frequency and severity of extreme weather events, and this amounts to fewer lives lost and lower levels of physical damages (with positive effects on, e.g., infrastructure, the value of assets, lower contribution rates in the global insurance sector).

- Climate neutrality will be largely a result of a global acceleration of innovation and the diffusion of technological progress as well as product innovations. From this perspective, there are new challenges to internalize enhanced international positive spillover effects from (green) innovations and R&D projects, respectively. This is a complex new policy field, namely international R&D co-financing, which requires the development of a broad scientific modeling of the size of international R&D spillovers and related positive international economic repercussion effects.
- To the extent that achieving climate neutrality brings about more reliable international cooperation, one might also expect politico-economic stabilization gains.
- As regards further research, there are many critical unsolved issues such as the challenge of a situation with slow progress toward climate neutrality and rapidly rising migration flows in certain regions of the world economy.

The politically critical question of identifying the costs and benefits (or losses and gains) from achieving climate neutrality cannot be answered adequately without further advances in modeling in several fields, including International Economics, Global Climate Research and examining household attitudes toward the potential trade-off between economic growth and climate policy progress.

References

Antholis, W. C. (2009, July 18). *India and Climate Change*. Op-ed for the Brookings Institution. Retrieved September 6, 2021, from https://www.brookings.edu/opinions/india-and-climate-change/

Committee on Climate Change. (2019). *Reducing UK Emissions–2019 Progress Report to Parliament*. Retrieved September 2, 2019, from https://www.theccc.org.uk/publication/reducing-uk-emissions-2019-progress-report-to-parliament/

De Haas, R., & Popov, A. (2019). *Finance and Carbon Emissions* (ECB Working Paper Series, No. 2318). European Central Bank. https://www.ecb.europa.eu/pub/pdf/scpwps/ecb.wp2318~44719344e8.en.pdf

Fankhauser, S., Gennaioli, C., & Collins, M. (2015). The Political Economy of Passing Climate Change Legislation: Evidence from a Survey. *Global Environmental Change, 35*, 52–61. https://doi.org/10.1016/j.gloenvcha.2015.08.008

Fankhauser, S., Gennaioli, C., & Collins, M. (2016). Do International Factors Influence the Passage of Climate Change Legislation? *Climate Policy, 16*(3), 318–331. https://doi.org/10.1080/14693062.2014.1000814

Federal Government of Germany. (2007, June 7). *Breakthrough on Climate Protection*. G8 Summit Heiligendamm. Retrieved September 6, 2021, from http://www.g-8.de/Content/EN/Artikel/__g8-summit/2007-06-07-g8-klimaschutz__en.html

German Council of Economic Experts. (2019). *Setting Out for a New Climate Policy*. Special Report, July 2019. Retrieved September 1, 2019, from https://www.sachverstaendigenrat-wirtschaft.de/fileadmin/dateiablage/gutachten/sg2019/sg_2019_en.pdf

Glachant, M., Dechezlepêtre, A., Fankhauser, S., Stoever, J., & Touboul, S. (2020). *Invention and Global Diffusion of Technologies for Climate Change Adaptation: A Patent Analysis*. The World Bank. https://openknowledge.worldbank.org/handle/10986/33883

ICAP. (2018). *Emissions Trading Worldwide: Status Report 2018*. International Carbon Action Partnership. https://icapcarbonaction.com/en/?option=com_attach&task=download&id=547

IPCC. (2021). Climate Change 2021: The Physical Science Basis, Contribution of Working Group I to the Sixth Assessment Report of the Intergovernmental Panel on Climate Change. In V. Masson-Delmotte, P. Zhai, A. Pirani, S. L. Connors, C. Péan, S. Berger, N. Caud, Y. Chen, L. Goldfarb, M. I. Gomis, M. Huang, K. Leitzell, E. Lonnoy, J. B. R. Matthews, T. K. Maycock, T. Waterfield, O. Yelekçi, R. Yu, & B. Zhou (Eds.). Cambridge University Press. In Print. (Approved version dated 7 August 2021). https://www.ipcc.ch/report/ar6/wg1/downloads/report/IPCC_AR6_WGI_Full_Report.pdf

Jakob, M., Flachsland, C., Steckel, J. C., & Urpelainen, J. (2020). Actors, Objectives, Context: A Framework of the Political Economy of Energy and Climate Policy Applied to India, Indonesia, and Vietnam. *Energy Research & Social Science, 70*. https://doi.org/10.1016/j.erss.2020.101775

Kade, C. (2008, August 31). Merkel Backs Climate Deal Based on Population. *Reuters.com*. Retrieved September 6, 2021, from https://www.reuters.com/article/uk-japan-germany-kyoto-idUKT26940120070831

Oates, W. E., & Portney, P. R. (2003). The Political Economy of Environmental Policy. In K. G. Mäler & J. R. Vincent (Eds.), *Handbook of Environmental Economics – Environmental Degradation and Institutional Responses* (Ch. 8, Vol. 1, pp. 325–354). https://www.sciencedirect.com/science/article/pii/S1574009903010131?via%3Dihub

Roeger, W., & Welfens, P. J. J. (2021). *Foreign Direct Investment and Innovations: Transmission Dynamics of Persistent Demand and Technology Shocks in a Macro Model* (EIIW Discussion Paper No. 300). https://uni-w.de/g9xs2

Welfens, P. J. J. (2019). *The Global Trump—Structural US Populism and Economic Conflicts with Europe and Asia.* Palgrave Macmillan.

Welfens, P. J. J. (2020a). Macroeconomic and Health Care Aspects of the Coronavirus Epidemic: EU, US and Global Perspectives. *International Economics and Economic Policy, 17,* 295–362. https://doi.org/10.1007/s10368-020-00465-3

Welfens, P. J. J. (2020b). *Corona Weltrezession—Epidemiedruck und globale Erneuerungs-Perspektiven* [transl. PJJW: Corona World Recession—Pandemic Pressure and Perspectives for Renewal]. Springer.

Welfens, P. J. J. (2020c). Trump's Trade Policy, BREXIT, Corona Dynamics, EU Crisis and Declining Multilateralism. *International Economics and Economic Policy, 17,* 563–634. https://doi.org/10.1007/s10368-020-00479-x

Welfens, P. J. J., & Bahlmann, J. (2021). *Environmental Policy Stringency and Foreign Direct Investment: New Insights from a Gravity Model Approach* (EIIW Discussion Paper No. 294). https://uni-w.de/4y04u

White House. (2021a, January 27). *FACT SHEET: President Biden Takes Executive Actions to Tackle the Climate Crisis at Home and Abroad, Create Jobs, and Restore Scientific Integrity Across Federal Government.* White House Briefing Room, Statements and Releases. Retrieved 26 April, 2021, from https://www.whitehouse.gov/briefing-room/statements-releases/2021/01/27/fact-sheet-president-biden-takes-executive-actions-to-tackle-the-climate-crisis-at-home-and-abroad-create-jobs-and-restore-scientific-integrity-across-federal-government/

White House. (2021b, April 22). *FACT SHEET: President Biden Sets 2030 Greenhouse Gas Pollution Reduction Target Aimed at Creating Good-Paying Union Jobs and Securing U.S. Leadership on Clean Energy Technologies.* White House Briefing Room, Statements and Releases. Retrieved April 26, 2021, from https://www.whitehouse.gov/briefing-room/statements-releases/2021/04/22/fact-sheet-president-biden-sets-2030-greenhouse-gas-pollution-reduction-target-aimed-at-creating-good-paying-union-jobs-and-securing-u-s-leadership-on-clean-energy-technologies/

CHAPTER 2

The Climate Challenge and Its Consequences

The challenges posed by the world's climate are confusing. At first glance it is not easy to understand both the main impacts and indeed the side effects. However, in the long run it is vital for the people of Earth to tackle the problem of the gradual and long-term warming of the Earth's atmosphere, which is essentially related to industrialization and the burning of fossil fuels over the last two centuries, head on. The rising of the surface temperature on Earth has important consequences, since rising temperatures for over a century threaten a rise in sea levels. Moreover, extreme weather conditions and instances of flooding are on the increase, and other new problems are also emerging in many regions of the world where the already high regional temperature continues to rise in the long term. Carbon dioxide emissions, which are related to energy generation, are an important problem here. Such CO_2 emissions are caused, for example, by the generation of energy particularly from fossil fuels. This type of energy generation is also promoted worldwide with gigantic subsidies every year, which is very contradictory with regard to climate protection. The CO_2 damage at home and abroad is more likely to lead to ever more expensive CO_2-intensive production processes or corresponding fossil energy production.

The climate challenge is caused by global CO_2 emissions. It does not matter to the climate where the CO_2 reduction which is necessary for climate stability occurs; in other words, the greenhouse gas problem, that is, global warming, arises through the interaction of the emissions of all countries, and only all countries working together could ultimately contribute to solving the problem. This idea of international cooperation is behind the 2015 UN Paris Climate Agreement. One can pragmatically limit the number of reform countries called for somewhat: the G20 countries, at least, are particularly challenged, because they are large in terms of the economy and in terms of emissions, and they are influential. From the perspective of the UN climate scientists, the task is to almost completely eliminate CO_2 emissions by 2050; in other words, to bring about a massive structural change in the global economy. This is no small tasks, and when you see how difficult it was in 2019 for the compact group of rich G7 countries to agree on a press release after the Canada summit, you can imagine that achieving meaningful cooperation at the G20 could be even more difficult. Moreover, it's difficult to just say that only market-based instruments are necessary; a meaningful mix of approaches is needed, a basic consensus of the G20 countries to work together internationally and reliably in core areas. If a common global goal can be achieved in this field by 2050, it may well initiate a phase of sustainable peaceful cooperation in other fields.

CLIMATE PROTECTION AS AN INTERNATIONAL PUBLIC GOOD

The climate problem looks more complicated than it really is. After a simplistic analysis, however, the basic structure of the key problems can be easily identified: protecting the climate is a global collective good, in which one cannot simply rely on national market solutions, but which actually requires both national and international politics. A form of international cooperation that would reliably cover the largest countries or CO_2 emitters is necessary—at what level or with how many countries one would have to start would have to be discussed. The Paris Agreement with 196 signatory countries (or 195 after President Trump withdrew the US) looks good on paper, but a better community of action would initially be the much more compact G20. However, this forum also seems to have only limited room for maneuver—again because of the US.

However, over the years, the G20 has also taken up important issues of climate protection, arguing early on that the enormously high global subsidies for fossil fuels could be rolled back. There was initial agreement here, but little seriousness in terms of the implementation of corrective measures. Climate protection policy means both accepting responsibility in theory and, in practice, introducing target-oriented policy measures nationally and internationally; above all, providing meaningful incentives for businesses and consumers and accepting the challenge of renewed, and broader, cooperation at a G20 level.

CLIMATE STARTING POSITION AT G20

In the years from 2014 to 2016, global CO_2 emissions stagnated. However, by 2017 they had already risen again by about 1.7 percent: in that year, 49 metric gigatons of CO_2 (more precisely: of CO_2 equivalent) were emitted worldwide, without any land-use change effects. This was communicated to the United Nations by the UN's own environmental agency in its 2018 emissions gap report. By 2030, however, global greenhouse gas emissions would have to fall by 25 percent if a maximum long-term global warming effect of just under 2 degrees were to be achieved (and by -55 percent if a 1.5-degree warming target is to be met by 2050). The basic problem over the course of the decade from 2020 to 2030 is that while OECD countries are likely to reduce their emissions, China, India and certain other G20 countries are likely to see a significant increase in CO_2 emissions. The path to lower emissions leads via CO_2 pricing which provides both incentives for savings and impetus for innovation to reduce CO_2 emissions. Possibly also for product innovations that incorporate CO_2 as production input into saleable new products. However, here we are only at the beginning of developing markets that could in time help turn a problem into a business.

If we simply assume that one could reasonably charge say €30 per metric ton of carbon emissions by way of a corresponding tax or a CO_2 certificate price—equivalent to the low-end estimate of the cost of damage of a metric ton of CO_2 (OECD, 2018, Table 3.7, p. 55)—then the highest CO_2 tax gaps would be recorded in the following countries, among others, in 2015: Russia (100 percent = $30 away from the reference value of one metric ton of CO_2), followed by Indonesia, Brazil, China, South Africa and India, all of which had a gap of over 85 percent; Turkey and the US were 75 percent, Germany 53 percent; and between 51 and 45 percent for Italy, the UK and France. According to this, the current pricing in the industrialized countries considered by the OECD, and the G20 countries, is far removed from what is required, that is, from a reasonable value. That is before one even considered that the actual damage of one ton of CO_2 may not amount to $30 but to $60.

It is clear that incentives should be given to reduce harmful CO_2 emissions, through appropriate financial burdens, if these emissions are not to increase further; in fact, they should decrease significantly. As the EU accounts for 10 percent of the world's emissions, it is also a question of how to get a critical mass of countries to cooperate together. At the UN, that would be almost 200 countries, which would then represent 100 percent of global emissions. A somewhat more manageable group is the G20, which stands for 80 percent of world emissions. The UN solution will be important in the long term, and in 2019 the UN General Assembly demonstrated by way of example that the United Nations is indeed an important forum for climate policy. It is also worth considering raising the issue of climate policy at the UN Security Council, of which the five permanent Security Council members are the US, Russia, China, France and the UK—as well as a further 20 countries, which will be replaced after two years by a further 20 countries (in 2019, Germany was one of the 20 non-permanent member countries in the Security Council; in budgetary terms, the two most important donor countries are the US and Germany). One can certainly argue that climate policy—or global warming as a problem—is an important issue for international security and belongs on the agenda of the Security Council. This in turn would provide a manageable action group in which free-rider behavior probably plays a lesser role than the behavior of countries at the UN General Assembly. Of course, there is also the risk that one of the permanent member states would veto decisions.

For pragmatic reasons, however, it seems preferable to organize international cooperation in climate policy primarily in the manageable and stable G20 group. What should the overall approach in a group of countries like the G20 be? Where do the common long-term interests lie, and where does mutual competition on world markets make a cooperative solution more difficult? Since the achievement of global climate neutrality is a process with a target date of around 2050, one can at least think about joint—long-term—basic research in scientific and social science projects: internationalized basic research on CO_2 reduction in the fields of, for example, buildings/transportation/agriculture. There is a lot to be done here by the G20 countries and beyond. Joint basic research projects can create a fundament of climate policy confidence within the G20, as all countries will benefit from the jointly financed projects. Since basic research is long term, short-term conflicts of interest between countries do not tend to play a blocking role for cooperation.

The G20 countries will account for about 82 percent of global emissions in 2030, but these emissions in the north of the global economy could cause serious problems in over 60 developing countries in the global South. It would be fair if the rich countries in the North were to pay for the damage to the south of the world economy and help the relatively poorer countries to cope with the problems of increased global warming, in particular through technology transfers in the area of climate protection. In this area, many things are actually already happening in terms of a North-South cooperation perspective. The World Bank as an institution is particularly committed to this.

According to the World Bank (2019), an additional 100 million people will probably end up in poverty by 2030 without comprehensive climate protection measures worldwide; by 2050 there could be up to 143 million climate refugees in developing countries. Extreme weather events could reduce global consumption by $520 billion, or 0.7 percent of world income. Very high levels of global environmentally friendly infrastructure investment are necessary—within 15 years about $90,000 billion, which corresponds to the world income of one year (in 2030). If the transition to a climate-friendly global economy is well managed, the global benefits could reach around 20 percent of annual global income (in 2030 terms) by 2030.

In private life, as well as in national and international economic policy cooperation, many measures can be taken and advantages are achieved albeit sometimes only after laborious changes, investments and innovations. It remains to be seen whether many people's own personal interests and framework conditions will then be such that the goals can be achieved in time. From a scientific point of view, climate neutrality is partly a problem of knowledge; from a politico-economic point of view, it is a problem of action; from a policymaker's point of view, it is a problem of explanation; and finally, there is the problem of global cooperation, since many countries would have to cooperate peacefully, meaningfully, efficiently and reliably.

Since the G20 countries account for 80 percent of global emissions in 2017 – with China, India and the US as the three principal emitters—a successful global climate policy depends on developing a meaningful, coordinated approach between the G20 countries on how to achieve climate neutrality by 2050.

Thus far, the G20 has been a group of countries that meet regularly, sometimes making a discernible difference. But the G20 is not a real international organization; there is no permanent secretariat, no budget. In the area of environmental policy, too, there is a lack of annual G20 summits—and later more frequently—only on climate policy. How best to integrate the G20 into UN activities in a meaningful way has not yet been discussed and decided either.

Two scientists, Robert Keohane and David Victor, have already discussed various possibilities for international cooperation in climate policy in 2010 (Keohane & Victor, 2010), and they stressed that the G20 was an early and active international discussion forum on climate issues. However, in the first few years since the activation of the G20 group at the level of heads of government in November 2008 – in the context of the banking crisis—it has shown a secondary focus on climate issues, as it did, for example, in 2009. Here, it is argued that this attention deficit can be fundamentally rectified from 2020 onward. The arguments developed in the book for the G20, or G20+, as the main climate forum for international cooperation are easy to understand. Indeed, in 2019 the G20 group organized its first summit at the level of environment ministers in Japan. However, how to mobilize the interests of the G20 more broadly for climate neutrality remains a challenge.

It is somewhat of a paradox that the G20 group was originally set up by the finance ministers of the countries concerned as an international discussion forum, which only in the year of the Transatlantic Banking Crisis became a globally relevant meeting of heads of government. From the meeting of the heads of government the forum was then differentiated in 2019 into an additional forum of environment ministers. This means that climate protection issues will indeed likely play a very important role at the G20 level in the long term. Incidentally, the G20's traditional focus on financial market issues (beginning in 2008 during the financial crisis) fits in very well with the idea of transactions on the CO_2 certificate markets in terms of content. This is important because this book stresses the link between certificate markets and financial markets—such as stock markets—as a relevant problem area for climate protection policy. Those who place too narrow a focus on climate protection policy and thereby overlook the related effects in terms of increasing economic inequality plus more financial market dynamics (which could also mean more financial market instability) are unlikely to be successful in politics in the end. Creating a good, functioning solution architecture for climate protection is a complicated national and global task. CO_2 certificate trading will necessarily play an important role here.

Trading in Emission Certificates

Emissions certificate trading as a CO_2 reduction system means that anyone who consumes (conventional) energy or coal in the course of steel production in the steel industry, or burns coal in a coal-fired power plant in the electricity sector, for example, must obtain as many pollution rights—that is, CO_2 emission units—as there are CO_2 quantities emitted in the production process. If a third company, a car manufacturer, also emits CO_2 (during the energy-consuming pressing process for body parts) in the example case considered here, the CO_2 quantities may be 50:30:20 units in the three companies. If the total emission quantity is to be reduced by 1 percent each year according to government regulations, then with unchanged production quantities, the total quantity would now have to be reduced to 99 units in total for the three companies of our model economy in the following year due to improved, more energy-efficient and CO_2-lighter production processes. This is the basic idea of certificate trading. If it is relatively easy for the car manufacturer to make the manufacturing process less CO_2 intensive through modernization and innovation—that is, to save about three CO_2 units—the car manufacturer can offer two surplus units of CO_2 on the CO_2 certificate market and the steel manufacturer, which is expanding its production volume, can buy two additional units. Every year, the competitive and market process determines which companies with strong investments and innovations can offer CO_2 emission certificates and which companies have to buy additional certificates on the market in addition to the often free initial allocation of CO_2 certificates. If one day the steel industry succeeds in switching from coal-based conventional steel-making technology to a new one that uses hydrogen instead of coal and electricity from renewable energies, then the steel industry could sell large surplus quantities of certificates on the certificates market. However, it should not be forgotten that the government is continually reducing the total amount of certificates available each year. If the transition to less CO_2-intensive technologies were to become increasingly difficult over time, the result would be that the market price of CO_2 certificates would continue to rise. This, however, increases the incentive for innovative companies to focus more on CO_2-light innovation projects.

Since certificate trading is the most economically advantageous form of CO_2 reduction, the EU—viewed through the lens of Californian—has achieved almost half of the possible CO_2 reduction far too expensively or indeed not at all. Of course, to a certain extent, a CO_2 tax could also be helpful as a CO_2 savings incentive for producers or consumers in those sectors that are not covered by certificate trading. An expansion of certificate trading should, however, be clear to the forefront of measures by 2020–2050, as this reduces the costs of climate protection. Above all, there are also additional opportunities for further cost reductions, namely if markets are integrated with other countries in the field of certificate trading. After all, Switzerland can be connected to the EU with its certificate trading system, which in turn could draw attention to California, parts of Japan, Republic of Korea, China, New Zealand and certain provinces in Canada, where such trading also already exists. Larger certificate markets ultimately bring advantages for everyone—including the climate.

THE CLIMATE ISSUE

The climate is the result of a complex interaction of conditions on Earth and solar radiation, as well as the rotation of the Earth. An easy-to-read introduction is the book by Mojib Latif, *Bringen wir das Klima aus dem Takt?* [PJJW: *Are We Destabilizing the Climate*] (Latif, 2007). According to Milankovitch's theory, the Earth will move toward a new ice age in the long term—in about 20,000 years (elsewhere, one finds the figure of 50,000 years) –, but significant global warming may occur in the meantime; the latter according to recent observations and climate explanatory approaches in which the IPCC expert group plays a major role. It is composed of experts from the World Meteorological Organization (WMO) and the United Nations Environment Programme (UNEP). Carbon dioxide and other "climate gases" therefore play a major role in global warming, while CO_2 alone is relevant for the declining CO_2 absorption capacity of the oceans due to acidification. Nitrogen and oxygen are the main components (99 percent) of air, in addition to so-called trace gases, which are vital. Carbon dioxide accounts for 0.038 percent of the air and is important for climate development. Apparently, due to man-made reasons, an increased concentration of trace gases has occurred since industrialization. The pre-industrial value for CO_2 was around 0.028 percent (or 280 ppm; ppm = parts per million). Compared to 1850, the concentrations of methane, which is also very harmful to the climate, and some other gases have also increased significantly, whereby methane can be converted into CO_2 equivalents with a view to global warming effects. Thus, you can add CO_2, methane (which is more "weighty" than CO_2) and other greenhouse gases together and speak of so-called CO_2 equivalents. CO_2 and other greenhouse gases lead to a warming of the lower atmosphere, the heat—coming to Earth via solar radiation—is less able to return to space, so that one has a kind of greenhouse effect: just as when the sunlight shines through a greenhouse made of glass, the heat remains trapped inside, so it is with the problem of global warming.

Higher CO_2 concentrations in the air make for thicker glass, as it were, and global warming gradually increases over decades and centuries. This has consequences for ocean currents and air circulation as well as for the melting processes of the ice sheets on Greenland and in the south in the Antarctic as well as the Arctic ice in the north. By the end of the twenty-first century, sea water levels could have risen significantly due to inland ice melting, and the risk of flooding in many densely populated regions of the world would then increase. The available scientific analyses have presented long-term computer models and simulations of climate development: a man-made climate problem in the early twenty-first century can be assumed with 95 percent probability. Even if man contributes only 0.2 percent to the global warming pressure of 30 degrees, that would be 0.6 degrees plus "from man"; if it is 0.5 percent, then the plus factor caused by man would be +1.5 degrees. The problem of global warming is scientifically well analyzed and follows the logic of physics and chemistry. How the concentration of CO_2 in the atmosphere or the challenge of better climate protection can be tackled in a meaningful way is primarily a politico-economic question. Here, there are important issues for economic policy, but also at the level of companies and even private households. Many large firms document their sustainability goals and climate protection activities in a sustainability report; one can look at Allianz or 3 M (such as the 3 M Sustainability Report 2019 from its German HQ) as examples of large companies—or, of course, at thousands of innovative medium-sized companies.

Since 30–40 percent of CO_2 emissions in Western industrialized countries originate from the energy sector—above all from electricity production—it is important that there should be a switch to a higher share of renewable energies in the energy sector of all OECD countries, but also in emerging and developing countries. However, it should not be forgotten that even in 2020, around 13 percent of humanity—around one billion people—still have no reliable access to electricity at all. A power connection and stable power supplies are important for satisfying many basic needs, for high productivity in production and for a high quality of life. If mobility technologies will in future be increasingly characterized by electromobility, which is based on the use of electricity, this will be even truer than ever.

From the point of view of parliaments and governments, the usual objective in industrialized countries is that prosperity, full employment, price stability and climate neutrality can be achieved simultaneously as long-term goals and that the degree of economic inequality does not rise beyond critical limits. Probably the most important contribution to climate protection will be climate-friendly innovations by companies and an integrated global emissions trading system. The basics of how it works, why it is such a good means to secure a CO_2 reduction at minimal cost and why an extended CO_2 certificate trading system (energy producers, industrial companies, etc., need CO_2 certificates which can be bought on the market to offset their CO_2 emissions) in the EU will be important in such a context are important aspects to explain clearly.

Figure 2.1 shows how the global average surface temperature has risen by about 1 percent since 1880; there is no doubt about the longer-term upward trend. Climate scientists agree, with very few exceptions, that part of global warming is man-made; without industrialization—and the enormous energy consumption associated with it—there would be no global warming of almost 1 degree between 1850 and 2020; whether the long-term increase observed is indeed caused by humans or is due to other reasons is only partially relevant: there is a discernible problem of global warming, to which humanity must find a suitable response. The man-made warming impulse may seem manageable, but systems can reach critical states and man-made impulses can lead to globally critical developments. A generally warmer planet creates significantly changed conditions for agriculture and marine use—agricultural yields and fishery yields could decline due to global warming. If hunger or even famine should become part of the climate change problem, new types of violent conflicts threaten some regions of the world.

Temperatures over the past 11,000 years have, despite some volatility over the centuries, been fairly moderate. What is likely to begin in the twenty-first century is a new hotter phase, when people in many countries will have to get used to much higher temperatures than before. A passive acclimatization is possible in moderation, but such a view is of course insufficient as a reaction on the part of the leading countries, including the G20. It is worrisome when temperatures in Australia reach 49.5 degrees in January 2019 and 45.5 degrees in the south of France at the end of June 2019; at least if these high temperatures are signals of what we should

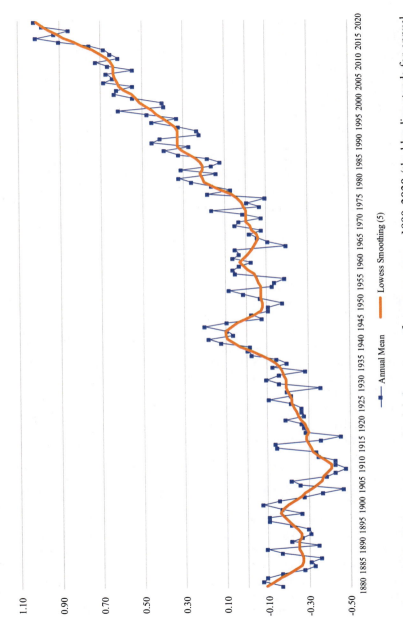

Fig. 2.1 The long-term increase in global average surface temperatures, 1880–2020 (the blue line stands for annual average temperature). (Source: Own representation of data from NASA's Goddard Institute for Space Studies. https://data.giss.nasa.gov/gistemp/graphs/)

expect to see again and again in future years. In parts of India, spring 2019 brought—not for the first time in recent years—temperatures of 50 degrees in some regions. Temperatures in the Arctic have been 3–4 degrees higher since 2010 than at the beginning of the twentieth century.

In Antarctica it is a little better, but in both polar regions there is a problem with regard to melting ice. When the Antarctic ice melts on a large scale, the global water level rises and important existing wind currents, which bring frequent weather changes—that is, keep away permanent heat as well as permanent rain—become unreliable. Warmer seas on a warmer Earth can absorb less CO_2, aggravating the greenhouse problem further. In addition, a warmer sea could weaken certain biological cycles and reduce the productivity of the seas for fishermen. More food shortages can result from inadequate climate protection in the longer term: not a comforting perspective given a world population that will continue to grow until about 2100. On the other hand, more heads—better educated than earlier generations—also means more understanding on Earth and more problem-solving ability; at least, one might hope so.

Longer and more frequent periods of continuous heat and heavy rainfall are a challenge for the affected regions and countries and for the people living there. CO_2 emissions play an important role in global warming, and the natural CO_2 concentration in the air has risen since industrialization. The concentration of CO_2 in the air in the late 1950s was 315 ppm (parts per million). The preliminary peak is 416 ppm in May 2019. CO_2 in the atmosphere is a relatively stable gas over the long term and has a lifetime of 80–100 years there. This, too, is an aspect that demands long-term thinking on the part of politicians, businesses and the electorate to a greater extent than in other policy areas. From an economic point of view, growth theory that takes into account natural resources and the climate is important.

Despite all the promises made at the UN Climate Conference in Paris in 2015, global emissions of CO_2—and similar effective greenhouse gases—which are decisive for global warming have continued to rise globally and will continue to rise for many years to come. Almost 50 billion tons of CO_2 equivalent emissions in 2018 is too much in the long run to mitigate global warming and prevent an increase of more than 1.5 degrees over industrialization (the more modest target often cited is the 2-degree mark, which was indeed a major focus at the Paris Climate Conference).

Based on the scientific analysis of ice core samples in the Arctic, we know approximately how high the CO_2 concentration has been over the past three million years. There is no doubt that the early twenty-first century represents a new record and that man-made emissions—such as from the combustion of fossil fuels such as coal, oil and gas—have contributed significantly to this. Thus, people should think about the problem quickly, change the policy framework conditions and set meaningful new incentives to develop low-CO_2 products and production processes: if necessary, also to remove CO_2 from the atmosphere and store it in a way that does not harm the climate.

Since global warming is essentially caused by emissions of CO_2 and other greenhouse gases, the question arises as to how much damage a ton of CO_2 emissions actually causes. If the production of good X requires the use of energy—more precisely the burning of fossil fuels—then the amount of (marginal) damage would be a starting point for a reasonable assessment of a CO_2 tax, for example. If a ton of CO_2 causes €110 damage, while the producer of the goods is not aware of this, then a possible response of the state to this situation would be that by introducing a CO_2 tax of €110, the producers would have to consider the damage caused by CO_2 emissions. What indicators of the level of CO_2 damage can be used? How could one react meaningfully in the event that companies produce in country 1 while the CO_2 damage occurs in country 2 (perhaps a neighboring country)? Should country 2 impose a CO_2 tax on the companies of country 1? This is hardly realistic and spells political conflict. It would probably be better—and this is something to which we should return—if there were a common emissions trading system. The particularly emission-intensive companies from country 1 (where countries 1 and 2 were EU countries) could act sensibly within the EU certificate system, namely by purchasing emission certificates from companies with surplus CO_2 certificates in country 2. But first let us talk about the amount of damage caused by one ton of CO_2 in Western Europe. Scientists are required to determine the amount of CO_2 damage according to certain standards, that is, how great is the damage caused by a unit of CO_2 emission?

The Cost of One Ton of CO_2 Damage in Western Europe: €60 or €180?

CO_2 is an important trace gas, too much of which causes economic and ecological damage. From a scientific point of view, the global CO_2 level has been too high since around 1950. What is cost of damage caused by an additional ton of CO_2 in Germany, Switzerland or other European countries? The German Federal Environment Agency (UBA) issued a press release on 20 October 2018 according to which the damage of one ton of CO_2 amounts to €180 per ton. This is an important figure which led to the statement that in 2016, the damage caused by CO_2 emissions amounted to €164 billion. This accounts for around 5 percent of gross domestic product (GDP)—the total economic output—in Germany. This figure should be discussed, as it seems excessively high. It is somewhat odd that the German Federal Environment Agency does not seem to take much note of similar such studies from neighboring Switzerland—studies have also been commissioned by the Swiss Federal Office for the Environment (FOEN)—although a scientifically sound analysis would generally have to consider comparative figures from comparable countries.

In any case, it is interesting to take a look at Switzerland, where the Federal Office for the Environment (FOEN) and the Swiss Federal Office of Energy (SFOE) commissioned and published a study by ECOPLAN/SIGMAPLAN (2007) in order to estimate the expected damage caused to Switzerland by rising temperatures: according to the study, the forecasted loss is still manageable until 2100 with a global temperature rise of 1 or 2 degrees, at about 1 billion Swiss francs per year. According to FOEN figures, CO_2 emissions in Switzerland in 2007 amounted to 21 million metric tons (Federal Office for the Environment, 2020). This level of emissions resulted in damages of 48 Swiss francs per ton, that is, about €44 per ton of CO_2 emitted in 2007. However, if the temperature rises by 3, 4 or 5 degrees, the cost of the associated damages increases dramatically in ECOPLAN's simulation analysis.

It is very implausible that in Switzerland one ton of CO_2 causes damage of around €60—extrapolated to 2016—while just over the border in Germany the corresponding figure is €180 per ton of CO_2. The per capita income in Switzerland is higher than in Germany, as is the price level. Obviously, there is not enough scientific discussion between scientists from European countries; otherwise such differences could not come about. The value determined for Switzerland seems more plausible than the German Federal Environment Agency's value, which is inexplicably also far removed from the CO_2 certificate price in the EU (at €25 per ton); it should be noted that Switzerland indirectly participates in the EU certificate trading system. The Federal Ministry for the Environment, as the superior authority of the Federal Environment Agency, has so far failed to address the contradictions identified—this is not a rational approach.

Nevertheless, the "key" figure in Germany is very influential in the debate: if, for example, the Fridays for Future movement adopts the €180 per ton figure—as was heard in August 2019 after the Fridays for Future Congress in Dortmund—then this pushes the climate protection discussion in Germany in too extreme a direction. A damage value of €180 per ton naturally requires much more decisive policy measures than a damage value of €60 per ton. It is advisable to objectify the often very emotional—and ideological—debate on optimal climate protection in Germany, the EU and the global economy. In any case, the German Agency's number is not sacrosanct, and apparently there is a lack of critical analysis in Germany.

It is noteworthy that the US climate macroeconomist and research pioneer William Nordhaus estimates damage per ton of CO_2 in the US at $31 per ton in 2015 (in 2010 prices) (Nordhaus, 2017). However, one can also point out that the figure of $37 per ton often quoted in the US was classified as being an underestimation of the true cost in a recent analysis—a new analysis assumes a figure of $220 per ton (Moore & Diaz, 2015). There may be different analysis results for individual scientists in the US. But in Europe it is again true that it can in any case be assumed that the damage per ton of CO_2 in Germany and Switzerland must be similarly high. Of course, you can also take a look at Austria (for an interesting report on the climate situation, see the Wegener Center (2017), The Greenhouse Budget for Austria, University of Graz) or the Netherlands, France or the UK; or Spain, Brazil, Russia, China and so on.

Since the media often functions according to the motto that "bad news is good news"—bad news means good (promotional) news with large attention-grabbing headlines—there is probably a temporary tendency toward exaggeration in the digital media society, which corresponds to a certain level of public commotion about climate protection. Developing a reasonable solution to the problem, however, requires a differentiated, critical, solid, fact-based analysis, which includes the results of more recent scientific findings. One should actually expect the scientific advisory institutions of national governments to work along these lines. It is, however, remarkable that in Germany, for example, at least one important advisory institution has developed a rather peculiar and ideological viewpoint—presented in 2019 as a major report. This situation is both strange and inappropriate, at least if one follows the approach of critical-rational science.

An Earlier Field of Success: Combating the Ozone Hole

The international response to climate issues is characterized not only by challenges, setbacks and failure; one can always look to previous problem areas for which international solutions were indeed found. In the case of the problem of the hole in the ozone layer and the 1987 Montreal Protocol against the use of CFCs (chlorofluorocarbons were considered to be the main drivers of damage to the ozone layer), two dozen countries and the EU signed an initial agreement, and in the end all 197 UN member states were on board. Through the hole in the ozone layer, the sunlight (ultraviolet radiation) penetrates through to the Earth much more strongly than usual, which is risky for both humans and animals—keyword: skin cancer. The successes with regard to the ozone problem are instructive. If a larger international starting group can be won over for joint action, then the other countries will also soon come on board over time. The successful fight against ozone depletion in any case is evidence of the possibilities when the international community cooperate.

The problems surrounding climate protection are not easy, at least when it comes to measures aimed at reducing CO_2 emissions. The conceivable planting of billions of additional trees around the world is also an admirable and long-term task; conceivable, feasible, but time-consuming. It would also be reasonable to merge the emissions trading systems of different countries, but that will hardly be possible before 2030 as so far, no political actor has set itself such a goal. It will not be an easy task to achieve, even if many large countries wanted to. According to the majority of climate experts, climate neutrality should be approached globally by 2050. Three decades to develop a novel climate protection policy of many countries, which should be coordinated in many fields from 2030, that is not much time for adaptation.

After all, increased climate protection must contribute toward solving another problem—that of inequality which has not yet been on the political agenda, and which can be attributed more to national than to international politics: it is not a question of existing income inequality in industrialized and emerging countries, but of the initially unavoidable increase in income inequality due to a rising differential in terms of the wages of skilled relative to those of the unskilled workers; for the correction and limitation of this inequality effect in the course of structural change in favor of more climate-friendly products and production processes, a sensible accompanying policy is needed in the G20, OECD and emerging countries. This triad of problems (national climate policy, international coordination and redistribution/social policy) needs to be explained fully, and successful climate policy will only exist if all three of these problems are tackled in a meaningful way and, in a large number of countries, at the same time.

Search for Solutions

According to UN climate experts (IPCC), CO_2 emissions should be halved by 2030. After 2050, CO_2 emissions should be "net zero": from a single country's point of view, you can have CO_2 emissions, but you would then have to compensate for them, for example, by funding the planting of forests in other countries. The EU summit in June 2019 showed that there is no agreement on tightening CO_2 targets in the EU28; above all, some Eastern European EU countries do not want to join in and do not want to become more ambitious with regard to target-setting for the future. Perhaps this is indeed not necessary at this point in time, since it is initially more important to reach the existing targets which were set for 2020 and to consider how existing target deficits can then be successfully addressed on the time axis up to 2030.

In fact, the EU28 countries have missed some of the energy efficiency and climate protection targets for 2020 – this was already apparent at the beginning of 2019. However, if all G20 countries (and ultimately all countries in the world) had comprehensive CO_2 certificate trading, then there is little to worry about. The question is how to get a G20 certificate trading system operating in a reasonable amount of time. The answer can be found in this book.

Quite a few EU countries are making good progress in reducing domestic CO_2 emissions, but there are also hidden CO_2 emissions abroad, for example, via flights by EU citizens to destinations outside Europe (more precisely, destinations outside the European Economic Area). Since 2012, flights within the EU have been included in certificate trading, but not flights outside the EU. Switzerland is also interesting here: in addition to the six tons of carbon dioxide emissions per Swiss citizen per year in Switzerland (in 2017), there are also slightly higher quantities resulting from various Swiss activities outside Switzerland. Similar considerations apply to citizens from many EU countries, North America and certain Asian countries.

In large OECD countries, the problem in this respect is not much different from those in Switzerland; in particular, the US has "offshore emissions" in China, for example, since a large proportion of China's CO_2-intensive exports go to the US (and the US has an overall current account deficit, with imports from China in particular exceeding exports in terms of value). If, for example, the US imports steel, aluminum or computers from China, the CO_2 emissions generated in China during production and the corresponding consumption of resources are actually attributable to the US; calculations can be found in the specialist literature on "embedded CO_2 emissions". In the international discussions at G20 level, it would therefore be appropriate, under the heading of burden sharing, to correct China's emissions accordingly and to correct those of the US and some other OECD countries upward in relation to the emissions of the respective country, provided that net foreign emissions are to be taken into account.

Whether one should introduce a border compensation tax for CO_2-intensive imports could also be discussed; this is not seen as promising here, since the best method is clearly to introduce CO_2 certificate trading in other countries as well. China is setting a good example here by implementing a single national certificate trading scheme from 2021 following pilot certificate trading schemes in a number of Chinese regions. The Chinese systems covers a lower proportion of emissions than in the EU, but in implementing a nationwide system, China is ahead of the US, where only California and a manageable group of nine other states (RGGI)—in the energy sector—are engaged in CO_2 emissions trading. EU countries could introduce a border equalization tax on imports from countries without adequate CO_2 certificate trading, which would be compatible with the rules of the World Trade Organization.

Unless sufficient annual CO_2 reductions are achieved in industrialized and emerging economies, intermediate targets toward the long-term goal of a climate-neutral economy in 2050 will not be achieved. In fact, EU countries have not developed a mechanism for achieving foreseeable missed shorter-term targets through significantly increased targets for annual CO_2 emission reductions in the EU in certificate trading (i.e., -5 percent annually from 2025 instead of the planned -2.2 percent from 2020), or for making reliable progress by gradually increasing CO_2 taxes in sectors other than those covered by certificate trading; Sweden has had a CO_2 tax since 1991 and also makes good contributions to climate protection through it. The CO_2 tax in Sweden affects those sectors where EU certificate trading does not work.

Germany has no such tax. Switzerland has had an automatic target attainment system for CO_2 tax rates for years. If the CO_2 emissions do not reach a politically defined target achievement path, a certain CO_2 tax increase will automatically take place—up to a capped maximum (politically determined) amount, with which one wants to create planning security for companies. However, Switzerland is not an island of the blessed either.

The "quasi-Swiss CO_2 emissions" generated abroad are slightly higher than those generated in Switzerland itself, namely 8 tons per capita. The total for 2017 for Switzerland is therefore 14 tons per capita (Federal Office for the Environment, 2018). In Switzerland, while the domestic CO_2 footprint (emissions per capita) has declined over time, Swiss foreign emissions have actually increased. It is clear that an increase in the price of CO_2-intensive production or intermediate products in Europe will incentivize companies to relocate the corresponding production or intermediate product manufacture processes abroad, that is, to countries where there is still no CO_2 pricing or where the CO_2 price—for example, in the form of an emissions certificate or a CO_2 tax—is still relatively low. We must not lose sight of this CO_2 leakage problem. It is becoming increasingly important to be able to introduce and expand CO_2 certificate trading systems in the vast majority of countries. By 2025, clear new directions are urgently needed here.

Many parts of the Earth will become rather uncomfortable for future generations unless a much better global climate protection policy is realized quickly. Emission-reducing innovations are important here, with regard to not only new products, but also more climate-friendly manufacturing processes. Every CO_2 emitter in the world is ultimately important. The atmospheric CO_2 concentration levels and the global warming problem depend on the global level of emissions. From an economic point of view, this means that climate protection is about a global collective good: all of the people of the world share the benefits of more climate protection; there is no rivalry in the use of a stable global atmosphere. A reasonable provision of an international collective good, however, is difficult to achieve, as experience teaches (and modeling shows). While almost everyone has an interest in a stable climate or in climate protection, there is also a tendency for actors to engage in free-rider behavior: individual countries may decide not to bear the burden but hope that others will ensure sufficient climate protection in time.

If one thinks of the world's major countries, then one would have to bring these main emitters to one table and agree on binding CO_2 reduction policies. The number of countries that are most important in this area is actually quite manageable, and helpfully, this group of countries also already meets regularly, namely the G20. These countries regularly adopt goals and recommendations which can be found in press releases. For example, it has been said for a decade that the huge subsidies for fossil energy use (i.e., coal, oil, gas) are to be removed. In global terms, they were about four times higher in 2018 than global spending on research and development.

This is a contradiction of titanic proportions: climate protection means that fossil fuel use must be significantly reduced in terms of energy production, especially coal and, in many areas, oil, while at the same time sources of renewable energies must be supported, at least in terms of research and development, through subsidies. Accordingly, there is a specialization in the export of environmentally friendly products in those countries that have relatively high per capita incomes and leading technology positions of many companies in "green technologies". The question of international competitiveness in environmentally friendly products will have to be addressed again—especially in the final chapter.

While the situation in Europe is reasonable, the same cannot be said about certain other industrialized countries. In the US, for example, President Trump took certain steps, at great expense, to restart coal production in the US; this makes no sense, economically or from a climate policy perspective. In some threshold countries, the initial starting point is not an easy one. In India, for example, expanded coal production is an integral part of the state economy: India's coal mines are part of a state-owned corporation that receives credit from state-owned banks for coal production, with the state-owned railway transporting the mined coal halfway through the country. Thus, there are many regional and national interest groups that want to continue producing coal. Australia is also a country with a question mark over its national coal policy. Germany is not much better because, despite the inclusion of coal-fired power generation—as part of the energy sector—in certificate trading in 2018/2019, the government is planning a kind of planned economic phase-out of coal, based on recommendations contained in a proposal of the so-called Coal

Commission at an unnecessarily high cost, as will become apparent in the near future.

At a global level, the primary emitters are China, the US, the EU, India, Indonesia, Japan, Brazil and the OPEC countries, and they are indeed active in the G20 with annual summits since the end of 2008. But whether this body is still able to act at all in matters of climate protection sometimes seems doubtful. At the G20 summit in Osaka in June 2019, there was for the first time a coalition of three countries opposed to comprehensive and rapid climate protection policy measures, spearheaded by the US, under populist President Trump, who temporarily brought Brazil and Saudi Arabia onto his side.

The Osaka G20 summit ultimately concluded with a 19:1 position in the final so-called Leader's Declaration document, where the 1 stands for Trump's US. Trump praised the quality of US water and air and told the TV cameras that he did not want to jeopardize US economic growth in favor of global sustainability or climate protection policy. This sounds like a short-sighted wealthy individual who does not want to invest in better flood protection but who will lose part of her fortune in the foreseeable next flood. Trump was also distanced from his own electorate at this point. After all, many US citizens are prepared to forgo some growth for environmental protection—this is shown by the results of the World Values Survey, a major international survey project.

Are there any previous global environmental protection projects that have been successful? The 1987 Montreal Protocol on Substances that Deplete the Ozone Layer—initially signed by 24 countries and the EU—with the 1985 Vienna for the Protection of the Ozone Layer, in response to the hole in the ozone layer which came about through the emission of CFCs (chlorofluorocarbons), is a remarkable success story. The hole in the ozone layer over Antarctica has been significantly reduced since about 2010, and the volume of CFCs in the atmosphere has declined. The industrialized countries raised around $1 billion in a special fund to enable developing countries to participate in conversion projects from the CFC economy or the use of CFC substances in the medium term.

In the case of CO_2 emissions, a conversion aid fund is also needed for poorer countries, but the issue of global warming is of much larger dimensions. The ozone layer issue shows, however, that success can indeed be achieved within three decades. However, this was before the age of populism in the West; the populist phenomenon in politics visibly affects not only the US during and after the presidency of Donald Trump and Brazil under President Bolsonaro, but also the UK (with the populist Brexit project) and Italy as well as some Eastern EU countries.

Climate protection depends not only on states, but also on investors and, of course, on the behavior of private households. After all, there has been an increased interest on the part of large investors in more sustainable investments since 2008. There are initiatives that allow companies to provide not only financial figures, but also information on their level of CO_2 emissions. From an investor's point of view, countries can be viewed in terms of their share of renewable energies, their international competitiveness in environmentally friendly products and the sustainability of the national "real" savings rate (for more, see the EIIW-vita Global Sustainability Indicator). Sufficient savings are necessary to preserve the capital base of companies and thus the basis for future production, and it should also be borne in mind that investment in education is a key part of preserving the substance of a society that wants to ensure that future generations have the same chances of enjoying living standards as good as the current generation.

GLOBAL WARMING, POLITICAL REFOCUSING AND FIRST LONG-TERM STUDIES

The year 2017 was the warmest in the history of modern, international temperature record-keeping with data available since 1800. The two previous years were the next warmest since 1800, but there was a particular wind phenomenon observed in South America, namely El Niño, which causes temperatures over land and sea to rise slightly (Olivier & Peters, 2018); the global average temperature over land and sea was 0.84 degrees above the average of the twentieth century—over land alone the increase was 1.31 degrees. Global warming and the climate problem are about long-term changes and prospects. In the political debate, a single year with significant heat waves may cause a spike in excitement surrounding the climate debate; however the climate problem is not about the short-term outcome of a single year.

The political excitement and attention in many countries in the twenty-first century will probably also be strongly determined by the weather; an election year which features extreme weather events in the run-up to polling will probably give environmental parties and parties with a focus on climate policy an increased share of votes. The European Parliament elections in 2019 provided a certain preview in this respect, the winners of the elections being environmental parties, liberals and populists. The latter, like US President Donald Trump, claim that there is no man-made global warming which should cause widespread worry. This is a naive misconception if you take the results of science seriously (see, e.g., Royal Society, 2009).

From the point of view of science—the predominant opinion of experts at universities, research institutes and laboratories worldwide—the global average temperature in the twenty-first century should reach *at most* 2 degrees above the level at the beginning of the age of industrialization; otherwise global problems threaten due to extreme heat, flooding, an increase in extreme weather events and the resultant problems, including millions of climate refugees. Some problems will be national and regional, but significant economic problems in large economies like US, EU, Japan or China will easily become an international challenge. Since one will not be able to simply move to the moon, Mars or other celestial bodies, one should limit the rise of global temperatures wisely and energetically by way of truly meaningful measures. The greenhouse gases important for this warming are CO_2 (73 percent) and methane (CH_4: approximately 18 percent). Methane and other emissions (e.g., NO_2 and F-gases) with warming effects are converted into CO_2 equivalents.

Sectors Reducing CO_2 Emissions and Sectors Increasing CO_2 Emissions

One of the most important starting points for CO_2 reduction is CO_2 certificate trading, where the EU has been a pioneer since 2005. Companies from the energy sector and industry must obtain CO_2 emission rights, only then can they produce. There is partly a free initial supply of emission rights for these companies—the state gives away some of the certificates—and further required CO_2 emission rights must then be bought by the companies on the certificates market at the market price; for example, an old coal-fired power plant buys emission rights from a modern gas-fired power plant that has surplus emission certificates. With certificate prices ranging from $15 to $50 per ton (or similar amounts in €), production becomes more expensive. In the EU, certificates can of course be traded across borders between countries. California's certificate trading system is linked to two provinces in Canada.

In the EU, there is—unsurprisingly—a big difference between developments in the emissions trading sectors (energy plus parts of industry: covering about 45 percent of emissions), where in 2017 emissions will decrease by 1.74 percent, as they will every year, according to the system's program; outside the emissions trading sector, emissions will increase by about 3.4 percent in 2017: with the overall result of an EU emission increase of 1.1 percent. The EU total emissions increase of 1.1 percent in 2017 and the differences between −1.74 percent and +3.4 percent show that the emissions trading sector reduces CO_2 emissions, and the system works. In addition, it becomes clear how problematic it is to have circa 55 percent of emissions occurring outside of a system of reasonable CO_2 pricing. In simple terms, this is a rising emissions sector.

California has set a policy of −3 percent per year as the emission reduction rate by 2020 for 85 percent of the emissions covered by the Californian emissions trading sector. Even if California had +3 percent emissions outside the emissions trading sector, the overall effect would be −2.1 percent. Although the EU is a pioneer in certificate trading, it still lags far behind what is possible and indeed necessary. One can already see here that the EU and other countries of the G20 group would be well advised to go to 85–90 percent emissions coverage for certificate trading and to set a programed annual reduction of the CO_2 limit of at least −3 percent in the medium term; as will be shown here, rather −5 to −6 percent would be more appropriate. In the sectors and areas that are not included in certificate trading, CO_2 taxes and regulations are needed; only where an overly complex and expensive system would be required can a small remnant of the economy and consumption remain without significant adjustment pressure. In principle, it is conceivable that in a two-state model economy (e.g., EU as "Country 1" and California as "Country 2", or EU and China, or the Global North and South; see Fig. 2.2), an integration of the certificate trading sectors would take place which would naturally result in a common certificate price. Integration can in theory be recommended if the degree of coverage of Country 1 and Country 2 in terms of emissions is roughly the same (EU at 45 percent is too low compared to the 85 percent of coverage in California—since 2015, after its launch in 2013). Although California has a greater degree of coverage than the EU, by mid-2019 the price in California is only about half as high as in the EU at the equivalent of about €14 per metric ton CO_2. An integration of the EU/Californian markets would result in a price reduction for the EU, with EU companies or companies from the Eurozone purchasing emission certificates from companies in California, thereby improving the US current account balance. In addition, there would also be an appreciation of the US dollar.

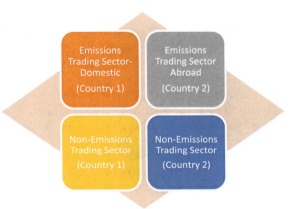

Fig. 2.2 The emissions trading sectors and non-emissions trading sectors. (Source: Own representation)

Five countries in the world economy, plus the EU, account for 63 percent of world emissions: Japan for 3 percent, Russia for 5, India for 7, the EU for circa 9, the US for 13, and China for 27 percent, respectively, in 2017. In terms of emissions, in 2017 the India recorded +2.9 percent, China +1.1 percent, the EU +1.1 percent, Russia +1 percent, Japan +0.3 percent and the US +0.1 percent (data according to Olivier & Peters, 2018). If all these countries had followed California's model, they would probably have had a reduction in emissions, that is, negative percentage rates of change. It should be mentioned that California, with 40 million inhabitants, recorded about three-quarters of the gross domestic product of Germany in 2018 and only half of the emissions, which means that the CO_2 emissions per unit of income were only two-thirds as high in California as in Germany. One part of the advantage for California comes from the stronger service orientation, but another part also from the more comprehensive emissions certificates approach—compared to the EU or Germany. Of course, from the point of view of a country introducing CO_2 trading, the expected loss of international market share would be lower if other countries were to introduce trading in the same sectors at the same time. However, the production cost aspect, which arises when certificates are purchased, is only one element of a firm's development. If, for example, the prices of manufactured products rise, firms' profits and returns could increase; this would lead to higher international capital inflows, which would lower the real interest rate and thus the investment costs—but would also make export business somewhat more difficult through an appreciation of the domestic currency (at flexible exchange rates). In any case, it is not enough to simply look at the cost side of companies when introducing certificate trading.

In the US, in addition to California, a group of nine federal states plus three other federal states have introduced a less ambitious system of trade in certificates; in addition, the EU, China—on a national basis from 2021 (previously a number of pilot trading schemes existed in various Chinese regions)—and Japan, which has a certificate trade in two regions (Tokyo and Saitama), all engage in certificate trading. Russia and India have no such system of emissions trading. The more countries have a certificate trade, the better for the climate; and the more advantageous also for suppliers and exporters of investments targeted at modernization projects and modern software. Better climate protection can be achieved only with better and newer production technologies. From this perspective, Germany, along with other EU countries, Japan, China and the US, is likely to be on the winning side internationally.

BCG/Prognos Study on Germany

There are only a few comprehensive models regarding CO_2 reduction toward reaching climate neutrality in 2050. There is a study by the Federation of German Industries (BDI); the modeling, carried out by the Boston Consulting Group and Prognos AG, is not easily comprehensible, and some obvious assumptions are questionable and, therefore, also some of the conclusions. In essence, the main finding is that an increased annual investment rate is necessary, which should increase by 1–2 percent; this is a very substantial increase that can be considered unrealistic. The conclusions of the BDI study can be summarized and translated from German as follows: "The direct additional economic costs, after the deduction of energy savings, would amount to about 470 to 960 billion euros by 2050 (about 15 to 30 billion euros per year), of which about 240 billion euros would be for existing efforts" (BCG/Prognos, 2018, p. 7). According to this, almost 0.5 percent of the gross domestic product per year would have to be assumed as the net cost of climate change for Germany over 30 years. With a significant external growth rate of 1.5 percent, this is considerable.

Cushioning Transition and Adjustment Costs Through Special State Funds

Given this magnitude, it seems sensible for Germany to set up a state-level climate protection investment and innovation promotion fund (CPIIPF), which would be financed in part by a climate protection solidarity tax surcharge. If the federal state were to borrow over €300 billion in 30-year bonds, such an earmarked amount could be financed by a new, special purpose institution at an interest rate of close to zero. The CPIIPF proposal, as developed here, would also be in line with other studies, such as the scientific studies submitted to the Federal Ministry for the Environment in 2019. However, the proposal made here assumes that the annual net costs of climate change will be lower than in the BCG/Prognos forecast, in particular because it should be possible by 2025 to merge the CO_2 certificate trading systems of EU-Korea-California-Canada (Quebec), China-Japan (Tokyo and Saitama), which will require several years of preparation and negotiations. It would probably be necessary to pay China some compensation for its participation in such a networked trading system, which ideally should initially comprise only a few actors—with more than 20 countries, there are often free-rider problems, and negotiating solutions is also a more difficult, costly and time-consuming process. Moreover, an annual reduction plan for CO_2 quantities would have to be made binding. The global efficiency of such a system is important for people around the world, as here a cost-minimal CO_2 reduction can be achieved.

However, it must also be examined whether fluctuations in the "global" CO_2 certificate price would have destabilizing effects on financial markets. If such an effect were to occur and be significant, it would be expected that the global investment rate and presumably also global innovation dynamics would decline due to rising capital and financing costs. This means that a stronger role for CO_2 taxes would have to be considered. However, consideration should also be given to introducing a tax on the return on equity volatility of banks and other financial institutions (as already suggested by the author in the context of the Transatlantic Banking Crisis), which may also reduce price volatility in financial markets.

Credibility Problems in Germany

There are economic policy contradictions in Germany that one should not overlook if one wants a sensible climate protection policy. The credibility and international influence of Germany and the EU will be weakened by the underperformance in terms of achieving the 2020 climate protection targets. In Germany, and some other EU countries, there is so far a high coverage of CO_2 emissions in industry and energy, but there is still a lot to do in the areas of mobility, housing and agriculture. Sweden, on the other hand, has confronted these sectors with important emission reduction incentives through a CO_2 tax introduced since 1991, with an increased use of district heating in buildings, for example, contributing to CO_2 reductions.

That government employees could also reclaim the costs of purchasing CO_2 compensation as part of travel costs for international flights outside the EU would, of course, have to be introduced at all levels of government independently of the CPIIPF, from the local authority level via the regional governments/federal states to the national level (federal government) and even the EU. These are just a few examples of simple policy points which could be tackled quickly and relatively easily. The federal and state governments in Germany, for example, are declaring a kind of climate emergency but at the same time are refusing to reimburse civil servants for additional CO_2 compensation costs for flights outside the EU as part of the flight costs. That is an enormous contradiction in Germany.

In Germany, the issue of district heating is also a nuisance for many households and firms, as there are very long contract periods of up to ten years and the intensity of competition is therefore low, which often leads to highly overpriced offers—also linked to municipal interests—to the detriment of customers (Sauga, 2019). While the electricity sector is subject to regulation by Germany's Federal Network Agency, there is no such institutional monitoring in the district heating market—the responsible state cartel authorities are generally inactive. There is therefore a clear need for reform here, but the German government was very silent about this in 2019. Contract periods should not exceed three years, and, in principle, customers should be free to switch to other providers/offers without significant problems. This is an exemplary reform policy for better climate protection policy.

Key Questions Recapped

The main questions, of course, is how to efficiently achieve a climate-neutral world economy by 2050 and how suitable existing approaches in the G20+ countries are? These countries stand for about 60 percent of the world's population, 80 percent of global income and 80 percent of global CO_2 emissions. Here, G20+ means the G20 club plus Nigeria (the EU is represented by some individual countries in the G20, as well as by the presidents of the European Council and Commission for the EU as a whole). What does one need to achieve climate neutrality? Much more than the G20+ – correctly constituted – addressing the following points is hardly needed to achieve global climate neutrality by 2050:

- Provided that the right new policy approaches are implemented quickly, some of which also already exist in the EU in the form of the emission certificate trading system for 45 percent of emissions—an extension to 85 percent in Europe would make sense.
- Provided that an appropriate adaptation speed—that is, annual CO_2 reduction speed in CO_2 emissions trading systems—is set: in the EU, California, China, Republic of Korea, Japan, Canada and the other G20+ countries.
- Provided sufficient support can be mobilized by the Fridays for Future movement.
- Provided that the appropriate global networking strategy for the national and regional certificate trading systems is implemented at a G20+ level—and that the actual influence of the EU countries and the cooperation options are used to the fullest extent.
- Provided that the distributional effects of global climate protection are reasonably limited and, at the same time, a stronger innovation promotion policy is pursued in good time.
- As long as every individual contributes in their own way and with enthusiasm, with many almost free possibilities for personal actions, for example, the whitening of roofs—which supports an improved albedo effect based on bright smooth surfaces. It would be wise to present such actions as something which is difficult to do, but to also

highlight the benefits and privilege of participation, following the wisdom of Tom Sawyer, who knew how to transform the penal work of fence-painting into a burden which became easy to share with others (in Mark Twain's book *The Adventures of Tom Sawyer and Huckleberry Finn*).

At the end of the book, all the main points are again summarized over two pages: one page of text and an overview as a conclusion of the whole study; a new view of the global climate protection problem.

Emissions Trading in the EU: An Innovative Approach

From an economic-ecological point of view, the climate protection problem is a manageable task: sufficient greenhouse gas savings are to be made, for which scarce resources—and technologies—must be used. In this task, the aim is to minimize the costs per ton of CO_2 saved, in other words, to maximize the reduction in CO_2 emissions per resource unit used. How can this be achieved? In essence, the answer is this: you need an emissions trading system that should function within certain political guidelines. Such a trading system for CO_2 emissions (or other emissions) brings an equilibrium price, which—if the system works sensibly and is not undermined by additional political intervention—tells all companies in the emissions trading sector up to what (marginal) costs are CO_2 saving measures worthwhile. A company that has higher (marginal) costs will buy CO_2 certificates from relatively innovative companies with surplus certificates. The surplus certificates will be listed by the innovative company as an asset in the balance sheet and valued approximately at the market price. This is a very simple system that provides reasonable incentives. It is worth thinking about it and understanding it, because it is the key to global climate protection. However, there is always a risk that impatient policy interventions may inadvertently (or indeed intentionally) bend this key—in which case the gateway to climate neutrality in 2050 will probably remain closed, which would be a global tragedy.

Box 2.1: Certificate Trading System
The key to climate protection is emissions trading (such trading systems have already been successfully used to achieve reductions of various pollutants, such as the reduction of sulfur emissions in North America and Europe). It is based on the simple idea that companies with CO_2 emissions—such as power plants that burn coal, oil or gas—must procure a corresponding quantity of certificates; if the state does not give away CO_2 certificates, they must be purchased on the certificate market. The suppliers on the market are those firms that have managed to reduce CO_2 emissions relatively easily through modernization investments and innovations: surplus certificates are then sold on the CO_2 emissions market to companies that have too few certificates. Since the upper limit of total permissible emissions is reduced by a certain percentage every year, there is a pressure to innovate in favor of less CO_2-intensive production technologies and the substitution of coal-fired power plants, for example, with zero-emission wind turbines. The value of emission certificates in the certificate market is determined by the interplay of supply and demand. The higher the certificate price, the greater the incentive to reduce emissions and innovate. By mid-2019, the price of certificates in the EU was around €26 per ton. In California, however, the corresponding certificate price was only the equivalent of around €14 per ton. Since only the total global emissions is important for the problem of global warming and thus the climate problem, climate protection can be made cheaper by interconnecting the certificate trading systems of the EU, the US, China and some other countries. Looking at the G20+ countries, which are all the G20 countries plus Nigeria—they account for 80 percent of global CO_2 emissions—it can be seen that more than half of the G20 countries do not yet have an emissions certificate system.

Figure 2.3 shows the simplified structure of EU climate policy. Apart from certain regulations—for example, on fleet consumption by car manufacturers—there is a trade in emission certificates. It accounts for about 45 percent of total CO_2 emissions (climate gases to be precise) in the European Union, across all EU member states, covering the energy sector

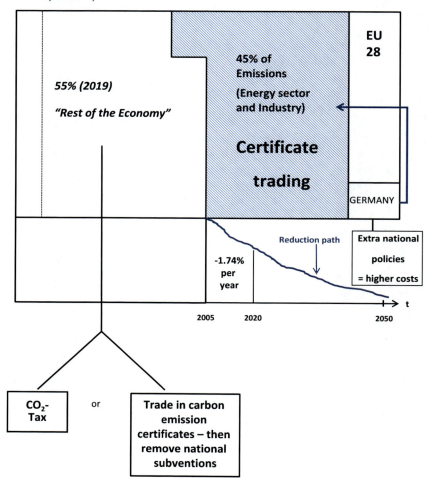

Fig. 2.3 Structure of climate protection policy in the European Union. (Source: Own representation)

and industry. For these two areas taken together, and for the EU as a whole, an annual maximum amount of CO_2 emissions will be set, which policymakers aim to reduce by 2030 and 2040, respectively. There are other regions and countries in the world where this certificate trading also takes place, partly also more comprehensively, as in California. In the medium term, the EU will have to decide the extent to which the existing certificate trading approach should be expanded; the control signal for certificate trading is the price for companies' CO_2 pollution rights on the market. If companies want to expand their production and have too few pollution rights, they can buy pollution rights from other companies. By reducing the combined maximum permitted amount of emissions for the energy sector plus industry in the EU over time according to a known reduction path, government can reliably reduce around half of the EU's emissions close to zero—the time horizon is 2050.

If the expansion of certificate trading into other production areas and perhaps even private consumption (e.g., personal/private automobile use) is extended, most of the economy can be managed accordingly for climate protection. Certain "residual sectors", not covered by the trading system, could also be provided with incentives to save CO_2 emissions by means of CO_2 taxes. If national governments in the field of energy and industry (both are included in certificate trading) launch additional national projects to reduce CO_2 emissions, this usually only has the effect of driving up the costs of climate protection. The situation is different in areas not covered by certificate trading—here the introduction of a CO_2 tax could possibly act as a "price signal" or incentive in favor of more climate protection. Figure 2.3 illustrates the points listed with a view to the EU, whereby government intervention is regarded as subsidies for companies with CO_2-light technologies in sectors outside the emissions trading sector. If the CO_2 emissions trading sector is expanded, such subsidies or other interventions by the state should be reduced (with the exception of subsidies for research promotion). Such interventions unnecessarily increase the cost of CO_2 reduction and weaken the price signal of the CO_2 certificate markets.

Reducing emissions is a standard economic problem, and policymakers in the EU, California and some other regions around the world have exemplary progress to show, namely the introduction of an emissions trading system:

- A maximum annual emission quantity is set for the EU in the energy and industry sectors—for 28 countries together (pre-Brexit).
- A corresponding quantity is then auctioned among the power plants and firms, which are allowed to trade the certificates among themselves (some of the certificates were given to companies in the export sector for nothing, as they did not want to weaken their international competitiveness). This results in a certificate market price in the EU. This market price provides important incentives: the higher the market price, the greater the incentives for CO_2 savings in the economy. However, it also makes no sense to bring about arbitrarily high prices. At the very least, the EU must be climate neutral by 2050, and the same must be achieved in other regions of the world.
- The EU reduces the upper limit of permissible emissions year after year—by about 1.7 percent annually, from 2020 by 2.2 percent (in California, the annual reduction is set at 3 percent, and emissions trading covers 85 percent of CO_2 emissions with Californian companies trading with companies from the Canadian province of Quebec).
- If a significant part of the economy—and of private consumption (leisure trips to the countryside with a gasoline-fueled car also cause CO_2 emissions)—is not included in emissions trading in the EU, one can think about CO_2 taxation, bearing in mind the side effects of the CO_2 tax and whether it is possible to motivate other countries to introduce a parallel CO_2 tax. That way, the number of threatened jobs in the correspondingly taxed sectors is lower than with a national solo effort. In sectors where a reduction in CO_2 per unit volume is very costly, large projects should be avoided from an economic point of view; it does not pay off for the economy. If, however, a country does take an economic policy approach here, then the economic costs in the form of income and job losses are high. Solid knowledge of cost structures in sectors and companies must therefore be mobilized: emissions trading does just that—companies with low CO_2 abatement costs will come forward to sell their surplus CO_2 certificates to other industrial companies with higher abatement costs. The carbon market reveals the relevant information, capabilities and needs. One can set up such a market locally such as in Japan for the prefecture of Tokyo (and that of Saitama), or in the US for California or for the EU28 countries as a political club, or for the whole world economy. Since climate protection is a global public good, a very large international market for emission certificates would indeed be

a sensible thing; in the end, even a global market might be possible, which, however, also needs a certain degree of regulation. In accordance with the principle of shipbuilding where bulkheads are intended to prevent complete water intrusion, one could also think of a number of regional emission certificate markets that could also be networked with each other according to certain rules. Here, there are obvious analogies to the financial markets, and it cannot be ruled out that only via a difficult learning process can one find out how to set the rules for large international markets wisely.

- If you undertake national emission reduction measures, in addition to the EU emissions trading system for the energy industry and industry, it may be well received as a headline on the front page of the newspapers, but—with very few exceptions—it is rather pointless. For example, if a national sectoral special measure achieves 20 million tons of CO_2 emission reductions in one year (e.g., by closing a coal-fired power plant in 2021), this would only mean that 20 million tons of emission units would be freed up for other firms in Germany or other EU countries because of the EU's total limit on emissions. Even the Renewable Energy Sources Act (EEG—in German the *Erneuerbare-Energien-Gesetz (EEG)*), introduced in Germany in 1999, is not without its problems—within limits it can be regarded as a globally useful impulse. The EEG stipulates that operators of solar and wind power plants (and other sources of renewable energies) will receive guaranteed electricity prices from the state for many years that are significantly higher than the market price. Electricity from renewable energy sources is fed preferentially into the grid. Household electricity customers essentially pay these subsidies of around €20 billion per year—that is €250 per capita per year—via artificially increased electricity prices. The electricity industry is one-fifth of the energy sector in Germany in 2018 but will continue to grow proportionately as the electric vehicle fleet expands. With the EEG, one can also say that the problem that CO_2 quantities "saved" in the energy sector by more wind and solar power do not contribute much to the climate in the European Union as, due to the EU's given total quantity, other enterprises in Germany or other European Union countries can now simply use the "quantity saved under the EEG" as new exempt quantity to be used. A good argument, however, can still be put forward for the EEG, because the corresponding plants are scale intensive: the higher the total production volume of solar plants or wind power plants over time, the lower the EU price or world market price of these products. The EEG therefore has the effect of making the use of solar and wind power cheaper in all countries of the world. This certainly helps in terms of contributing to climate protection, especially in countries outside the EU. Since energy production worldwide accounts for about one-third of CO_2 emissions, Germany and other EU countries with corresponding guaranteed feed-in prices for renewable energies can take a kind of external climate protection effect (the opposite of the CO_2 leakage effect) into account. By 2019, the prices for wind and solar power had fallen to such an extent that in the EU and other regions of the world wind power plants can now be built without government subsidies; in India and some other countries of the world, solar power production can also be installed without subsidies (in Germany this is probably not even possible in sunny Freiburg for the time being). It is a very important insight that additional sectoral CO_2 saving actions undertaken by national policymakers are generally a pure waste of taxpayers' money within the framework of an EU Emissions Trading System. Anyone who wastes €45 billion with no effect to show due to such interventions is acting irresponsibly or simply wants to generate good headlines at the expense of, for example, the 82 million taxpayers in Germany who are secretly asked to pay €500 each—as in the case of the phase-out of coal according to the so-called Coal Commission. It would be much better if everyone received €500 as a voucher for further education or as a holiday allowance for the children in the case of large families or single parents.

- Actual EU CO_2 emissions in the energy and industry sectors have never been higher than the ceilings set by the EU, as Fig. 2.4—based on Weimann (2019)—shows.

The introduction of the EEG was a manageable success in Germany in view of the drop in emissions in the energy sector. It has been agreed at EU level that the annual maximum amount of CO_2 must be reduced by 1.74 percent by 2020 and by 2.2 percent from 2021 on. The CO_2 emission reduction in 2030 should be 43 percent compared to 1990 in the combined emissions trading sectors of energy plus industry. The amount of emission rights actually used – that is, redeemed – by both sectors was below the volume of emission rights issued from 2005 to 2018. One

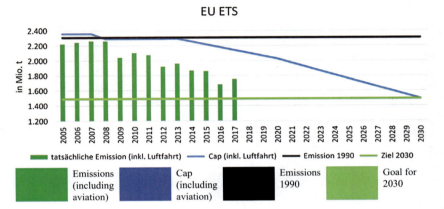

Fig. 2.4 EU certificate trading (ETS = emissions trading system): maximum emission quantities and planned reduction path (blue). (Source: Weimann (2019, p. 19))

reason for this was the Great Recession, that is, the financial crisis of 2008–2010. By 2016, a 25 percent decline compared to 1990 had already been achieved. Emissions trading had also been reformed: so-called backloading was carried out in 2014 so that 900 million tons of CO_2 emission rights were not auctioned in 2014–2016 – this was to be made up in 2019/2020. The situation was different, as a "market stabilization reserve" was already decided in 2015. The 900 million certified tons withheld were placed in this reserve, which should be replenished as a rule: as soon as the aggregated surplus exceeds 833 million tons, 12 percent of the total surplus should be placed in the reserve. As a result of these and other reforms, emission allowances of about 1.2 gigatons of carbon dioxide emissions will be canceled in 2023 (for details and the following aspect, see Weimann, 2019).

The additional national CO_2 reduction efforts thus create a double "redundancy problem" – a kind of overachievement problem in CO_2 reduction: the first redundancy aspect consists of the fact that national feed-in tariffs for renewable energies actually stand for CO_2 reduction costs that are much higher than the CO_2 certificate price. Second, a national reduction in CO_2 emissions achieved with specific projects in one EU member country generally ensures that the other EU countries can then realize as many additional emissions as were reduced elsewhere. If new additional national (political) reduction projects repeatedly result in emissions falling well below the EU's upper limit, the CO_2 certificate market prices will then no longer be of economic significance: the market price signals cannot then exert their full efficiency-enhancing power. Instead, there is a kind of climate protection policy with planned economy aspects. If the government wanted to buy the 250 million tons of CO_2 emissions from the market by 2038 by making a steady annual purchase of CO_2 certificates, which by 2038 would correspond to the 250 million tons of emissions of coal-fired electricity generation, the cumulative certificate purchase costs – according to Weimann (2019)—would amount to €47 billion.

Angry Protests in Lignite Mining Areas Are Little Help to the Climate

There are regularly new protests against lignite opencast mining in Germany. In the summer of 2019, the coal action alliance "Replace Coal" called for a blockade action. Behind the protests of many young people is genuine concern about the climate, and coal-fired power generation is a symbolic opponent, even though the entire energy sector and industry have been involved in EU emissions trading since 2005, with an annual cap which has been set by the EU countries whereby with the emissions ceiling is currently falling by 1.74 percent annually until 2020, thereafter by 2.2 percent annually. This emissions trading system, which applies to 45 percent of emissions, reliably reduces CO_2 emissions in the combined emissions trading sector (energy plus industry) to ever lower levels: by 2030, a target of -43 percent compared with 1990 is set, and the target of around -27 percent by 2020 is already well on the way to being achieved. The system works similarly in California, where 85 percent of emissions is included in the certificate trading system. This certificate trading induces companies and power plant operators with high (marginal) costs of emission avoidance in the market to buy certificates from other companies with low costs of emission reduction.

As a result, via an emissions market, emissions are reduced at the lowest possible cost to the national economy in the same way as the state has stipulated for the maximum quantities—the market price for a certificate is €26 per ton of CO_2 in mid-2019. The simple and convincing logic of emissions trading, which is also being implemented in the Republic of Korea, China and parts of Japan, naturally has a clear consequence in the case of the EU for additional lignite decommissioning: if, in 2038, around 250 million tons of emissions from the lignite and hard coal sector in Germany are eliminated as a result of decommissioning according to the plan of the Coal Commission, this will be done at unnecessarily high costs.

From an economic and climate protection policy point of view, it does not make sense to remove the largest emission companies from the market—even if this may seem an emotionally plausible response to one's own climate fear. The smartest way to help the climate is to massively reduce emissions where the costs of reducing emissions are lowest. This is precisely what emissions trading achieves. More emissions trading in the EU and worldwide is desirable. The YouTuber Rezo is correct in his (famed in Germany) video comments on YouTube before the European Parliament elections in 2019 when he criticizes the insufficient efforts of the German government in the field of climate policy. If California could cover 85 percent of its emissions with CO_2 certificate trading since 2015, this could have been done long ago in the EU. In 2018, there was nothing to be heard from the federal government in Berlin about this; in the end and following the European elections in 2019, there was a timid debate in parts of the federal government in response. In the European elections, the climate issue was seen by German voters as the third most important issue, as the analysis by a German electoral research group (*Forschungsgruppe Wahlen*) has shown.

A visit by Swedish activist Greta Thunberg to the lignite protests in North Rhine-Westphalia on 10 August 2019 brought the call that one should stop using lignite to generate electricity earlier than 2038. That somehow sounds like a good idea, but it's not reasonable. On the other hand, it is worth demonstrating that the annual reduction of CO emission ceilings in the EU—in certificate trading—will be higher than the planned 2.2 percent by 2025. This order of magnitude is still too small, however, to achieve climate neutrality in the longer term (by 2050). A -5 percent annual reduction target in terms of the CO_2 emissions cap from 2025 would be a figure worth striving for in the EU. A similar logic applies worldwide.

A broad exit from coal and oil—and later also from natural gas—is not available for free. First of all, such an exit means that part of the capital stock is devalued; an earthquake would have similar economic effects. There will be winning and losing sectors in a transition to CO_2-light production; structural change will accelerate and job losses in some sectors will also occur, while new jobs may be created in other sectors.

Prospects for Renewable Energies in G20 Countries

Since at least the G20+ countries will have to cope with such a transformation more or less in parallel, there are also some profits arising from this dynamic and networking; think of the mass production advantages that arise when solar and wind energy production is increasingly developed in the G20+ countries.

The expansion opportunities for renewable energies are great worldwide. The US is just starting out with large offshore wind farms. South Africa—at times fascinated under President Zuma by the possibility of having six nuclear power plants built by Russia—has decided under his successor to go back to the earlier major expansion project in renewable energies. South Africa has unique natural conditions for solar and wind energy, but of course the South African power grid needs to be expanded and modernized.

India can probably undertake a rapid expansion of its solar power production by 2030 and beyond, with India itself likely to become an exporter of solar systems. China will play a strong role in renewable energy production as the Chinese domestic market is large and air quality in many major cities can be significantly improved by shutting down coal-fired power plants, especially by replacing coal-fired heating with natural gas heating. This can also be an important aspect in parts of India, where better air quality and CO_2 reduction go hand in hand.

Russia has carried out some energy modernization projects with the EU, but due to its abundance of fossil energy resources it is probably only willing to develop wind energy and solar power, as well as hydroelectric and geothermal power production, to rather a limited extent. The production of coal will probably be abandoned in the medium term. For Russia, but also for Turkey, what was already true for the US in the twentieth century applies to coal production today: fatal accidents are relatively frequent; the US recorded 100,000 deaths in the coal-mining industry in a century.

There are some G20 countries for which the expansion of renewable energies could be an impulse for modernization and growth. These include Argentina and Indonesia. Argentina has enormous potential in terms of wind power; the country, which for years has been teetering on the brink of bankruptcy, can use the help of the Inter-American Development Bank and the World Bank, as well as the EU and EU countries, in particular Spain, to modernize its energy sector.

Canada and Brazil are leading G20 countries in the area of renewable energy, with hydropower playing an important role in both countries. Brazil could fall behind in climate protection policy for political reasons, as the current populist president Jair Bolsonaro also talks down or simply denies the problem of man-made global warming.

Germany, France, the UK and Italy, with their experience in EU emissions trading (since 2005), could play a positive role in encouraging other G20 countries to introduce and progressively expand emissions trading systems. These four countries could also join the G20 in making Nigeria the 20th country to join the existing group of 19 and EU, with the EU representing the other EU countries. Nigeria has great potential for solar power, presumably also for wind power. Like the EU countries, Japan and Republic of Korea should be able to play a significant role as suppliers of technology for renewable energies in many G20+ countries. In the case of wind power plants, Germany is particularly well positioned offshore—as with onshore wind plants in coastal areas; suppliers from Germany and the EU are international leaders, especially in large wind power plants, together with Japan. Saudi Arabia has so far had relatively little experience with renewable energies, but of course a high proportion of such energies can also be realized in that country in the long term, provided that appropriate investments are made. Even an oil-rich country like Mexico faces special challenges and opportunities, although the political course has already been set for an emissions trading system there.

The G20 countries have so far paid little attention to climate protection as a group, apart from a critical press release on fossil energy subsidies at the 1999 G20 summit in Seattle. A meeting of the environment ministers of the G20 countries first took place in 2019, twenty years after the Seattle summit. The meeting of environment ministers in Japan may have been useful in several ways. However, no concept of a common or coordinated strategy is discernible in the decisions. With a view to the time horizon for climate neutrality in 2050, there is little time for the G20 (or G20+) to organize itself sensibly in terms of climate protection policy and also to ensure the availability of a substantial number of technical and policy papers as impulses for conceptual progress.

The transition to climate neutrality will at times bring considerable costs and pressure to adapt to structural change for all G20 countries. The challenge of global warming and climate protection may also bring important benefits:

- The topic of global warming could help to push back against the populists who dispute climate change; since populism means nationalism and protectionism, this would result in an improved basis for international policy cooperation in general—and economic cooperation gains can be substantial for many countries and have a positive effect on growth and jobs. Better conditions for free trade could lower the costs of the transformation to CO_2-light production technologies and production worldwide.
- The benefits of cooperation in the G20 area (and G20+) could be significant in many areas: if international cooperation is strengthened through networked G20 climate protection policy, improved opportunities for a common competition policy at the global level could presumably emerge and there could also be meaningful Internet framework regulation, thereby strengthening prosperity and stability. Sensible minimum regulations for banks and financial markets could also be a benefit. These benefits could far outweigh the cost of the steps toward climate neutrality.

Against this background, it is important that Germany and other EU countries do not pursue a strategy of navel-gazing in terms of climate protection policy, but instead to view this policy area from the outset as an opportunity to establish a sustainable global market economy. If Germany overcomes its internal contradictions in renewable energy policy, this will strengthen the global capacity of Germany and the EU to act. Germany is also a contradictory country when it comes to wind power because due to insufficient expansion of north-south power lines in Germany—there is also some resistance here from local environmental groups—the wind power generated by plants in the North Sea can sometimes feed nothing at all into the broader grid. Germany then has to pay compensation to the wind turbine operators. When restructuring the energy sector in the direction of renewable energies, a system approach must be implemented, since it is not only individual points of the necessary modernization that should be considered, but the totality of all necessary restructuring elements.

It would simply be much cheaper and better if the German government were to advocate for CO_2 certificate trading to be expanded in terms of emission coverage from 45 to 85 percent—or even 90 percent—and that from 2025 the annual decline in the EU's maximum quantity of emissions be -5 percent. Radical administrative steps to phase out coal in Germany may feel good from an ideological perspective and are thus acceptable for a corresponding ideologically driven code of ethics, whereby without reference to costs or alternatives, one only asks oneself what noble goals are at stake. But anyone who really wants to achieve something sensible in climate protection in the long term, for either themselves or for the generations of children and grandchildren to come, while taking into account both the main and side effects, will also want to consider the central cost-benefit aspects and the best way to achieve climate neutrality by 2050 in the sense of an ethos of responsibility, and in doing so will want to recognize the need for truly global cooperation among many countries.

References

BCG/Prognos. (2018, January). *Klimapfade für Deutschland* [Climate Paths for Germany]. Study for the Federation of German Industries. Retrieved September 6, 2019, from https://www.prognos.com/uploads/tx_atwpubdb/20180118_BDI_Studie_Klimapfade_fuer_Deutschland_01.pdf

ECOPLAN/SIGMAPLAN. (2007). *Auswirkungen der Klimaänderung auf die Schweizer Volkswirtschaft (nationale Einflüsse)*. [transl. PJJW: Effects of Climate Change on the Swiss Economy (National Influences)]. Commissioned by the Swiss Federal Offices of the Environment (FOEN/BAFU) and Energy (SFOE/BFE). http://webarchiv.ethz.ch/vwl/down/v-schubert/oekonomie1/Artikel/Ecoplan2007.pdf

Federal Office for the Environment. (2018). *Switzerland's Climate Policy – Implementation of the Paris Convention*. Environment Information 2018, Federal Office for the Environment, Swiss Confederation, FOEN: Bern.

Federal Office for the Environment. (2020). *Emissionen von Treibhausgasen nach revidiertem CO2-Gesetz und Kyoto-Protokoll, 2. Verpflichtungsperiode (2013–2020)* [tranls. PJJW: Emissions of Greenhouse Gases According to the Revised CO2-Law and Kyoto Protocol, 2. Implementation Period (2013–2020)]. Federal Office for the Environment, Swiss Confederation, FOEN: Bern.

Keohane, R., & Victor, D. (2010, January). *The Regime Complex for Climate Change. The Harvard Project on International Climate Agreements*, Harvard Kennedy School (Discussion Paper 10–33). Retrieved September 6, 2019, from https://www.belfercenter.org/sites/default/files/legacy/files/Keohane_Victor_Final_2.pdf

Latif, M. (2007). *Bringen wir das Klima aus dem Takt? Hintergründe und Prognosen*. [transl. PJJW: Are We Destabilizing the Climate? Background and Prognoses]. Forum for Responsibility. Fischer Taschenbuch.

Moore, F., & Diaz, D. B. (2015). Temperature Impacts on Economic Growth Warrant Stringent Mitigation Policy. *Nature Climate Change, 5,* 127–131. https://www.nature.com/articles/nclimate2481

Nordhaus, W. D. (2017). Revisiting the Social Cost of Carbon. *PNAS, 114*(7), 1518–1523. https://doi.org/10.1073/pnas.1609244114

OECD. (2018). *Effective Carbon Rates 2018, Pricing Carbon Emissions Through Taxes and Emissions Trading.* Organisation for Economic Cooperation and Development.

Olivier, J. G. J., & Peters, J. A. H. W. (2018). *Trends in Global CO_2 and Total Greenhouse Gas Emissions: 2018 Report.* PBL Netherlands Environmental Assessment Agency.

Royal Society. (2009, September). *Geoengineering the Climate – Science, Governance and Uncertainty.* The Royal Society, RS Policy Document 10/09, London.

Sauga, M. (2019, July 20). Unheilige Allianz [transl. PJJW: An Unholy Alliance]. *DER SPIEGEL*, No. 30.

Wegener Center. (2017, October). Das Treibhausgas-Budget für Österreich [transl. PJJW: The Greenhouse Gas Budget for Austria]. University of Graz.

Weimann, J. (2019). Der Ausstieg aus der Kohle: Alternativlos oder verantwortungslos? [transl. PJJW: The Exit from Coal: No Alternative or Irresponsible?]. *Perspektiven der Wirtschaftspolitik., 20*(1), 14–22. https://www.degruyter.com/downloadpdf/j/pwp.2019.20.issue-1/pwp-2019-0011/pwp-2019-0011.pdf

World Bank. (2019, April). *World Bank Climate Change Overview.* Updated April 2019, Retrieved 15 September, 2019, from https://www.worldbank.org/en/topic/climatechange/overview

CHAPTER 3

Climate Protection Problems and Options for Action

If the problem of climate protection in Germany, Europe and the world economy is to be taken seriously, then it is necessary to assess the extent of the challenge worldwide and the extent to which individual countries and regions are affected—as well as the shares of individual countries in CO_2 emissions. If some climate policy opponents argue that Germany, for example, with its 2 percent share of global emissions, is too small to be problem relevant in terms of global warming, then this is not a sensible objection: 50 × 2 percent = 100 percent, that is, you only need to add up 50 similarly "small" emission countries, then you have roughly the level of total global emission. In reality, it is in fact a bit easier, since the G20 countries would have to be mobilized—where Germany is also involved—to tackle 80 percent of the world's carbon dioxide emissions (it is further argued that actually the G20+ is needed, namely Nigeria would have to be added to the G20). If the G20 countries could reduce emissions by 2050 by 90 percent compared to 1990 levels, the G20 alone would have reduced global emissions by 72 percent. Here, the EU representation at the G20 is classified in such a way that ultimately all the EU member countries are represented at a G20 level, which also makes sense in terms of EU certificate trading as this is where all EU countries already cooperate. Together with the contributions of the many really small countries, the G20 will then achieve the necessary overall reduction of about 90 percent by 2050. However, it cannot be assumed that the G20 will be an actor capable of

© The Author(s), under exclusive license to Springer Nature Switzerland AG 2022
P. J. J. Welfens, *Global Climate Change Policy*, Sustainable Development Goals Series,
https://doi.org/10.1007/978-3-030-94594-7_3

taking decisive action in climate policy from 2025 or 2030 without reliable decisions in the short term on a better cooperation strategy.

Moreover, Germany, together with other OECD countries, can use multilateral banks—where EU countries and other industrialized countries are members—to provide incentives and to build up pressure worldwide to ensure that climate policy by governments in all regions of the world economy makes a reasonable contribution to solving the problem. In Germany, populists who are opponents of climate policy like to argue that Germany cannot make an important contribution to climate protection policy with its 2.2 percent share of global CO_2 emissions. However, that is not a solid or valid argument; it is nonsense. In the case of all international public goods—for example, NATO in terms of defense or free trade (via the membership of some 150 countries in the World Trade Organization)—many countries have enjoyed a common benefit, although in the case of dozens of member countries, or even more than 100 member countries in some cases, the contribution of individual countries may look small in isolation. However, no one will want to abolish flood protection in countries with coasts threatened by rising seas either, just because floods usually cause flooding problems in only a few villages most years (with the exception of more rare major flood events, as was the case in the Netherlands in 1953, when there was a flood catastrophe with many deaths and flooding in larger regions of the Netherlands). In the case of collective goods, market solutions do not work; the actual decision to provide flood protection, for example, must be taken by political actors; on this basis, market players can then implement flood protection projects in competition. In Frisian villages, in northern Germany near the coast, there is a saying which essentially means that if you don't want to collide, you have to give way; if you don't want to make a financial contribution to flood protection, you have to move elsewhere. In climate protection, such a sanction is not easily possible because those inhabitants who do not want to contribute to climate protection cannot simply be sent to an international space station or another planet. The only thing that is clear is that populists who reject scientific findings on global warming for no apparent reason are acting irresponsibly and are ultimately free riders in terms of climate protection. This does not preclude populists in some countries from gaining a political majority in elections. However, in the long run, populism is probably not conducive to life on earth and is certainly not compatible with Kant's categorical imperative (simplified: do unto others as you would want all others to do unto everyone).

Key Points of the Climate Protection Debate

If you formulate a few key points for the climate protection debate, you will immediately see that national and international climate protection policy must decide on various alternatives. And that a focus on climate protection policy alone will not be sufficient from an economic policy perspective, because the simultaneous climate protection policies in many countries have important economic effects. For an understanding of the climate protection perspectives, a number of fundamental points are important, whereby the focus is first on CO_2 emissions, but also on other equivalent emissions (one therefore speaks of CO_2-equivalent emissions).

- According to the German government, the reduction in CO_2-equivalent emissions in 2020 should have been 40 percent compared to 1990, whereby the effects of the corona pandemic has clearly flattered the German figures for 2020. The achievement of the climate targets for 2030—a reduction by 55 percent compared to 1990 – and 2050 (a reduction of 80–95 percent) cannot be reliably expected. Not even symbolically, the federal government's own vehicle fleet is up to date with contemporary vehicles; however, as of the beginning of 2019, the share of electric vehicles in the fleet is below 10 percent.
- Since 2005, the energy sector and industry have been subject to mandatory participation in EU emissions trading for relatively large companies. The policy defines the EU-wide reduction path for CO_2 emissions for participating sectors, whereby the companies concerned trade with each other on the basis of the available or allocated (or also auctioned by the state) emission certificates in order to produce regularly and reach their own company targets in a favorable way through structural change in the product mix and CO_2-reducing emissions. Since there are no quantitative emission limits for transport, housing and agriculture—there are, however, emission targets for the vehicle fleets produced by car companies and thus indirectly for part of the transport sector—an expansion of emissions certificate trading is necessary in the medium term, or incentives to reduce sectoral CO_2 emissions would have to be introduced via a sectoral (or cross-sectoral) CO_2 tax. It would hardly make sense for both CO_2 taxation and emission certificates to be implemented in one sector at the same time—a minimum price for emission certificates can, however, be regarded as the lower quasi-CO_2 tax rate. From around

€25 in the first years of EU emissions trading, the price per ton of CO_2 has at times fallen to barely €5 per ton, then increased significantly again in 2018/2019 and should be around €27 per ton in the course of 2019. An auction of CO_2 certificates generates one-off revenue for the state—in the Eurozone, or the EU, this could also generate a broader revenue base. CO_2 volumes in the EU will be reduced over time, which will stimulate CO_2 savings in those sectors of the economy included in the trading of allowances (for the US approach in California, see the information box in Appendix 1; in the period 2015–2020, the allowable emissions will decrease by 3 percent annually, from then on by an expected higher rate).

- CO_2 tax rates give clear signals to consumers and businesses as to the extent to which CO_2 reduction is worthwhile in certain activities, and if an increasing tax rate path is announced, this is likely to be all the more true. However, a CO_2 tax is a relatively imprecise instrument, since the legislator has to assess the technology adjustment and ultimately the quantity reaction of the companies in the sector concerned or of the relevant private households. In the long run, however, a CO_2 tax has a certain effect if it increases significantly over time. In order to achieve a fair distribution of burdens, it makes sense to largely reimburse private households for the revenue from a CO_2 tax.
- From 2020, failure to achieve emission reductions will have financial consequences, as EU countries that fail to achieve agreed emission reductions will then have to purchase emission certificates from other countries. Since only very few EU countries exceed their targets, countries such as Germany or Spain could face considerable government budget burdens as a result of billions of euro in purchases of foreign emission certificates.
- It cannot be ruled out that new synthetic CO_2-neutral fuels for mobility with cars, ships and aircraft will play a certain role in the long term. Germany is an international leader in the field of research here.
- The expansion of CO_2 certificate trading is economically preferable to a CO_2 tax in many sectors for reasons of efficiency. However, it has to be examined whether the volatility of the CO_2 certificate price in the EU has an exacerbating effect on the volatility of the share price index, which in turn could impair investment and innovation

dynamics. In the case of such a positive correlation, CO_2 taxes could play a greater role than usual.
- The consequence of fundamentally tougher climate protection worldwide in the decades from 2020 to 2040 will be an increased demand for climate-friendly products, which will drive up the prices of these products EU-wide and ultimately worldwide—especially since climate protection policy is also being pursued in other countries and regions. Since climate-friendly products require a relatively large amount of skilled labor in production, the wages of skilled workers are increasing compared to those of unskilled workers, so that there is a risk of increased inequality in almost all countries; politicians must find an answer to this question.
- Germany and the EU have many opportunities to link EU emissions trading with the corresponding trading systems of other countries (or regions or cities) and thus to achieve a reduction in emissions more cheaply on a global scale; moreover, more countries could be won over to emissions trading.
- The promotion of climate-friendly innovations is very important, since it is here that decisions are made on the share of emission reductions that is ultimately to be achieved through emissions certificate trading and CO_2 taxes. Such innovations can be promoted not only in OECD countries but also worldwide, with Germany and the EU countries having good opportunities to provide significant impetus through memberships in many regional multilateral banks and the World Bank, a policy option that has hardly been explored to date. The argument occasionally heard in the debate that Germany or the EU have no means of influencing a sensible global climate protection policy is both false and misleading.
- If the EU certificate trading system could be merged with that in the Republic of Korea, China, California and Japan (Tokyo and another region) as well as Canada (various regions), the costs of CO_2 reduction would be reduced especially in the EU countries; Germany could then purchase the necessary additional certificates cheaper outside the EU in the medium term. However, the integration of different certificate trading systems must be carefully organized, and international political cooperation is indispensable.
- Measures to cool the atmosphere are conceivable within the framework of so-called geoengineering.

- In Germany, the state acts in a contradictory fashion when it comes to climate protection policy at both federal and state levels, since federal and state employees who buy emission certificates as a form of carbon compensation for extra-European flights cannot claim the cost back on business travel accounts (in the EU, only intra-European flights are part of emissions certificate trading); many parties in the various governments are involved in this contradiction.

For the Federal Republic of Germany, there is a BDI study (BCG/Prognos, 2018, see Box 3.1) which provides a number of interesting insights: by 2050, a 61 percent reduction in greenhouse gases compared to 1990 should be achieved if current efforts are continued and foreseeable technologies are taken into account. Compared to the German government's target, this would probably leave a gap of about 30 percent in 2050. However, the target of climate neutrality can in fact be achieved by expanding certificate trading, which could cover about 90 percent of emissions in the EU, and by promoting innovation more strongly by 2050. A target gap that may remain can be dealt with via special measures: for example, measures to cool the climate via geoengineering. That will have to be discussed.

Global Renewable Energy Perspectives

In so far as the expansion of renewable energies is seen as key to major steps toward long-term climate neutrality, the investment and performance data for renewable energies in 2018 are encouraging in some respects. According to IRENA (the International Renewable Energy Agency—an organization based in the United Arab Emirates), the installation of new renewable energy capacities in 2020 amounted to 260 gigawatts (GW). Solar and wind power expansion accounted for over 90 percent of global renewable energy growth in 2020, with both forms of energy making up over 50 percent of total installed renewables capacity. Asia accounted for circa 65 percent of additional renewable energy installations, with emerging and developing countries leading the expansion of renewable energy in 2020. Broken down by the type of renewable energy, the developments in the global economy were as follows:

- Hydropower: relatively weak global growth, but China at least has made a significant expansion steps (+12 GW capacity, equivalent to about 12 standard 1 GW nuclear power plants).
- Global wind production capacity increased by 111 GW in 2020, with China and the US expanding capacities the most, namely by 72 GW and 14 GW respectively. Expansions of about 2 GW took place in Brazil, with France, Germany, India and the UK adding about 1 GW in wind energy capacity.
- Three countries expanded relatively strongly in the field of bioenergy, namely China (circa 2 GW), India (0.3 GW) and Finland (0.4 GW).
- Solar energy capacity expanded by 126 GW, which corresponds to over 20 percent growth. Asia occupied first place in terms of expansion with an increase of 78 GW, representing about 60 percent of global expansion, with China, India, Japan and the Republic of Korea to the forefront—continuing previous trends in Asia. The US, Australia and Brazil also expanded significantly, namely by +14.9, +4.4 and +4.2 GW, respectively. Other major expansion countries were Brazil, Egypt, Pakistan, Mexico, Turkey and the Netherlands.
- Geothermal power generation: Increased by 0.16 GW, with Turkey, Italy, the US, Mexico and New Zealand leading.

Worldwide capacity reached 2799 GW in 2020, or one-third of installed capacity. Hydropower accounted for 1332 GW, that is, about half of renewable energies. Wind and solar energy accounted for 733 GW and 714 GW, respectively; bioenergy stood for 127 GW and geothermal energy for 14 GW (all data from IRENA, 2021). The mass production advantages of wind and solar energy will bring further cost reductions for these two types of renewable energy in the longer term, with an increasing share of renewable energy naturally also requiring progress in storage options—that is, batteries or pumped storage power plants (where, in the case of surplus electricity production, water is pumped into a higher reservoir, which can be emptied later to produce electricity if and when required). As the global automotive industry has only gradually started to address the issue of electromobility in 2015, newly developed battery technologies from the automotive sector available as of 2025 or so and new mass production advantages should also significantly advance progress in the battery sector in power generation. One can argue that more electromobility will strongly increase the demand for electricity in many countries of the world; but in the OECD countries, autonomous driving should become an important issue in reality around 2030, and from 2040 on, one can expect extended systems for autonomous driving. Of course, this presupposes that adequate mobile broadband communication networks are actually available throughout the main regions in the EU, Europe, more broadly, China, Japan, the US, Russia and so on. However, since a considerable proportion of households will then no longer buy their own cars but will instead increasingly rely on transport services from various providers (i.e., Transport as a Service (TaaS) such as shared cars, ride hailing apps), the number of cars sold could fall considerably. Huge numbers of high-quality (with regard to location) parking spaces in cities will then become available and living and mobility could be completely redefined in newly built city districts. With a view to the early 2020s, broadband mobile communication coverage in Germany is inadequate, the patchwork of areas with no coverage at all is unsustainable, and since tenders and contracts with mobile network operators do not include reasonable fines for black spots and dead zones, there is likely to be no truly usable network for autonomous driving in Germany before 2030. Given this situation, just how Germany's innovative car manufacturers intend to become global market leaders in autonomous driving is somewhat unclear.

Wind Energy Prospects

Germany also has problems with respect to the expansion of wind energy, as in many regions the necessary new power line infrastructures are being delayed and prevented by public opposition. However, the prospects for the global development of renewable energies are still favorable, especially for wind energy. The Global Wind Energy Council expects new capacities of 59,000 megawatts (MW) to be built in 2019. This corresponds to the output of 59 nuclear power plants. In 2018, investments in wind energy amounted to $129 billion, an increase of 3 percent; with falling prices of one kilowatt-hour of wind energy, 3 percent would represent a significant real increase over 2017. For the period of 2019–2023, the Global Wind Energy Council expects the onshore expansion of wind energy in Asia to be 145,000 MW, while Europe along with North and South America is expected to add about 59,000 MW.

With larger wind turbines, wind energy can be expanded over time through "repowering", although in densely populated countries there are also limits to the level of noise emissions from wind farms. There are corresponding minimum distance regulations for wind turbines with a view to houses and villages. The minimum distance requirements also partly play a role in wind farms in the sea, where Germany requires turbines to be located at much greater distances from beaches than, for example, the UK. When expanding wind energy, a similar problem has to be considered as with solar energy. Due to the temporary lack of continuous wind and solar energy, more has to be invested in power grids, while the importance of the international trading of electricity is also increasing: in the case of surpluses in country X, it should be easy to supply surplus electricity to neighboring countries; if there is little wind and hardly any sunshine in country X, it should likewise be technically possible to import electricity without problems. Here, however, there is often a lack of sufficiently dimensioned power coupling points at the borders of neighboring countries in almost all regions of the world. Here, too, more international cooperation makes sense and is necessary. The Scandinavian countries have shown for decades that it is also possible to create successful cross-border power exchanges.

EXPANSION OF THE EU EMISSIONS TRADING SYSTEM, FRAUD AND FINANCIAL MARKET PERSPECTIVES

The EU emissions trading system is a very good instrument for the efficient reduction of CO_2 emissions. Every large company that consumes energy (i.e., electricity from non-renewable sources) and fossil fuels directly (e.g., steel producers that usually use coking coal in the production process and then emit CO_2) must obtain allowance certificates equal to the expected volume of CO_2 emissions for each production year. The data, statistics and figures on emissions must also be reported to the relevant authorities. If the company does not receive the necessary certificates as a free allowance from the state, it must purchase the required additional certificates from other companies in the emissions trading sector (energy plus industry). At a certain price, innovative companies that have been able to reduce energy consumption and CO_2 emissions through better technologies will offer a sufficient number of "surplus certificates" for sale. Supply and demand for certificates thus result in an equilibrium market price for CO_2 certificates: supply and demand are then balanced, and at the same time, a signal is sent out over time to companies with regard to undertaking more or less CO_2 innovation projects. If certificate prices rise over time, there is a strong incentive to realize more such innovation projects and to invest accordingly in research and development. Since the quantity available in the EU Emissions Trading System decreases year by year—due to the requirements of the EU or of individual EU member states—there may be upward pressure increasing the price of certificates. However, this is counteracted by the innovation dynamics of companies that introduce production processes with lower CO_2 emissions.

Since the EU covers 45 percent of emissions through its ETS, an early expansion of this trade is urgently desirable. This is a task that should be taken up by the von der Leyen Commission, the European Council (comprising heads of state and governments) and the European Parliament. It would be conceivable that individual EU countries, such as Germany, would first temporarily expand certificate trading to other sectors nationally and wait for the EU to expand certificate trading more broadly in the medium term. However, this could also cause problems in the transport sector, for example, as the resulting rise in fuel prices will trigger increased German "fuel tourism" in neighboring EU countries. It would certainly be better if efforts were made at EU level to rapidly and significantly expand certificate trading for all member states step by step: up to at least 85 percent by 2025.

One serious problem with emissions trading in the European Union is fraud, as has been shown in various EU countries. An example of this is a case from France where over many years, fraudsters who bought and sold certificates—without and with VAT—caused billions in losses for the French state coffers, as one could see from an AFP news release in September 2019. The fact that a new field of fraud of considerable magnitude is emerging here should be viewed with concern. The extent to which extensive market speculation with certificates will also take place internationally in the longer term will also have to be examined and subjected to careful scientific research.

A liberal market environment may be useful for some purposes, but the 2008/2009 Transatlantic Banking Crisis can be regarded as a warning signal with continuing effects on international financial markets today. A critical look toward the US under President Trump and the UK (under Prime Ministers May and Johnson) in the years 2017–2019, however, raises doubts about overall prospects, as both countries have discussed the possibilities of new financial market deregulation on the government side, and the US has indeed implemented the first steps in that direction. Sooner or later, CO_2 certificate trading will make up a substantial part of securities trading in industrialized and emerging countries, a position it will occupy for many decades, so this new issue should be seriously addressed in the short term. This may well mean new international challenges, for example, with regard to the industrialized countries and the G20:

- If the certificates trading systems of the EU, China, the US (possibly only California), Japan (possibly only a few prefectures), Republic of Korea and other countries were to be integrated into an overall system, then not only would this institutional challenge have to be tackled carefully, but it would also be advisable to coordinate the financial market supervisory rules more closely.
- Since the Bank for International Settlements (BIS) has been active for years, at least with a view to framework regulation of the major banks in industrialized countries, one could consider involving the BIS at an early stage both in terms of financial market regulation and in terms of the regulation of transactions on CO_2 certificate trading markets; however, it should be kept in mind that not all G20 countries are members of the BIS, so that a broader membership base of the BIS would also have to be created. This, too, is a challenge that has not even been considered to date.

Of course, it can be argued that with more broadly based and experienced international organizations—such as the BIS—new contributions to solving the challenge of climate neutrality in the global economy could also be mobilized. The EU countries are invited to develop appropriate initiatives here, together with partner countries from the G20 (or the G20+) area.

Firms' Progress Toward Climate Neutrality: New Concepts Necessary

Large companies are frequently required by law to publish information on sustainability measures as a supplement to their balance sheets. However, the majority of companies are, of course, small- and medium-sized enterprises (SMEs), while in the service sector (e.g., software companies, insurance companies and banks) there is often little orientation toward climate neutrality and sustainability. Conversely, a global warming trend must concern companies with regard to their employees and the stability of business and political perspectives:

- Employees could become ill more frequently (from the point of view of health insurance companies, this naturally also applies to customers).
- Disruptions could occur to production and in international and national production and logistics chains.
- Losses in real estate and other assets are conceivable—for example, due to extreme weather events.
- Economic policy could become less reliable as a result of ever new climate policy tasks in the standard areas of activity, and there is also the threat of higher CO_2 tax rates or rising certificate prices.

Every company can easily conduct its own climate policy in key areas:

- The production and distribution of goods/services and the transport/mobility of the workforce should be designed to be CO_2-light, which will have consequences, for example, for the purchase/leasing of vehicles, but also for the selection of new technologies. The question of enabling home office work for employees should be seen in the light of family, motivation and climate protection aspects. Those who work at home do not have to commute to work by car or train. Here, again, a lot of raw data, information and calculations are necessary, since otherwise one cannot represent the progress elements realized later for communication to and by the enterprise appropriately—however, this is important in terms of both internal and external relationships.
- In the field of information and communication technology (ICT), new well-thought-out concepts are necessary, and the awareness of employees of the relevant interrelationships in saving energy and emissions needs to be heightened.
- All buildings and construction measures must be checked for CO_2 intensity and sustainability aspects, and modernization measures for new lighting, heat and electricity use concepts should also be considered from this perspective.
- When selecting partner companies and suppliers, CO_2 aspects must be taken into account, and new information must also be obtained here.
- If one is or becomes involved in CO_2 certificate trading, appropriate balance analyses—including simulations—are useful, for example, to correctly classify the effects of the allocation of free certificates and of

rising and falling certificate prices. An optimal certificate procurement and certificate sales strategy must be developed.
- The firm's communication strategy plus marketing must be realigned and supplemented by climate policy aspects and activities within the company. This is not just about developing the identity of the company, but also about image enhancement and signaling to customers, employees and business partners in advertising.

For many years now, millions of companies in industrialized and emerging countries have faced a host of important challenges here.

> **Box 3.1: The BDI Study: Climate Paths for Germany (BCG/Prognos, 2018)**
> "With a continuation of current efforts in the form of existing measures, agreed political and regulatory framework conditions and foreseeable technological developments ("reference path"), by 2050 a reduction of approximately 61 percent of greenhouse gases (GHG) compared to 1990 will be achieved. This leaves a gap of 19–34 percentage points to the German climate targets.
> - An 80 percent greenhouse gas reduction is technically possible and economically feasible in the scenarios considered. However, implementation would require a significant increase in existing efforts, political changes and effective carbon leakage protection without a global climate protection consensus.
> - A 95 percent greenhouse gas reduction would be at the limit of foreseeable technical feasibility and current social acceptance. Such a reduction (by three quarters more than the 80% path) requires practically zero emissions for large parts of the German economy. In addition to largely eliminating all fossil fuels (solid, liquid and gaseous energy sources), this would also mean the import of renewable fuels (power-to-liquid/-gas), the selective use of currently unpopular technologies such as carbon capture and storage (CCS) and even fewer emissions from livestock – successful implementation would only be conceivable with similarly high ambitions in most other countries.

(*continued*)

(continued)
- Several game changers could potentially facilitate the achievement of climate targets in the coming decades and make them more favorable (including technologies for the hydrogen economy and carbon capture and utilization processes). Their operational readiness cannot yet be predicted with certainty and is therefore not assumed for the achievement of the targets. However, they should be researched and developed as a matter of priority.
- From today's perspective, the cost-efficient achievement of the climate paths would require additional investments of 1.5–2.3 trillion euros by 2050 compared with a scenario without increased climate protection, of which about 530 billion euros would be needed to continue existing efforts (in the reference path). By 2050, this corresponds to average annual additional investments of approximately 1.2–1.8 percent of the German gross domestic product (GDP). The direct additional economic costs after deduction of energy savings would be about 470–960 billion euros by 2050 (about 15–30 billion euros per year), of which about 240 billion euros for existing efforts. Additional investments include all extra investments required to achieve the climate paths beyond those made in the reference scenario. To calculate the additional costs, these were annualized at a real economic rate of 2 percent over the life of the respective capital asset. Energy cost savings and expenses were offset. Cross-border prices for fossil fuels and electricity system costs were used for this purpose. Moreover, the additional investment and costs for non-economic measures in the reference scenario have been roughly estimated.
- With optimal political implementation, the macroeconomic effects of the climate paths under consideration would nevertheless be neutral ("black zero"); in the 80 percent climate path under consideration, this would even be the case in the scenario without global consensus. However, a more extensive protection of endangered industries would be necessary in order to counter the risk of a weakening of industrial value creation – in the form of effective carbon leakage protection and long-term reliable compensation arrangements for industries in international competition.

(*continued*)

(continued)
- Successful climate protection efforts would be linked to a comprehensive renewal of all sectors of the German economy and could open up further opportunities for German exporters in growing "climate protection markets". Studies expect the world market volume of the most important climate technologies to grow to 1–2 trillion euros per year by 2030. German companies can strengthen their technology position for this global growth market.
- At the same time, the forthcoming transformation process will present Germany with considerable challenges for implementation. The considered climate paths are economically cost efficient and assume an ideal implementation in terms of cross-sector optimization and "right decisions at the right time". Misconduct in implementation – as can be observed, for example, in the transformation of energy systems through over-funding and the delay in grid expansion – can significantly increase costs and risks or even make the goal unattainable.
- Successful climate protection in Germany could, on the one hand, motivate international imitators. On the other hand, in the case of significantly negative economic impacts, German climate protection efforts would even be counterproductive, as they would deter other countries, while the German share in global GHG emissions (around 2 percent) alone does not significantly influence the climate. An internationally comparably ambitious implementation, at least in the largest economies (G20), would significantly reduce these risks and also open up broader export opportunities for German companies.
- A successful achievement of the German climate targets and a positive international multiplier effect are therefore a political, social and economic feat of strength. What is needed is a far-sighted climate, industrial and social policy "from a single source" that focuses on competition and cost efficiency, distributes social burdens fairly, ensures acceptance of the measures and prioritises the maintenance and expansion of industrial value creation. This requires long-term political support for the "major climate protection project"".

Climate Change Situation in the EU

There is a clear starting point for climate protection policy in Western Europe, namely that 45 percent of emissions—with coverage of the energy and industrial sectors—are included in the EU's CO_2 Emissions Trading System. California demonstrates that 85 percent coverage is possible, which the European Commission and the European Council could set as a target within a few years. It is likely that 80–90 percent coverage can also be achieved in the EU, with this approach being the most cost-effective in terms of reducing CO_2 emissions—with a given total emissions quantity (decreasing over time). However, geoengineering to cool the atmosphere and afforestation also remain as viable options, as proposed in particular by a study of scientists at ETH Zürich. The last two approaches are only partially explored by policymakers.

In Germany, the Council of Economic Experts argued in its 2019 Special Report (German Council of Economic Experts, 2019) that a CO_2 tax could be introduced on a transitional basis in sectors without certificate trading in view of the suspected protracted negotiations at EU level. The revenue generated by such a tax should be returned to the citizenry. A residual area of the economy will probably be targeted exclusively or additionally with regulations in order to bring about a specific reduction in CO_2 emissions there as well (Fig. 3.1). From an economic point of view, regulations aimed at CO_2 reduction are often not very exact and can be expensive if one considers the side effects and consequences. What level of

Fig. 3.1 Three approaches to climate protection policy. (Source: Own representation)

certificate trading is needed at what prices depends essentially on an innovation policy that promotes climate protection; as long as innovation-induced CO_2 reduction is cheaper than the emission certificate price, the corresponding funding for research should be expanded—of course with an essential focus on corresponding basic research. The promotion of innovation should be given a high priority.

Moreover, the price of emission allowances could fall significantly once the EU and China should form a common allowance trading area; the EU could offer China a significant transfer of environmental and climate change technology if China agreed to a common allowance trading area. In 2019, the emission certificate price in China is significantly lower than in the EU. It does not matter to the atmosphere in which countries CO_2 emissions are reduced.

CO_2 TAX RATE DOES NOT WORK LIKE CO_2 CERTIFICATE PRICE

A CO_2 tax rate—with a tax amount per ton of CO_2—can be set by the state at a certain level. The idea behind this is that producers (or consumers) of CO_2-intensive goods should be given an incentive to switch to other, less CO_2-intensive goods and technologies. As a result, CO_2 emissions are reduced. In principle, the same incentive is obtained by using certificate trading: as a company, you have to buy a CO_2 certificate at the market price on the certificate market that entitles you to emit one ton of CO_2 (or X tons if you emit a lot of CO_2 during production); sellers of the certificates are companies with a surplus of CO_2 certificates. Alternatively, you can reduce emissions by one ton by investing in new machinery or technologies. Naturally, each enterprise will accomplish the same end with the alternatives of buying CO_2 certificates or undertaking their own investment for CO_2 reduction. Firms need to look at both—how much does a certificate cost on the one hand and how high are the costs of financing one's own CO_2-reducing investments. If, for example, the certificate price is €25 per ton, then it would be worthwhile for any company with lower CO_2 reduction costs to make additional investments itself or to introduce new CO_2-lighter technologies.

In the end, in a market equilibrium, one will have a situation in the certificates market where one of the companies has minimally higher CO_2 abatement costs than the market price of €25 per ton. In somewhat simplified terms, it can therefore be said that the market price indirectly provides information regarding how high the avoidance costs (for the next unit of CO_2 reduced) of companies are. Avoidance costs are an important factor in climate protection policy.

The fundamental difference (apart from the fact that in important sectors the state often gives companies a free initial supply of certificates) between pricing via a CO_2 tax and CO_2 certificate trading should be understood. The difference between the CO tax rate and the CO_2 certificate price lies in the fact that a certificate system of different countries can be merged—"integrated"—into one system, which leads to lower CO_2 reduction costs worldwide. With a then globally uniform CO_2 certificate world market price, the average costs of CO_2 reduction in the global economy are significantly lower than in the case of the use of CO_2 taxes (the word average refers to the average cost level of the countries). CO_2 tax systems of different countries cannot be integrated as parliaments from different countries will probably never agree to setting a common global tax rate for CO_2 taxation. Also, a parliament will not allow other countries to set tax rates in the country. If the whole world were a single state, the situation would be different.

Only at first glance do both types of CO_2 pricing appear very similar or indeed equivalent. Because one could argue that it matters little whether a company pays €30 CO_2 tax or €30 Euro CO_2 certificate price per ton. However, both approaches, CO_2 tax or certificate prices, are not equivalent as a system in a global economy with open economies with innovation dynamics. Only if the world economy were a single country or if the (marginal) avoidance costs of one ton of CO_2 were the same in all countries would it make no difference to the economy and CO_2 reduction whether one has a CO_2 tax or a CO_2 certificate system. However, the global economy consists of circa 200 countries, each of which has different CO_2 reduction costs. It should suffice to illustrate the big difference between CO_2 tax and CO_2 certificate price in a simple two-country case.

A look at the EU, California and the Republic of Korea in the summer of 2019, where the EU recorded a certificate price of a good €25/ton of CO_2, for example, shows that the abatement costs already vary considerably within the OECD country group. In California, the price of a CO_2 certificate in the certificate trading system there was only around €15/ton of CO_2 (in Korea the certificate price was lower again than in California). The Californian certificate trading system covers 85 percent of CO_2 emissions, almost twice as much as the EU. It must be made clear that in the

EU, the price of a certificate for one ton of CO_2 of €25/ton means that the CO_2 avoidance costs (for the last purchaser of a CO_2 emission certificate) are apparently just €25 per ton. Otherwise the corresponding company would not buy the certificate, but would reduce emissions by a further unit through its own investments in CO_2 avoidance innovations. As soon as the company's own CO_2 avoidance costs are higher than the certificate price (here €25/ton), the company in question prefers to buy a certificate unit in the certificate market: a pollution right for an additional ton of CO_2. If there are national or regional CO_2 trading systems, then the certificate market price also provides information on how high the (marginal) avoidance costs are, that is, the costs for avoiding another ton of CO_2 in companies. To simplify matters, it is assumed below that in California the politically prescribed annual CO_2 reduction rate is the same as in the EU (e.g., 3 percent per year).

So, if, as an example, a politically decided integration of the EU-Californian certificate markets took place, then in the EU—with an initial certificate price of €25/ton—as the "country" with the initially relatively high certificate price, an import of certificates from California will take place (there, the certificate price of €15/ton is lower than in the EU with the aforementioned €25/ton). The price of certificates in California will rise significantly, from €15/ton to €20/ton. This makes it worthwhile for more companies in California to invest more in avoiding CO_2 emissions or to launch corresponding innovation projects to reduce CO_2 emissions. The costs for this are initially lower than in the EU (see mirror image of the initially low certificate price of €15/ton).

In the EU, on the other hand, companies benefit because importing certificates from California is cheaper in the integrated EU and California system than without market integration: about €20/ton instead of the starting cost of €25. The transatlantic trade drives the EU certificate price down to €20/ton, so that the certificate price in California and the EU is ultimately the same and reaches an equilibrium at €20 (this is analogous to the world market goods price for tradable goods in a conceivable free trade system of two countries).

If the upper limit for CO_2 emissions in the combined certificates trading area is -3 percent annually, this reduction will be achieved in the integrated trading system as a whole, but in a geographically different combination than in isolated certificates trading systems or national CO_2 taxes: there is more CO_2 reduction in California, less in the EU. It doesn't matter to the climate, but it makes a difference to the combined

EU-California economic area. For the EU economy, this means that more can now be produced due to the lower cost achieved through international certificate trading, and the standard of living is therefore higher than without an integrated certificate trading system.

For the US economy and in California, respectively, this means that companies have greater profits than usual—also from the export of CO_2 certificates to Europe: that pleases the shareholders, often the pension funds related to certain occupational groups, such as teachers or firefighters, who are now profiting. More profitable companies usually also pay relatively higher wages. Moreover, the US economy also profits in the form of higher exports of goods and thus a higher real income, since the reduction in the price of emission certificates in the EU has a positive effect on production and employment in the EU; more will then be imported—including more from the US. The expansion of the US export economy increases US real income, and then the EU can also export a little more to the US.

How high are the worldwide CO_2 reduction costs for CO_2 taxation in the global economy—again for simplification with two countries—compared to the general application of certificate trading in the integrated certificate trading system? Let us now assume that there are two countries in the world economy: the "North" (two-thirds of the world economy, with a high per capita income and relatively high price and cost levels), and the "South" (one-third of the world economy, with a low per capita income and low price and cost levels), each with an isolated certificate trading system or a national CO_2 tax: €40/ton CO_2 in the North, €10/ton in the South for both pricing cases; that is, a CO_2 tax or a certificate trading system. Price and cost levels are higher in the North than in the South, mainly because the prices of non-tradable goods are higher than in the South. The initial global emission level is 40 billion tons of CO_2.

If the avoidance effort for CO_2 emissions in the North corresponds to the share of the global economy (i.e., two-thirds or 0.67 for the North, and one-third or 0.33 for the South), then the global CO_2 avoidance costs are simply given by $(0.67) \times 40 + (0.33) \times 10$, which corresponds to an average cost of €30/ton. This means a global cost of €30/ton × 40 billion tons of global CO_2 emissions, that is, €1200 billion – around $1300 billion US dollars—avoidance costs for the global economy per year. That corresponds to 1.6 percent of world income in 2018, which is a considerable amount.

If you have an integrated certificate system, you would get a world price of €20/ton. Again, assuming 40 billion tons of CO_2 emissions per year, an integrated certificate system (North + South; corresponds to about G20 countries) would cost €800 billion to reduce CO_2 emissions. That's 1.1 percent of the world income. The use of an integrated certificate trading system thus results in a saving of the global CO_2 avoidance costs by €400 billion: that is, one-third of the costs incurred by a system with separate systems. Only in an integrated certificate system can such enormous efficiency gains, that is, cost savings, be achieved. It would be economically and also morally—if one is against wasting resources—indefensible, therefore, if one did not strive to establish a broad, internationally integrated certificate trading system.

Similar efficiency gains in a global economy with different national CO_2 tax systems are not possible. A CO_2 tax system would only have a similar effect as the integrated certificates trading system if the parliament in the North wanted to decide that a large proportion of its own CO_2 tax revenues would be transferred to the poor South for CO_2 reduction measures; this is a far-fetched notion and is also likely to lead to enormous corruption problems. Since the North—apart from Norway and a few other countries—has been struggling for decades to transfer even the 1 percent of gross domestic product promised at the UN to the South to support development, one will want to be realistic. It cannot be assumed that further increases in payments from the North to the South are feasible: this time, however, also for concrete, useful compensatory measures for the North or the world economy, namely CO_2 reduction.

Finally, let us assume, for further clarification, that saving one ton of CO_2 in India costs only half as much as in the US or the EU. With an integrated CO_2 trading system, this will result in US and EU companies that need certificates buying cheap certificates from India. This will then lead India toward a structural change involving CO_2-light services and corresponding industries earlier than Western countries. Imagine that India is about two decades behind a Western analog country in a 2020 structural comparison; then the Indian economic development from 2021 onward will not be a simple imitation of the development of a Western country, where over time the share of services in total value added has risen by X percent per year; rather, India's economic development will move toward CO_2-light production structures much earlier—compared to the earlier historical development in the US and the EU.

Satellite and Sensor Image Analysis for Latin America in 2019

In August 2019, slash-and-burn farming practices and fires in Brazil's forests attracted considerable media attention all over the world, as the large forests in Brazil, Bolivia and other Latin American countries are of great importance in terms of climate stability. These and other forests in the world absorb large amounts of CO_2—and the ocean is also a sink for carbon dioxide. As can be seen in the satellite/sensor image evaluations shown in Fig. 3.2 and Fig. 3.3 (from Sentinel 2 satellites from the Copernicus program), the development of smoke in August was quite considerable; the development of particulate matter associated with the spread of fires, which is detrimental to health, can also be seen very well from the second image.

Thanks to modern satellite and sensor technology, the implementation of nature conservation and environmental protection and, ultimately, some of the facts relevant to climate policy can be observed quite precisely in real time. This opens up completely new possibilities for realizing meaningful regional, international and global policy cooperation, from climate protection to water protection; it would be desirable if Germany or the EU could become more active here, since the benefits for economic and climate policy are likely to be very considerable. In addition, a much stronger climate awareness can emerge in the public on the basis of satellite image-based visualized correlations.

On the basis of satellite data, Thomas Crowther and other researchers from ETH Zürich have determined what role a global reforestation policy could play as a climate protection policy (Fig. 3.4): estimates suggest that a committed reforestation policy would absorb two-thirds of the CO_2 emissions of around 300 billion tons since industrialization. However, this presupposes reforestation and forest growth periods of about half a century, while in reality the global amount of forest decreases year after year due to deforestation. If we include the ETH researchers' approach to reforestation, the principal reforestation countries should be Russia (151 million hectares), the US (103 million hectares), Canada (78 million hectares), Australia (58 million hectares), Brazil (50 million hectares) and China (40 million hectares).

3 CLIMATE PROTECTION PROBLEMS AND OPTIONS FOR ACTION   135

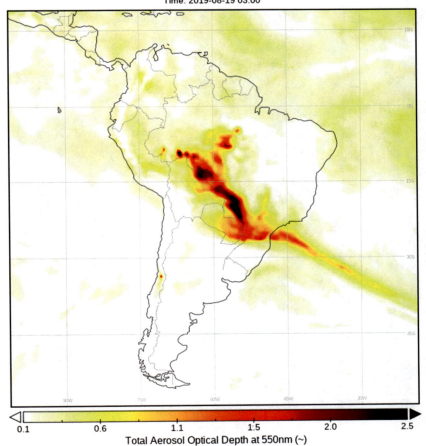

Fig. 3.2 Smoke development in Brazil on 19 August 2019 (with influences from fires in Bolivia). Note: The author would like to thank EDEO GmbH, Roding, Germany, for kindly providing this graphic which was created using Copernicus CAMS data 2019. (Source: EDEO GmbH (with project funding from StmWi Bayern)

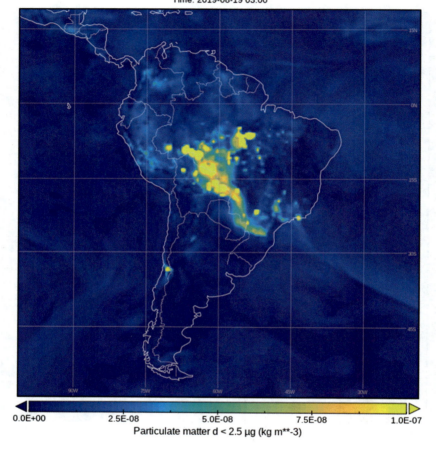

Fig. 3.3 Regional distribution of particulate matter in South America on 19 August 2019. Note: The author would like to thank EDEO GmbH, Roding, Germany, for kindly providing this graphic which was created using Copernicus CAMS data 2019. (Source: EDEO GmbH (with project funding from StmWi Bayern)

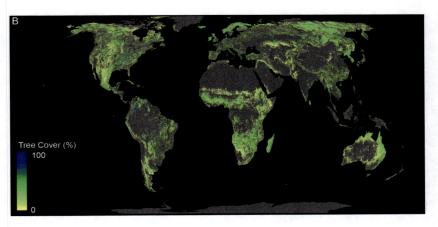

Fig. 3.4 Afforestation possibilities worldwide (bright areas = afforestation reserve or desert). (Source: ETH ZURICH/CROWTHER LAB (2019) and Bastin et al. (2019), https://ethz.ch/en/news-and-events/eth-news/news/2019/07/how-trees-could-save-the-climate.html)

Facts About Germany and International Energy Market Perspectives

In addition to the energy sector and industry, as well as the transport sector, private households account for 10 percent of greenhouse gas emissions; households were able to reduce emissions by 31 percent in Germany between 1990 and 2016. Agriculture has been a problematic sector with an 8 percent share of greenhouse gas emissions in 2016, whereby the share of total economic value-added amounts to just 1 percent. Agriculture is lagging behind in the reduction of CO_2; in the period 1990–2016 the decrease was about 20 percent. According to the German Federal Government (Federal Ministry for the Environment, Nature Conservation and Nuclear Safety), the land use, land use change and forestry sector has reduced net CO_2 emissions by 14.5 million tons of CO_2 equivalents. Due to the intensive management of soils, their storage capacity for greenhouse gases in 2016 was still half as high as in 1990. The German greenhouse gas emissions of 905 million tons of CO_2 equivalents in 2016 represent a decrease of 27.3 percent compared to 1990, with the energy industry accounting for the highest share of total German emissions in 2016 at 37.8 percent. The transport sector accounted for 18 percent of emissions in Germany in 2016—a rise again for the first time since 2004 compared with 1990 levels.

Global CO_2 emissions in 2016 were 4.8 tons per capita on average, with Asia, Brazil, North Africa, India and sub-Saharan Africa below the global average. For the EU—excluding Germany—the figure was 6 tons per capita, Germany a good 9 tons per capita, Russia and Australia about 12 tons per capita and the US and Canada at 16 tons. If the Western industrialized countries and Japan, as well as Russia, China and some other countries, quickly reduce their CO_2 emissions in absolute terms, this will have an economic and ecological benefit for these countries and the whole world and also reduce the causes of migration caused by climate change. But because each individual country contributes relatively little to the world's climate problem, the incentive to get involved in climate protection is basically rather weak. Progress already requires a certain social and political rationality on the part of many countries, or in the political systems of many countries, and increased climate-friendly innovations are also needed. Innovative entrepreneurship worldwide and the participation and involvement of private households are also important.

For 2025, the federal government in Berlin assumes that 50 million tons of CO_2 equivalents can be saved through increased digitization. For the first time, Germany's Climate Protection Plan 2050—as the Federal Ministry for the Environment, Nature Conservation and Nuclear Safety (2018) stresses—also sets CO_2 reduction targets for individual sectors. For sectors of the economy, target corridors have been set until 2030, with a 55 percent reduction compared to 1990 to be achieved by then. This goal has been reinforced via new legislation in June 2021, which has increased the reduction rate to 65 percent. Sectoral reduction targets are peculiar from an economic point of view, since such targets make climate protection unnecessarily more expensive; the climate does not care which sectors make which contribution, as long as overall greenhouse gas emissions are reduced. Politicians cannot know what the respective sectoral CO_2 reduction costs are, in other words, how to minimize climate protection costs. This is what certificate trading does.

The inefficiencies in German climate policy can probably be estimated as amounting to at least 1 percent of the gross domestic product, which is as much as all innovation promotion expenditures of the federal and state governments. After all, the German government supports more than 500 projects in developing countries in the context of international climate protection. The highest shares of renewable energies in gross electricity generation by energy source in Germany in 2017 were wind power (48.8 percent), biomass (20 percent), photovoltaics (18.3 percent), hydropower (9.3 percent) and domestic waste incineration (2.7 percent). Wind power projects in the sea could also be agreed in 2017 mainly without state subsidies within the framework of tender procedures. This makes wind power competitive. It would be even more so if nuclear power in Germany were not to run practically without any significant liability insurance—in other words, if it were not to be subsidized in a hidden way. If a nuclear power plant had to be insured with €200 billion instead of €2.5 billion in liability insurance—this is the order of magnitude of a serious accident like in Fukushima—then the nuclear power plant would already be closing before the legally prescribed expiry year 2022. On the issue of nuclear power plant liability insurance, I myself made a statement in an article in the *Handelsblatt* newspaper, which stimulated the discussion in Germany very much and drew attention to the fact that nuclear power plants could not obtain an insurance policy on the market for comprehensive liability insurance (Welfens, 2011). The *Handelsblatt* editorial team decided at the time to ask the chairman of the Board of Management of Allianz whether a comprehensive liability insurance policy for a nuclear power plant could be purchased from Allianz: the answer then was a clear "no" (Flauger & Stratmann, 2011). However, Japan's government has not learned from the Fukushima disaster with damages of more than $100 billion in Japan (most of the cost covered by the Japanese taxpayer). Since at least a century, the risk of tsunamis is well known in Japan so that a nuclear power plant should never have been built on the side of Japan's islands exposed to the Pacific, and post-Fukushima any plants in those regions should have been shut down if one follows the basic logic of risk, but this did not happen.

It is not only nuclear power which is heavily subsidized in almost all countries with nuclear power plants. On the contrary, there is also the mind-boggling worldwide subsidization of fossil fuel energies. In 2013, this figure was an enormous 6.5 percent of world income. In 2015, subsidies still amounted to $4700 billion worldwide, or 6.3 percent of world income (Coady et al., 2015, 2019).

To date there are only indirect market signals on the global warming risk. It is clear that reinsurance and insurance companies will face more long-term losses due to extreme weather conditions, and millions of property owners will have increased losses—including uninsured cases. It would be desirable for climate risks to be visibly priced into real estate insurance policies in a formulaic manner. Conversely, this would mean that worldwide progress in climate protection policy would lead to lower property insurance prices and lower rent increases: understandable for everyone. In some cases, the liability risk of coal-fired power generation, for example, could become so high that coal is no longer used to generate electricity. This is conceivable, for example, in the US. The damages that cigarette manufacturers, for example, have had to pay in the past could one day be paid in even higher dimensions by the owners and operators of coal-fired power plants.

With regard to the expansion opportunities for wind, solar and wind power plants, for example, it is very important that manufacturers of electricity from renewable sources have access to the power grid. As cases in China and Argentina and also in Europe show, this is by no means a matter of course. The International Monetary Fund should publish an annual overview for all member countries. This is because macroeconomic growth and stability aspects are also at stake here. In this way, political pressure could be built up—namely through transparency and international comparisons—so that network monopolies do not artificially obstruct important progress in climate protection.

References

Bastin, J. F., Finegold, Y., Garcia, C., Mollicone, D., Rezende, M., Routh, D., Zohner, C. M., & Crowther, T. W. (2019). The Global Tree Restoration Potential. *Science, 365*(6448), 76–79. https://doi.org/10.1126/science.aax0848

BCG/Prognos. (2018, January). *Klimapfade für Deutschland [Climate Paths for Germany]*. Study for the Federation of German Industries. Retrieved September 6, 2019, from https://www.prognos.com/uploads/tx_atwpubdb/20180118_BDI_Studie_Klimapfade_fuer_Deutschland_01.pdf

Coady D. et al. (2015). *How Large Are Global Energy Subsidies?* (IMF Working Paper). International Monetary Fund.

Coady, D. et al. (2019). *Global Fossil Fuel Subsidies Remain Large: An Update Based on Country-Level Estimates* (IMF Working Paper). International Monetary Fund.

ETH Zurich/Crowther Lab. (2019, July 4). *How Trees Could Save the Climate.* Press release. Retrieved September 6, 2021, from https://ethz.ch/en/news-and-events/eth-news/news/2019/07/how-trees-could-save-the-climate.html

Federal Ministry for the Environment, Nature Conservation and Nuclear Safety. (2018). *Klimaschutz in Zahlen – Fakten, Trends und Impulse deutscher*

Klimapolitik [*Climate Protection in Numbers – Facts, Trends and Impulses of German Climate Policy*], Issue 2018, Federal Ministry for the Environment, Nature Conservation and Nuclear Safety. https://www.bmu.de/fileadmin/Daten_BMU/Pools/Broschueren/klimaschutz_in_zahlen_2018_bf.pdf

Flauger, J., & Stratmann, K. (2011, March 24). *Die wahren Kosten der Kernkraft* [tranls. PJJW: The True Costs of Nuclear Power]. Handelsblatt (p. 1). *Handelsblatt* Media Group: Düsseldorf.

German Council of Economic Experts. (2019). *Setting Out for a New Climate Policy*. Special report, July 2019. Retrieved 1 September, 2019, from https://www.sachverstaendigenrat-wirtschaft.de/fileadmin/dateiablage/gutachten/sg2019/sg_2019_en.pdf

IRENA. (2021). *Renewable Capacity Statistics 2021*. International Renewable Energy Agency, IRENA.

Welfens, P.J.J. (2011, March 24). Atomstrom ist extrem teuer [transl. PJJW: Nuclear Power Is Extremely Expensive]. *Handelsblatt* (p. 38).

CHAPTER 4

Global Warming Perspectives

Global warming is a serious challenge facing billions of people in the twenty-first century. In 2020, Germany fell short of meeting its climate targets (if one accounts for the fall in emissions resulting from the corona shock), the EU as a whole is faring somewhat better; the world, however, is falling short of the targets foreseen in the UN's Paris Climate Agreement. How exactly one hopes to reach the goals set for 2030—which is the next cliff edge and benchmark target—is rather unclear. There is no lack of models in economics, particularly since the 1970s, which show how CO_2 emissions can be reduced in a sensible way. Economists such as William Nordhaus and Thomas Schelling, for example, highlighted the energy aspects of production and consumption very early on. Numerous economists, climate researchers, physicists and engineers have analyzed the mechanisms of global warming caused by CO_2 and other greenhouse emissions, for example, in relation to power generation from fossil fuels such as oil, coal and gas. That human activity is playing a major role in exacerbating global warming appears to be an uncontroversial position among scientists. That natural fluctuations affecting global temperatures are more responsible for warming than the increased levels of global CO_2 emissions since 1850 due to industrialization is an argument which has not been made in any serious context.

It is as yet unclear how quickly economic policy in industrialized, emerging and developing countries could—and should—respond to the challenge with vigorous and coordinated countermeasures. It is hard to overlook the fact that the problems of climate change in the twenty-first century are a serious issue; of course, government impulses and sensibly channeled market forces could fundamentally achieve a timely adaptation of the global economy. However, it will not be easy, because—at the very least—the 20 largest CO_2-emitting economies around the world would have to cooperate. Moreover, in the period between 2019 and 2030, a very significant acceleration in the reduction of emissions compared to the period from 1990 to 2018 is required. Even though market economies are innovative and powerful, the question must be asked as to how the necessary acceleration in the reduction of climate gases such as CO_2 and methane in the atmosphere can be achieved.

From a scientific and economic policy point of view, the climate problem has been a major issue since the United Nations Kyoto Agreement of 1997: CO_2 emissions, which are caused by the burning of fossil fuels such as oil, coal and gas, for example, have contributed massively to global warming since the age of industrialization began in earnest in the nineteenth century. Increasing warming, on the other hand, leads to the melting of ice caps and glaciers in the Arctic, Greenland, the high mountains of Europe, Asia and Africa as well as at the southern polar cap: in the North, the polar bear is forced to swim, while in the South, the penguins can only stand on shrinking ice fields. New York, Baltimore, San Francisco, Yokohama, Tokyo, Manila, Shanghai, Rotterdam, Hamburg, Venice and many other port cities face the problem of severe flooding in the long term.

High economic losses globally are not only caused by flooding, but also by an increase in extreme weather events—heavy rainfall, hailstorms, electrical storms, tornadoes and hurricanes. In the 2006 Stern Review on the Economics of Climate Change (Stern, 2006), the costs of global warming were roughly quantified, and since these costs are extremely high, it is worth investing in climate protection globally now. Do the income losses of 10–15 percent of world income, shown in the Stern Report in the absence of an energetic climate policy, mean that people in many countries will develop a clear impulse for a more urgent climate policy? There is certainly no clear positive answer to this question. The decision in the UK to leave the European Union in the Brexit referendum of June 2016, and the subsequent debate, showed that the proponents of a hard Brexit were little impressed by or affected by the expert forecasts of Brexit-related expected income declines of 10 percent. The populist Brexit issue is, after all, about the economic and political costs of the British withdrawal from the EU in the long run, which the British themselves can digest. How are the expected global real income losses to impress observers in the event of further significant global warming, when it can be assumed that industrialized countries will in many cases be able to arm themselves against rising sea levels and more flooding phenomena as well as extreme weather by means of higher dikes and other measures? According to the Stern Report, the majority of related damage will occur in developing countries. If, for example, there are suddenly millions of climate refugees in Africa who are pushing toward the North, toward EU countries, and also toward Asia, then the resulting adaptation problems in preferred immigration and asylum destination countries will affect only a few countries.

That government economic policy advisors really deal with the topic of climate protection is—with the notable exception of the Stern Review in the UK—rather a rare case. The US Council of Economic Advisors, for example, has included very little on climate-related aspects in its annual reports to the US President, and the German Council of Economic Experts has only marginally addressed the issue (however, in 2016 and 2019 there were special reports). Criticism of Germany's so-called Grand Coalition, a government formed of the center-right and center-left parties, with its inadequate climate policy increased significantly in the run-up to the European Parliament elections in 2019. A viral video by YouTuber Rezo, who originally comes from the music scene, in which he unleashed a political broadside, particularly of the CDU (German Christian Democratic party), targeting young voters just two weeks before the elections, was interesting, technically well done and partly missed the key economic arguments—but essentially it was an apt criticism of Berlin's climate policy. In any case, with over five million views during the days leading up to the European elections, Rezo created a political earthquake beneath the Grand Coalition, presumably helping the Green Party, which indeed went on to achieve very good election results.

It seems strange that the World Trade Organization, for example, last had a major publication on environmental issues in 1999, namely a document titled "Trade and the Environment". Of course, foreign trade issues are important with regard to climate problems—one only has to consider extended global value chains and transport needs: with intermediate and end products transported around the globe predominantly by ships powered by heavy fuel oil and with very high emissions. In addition, in the case of CO_2 taxes, the question with regard to the extent to which such taxes should be levied on imports in certain sectors and what innovation and structural effects could arise here. It can be seen as a positive development that exemplary innovations in the field of climate-neutral living have been realized in Austria: the country has gained a head start in the construction of such climate-neutral houses in Europe and worldwide (Dachs & Budde, 2019).

The issue of the appropriate pricing of CO_2 emissions is not difficult to solve economically. The average and marginal costs of one ton of CO_2 emissions have to be determined. The Federal Environment Agency in Germany published a publication in 2018 stating that the damage caused by one ton of CO_2 could be estimated at €180. For 2016, CO_2 emission losses of €164 billion were calculated for Germany; that would be about 2 percent of the national income. If it were possible to significantly reduce CO_2 emissions in Germany and worldwide, there would be reduced environmental damage and associated health costs. How high should one set the price for one ton of CO_2 in order to achieve a reasonable CO_2 reduction path by 2030? If one follows the level of the CO_2 tax in Sweden and Switzerland in 2016, then it should probably be a good €100 per ton. In the optimal economic equilibrium of an economy, the damage caused by an additional ton of CO_2 is just as high as the price of a CO_2 certificate or CO_2 tax. The emission certificate price of about €20 in the EU at the end of 2018 is thus comparatively low. It would be possible to push up the certificate prices on the part of EU countries to about €60–100 by purchasing CO_2 certificates from the state or at an EU level. This would, of course, be associated with government purchase costs for the CO_2 certificates to be skimmed off and removed from circulation. Many companies with surplus certificates to sell would have book profits in their balance sheets; the returns of innovative companies—with a low CO_2 intensity of production—would increase.

With regard to CO_2 emissions and other climate-damaging gas emissions, it does not matter which country they come from. All countries are therefore called upon to cooperate internationally in the field of climate policy. However, from an economic point of view, climate protection is a global public good, so that the incentives for individual countries to express their real need for climate protection are not high. All the more so as there are no high incentives to commit oneself financially or via one's own costly reforms to climate protection. Given this, there are clear free-rider problems in which any single country is not incentivized to make its own efforts to protect the climate but could simply wait for other countries to massively reduce their CO_2 emissions and still enjoy the benefits of a better climate overall. Since climate protection is a global public good, effective global cooperation between all countries is essential in the long term.

It may be difficult to get 200 countries around one table. However, the leading industrialized and emerging countries could actually work together in an exemplary manner: the G20 countries, for example, which in 2018 stand for about 60 percent of the world's population, 81 percent of world income and 80 percent of world CO_2 emissions, could and should cooperate relatively easily. This group is manageable in size, already meets annually to discuss global challenges and also has the main emitters on board with the US, China, India, the EU and Japan all represented. However, this grouping of countries is economically very different, for example, with regard to per capita income; in turn, there is little inclination to even in this more limited setting to cooperate from different positions.

In the case of a climate challenge that calls for energetic reform and cooperation policies by 2030 and 2040, the failure of the US as the global superpower—major political and economic actor—to take up a leadership role is a serious problem. However, climate protection policy is not only pursued at the level of national states, but there are also federal states—in the US, for example, California, there are also national and international city networks that pursue a committed climate policy. The unresolved climate problem had a strong influence on the results of the European Parliament elections in 2019, and shortcomings in the federal government's actions in Berlin lead to a broad public debate in Germany. The poor election results for the traditional, mainstream centrist parties almost broke the governing coalition in Berlin. However, there are also persevering forces within these parties who still think that one could sit out the climate problems for a few more years. This approach is hard to comprehend, as with intensifying global warming, the earth or mankind will ultimately run out of time.

On the issue of how to achieve important climate targets nationally and globally, there have been and continue to be heated debates in Germany, Europe and the US. Many countries, including China, can point to the fact that the CO_2 emission intensity of their economies is declining. Over time, generally speaking less (fossil) energy is being used per unit of production, and therefore the specific CO_2 emissions, that is, the "climate pressure" per unit of output, decrease. If, however, the production volume rises sharply, the climate problems will continue to increase. If the global warming headline limit of 1.5 degrees is exceeded—compared to the time of industrialization, that is, around 1850—this can have dramatic consequences for the earth. Global warming means not only that there will be more floods, but also that the number and intensity of extreme weather events will also increase in many regions of the world: economically significant loss events for the individual, for regions and countries, and, of course, also for insurance companies; whereby one can assume that less than a third of global loss events are actually insured. However, even that is enough to ensure rising insurance premiums in the relevant market. Production disruptions, a damaged housing stock and the pressure of possibly millions of climate refugees could contribute to serious political and economic instability.

The longer-term global production growth rate is around 3 percent, which means a ninefold increase in world production within 75 years. If there is no radical decoupling of production and emissions, there is the apparent threat of a climate disaster for the world -0 because climate quality is a global phenomenon. A limiting of global warming dynamics requires an absolute reduction in CO_2 emissions and similar emissions (even worse, per emission unit, is methane). Where reductions are not possible, compensation can be provided, for example, through the planting new forests, that is, reforestation. That would then at least be climate-neutral, and Germany's federal government under Chancellor Merkel, herself a scientist, is aiming to achieve this by 2050. The fact that the German government would have missed its own 2020 targets by a rather wide margin in the absence of a global pandemic shows, amongst other things, the shortcomings of the Grand Coalition; since the traditional middle-of-the-road parties in the government have not organized themselves enough over many years to engage in a coherent response to climate issues, there is no strong opposition that can give the government a push when it comes to climate policy. The largest opposition party in the German Bundestag, the AfD (*Alternative für Deutschland*, i.e., the Alternative for Germany), is full of climate change/global warming deniers and thus is reluctant to act on climate protection and therefore a total failure at holding the government to account on this (its right-wing populist tone often makes it untrustworthy anyway). After the 2017 federal elections, the Greens had entered the Bundestag as the smallest opposition party.

Only with the European Parliament elections in 2019 did the Greens see a nationwide surge in support, which saw them become the second strongest party with over 20 percent of the votes. At the end of May 2019, the Greens in Germany were ahead of the CDU/CSU for the first time in a survey (Forsa for RTL/n-tv), which shows that the Greens' own program, on the one hand, and the subjectively perceived climate pressure, on the other, combined to cause significant shifts in voter orientation. The German government, with a "climate cabinet" since 2019, is falling behind what is required with its speed of reaction; the pace of work is too slow, and the dislike of thinking outside the box, which are evident in parts of the German government regarding the expansion of certificate trading and the role of CO_2 taxes, is strange and reflects too traditionalist a response. In Germany, one of the world's leading export and technology nations, the national policy layer, in particular, was the government's primary focus in terms of climate policy in 2019, although this cannot be efficient and successful without a strong international cooperation component. It is commendable that several different ministries are working together within the framework of the "climate cabinet"; however, the fact that the Germany's Foreign Office is not one of them is incomprehensible and already points to a fundamental conceptual deficiency. An intelligent climate policy of a large EU country would always seek a coherent EU anchoring and also consider the possibilities of a G20 strategy—that is, how the world's leading countries can ultimately be included in a cooperation forum that makes sense in terms of trade and innovation policy as well as regulatory policy and as a basis for globally integrated certificate markets. If the framework conditions are sensibly anchored in the national and global markets, then globally integrated certificate markets of the G20 countries are the key to achieving global climate neutrality efficiently (i.e., at low cost).

A temporary decline in Green votes can be assumed as part of normal policy dynamics, but the policies of the Grand Coalition in particular have resulted in the government distancing itself too far from Germany's youth. In any case, many voters have indicated that the climate issue was particularly important to them with a view to the European Parliament elections: with a view to the role of the EU and the European Commission, this makes sense.

The YouTuber Rezo put the parties under massive pressure two weeks before the European Parliament elections with his YouTube video titled "The Destruction of the CDU". In the 55-minute video clip, the young man—then with 155,000 followers—took a critical look at the policies of the Grand Coalition, not only focusing on economic inequality but also touching on the military policies of the US and Germany, and on climate policy, which he argued was very inadequate and ignorant with regard to the findings of international climate research. Voters were discouraged from voting for the CDU and SPD (as the center-left partner in the coalition government) as well as for the AfD. Within a few weeks, the video had been viewed almost 15 million times, and the particularly criticized CDU had nothing to offer to counter the video apart from an 11-page written statement—there was also an offer to talk and engage with Rezo, which as it happens, came from the SPD.

Since the Greens won the majority of votes in the European Parliament elections among the under-60s, the previous popular centrist parties are facing a potential existential crisis. With the climate-related Fridays for Future movement of school students, who demonstrated for better climate policy worldwide with Friday demonstrations in European countries in 2018 and 2019, the established parties in a number of countries are coming under new pressure to adapt; globalization, digitalization and the confused US policy (at least under President Trump) are already causing major problems in many fields of action simultaneously.

Progress in terms of emissions in many OECD countries and in China can be observed at times. However, to reduce the absolute level of CO_2 emissions globally, which is crucial for climate change, these advances are not enough. This is perhaps unsurprising given the high growth rates of real income in many Asian countries and the sharp increase in the global population: from seven billion people in 2010 to an estimated nine to ten billion by the middle of the twenty-first century. In the longer term, sustainable CO_2 emissions per capita should not exceed 1 ton of CO_2 emissions per year, but the global average in 2018 will be a good 4 tons of CO_2 emissions.

Only three decades remain to make very significant progress by 2050 in, for example, OECD countries. An important contribution to this end can be the transition to renewable energies across the board, but new power lines must also be built. If, for example, considerable investments are made in wind farms in the North and Baltic Seas in Germany, this would only make real sense if there are also new power lines connecting wind farms in the north to the main industrial consumers in southern Germany. However, many municipalities and local protest groups are blocking the expansion of the infrastructural networks required. Moreover, the phasing out of nuclear power—planned for Germany in 2022—and coal-fired power by 2038 is a major and expensive challenge, with large write-downs on machinery and equipment and job losses occurring prematurely.

What is to be done on the part of economic policy at the national and international levels? From an economic point of view, it is necessary to think about more trading in emission certificates, which has so far only been achieved in the EU, China and a few other countries; additionally, it is about climate-friendly innovations and the question of introducing a CO_2 tax in certain economic sectors—coupled with a partial or complete recycling of the CO_2 tax revenues generated back to private households. The latter aspect corresponds to the approach in Switzerland and Sweden, with the Swedish model achieving a 25 percent reduction in emissions in the 25 years since the introduction of a CO_2 tax in 1991. And that despite a simultaneous increase in production of 75 percent between 1991 and 2016.

In Germany, it is planned to phase out coal-fired power generation and thus coal production by 2038—the phasing out supported with around €40 billion in adjustment aid for the coal-producing regions from tax revenues. How Germany can develop a smart CO_2 reduction policy remains a controversial issue. The trading of CO_2 pollution rights (i.e., CO_2 certificate trading), an innovative development carried out in the European Union, has certainly had some effects over time. However, a phase of low prices for certificates permitting a ton of CO_2 emissions has temporarily denied the approach a large part of the hoped-for positive effect. In addition, certificate trading in the EU system covers barely half of the economy. The fact that there have been good successes with a combination of certificate trading and CO_2 taxation can be well understood in Sweden, where the CO_2 price rose to around €110 per ton between 1991 and 2019. However, neither Sweden, nor Switzerland nor Germany alone can tackle the climate problem. The global emission of CO_2 and "CO_2-equivalent" gases (e.g., methane, which is important in agriculture, among other things) is decisive for global warming. However, if some countries make very good progress in reducing CO_2 emissions, then they can nevertheless serve as models and benchmarks for other countries looking to reduce emissions.

Policy innovations with a global focus are needed. It is conceivable and sensible to jointly agree on certain innovative measures at an international level. A common goal could be to implement an overarching and groundbreaking scientific research initiative between Europe, the US, China, Japan, Brazil, India and South Africa. It is worth considering, for example, that each country would gradually introduce CO_2 taxes or increase CO_2 emissions trading approaches and by 2025 would contribute 0.1 percent of GDP from the resultant revenues to a global innovation promotion fund. The US, the EU27 (plus UK) and China would then have to pay roughly equal shares into a subsidy pot around 2020 for which companies and consortia of companies from these countries could apply. The patent terms could be shortened in the interest of a faster diffusion of emission-reducing technologies, with companies receiving some compensation from tax revenues for the reduction of the patent term from 20 to 10 years. If the climate protection targets can then gradually be achieved without shortening patent terms, we could revert to applying the usual 20-year patent term once again.

Many scientific analyses of climate change show the seriousness of the global situation in the medium and long term. Not even climate change skeptics can deny the old postcards from Switzerland and other Alpine countries in Europe which featured extensive glaciers from around 1900 while only smaller localized glaciers exist in the same mountain areas from around 2000, and nobody with an ounce of sense will be able to ignore the photos that NASA, for example, has taken of the Arctic sea ice at various times: with clear findings, namely that in the longer term the extent of the ice sheets will decrease, that is, through melting. According to a good 90 percent of climate researchers, global warming is essentially the result of man-made changes since about 1825, namely since the onset of industrialization with its enormous hunger for energy—almost always energy in the form of fossil fuels with significant CO_2 emissions. In addition to carbon dioxide, however, there are other gaseous emissions that are also regarded as impulses for global warming, such as methane.

There are various ways of combating global warming; some measures in households and the wider economy generate costs, some measures require international cooperation in economic policy, while some measures are almost free of charge, but at least require a rethink and some knowledge beforehand—such as exploiting the albedo effect, which suggests bright roofs on houses, cars, trains, buses, trucks to reflect more sunlight than before. Each individual can make his or her own decisions with regard to adopting behaviors conducive to more climate protection, but of course it is the political leaders who are called upon to make adopt a more reliable climate protection policy, which not only sets goals, but also makes a well-thought-out and transparent effort to achieve them. Some activists in the field of climate policy want to frighten people and politicians in particular into changing, such as the young Swede Greta Thunberg, who since 2018 has initiated a Fridays for Future protest movement in large parts of Europe and has also been invited to speak at prominent institutions. This approach may accelerate climate policy.

Melting of Inland Ice as a Long-Term Problem

The 2012 NASA photo below shows that the extent of the Arctic ice field has shrunk enormously compared to the average of the previous 30 years—yellow line (Fig. 4.1). A large part of the long-term decline of the ice sheet is due to global warming. If extensive sections of the Antarctic and Greenland ice sheets melt, sea water levels globally could rise by 1–3 meters within a century. Previous wind currents around the globe could change significantly; important ocean currents, such as the Gulf Stream, which is important for Europe, are also likely to become unstable. The Boucher painting below (Fig. 4.2)—from 1748, on view in the Princeton University Museum—creates an association of thoughts that should be obvious. If icecaps and glaciers melt significantly over the next 50 years, floods in many parts of the world will become a serious problem (Boucher's

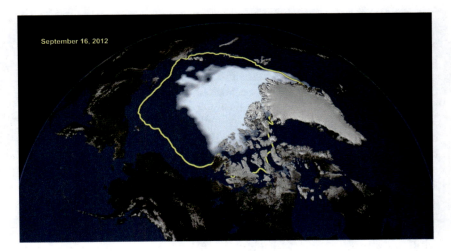

Fig. 4.1 Extent of the Arctic ice field in 2012 (the yellow line stands for the average of the 30 previous years). (Source: NASA/Goddard Scientific Visualization Studio. https://www.nasa.gov/topics/earth/features/2012-seaicemin.html)

Fig. 4.2 Arion on the dolphin (1748), painting by François Boucher. (Source: Arion on the Dolphin, 1748, François Boucher, Oil on canvas. Princeton University Art Museum purchase, Fowler McCormick, Class of 1921, Fund)

picture is of Arion, who was forced overboard and into the sea by his disagreeable, rapacious fellow ship passengers, upon which he is rescued by a passing dolphin—the beautiful siren Leucosia can also be seen, with whom the young castaway fell in love. His greedy fellow travelers, however, have themselves become shipwrecked because of the storm. The painting is said to be allegorical with Arion representing the French king Louis XV).

The rise in sea level has considerable political consequences, not least because entire atolls and islands could disappear—and with them the territorial claims of certain countries: those who regard themselves as the owners of these islands and atolls. Thanks to research at the University of Tokyo, the Japanese government has been promoting the cultivation of corals for years to counteract rising sea levels. Japan's southernmost territory is the Okinotori atoll—referred to as an island by Japan (as the designation provides more resource use rights around this latitude, almost 1800 km south of Tokyo)—which is artificially maintained and extended via coral breeding in Japan and therefore could be saved from extinction despite rising sea levels. Japan could thus maintain large marine area claims thousands of kilometers south of the main Japanese islands; this is about fishing waters and natural resources in the sea and seabed; in the case of doubt, interest in the locations is also cultivated by the navy, air force and military.

When islands or coral reefs disappear, or indeed reappear in the sea, the political power of countries and regions changes; this can have a destabilizing effect on security policy. Environmental and climate policy is therefore also geopolitical and intertwined with great power politics. According to Article 121 of the United Nations Convention on the Law of the Sea, rocks protruding from the sea which are unsuitable for human habitation or which do not allow an economic life of their own may be said not to give rise to an exclusive economic zone or a continental shelf claim.

Differentiated Perspectives on the Climate Problem

There are obvious climate challenges in the early twenty-first century, but there is also no lack of positive private initiatives in many climate-related fields: For example, in the conservation of the rainforest, where large areas have been cleared since 1900—about as much as the area of Germany plus Italy—but where millions of hectares of forest have also been protected by private foundations and through the purchases of individual investors. In Western Europe, the quality of the water in many rivers and lakes has improved significantly since about 2000, and the number of endangered species at sea and in mountainous regions has recovered—such as gray seals or chamois. In Latin America, there are also huge forests and large river systems such as the Amazon or Orinoco, which Alexander Humboldt was particularly interested in during his research trips. The Orinoco is a huge river that carries about ten times as much water as the Rhine and, as Humboldt found out, is also connected to the Amazon by a tributary river. On New Year's Eve 1978, I myself stood close to the jungle on the banks of the Orinoco in Venezuela (near Ciudad Guyana), where a Swiss company wanted to build an aluminum plant—at the time, I was visiting my parents over the Christmas period and was immediately impressed by the Orinoco through its sheer size. The breadth and depth meant that even ships with a high draft could journey up the river and first deliver materials to an aluminum plant and later transport the aluminum—which is also produced using hydropower—back down the river and on to the markets of the world. The production of new aluminum is very energy-intensive, while production on the basis of recycled aluminum is much less expensive, and 90 percent of world trade is conducted by sea.

Just as in the case of the enormity of the river, I found the incredible vegetation at the edge of the jungle fascinating, and the friendliness and cheerfulness of the Venezuelan people left a lasting impression on me although I found the daily repetitive playing of the national anthem on the national TV channel rather strange.

The fact that Venezuela would find itself in an economic crisis under President Maduro was obvious. The populist hero Hugo Chavez had already failed to deliver sustainable policy, as he dismantled a sound ideological framework of economic policy for a decade, while allegedly working in favor of the poor. By the beginning of 2019, many people in the capital Caracas had resorted to drinking water from the sewers because of the temporary collapse of electricity and water supply systems. Incidentally, petrol in 2019 was just as incredibly cheap as it was in the late 1970s: just a few cents per liter, which even in the 1970s had resulted in one unhealthy development in Venezuela, namely that the country was filled with large, gasoline-thirsty US-made cars.

Economic growth in Venezuela in the 1970s was already strongly centered around government oil revenues—there is a whole body of literature on the dubious advantages of countries rich in natural resources. Such natural bounties may well be advantageous in the long term if economic policy is wise, but the many negative experiences of countries in such areas regarding the explosion of corruption, low educational incentives and weak innovation dynamics give pause for thought. Are resource-rich countries important drivers of technological progress, greater energy efficiency and good climate policy? Here, a differentiated picture is to be drawn. Overall, the G20 countries have, for example, surprisingly high energy subsidies. This is precisely the opposite of what is required to protect the environment, since the energy subsidies involved usually relate to fossil fuels: The state thus provides incentives for increased energy consumption and thus also for artificially increased CO_2 emissions.

It is obvious that climate policy itself also contributes to international conflicts. Under President Trump, the US withdrew from the Paris Agreement of 2015, and the question of how to deal with larger numbers of climate refugees is also looming on the horizon. It is already known from the EU refugee debate of 2015–2018, for example, that destination countries cannot easily agree on the distribution of a large number of refugees. Global warming may also bring economic benefits for some countries and regions of the world, but even that can become an international problem. If the winners of global warming were economically leading countries in the world economy, this would create greater international migratory pressures. In order to understand and solve the climate problem globally, one has to look at many different aspects. Of course, the Fridays for Future protest wave must also be considered, which at least gives policymakers an impetus to act: at any rate, it increases the pressure on governments to comply with the climate targets set both nationally and internationally. However, the climate protests also indirectly overlook where the largest emission lobbyists sit, namely on the boards and in higher management positions of some of the largest automobile manufacturers and of course oil companies all over the world; at a conference in St. Petersburg a few years ago, energy and climate issues, among other items, were discussed. However, a representative of the Russian Ministry of Energy stated that global warming would in fact bring advantages for Russia—with access to fossil energy resources in the polar regions and an ice-free Northern Passage (from Japan, one could then conveniently trade by ship along Russia's northern coast to the east coast of the US), which would mean cutting the distance to be covered between Japan and the US by two-thirds compared to the previous route through the Suez Canal. Global warming would also, however, mean that the melting of the permafrost soils in Siberia would increasingly allow methane to escape into the atmosphere and, at the same time, homes, factories and crucial infrastructure could sink into the thawing ground. The softening of permafrost soil could also become a serious problem in parts of North America.

Since around 1900, oil has shaped mobility in the global economy, and there are still high global reserves relative to global consumption. The claim that we will soon—within a few decades—be running out of oil is a widespread misconception in parts of environmental research. However, we should still be wise enough to cut back on worldwide oil production significantly as the use of fossil energies for electricity generation and transport goes hand in hand with increased CO_2 emissions. Oil and gas could continue to play (and increasingly so) a role in the chemical industry.

How can the world's hunger for energy be satisfied with more and more people inhabiting our planet? Here, too, the answer is not easy: whether it will be possible to build up sufficient renewable energy capacities sufficiently quickly is something that needs to be considered—along with how high the associated costs will be. Is the situation desperate? Is there cause for panic? It is apparent that there is indeed cause for concern, but there are also many good approaches to limiting global warming, including a temporary decline in consumption in affluent countries. It should be borne in mind that long-term challenges are at stake: climate change is a long-term phenomenon; short-term weather problems are less important with regard to the climate—even if they are likely to be difficult for those most affected to cope with, as increasing extreme weather problems are associated with prolonged global warming.

The Stern Report has already stressed that the relatively poor countries will be among the losers of global warming; people in the countries of Africa in particular are facing considerable problems. The Stern Report also, rightly, argued that we should strive for an expansion of emissions certificate trading globally. However, since 2006 little has happened globally in that area, apart from relatively limited initiatives and pilot schemes in California, China, the Republic of Korea and some other countries and regions. With regard to the G20 countries, more is certainly possible, and the EU countries should also make a serious commitment here for many years to come. The situation with regard to the global emission structure in the year 2000 was such that worldwide, CO_2 emissions from the energy sector represented 24 percent of emissions with industry and transport standing for 14 percent each. As Fig. 4.3 shows, buildings and agriculture also make a significant contribution to CO_2 emissions.

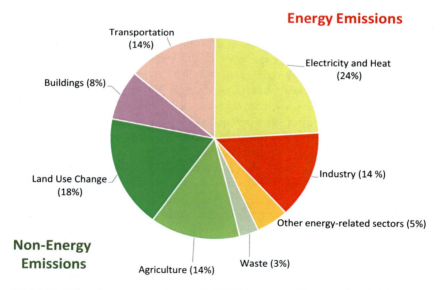

Fig. 4.3 Greenhouse gas emissions in 2000 by source. (Source: Created by Stern Review using data obtained from the World Resources Institute Climate Analysis Indicators Tool (CAIT), online database version 3.0)

REFERENCES

Dachs, B., & Budde, B. (2019). Fallstudie Nachhaltiges Bauen und Lead Markets in Österreich. In Welfens, P. J. J. (Ed.), *EU-Strukturwandel, Leitmärkte und Techno-Globalisierung* [transl. PJJW: A Case Study in Sustainable Building and Lead Markets in Austria. In Welfens, P. J. J. (Ed.), *EU Structural Change, Lead Markets and Technoglobalisation*]. Oldenbourg.

Stern, N. (2006, October). *The Stern Review on the Economics of Climate Change-Commissioned by Her Majesty's Government of the United Kingdom*, London.

CHAPTER 5

Perspectives on the Climate Debate and International Economic Aspects

The Climate Policy Debate and Wider Problem Perspectives

One can approach long-term climate issues in many different ways. One conceivable method is to look back over the previous 200,000 years or so, since—according to the current state of research—Homo Sapiens, that is, the forebearer of the modern human being, walked the earth. Since the industrialization of Europe around 1850, however, prospects have changed significantly. The many innovations in the relatively brief period since have produced sustained economic growth: the agricultural revolution (such as the use of fertilizer, but also of tractors) has enormously increased the productivity of the agricultural sector and led to a labor surplus in the countryside, so that the industry in towns and cities—more precisely, mostly on the outskirts of towns and cities—was able to thrive as a result of an abundant supply of labor. With the help of labor, capital and energy, at any rate, the Industrial Revolution was about making progress; the leading country globally around 1860 was still the UK, with Germany catching up strongly around 1900. Even before that, around 1880, the US had already risen to become the largest economic power, albeit without actively participating in international policy development for a long time. This only changed with the first international Washington Naval Conference and ensuing treaties of 1921/1922, which brought the world

© The Author(s), under exclusive license to Springer Nature Switzerland AG 2022
P. J.J. Welfens, *Global Climate Change Policy*, Sustainable Development Goals Series,
https://doi.org/10.1007/978-3-030-94594-7_5

powers of the UK, France, Japan and the US, among others, around one table and which for the US resulted above all in an important recognition of its position as a power in the Pacific region. The US as a truly global power was conceivable then for the first time—no world power position was possible without great naval fleet power. Of course, US President Woodrow Wilson had already appeared as an influential politician at the post-World War I peace talks in Versailles in 1918, and many elements of the agreed post-war order indeed came from Wilson's plans. It was only the fact that the US Congress refused to ratify the Versailles Treaty or agree to US membership of the newly founded League of Nations which undermined Wilson's position. Post-1945, however, the US indeed became the leading country in promoting and supporting international organizations and also supported European integration over more than six decades. Even more recently under President Obama strong transatlantic cooperation in the fields of climate change and environmental policy was apparent.

In the climate policy debate in Europe, the US, Asia and worldwide, the first question is whether CO_2 emissions from production and consumption will present a long-term climate challenge that is likely to be essentially wide ranging in nature:

- Rising sea levels and the resulting disappearance of certain inhabited islands and coastal regions around the world and, of course, increased flood risks elsewhere; property assets in flood-prone areas will decline, and insurance premiums will rise.
- An increase in extreme weather events associated with global warming; here, there is a threat of production declines and asset losses for affected individuals and regions. In addition, global warming will lead to rising health care costs, so that social security contributions and labor costs will rise to the detriment of jobs and employment.
- An increase in the number of climate refugees, who are likely to move mainly from the Global South, or developing countries, toward Europe, developed Asia and North America. If one considers the temporary political destabilization of Germany in 2015, in the course of the poorly organized opening of the border for civil war refugees from Syria and refugees from other countries, then a conceivable climate migration problem could at least bring about similar political destabilization impulses in host countries.

- Strong structural change required in many countries will account for part of the substantial adjustment costs associated with significant global warming; however, some regions or countries could even benefit from global warming.
- Questions about the national climate protection policies of large CO_2-emitting countries and the international debate about measures in different countries needed to adapt to live reasonably with increased warming (e.g., the increased use of air conditioning equipment in homes and factories) can lead to completely new international conflicts and destabilize old alliances. One can hardly imagine, for example, that the EU countries could continue to have good long-term relations with the US if the administration, as was the case with Trump administration, would demonstratively set the course for a prolonged use of coal-fired power plants—with even more generous emission regulations which largely reversed the previous Obama administration's policies—and if the populist Trump's successors were to make US energy policy even more short-sighted than already discussed within the Trump administration during 2018–2019. It was a clear signal to many when President Trump chose a former coal lobbyist to be his head of the national environmental authority, the Environmental Protection Agency. If the US were to emit relatively high levels of CO_2 unnecessarily, this would be seen by large sections of the public in the EU as a US attack on prosperity and stability in Europe and the world as a whole. Of course, everyone understands that climate protection is a global challenge for all countries.
- From an economic-ecological point of view, one cannot stop at the question of national climate policy, because in open economies there is often also an international CO_2 shifting problem: incentives to reduce CO_2 intensities in many EU countries create at the same time an incentive to outsource a larger share of production abroad—especially to countries where the CO_2 emissions issue is approached rather softly by politicians; in the specialist literature, this issue is dealt with under the heading of carbon leakage (i.e., the CO_2 leakage problem). In their analysis, Peters et al. (2011) have shown that the share of CO_2 emissions from global trade has increased in the longer term from 20 percent in 1990 to 26 percent in 2008; due to increased international trade, the share of developing countries has increased from 0.4 gigatons of CO_2 emissions to 1.6 gigatons over the same

period; there is certainly a carbon leakage problem; however it is manageable. Moreover, even in the case of China—with its large export surplus vis-à-vis the US for many years—it will be possible to assume that about one-third of the country's CO_2 emissions are actually attributable to trading partner countries; some of the emissions in China that can be attributed to the US (via input-output tables for the production of goods which are ultimately exported from China to the US) would indeed have to be regarded as essentially a US problem. This issue is exacerbated by the fact that 90 percent of world trade is transported by ship, with most freighters using emission-intensive heavy fuel oil; it is only since around 2018 that many shipowners have stepped up their efforts to use relatively cleaner marine diesel or LPG in converted ship engines or intentionally designing for such gas usage in newly built freighters.

- If US protectionism affects world trade, this could reduce China's export surpluses over the US and at the same time increase US CO_2 emissions. US protectionism is also likely to reduce global technology transfers including of CO_2 abatement technologies. Protectionism therefore also results in climate-related effects, and because of the reduced global production efficiency, the connection is likely to be negative: protectionism leads to less climate protection.
- Thus, an isolationist climate policy perspective is inappropriate. This is because climate policy is not free of charge, and increased economic pressure in industrialized and emerging economies to increase low-carbon production or to reduce the intensity of CO_2 emissions in production has considerable consequences for structural change—this must be taken into account by economic policymakers: if there is increased demand for low-carbon products, and these products are produced in a skill-intensive manner (i.e., in the corresponding sectors, the proportion of skilled workers in production is high relative to unskilled workers), then the demand for skilled workers in the labor markets increases. This is where governments' education and training policies are called upon to play their part, and immigration policy naturally also plays a role. If there is a significant increase in the immigration of skilled workers in key migration destination countries, it will be relatively uncomplicated in view of the necessary availability of qualified workers to actually initiate more climate protection-oriented economic development from both a political and social perspective.

- The extent to which voters are willing to accept the warnings of global warming, clearly formulated by scientists in the IPCC, could also be shaped by their own interests—for example, it could be investigated whether diesel car owners (who will probably suffer a particular loss of wealth in terms of their assets (i.e., their cars) if local or regional diesel driving bans are imposed) are more skeptical about the thesis of global warming than are, for example, the owners of petrol cars or those who own only bicycles. For a promising climate policy mix, a wise sequence of policies would be essential in such a context. Among other things, it would be important for policymakers to take a consistent and unambiguous approach to cases of fraud concerning diesel engines in the automobile industry first, with a clear focus on consumer protection. If the political system of Western countries loses the confidence of large sections of the electorate, the global political steering capacity of these countries will decline significantly; this confidence is already being weakened by the expansion of the Internet, which is causing a much more fragmented public than before. In addition, there is probably also a larger part of the lower strata of society—often climate skeptical—with a new-found voice in the political debate, which indirectly stimulates the expansion of populist parties which aim to appeal to less educated voters. In democracies, an Internet-driven increase in voter turnout is, of course, welcome even if the relative weight of the lower strata representation among voters increases; certain worries may arise on the part of the ruling elites, but then there is also an increased need for politicians to invest more in education and further training. In aging societies, however, this may often be difficult as political majorities are more likely to be mobilized in support of pension increases rather than an expansion of the training budget for younger cohorts. From a demographic point of view, Germany, Italy, Spain, Portugal and Greece could face significant problems from about 2025 onward with regard to the expected aging of the population, in contrast to France and the UK, for example, with younger populations. It can be assumed that even within the EU, cooperation will become more difficult from about 2025 onward.
- Will global population growth play an aggravating role in terms of climate protection until 2050? The answer of Bretschger (2019), in the context of a demanding growth model with endogenous innovations (i.e., innovation dynamics and economic growth are explained

in the model) is a cautious no: an increase in the global population also means that it will be easier to expand the research sector thanks to the availability of more qualified people in labor markets. It is conceivable that the increase in the global challenge due to a growing population—this means, among other things, more production and therefore also more energy consumption and thus higher CO_2 emissions—will at least be compensated by an increased expansion of research and innovation dynamics. The Bretschger contribution, which is a multi-sector growth model, means more climate challenges can also bring more "climate-beneficial" innovation dynamics if the research sector of the economy grows: the long-term growth rate of per capita consumption depends positively on the rate of innovation growth and is relatively high if the production elasticities (such an elasticity indicates how much production increases in percent, if the input of a factor of production is increased by 1 percent) of labor and capital are high for end products, and that of labor in the research sector are high and the time discount rate is low. A low time discount rate means that households' preference for present income is not very high: that is, households are prepared to forgo a unit of present consumption if this—that is, through saving rather than consuming now—allows a somewhat higher level of consumption to be achieved in the future.

Thus, there are many good arguments in favor of a broader view of the climate problem and sensible modeling responses, and there is no real reason for a general sense of skepticism. However, only limited insights into climate protection and economic policy as a whole should be expected from selective partial analyses.

82 Billion People Since the Beginning: Industrialization Since 1850

Earth, according to astronauts who have described its appearance from outer space to people, is a blue planet. It is estimated to be circa four billion years old and has about as many years ahead of it again, if you trust modern physicists—after another four billion years, at least, the power of the sun will be expended. People, broadly speaking, have been inhabiting the Earth for only around 200,000 of those years. In total, an estimated

82 billion people had called this planet home by about 2000 during this period (Lesch & Zaun, 2008). The Earth's population is expected to continue to rise until about 2050—about 10 billion people could by then inhabit the Earth (Fig. 5.1); by 2100, the population is expected to reach 11 billion people or so.

Every living person needs food, energy, transport and telecommunication or Internet services, a roof over their heads and consumer goods. This already addresses the reasons behind growing energy consumption and rising emissions of CO_2 or similar climate-damaging gases. With an additional two to three billion people, will living together on Earth become more difficult and more conflict-prone? Or will the world's best educated populations solve existing problems and respond to new challenges better than previous generations? Will there be enough technological and climate-friendly green progress?

How much research funding is needed? Is the existing level of public funding for research and development (R&D) sufficient or appropriate? Is there sufficient cross-border R&D cooperation, that is, sufficiently strong cooperation between multinationals in innovation projects and sufficiently strong internationalization of R&D on a personal level? Whereas in the past every IBM subsidiary abroad was essentially a small, localized offshoot of IBM in the US (with its headquarters near New York), following

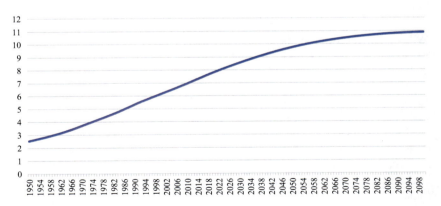

Fig. 5.1 UN world population forecast up to 2100 (medium variant). (Source: Own presentation of UN data; United Nations, DESA/Population Division, World Population Prospects 2019 https://population.un.org/wpp/)

a crisis in the 1990s, IBM built a new "global IBM"—a network of nationally specialized, highly independent knowledge teams. Every IBM subsidiary in the world must then make a "team contribution" to the overall performance of the IBM Group. This makes IBM's overall competence even better, but also more vulnerable, as different IBM subsidiaries in different countries need to work together efficiently and seamlessly to deliver optimal IBM services to often mobile or international customers: clients actually want fewer mainframe computer systems, but more and more digitized, innovative computer-based services. The modern world economy is characterized by an international division of labor in the sense that the production of various goods (and parts thereof) in many different countries, with knowledge-intensive and capital-intensive production, is gaining in importance worldwide.

China became an increasingly important player once it opened to the world economy in 1978, and by 2018 the real gross domestic product values—in comparable purchasing power parities—of the US, the EU28 and China were already roughly the same: about a 17 percent share of global output each. The G20, which represents an influential group of 20 large and powerful countries (plus the EU, which is represented by the president of the European Commission), account for around 80 percent of the world economy as far as real gross domestic product is concerned. Can the G20 or the United Nations, with over 190 member countries, succeed in solving global climate problems?

A notable early high in terms of world population occurred around 1900 when the number of global inhabitants exceeded about 1.5 billion. Since about 1980, many critical reports have emerged in the field of climate research that mankind should prepare for global warming in the twenty-first century. Through their own actions, people in Europe and North America in the nineteenth and twentieth centuries, and since about 1950 also in Japan, the Republic of Korea, India and China, have contributed massively to CO_2 emissions, which is continuously exacerbating the challenge of global warming. The emission of CO_2 and equivalent gases into the atmosphere, such as those produced during the combustion of coal, oil and gas—and also naturally, such as during a volcanic eruption—causes an increase in the mean temperature on Earth, including the temperature of the oceans.

An increased concentration of CO_2 in the atmosphere reduces the reflection of solar heat, radiating onto the surface of the Earth, back into space, instead trapping heat in the atmosphere: this results in a kind of greenhouse effect on Earth which is not without consequences. For glaciers, and ice sheets in the Arctic and Antarctica, prospects for the future are not good, and because meltwater then causes the level of the oceans to rise, the prospects for major port cities and many coastal regions across the world are also apparently quite bad. In many coastal countries, the majority of the population live less than 100 km from the sea. The consequences and risks of rising sea levels can be partially limited by certain construction works and protective dike measures. An increase of the global temperature by more than 2 degrees will, however, be difficult to manage on Earth in the twenty-first century. On the contrary, millions of climate refugees could be expected by the middle or end of the century, and massive conflicts between countries and even regions are conceivable.

It is obvious that protecting the climate as a global phenomenon requires the cooperation of all, in particular the larger, countries, thus it appears threatening when, for example, a populist US president such as Donald Trump positioned the US to take action against numerous countries, including traditional allies, both economically and politically and, on top of that, tried to undermine the EU as an integration club. If one assumes that the Stern Report made a more or less correct forecast (Stern, 2006), that is, that in the long run a global real income decline of 10–15 percent is to be expected if the 2-degree target is not met, then it must be clear that the magnitude of this decline is likely to be threatening and possibly existential, even if the decline in income is spread over a longer period of time than, for example, the income declines in the US and Western Europe in the early 1930s during the Great Depression.

How can we contribute to climate stabilization? Obviously, emissions of CO_2 and gases with similar effects should be significantly reduced; flanking measures are also necessary for countries or regions of the world negatively affected by climate change. The problem, however, is that according to scientific studies at least, the period available to adapt is quite limited: less than about two to three decades remain in order to achieve an effective decarbonization of the global economy. This will simply not be possible without urgent targeted measures and intelligent cooperation at an international level.

There will also be some regions which could be "winners" of global warming—but their numbers will be limited. What physicists, chemists, geologists, marine researchers and meteorologists have so far contributed to climate research is, in simple terms and on the basis of the Stern Review, essentially the following:

- In the twenty-first century, there is a very serious danger that global warming will exceed the critical 2-degree mark—measured as an increase in temperatures compared with 1850. An increase of about 3 degrees would probably result in an accelerated and irreversible process of destabilization for the global climate and thus economic development; at any rate, there would be serious new risks to life globally and regionally. A nationally, regionally, or even globally destabilizing international mass migration could result on the basis of climate crises. The result would be completely new serious international conflicts.
- There is only one global climate and that is a long-term phenomenon. It is possible, but not entirely easy, to counter the climate change challenge or the greenhouse gas effect through political intervention: large emitting countries would have to lead the way through climate-friendly innovations and corresponding investments; a minimum number of countries from the Global North and South as well as East and West would have to work together in new ways. This will likely be difficult to achieve, as was the case with the US following the election of Donald Trump in November 2016 and with Brazil since the election of populist President Jair Bolsonaro. Populists are nationalists, protectionists and egoists—the opposite of what is required of world leaders if we are to see increased international cooperation.
- Some leading climate protection countries, such as Sweden and Switzerland, have already achieved demonstrable reductions in CO_2 emissions within two decades as a first step, as has the EU in the area of tradable CO_2 emission certificates—but the EU system covers less than half of the economy. Some countries have set themselves ambitious targets for 2020—but missed them. Policymakers now want to refocus on 2030 but are unlikely to achieve these goals either without new approaches. What does this mean for younger generations?
- Some important countries with regard to the climate, such as China and Russia, are still relatively uninvolved in global efforts to reduce emissions. Of course, these countries can also contribute to climate stabilization measures through technical progress, economic structural change and promoting changes in the behavior of their citizens. Whether and how this can be achieved, however, is unclear. Under President Trump, US relations with both aforementioned countries deteriorated, and the US withdrew completely from the Paris Climate

Agreement—rescinding its prior signing by President Obama (although California, as a federal state, and some other cities and regions within the US committed to meeting their targets).

It should also be kept in mind, as previously mentioned that around 1900 the global population was about 1.5 billion. By 2050, the world population is expected to reach a historic peak of around ten billion, after which, according to UN forecasts, it will rise at a much slower pace. At first glance, you can do very little with such large numbers. However, it is clear that the Earth has had to cope with considerable population growth since the Industrial Age had flourished, that is, since around 1850. Two hundred years of burning fossil fuels in enormous quantities will not simply pass without leaving significant traces in the atmosphere by 2050. Of course, there have also been earlier phases with considerable increases in the CO_2 concentration in the Earth's atmosphere but not caused by human activities.

European Union countries have pledged to cut CO_2 emissions by 2030 by 40 percent compared to 1990 levels. By 2020, the EU should already have reduced CO_2 emissions by 20 percent, renewable energy should account for at least 20 percent of the energy mix by 2020 and energy efficiency should have increased by 20 percent. What became of the 20:20:20 target of the EU? Has it been achieved? If the objective has not been achieved, where lies the problem, and what is the situation in other large economies such as the US, China and Russia? As far as Germany's climate targets for 2020 are concerned, namely, to reduce CO_2 emissions by 40 percent compared with 1990 levels, the failure to meet the target is very clear. For this reason alone, pressure is building up regarding climate policy on the one hand and economic policy in general on the other. Successive German governments had set relatively ambitious targets as the reference year of 1990 was just the first year in which the former socialist German Democratic Republic, also known as East Germany, a country with little energy efficiency, was counted in the reunified Federal Republic of Germany's statistics. At the same time, the hope in Berlin was that the high level of technological progress and innovation in Germany would make it relatively easy to reach the target.

In addition, targets concerning emissions improvements had been agreed with the other EU countries, with targets for the trade in emissions certificates to cover circa 45 percent of CO_2 emissions. In principle, the achievement of these targets can be obtained via the administrative decommissioning of certificates or the state purchase of "surplus" emission certificates, provided that EU countries agree on when and to what extent the number of emission certificates available to companies are to be reduced. In the first round of emission certificates issuance, the EU and member countries were relatively generous toward industrial companies, as they did not want to impair the international competitiveness of European companies through unduly low numbers of trading emission certificates or high certificate prices. The primary focus here was therefore on the production and employment interests of EU countries which were initially to the forefront of economic policy.

Certificate trading provides efficient emission reduction incentives for companies with CO_2-intensive production processes. Millions of companies have a special knowledge of how high the (marginal) avoidance costs of CO_2 emissions are for their own production processes. The pricing of pollution rights (i.e., CO_2 emissions) triggers an adjustment process millions of times over—mobilizing the relevant knowledge of companies. Therefore, companies can react by undertaking suitable technological modernization measures and implementing innovations in the direction of reducing CO_2 emission or purchasing additional emission certificates from other companies in the EU. This brings about a cost-efficient reduction of emissions, but possible issues are that the CO_2 certificate price is very low—which means insufficient incentives for technical progress. Or, the relative certificate price (the certificate price divided by the macroeconomic price index, i.e., the national product deflator; see Figs. 5.2 and 5.3) fluctuates with such volatility that companies have no reasonable orientation for their innovation and investment policy going forward.

As the graphs show, the price of emission certificates in the EU has fallen sharply from an initial level of approximately €20 per ton, primarily due to the Transatlantic Banking Crisis, which caused the price of certificates to fall for several reasons, in particular as overall production in many EU countries, including the corporate demand for certificates, fell significantly after 2008. Emission certificates have certainly also provided incentives for innovation and certain investment incentives, such as the expansion and diffusion of low-carbon technologies.

In the UK, a minimum price for CO certificates has been introduced for energy producers—this gives companies a certain stability in emissions planning. In 2019, it was expected that if UK companies left the EU, British companies would take with them a surplus of allowances which—without a negotiated EU-UK continued integration settlement—would

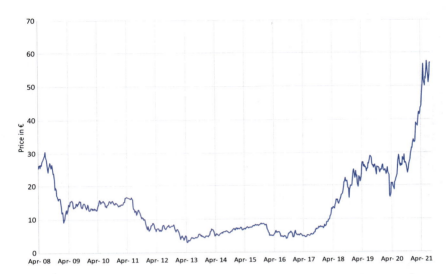

Fig. 5.2 Nominal CO_2 certificate price in the EU ETS from April 2008 to April 2021, weekly data points, price in €. (Source: Own presentation of data from Sandbag Smarter Climate Policy, https://sandbag.be/index.php/carbon-price-viewer/ (last accessed 01.06.21))

no longer be available for trading on the EU emissions allowance market in the future. Therefore, an increase in certificate prices in the Brexit context, at least a temporary increase, is to be expected in the EU.

In principle, a global trade in emission certificates is desirable, which would lead to a globally uniform price. But for the time being, this is far from being the case. However, some positive signs are there, and there is, for example, partial certificate trading across North America, where California trades certificates with some federal states in Canada. Basically, this example shows that certificate trading can have a direct and an indirect influence on the current account position of countries. If Canadian companies have a net import of certificates from California—that is, buying US pollution rights for production in the Canada—this initially means that Canada's bilateral trade position or current account balance will deteriorate and that of the US will improve.

If the US and Canada could establish a common emissions trading area incorporating both countries completely, this would lead to an improvement in the US current account balance and, with sound US economic

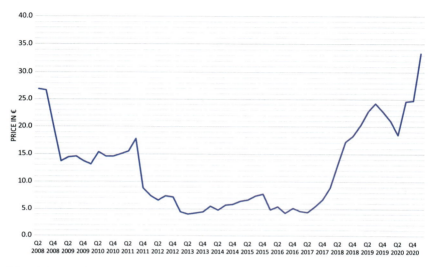

Fig. 5.3 Real CO_2 certificate price in the EU ETS from Q2 2008 to Q1 2021; quarterly data points, price in €. (Source: Own calculations and presentation; data from Sandbag Smarter Climate Policy, https://sandbag.be/index.php/carbon-price-viewer/ (last accessed 01.06.21) and Eurostat; relative price—nominal certificate price divided by national product deflator)

policy, a sharp decline in global CO_2 emissions. After all, the US was the second largest CO_2 emitter in the world after China in 2018. Of course, China could also be included in emissions trading or a common emissions trading area could be established between the US, Canada, the EU, China and Japan, which would require corresponding international cooperation. In fact, all of the G20 countries, which account for about 80 percent of world income, could agree on such an emissions certificate trade in the longer term.

Not all of the G20 countries currently have emissions trading. China has started a national emissions trading scheme in 2021, after having initially implemented a number of regional emissions trading pilot schemes for several years. Whether a G20 certificate trading system is realized—which of course could then be joined by other countries—depends on whether the will to establish such a trading system exists in the G20 countries, in practice probably also on the fact that, at least initially, the international price differences are not too large. A G20 trading system would of course ultimately lead to a uniform price, and accordingly, in countries with high certificate prices, there will be a strong import of certificates which tends to favor the production and export of emission-intensive goods—assuming that the prices of emission certificates will fall for many countries when a global trading system is established; for some other countries, there will of course be (relative) certificate price increases compared to the initial situation. This will lead to increased incentives to reduce CO_2 emissions through innovation and structural change, which in turn will provide an impetus to reduce exports of emission-intensive goods—the overall trade effect is unclear. The global economy in 2020 is probably still at least a decade away from global emissions trading, but it would certainly be sensible to set course in this direction in terms of economic policy in North America, Europe, Asia, Australia, Africa and Latin America.

One important issue in the EU when it comes to reducing CO_2 emissions is the sectors that are not included in emissions trading: building management (housing use), transport, agriculture, air transport (outside the EU), shipping, which raises some complicated questions—should such sectors be subjected to a CO_2 tax by the state, or should such sectors be included in a new and expanded national or EU-wide system of CO_2 certificate trade? Of course, each individual can also trade emissions certificates herself or himself. I compensated for the emissions of a flight to Washington, DC, and the return flight from the US CO_2-wise by buying a certificate online from the company Atmosfair, whereby one could only buy the CO_2 emission for the first leg of the trip from Frankfurt-Washington, DC; with a view to the actual route, which was Frankfurt-Washington, DC, and return from New York-Frankfurt, I bought a certificate that, according to Atmosfair, compensated for about 95 percent of "my" emissions for the (so-called open-jaw) flight; an open-jaw trip cannot be compensated for exactly as yet via Atmosfair. Out of interest, I sought to have the cost of this CO_2 neutrality certificate reimbursed via the budget of my chair—unsuccessfully. At many (presumably all) universities in Germany, the university administrations do not accept such emissions-related expenses as being valid business travel expenses; this is, of course, a major policy contradiction. This means that national and international policymakers want actually climate protection policy, but if civil servants and employees within the state system want to take emissions resulting from work-related air travel seriously, such costs will not be recognized as a valid expense. It is an unsustainable contradiction.

Are the people or countries of the world well prepared to counter global warming? On the one hand one could say yes, as there are more well-educated people on earth than ever before. On the other hand, one could also say no, as there are around 200 countries and jurisdictions across the globe, and the tendency for a large number of them to work together reliably on issues like international climate protection is relatively limited. The significant number of countries required for a meaningful response means that it is difficult to adequately provide the international collective good of climate protection quickly enough to be effective or to organize sustainable global cooperation. It was laborious enough for the United Nations to organize the world climate conferences and actually reach an agreement of all countries in 2015—and then the US subsequently withdrew from the global climate protection agreement reached in Paris under President Trump. This not only displeased France and the Europeans more broadly, but also many people in all regions of the world. Former President Trump tried to pursue his goals by reducing nature conservation in the US, distancing the US from its international climate protection obligations and increasing US oil and gas exports in order to, among other things, reduce the trade deficit. However, this all comes at a high price for the US and the entire world economy, as global warming will continue to rise significantly and extreme weather phenomena and flooding will become more commonplace. This will cost human lives, reduce global real income and increase the global cost of climate change due to rising losses in the insurance industry.

What can be done in principle to limit global warming in a sensible way? CO_2 emissions should be sufficiently decreased in the production of goods and with regard to consumption, with some sectors levying taxes on CO_2 emissions (or on the emissions of CO_2 equivalents), or there should be regional or global emissions trading—with the trading of emissions certificates in the EU, companies must either possess sufficient emissions certificates in the industrial and energy sectors to cover emissions resulting from their own production targets or they must purchase additional CO_2 emissions certificates from other companies with surplus emitting rights.

Many young people in Europe and around the world are concerned about global warming and the economic and climate policies of both industrialized and increasingly of emerging countries, including China. The focus is on the next 100 years or so, that is, the twenty-first century.

If one follows the arguments of Greta Thunberg and other climate activists, then there is good reason to engage in climate-related panic. On 1 May 2019, the British House of Commons declared a climate crisis situation, giving the parliament a welcome but brief distraction from the eternal hot topic of Brexit. Only a few weeks later, Donald Trump was welcomed on a state visit to the UK—the leader of the free world who had denied that global warming was a man-made problem. The country with the largest population in the world, that is, the country potentially most affected by climate change, will also be the largest emitter of greenhouse gases in 2018, namely China. After all, China has promised to make the new "Silk Road", or the "One Belt One Road" initiative, climate friendly. The new transport links between China and Europe, by sea and by land, are not intended to further increase global warming.

However, China itself will still emit more and more greenhouse gases, that is, CO_2 emissions, for at least the next decade. The climate problem, therefore, is not going to solve itself, especially as other countries are also recording rising CO_2 emissions; on the other hand, one also has to recognize that there are indeed some countries that have been recording falling CO_2 emissions for years. For global warming it does not matter from which countries the CO_2 emissions come; every ton of additional CO_2 in the atmosphere contributes to global warming. According to international experts, however, this should be stopped at all costs: according to the 2-degree target, there should be an increase of no more than 2 degrees Celsius in the mean temperature of the Earth compared with pre-industrialization levels; better still, warming should be capped at 1.5 degrees if possible. Only then would there be a chance to avoid a critical rise of the oceans and drastic ecological and economic problems.

Perspectives on the challenge of global warming are very different: in its demands, the Fridays for Future movement follows Germany's Federal Environment Agency, which argues that a price of circa €180 per ton of CO_2 is required in order to reduce CO_2 emissions by more than half by 2030 and to net zero by 2050; Britain's Energy Transitions Commission (ETC), on the other hand, believes that only small price increases for energy-intensive goods are necessary to achieve the 2 degree target (Häring, 2019)—Clive Spash and Tone Smith in a special issue for the journal *Real-World Economics Review* titled "Economics and the Ecosystem" (Spash & Smith, 2019) are skeptical that the major changes in the economic system necessary for climate stabilization could be adequately recorded with the usual marginal analyses, with Herman Daly also expressing skepticism in the same special issue (Daly, 2019), as global energy and resource consumption continues to rise. CO_2 emissions have been falling for many years in Switzerland and Sweden: CO_2 emissions have been reduced by way of a CO_2 price in Switzerland through an additional tax of around €80 per ton; if CO_2 emissions do not continue to fall according to a government-specified reference path, the tax rate will automatically increase up to an upper cap.

Economic Catching-up Processes and the China Shock

In the 1970s, Western market economies and Japan were hit by fourfold increases in crude oil prices in 1974 and again in 1979/1980: These politically induced OPEC price shocks led to considerable instability in many OECD countries and also increased unemployment rates and resulted in rising inflation rates. The oil price shocks, however, also acted as behavioral incentives: consumers and producers placed much more emphasis than they had before the crises on energy-efficient products and production processes. By 2015, the energy intensity of production in the EU was only about half as high as in 1980. Relative price changes triggered adjustment processes among consumers and suppliers alike, many energy-saving innovations were developed on the part of producers of goods and oil producers were able to develop new oil fields—including those in coastal waters and in deeper waters of the world's oceans. Are we running out of oil—or coal and gas—soon? That's not something one can say with any certainty.

If one has followed, for example, the BP World Energy Report over many years and indeed decades, then the ratio of world reserves—usable at the prevailing world market price—to world demand has indeed increased for decades: the order of magnitude of the ratio is about 40 for oil, about 60 for gas and about 200 for coal; the current global reserves would still be sufficient to meet demand at the current global level of consumption for many, many years to come. It is also gratifying to know that this global inventory ratio is likely to rise further, above 40, as oil and gas prices continue to rise. However, it is inadvisable to continue to use oil and coal reserves in the longer term—certainly not with the current technologies. Global CO_2 emissions would soon be so high that high points critical for the climate—as identified by climate scientists—would soon be surpassed. The resultant global warming would result in high global income and wealth losses, while the destabilization of the world economy and political sphere in many regions of the world could have further (negative) consequences.

Until about 1978, the global economy for the most part looked economically stable in a long-term perspective (i.e., over decades)—with a poor and populous China in Asia. Since that year, China has opened itself to the world economy and introduced a market economy with many state-owned enterprises: within 40 years, the country has risen to become the largest economy in terms of national output or real gross domestic product in terms of purchasing power parity. China at the beginning of 2019 was as large as the EU28 or the US; and the number of people in poverty in China has fallen from about 900 million in 1978 to less than 80 million in 2018, and in less than a decade, poverty in China is likely to have largely disappeared. However, China's per capita income in 2018 was still just under a third of that of the US or Western Europe. It can therefore be expected that China will continue to catch up economically with the US and Western Europe until around 2050; ecological progress can also be expected—it remains to be seen, however, whether it will be sufficient to make a strong contribution to sustainability progress. The fact that China's share of world production and exports rose sharply between 1978 and 2018 is acting as an economic adjustment shock to the West and other parts of Asia. At the same time, China's markets are large and growing, making China the largest sales market for many top companies from Europe and the US since around 2015. Thus, China is now an economic powerhouse driving the world economy.

Near Shanghai there is a new model city with a population of about 100,000, namely Lingang New City, which is CO_2-neutral. There is no lack of large projects in China, for example, in the field of e-bus mobility, where developments relevant to climate protection have been initiated at least regionally. Europe would be well advised to cooperate with China on such projects.

As Fig. 5.4 shows, China made enormous progress in the field of renewable energies in 2006–2011 compared to the previous decade—improvements in solar energy were particularly impressive.

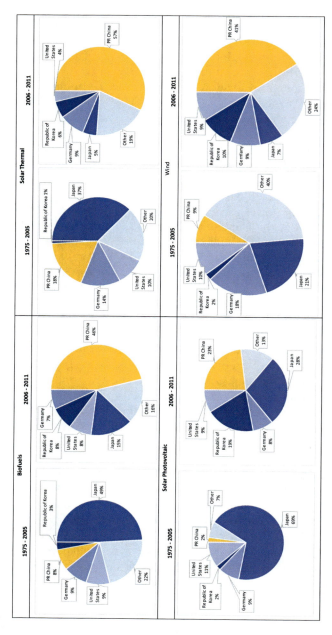

Fig. 5.4 China's patent dynamics in renewable energies: shares of patents by technology based on Office of First Filing. (Source: Own representation based on Figs. 7, 11, 14 and 17 in Helm, S.; Tannock, Q.; I. Iliev, I. (2014), Renewable Energy Technology: Evolution and Policy Implications—Evidence from Patent Literature, Global Challenges Report, WIPO: Geneva https://www.wipo.int/edocs/pubdocs/en/wipo_pub_gc_3.pdf)

The Fridays for Future Impact and International Climate Protection Perspectives

An overwhelming majority of natural scientists from all over the world—that is, those who deal with climate issues—have come to the consensus that the climatic global warming effect observed since 1900 is essentially man-made and ultimately a side-effect of industrialization, and thus also of the use of fossil fuels. The burning of huge quantities of coal, oil and gas has released enormous amounts of CO_2 into the atmosphere since 1850, with 1.5 billion people contributing to this effect around 1900; but with slightly better technologies, it was circa 7 billion people in 2018.

In 2018, Greta Thunberg's own protests before the Swedish Parliament—directed against what she saw as an inadequate climate policy—provided a signal and an impetus to millions of young people across Europe and in other regions of the world. Spread through traditional media channels and, in particular, via the Internet, protests by schoolchildren during school hours on Fridays became an international phenomenon—in Germany and in other EU countries, as well as in other countries—which, in turn, were well received and reinforced by the media. In 2019, the Fridays for Future movement increased its campaign capability in Germany by holding a congress in Dortmund. The movement claims that it has the support of thousands of scientists. The website says (https://fridaysforfuture.de/; original German text translated by the author):

> Why build on a future that will soon no longer exist? Our answer to this question is the climate strike: We are striking for an effective policy that does justice to the scale of the climate crisis. We have ten years to achieve our goals. Let's go!

> In the name of science: Over 27,000 scientists in German-speaking countries alone stand behind us and support our demands. We demand nothing more from politics than the consideration of scientific facts.

Thunberg is indeed not only a likeable teenager, but occasionally also a great facilitator. The fact that she initially protested against Sweden's climate policy seems a little strange nevertheless. Sweden is one of the most successful countries in the world in the field of climate protection. Thanks to the interaction of a CO_2 certificate policy and a CO_2 tax (since 1991), plus some other measures, Sweden achieved an impressive 26 percent reduction in CO_2 emissions between 1991 and 2016 (at the same time, real gross domestic product rose over the same period by 75 percent). This is one of the strongest reductions of emissions in the EU in this period, comparable with the UK. The Green Party's share of the Swedish vote in the 2019 European Parliament elections showed hardly any effect. On the contrary, in Germany and some other EU countries, the increase in Green votes was considerable. All in all, the Greens were the big winners, alongside the liberals, in the European elections in 2019. One can assume that persistent extreme weather events in EU countries and other parts of the world will further increase the climate concerns of many people in the long term, and environmental and climate policy should therefore be strengthened in the policies of democratic countries in Europe.

Quite a few politicians took a rather paternalistic and even patronizing approach toward the Fridays for Future protest movement, for example, when the leader of the classically liberal Free Democratic Party in Germany, Christian Lindner, said in spring 2019 that climate policy was a matter for experts. This is an elitist and dismissive view that also implies little willingness to engage in public policy dialogue with young people.

Greta Thunberg's broad self-empowerment can however also be seen as somewhat problematic. On 12 June, she tweeted a call for a general strike to support the student protests planned for September 2019. An exaggerated tendency can be seen in some of Thunberg's protest activities, and presumably there are significant gaps in the knowledge of many pupils on the subject of climate protection—although this is often a difficult accusation to level, since in Germany, for example, the federal government has provided hardly any information on a nationwide basis on the subject of climate protection since 2005; only a few federal states have taken it upon themselves to incorporate the topic of climate protection into their school curricula. Greta Thunberg's appeals to managers and politicians at the Davos summit in 2019—namely that she is panicking over the climate and that she wants them to feel her panic as well—can be taken seriously; but this could also be dangerous. Do people want their doctor or train driver or manager to be motivated by panic? Panicking people usually do not make the most sensible decisions.

In view of the visible progress made in climate protection in some industrialized and emerging countries, there is also little call for panic. However, there is cause for concern, as overall climate protection progress globally is too slow to achieve the 2-degree target set by scientists for the period 2030–2050. Not to mention meeting the 1.5-degree target.

Since the problem of global warming is essentially caused by the emission of CO_2 (and other greenhouse gases), the basic starting points for solving the problem need to be considered:

- Reducing CO_2 emissions; economic incentives are necessary here.
- CO_2 absorption through forests or afforestation, so that more CO_2 can be stored naturally.
- Finally, one can increase the reflection of the sun's rays on earth—that is, the "albedo effect", black surfaces have a zero reflection effect, while white surfaces have a reflection effect of close to 100 percent. The naturally occurring global albedo effect is around 30 percent. One can try to counteract global warming by increasing the number of white surfaces on earth, for example, by choosing white for the roofs of houses, cars, etc., or by providing light-colored road surfaces. Global warming can be also neutralized by switching from 30 to 34 W/m^2 of solar reflection on earth. According to Lenton and Vaughan (2009), the use of an improved albedo effect on 2.3 percent of the earth's land surface produces a global cooling effect of about -0.2 W/m^2; this would be a cooling effect equivalent to 5 percent of the total cooling requirement—if CO_2 emissions themselves were not reduced. The Royal Society (2009, p. 25) claimed that the annual cost of such a "whitening" of one percent of the earth's surface (about 10^{12} square meters) would be about $300 billion dollars per year. This view is wrong, as new buildings such as houses would not incur any additional costs if there were a regulation stipulating a bright or white roof. Roofs in existing properties must be replaced or repainted every 40 years or so anyway. One can assume at most additional cleaning costs for brighter roofs. However, their use makes little sense in terms of climate policy at northern latitudes. The reflection intensity of the atmosphere can also be increased through geoengineering, such as first using a sulfate injection in the stratosphere and second by means of a "salt spray" in the clouds above the sea, whereby the two methods lead to changes in the mean surface temperature, extreme temperatures as well as precipitation. Both methods actually lead to improved global albedo effects, but then there could regional climate problems, which bring additional social and political conflicts (Aswathy et al., 2015). Figure 5.5 shows the possible starting points for climate protection.

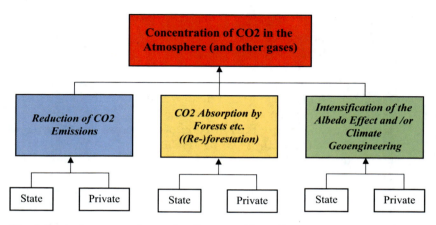

Fig. 5.5 Action approaches to the climate problem. (Source: Own representation)

INTERNATIONAL FREE-RIDER PROBLEMS

If you want to record the demand curve for particular beverages, this is not really a problem in any city, region or country. You need to conduct a survey in the local market and try to find out by way of questionnaires what the demand would be at different prices. If suppliers or beverage producers have such information at their disposal, they will provide a reasonable offer. The result on the market is an equilibrium price. Those who are willing to pay at least the price offered by suppliers, or more, they will be supplied with the drink.

In the case of public goods, collective goods such as the light output of a lighthouse at the entrance to a port with a dangerous rock formation directly in the approach area, a survey of ship captains is of little help. Hardly anyone will give her or his true demand for lighthouse light; everyone may hope that others will already pay. Once the lighthouse is there, anyone looking for the safe approach to the port can benefit from the light. Think of flood protection in a place on the coast where there have been frequent floods recently—is there a need to raise the flood wall? If a marketing institute distributes questionnaires to find out how strong the demand for increased flood protection is, one will distribute a sheet with the question: are you interested in increased flood protection? Answers are (A) Yes—the costs per citizen are about €1000, payable in 10 annual installments (via increased local taxes/fees); (B) No. It could be that all citizens would like more flood protection and would also be willing to pay more than €100 per year. But all the completed questionnaires collected during the survey show crosses at (B). Here, of course, strategic demand behavior is the problem. As this is to be expected, the supply of local or national public goods will be decided politically in the respective local legislative bodies and national parliaments. In terms of climate protection, the problem of recording demand is in fact a global challenge because there is only one climate for all countries and all people of the world together. Is there a world parliament? First of all, the answer to the latter question is still no.

Who are the major CO_2 emitters, the causers of the greenhouse effect? How could the main emitters—or even all of them—be persuaded to make their fair contribution to climate stabilization? Here, there is the problem of national climate policy and international climate policy.

Among the important starting points for climate policy are particular policy instruments (see also Fig. 5.6):

- CO_2 certificate trading: as a rule—and in any case within the EU—this takes place across borders and provides incentives for a cost-minimizing reduction of CO_2. The companies that have high CO_2 reduction costs buy certificates (i.e., emission rights for CO_2) from companies with relatively low CO_2 avoidance costs. EU member states have favored sectors with strong international competition in the first round of certificates trading by allocating a certain share of emission certificates to them largely free of charge. In the longer term, however, this is not a sensible strategy in the EU, China, North America and other regions of the world. It is important that as many trading sectors as possible are included in a regional, or better still global, certificate trade. However, if CO_2 prices are high in one country and low in another, production is shifted to countries with low CO_2 prices (or possibly zero prices), which leads to increased global emissions and is known as the carbon leakage problem.
- A CO_2 tax can be introduced in areas not covered by certificate trading, so that meaningful incentives for the internalization of negative external effects can also be created there. However, how this can be done in a meaningful way, especially in the important areas of transport and housing is apparently unclear to policymakers thus far. Illusory objectives, for example, in German transport policy—first announcing a plan for two million electric cars on the road by 2020,

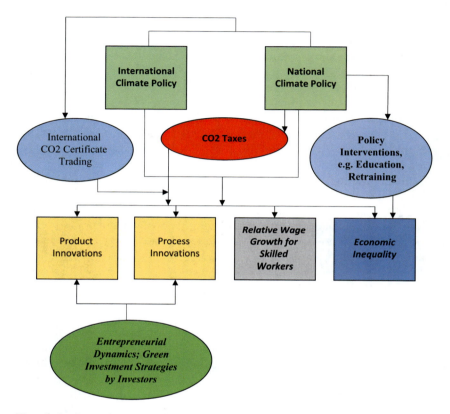

Fig. 5.6 Strategic approaches to modern integrated climate policy. (Source: Own representation)

then a plan for one million such cars by that year and ultimately reaching barely 100,000 cars in reality—contribute to political frustration, populism and climate protests.

- CO_2 tax revenues provide incentives for innovation, in particular for new, low-emission products and production processes. Part of the tax revenue can also be channeled into increased green innovation promotion, that is, innovation projects that promote climate protection. Since climate protection is a global challenge, one could also consider organizing cross-border funding for certain projects. More green innovations can also be achieved through more entrepreneur-

ial dynamism, especially if the focus is on environmentally and climate-friendly start-ups or investment strategies.
- Since the increase in prices for climate-friendly products—usually produced in a skill-intensive manner, using a relatively large number of skilled workers—leads to increased demand for skilled workers in industrialized countries, economic inequality in these countries is rising: the unskilled workers will face a worsening relative income position over time; it is also conceivable that their income may even temporarily fall in real terms.
- If the unskilled in society are to be included in climate policy, appropriate political decisions must be taken, such as increased initiatives for further training as a starting point for limiting economic inequality. Many EU countries—and even more so the US—are far removed from leaders in terms of government spending on continuing education such as of 0.5 percent of GDP in Denmark.

If one promotes green innovations, this results in a double internalization: positive external effects in innovation services are internalized or, thanks to public research funding, more innovations are created than usual. As the innovation projects reduce emissions—especially CO_2 emissions—the application of green product and process innovations leads to an internalization of negative external, climate-damaging, effects. All industrialized and emerging countries could probably do more in this area. In Germany, the federal government and the states are facing increasing demand in terms of research funding, and the same applies in Austria and Switzerland with regard to the interplay between national and regional innovation funding. Ultimately, all EU and G20 countries are called upon to act.

References

Aswathy, V. N., Boucher, O., Quaas, M., Neimeier, U., Muri, H., Mülmenstädt, J., & Quaas, J. (2015). Climate Extremes in Multi-model Simulations of Stratospheric Aerosol and Marine Cloud Brightening Climate Engineering. *Atmospheric Chemistry and Physics, 15*, 9593–9610. https://doi.org/10.5194/acp-15-9593-2015

Bretschger, L. (2019). *Malthus in the Light of Climate Change* (CER-ETH – Center of Economic Research at ETH Zurich Working Paper 19/320).

Daly, H. (2019, March 19). Growthism: Its Ecological, Economic and Ethical Limits. *Real-World Economic Review* (87), 9–22. http://www.paecon.net/PAEReview/issue87/Daly87.pdf

Häring, N. (2019, April 28). Experten-Kommission halt Klimarettung aus der Portokasse für möglich [transl. PJJW: Expert Commission Considers Climate Rescue from Petty Cash Possible], *Handelsblatt Online Edition*. Retrieved 17 July, 2019, from https://www.handelsblatt.com/politik/deutschland/umweltpolitik-experten-kommission-haelt-klimarettung-aus-der-portokasse-fuer-moeglich/24260878.html?ticket=ST-10234801-U7otBXQIoXKfZMeEqHWN-ap3

Lenton, T. M., & Vaughan, N. E. (2009). The Radiative Forcing Potential of Different Climate Geoengineering Options. *Atmospheric Chemistry and Physics Discussions, 9*, 2559–2608.

Lesch, H., & Zaun, H. (2008). *Die kürzeste Geschichte allen Lebens* [transl. PJJW: The Shortest History of Life]. Piper: Munich.

Peters, G. P., Minx, J. C., Weber, C. L., & Edenhofer, O. (2011). Growth in Emission Transfers Via International Trade from 1990 to 2008. *Proceedings of the National Academy of the Sciences of the United States of America, 108*(21), 8903–8908. https://doi.org/10.1073/pnas.1006388108

Royal Society. (2009, September). *Geoengineering the Climate – Science, Governance and Uncertainty*, The Royal Society, RS Policy Document 10/09.

Spash, C.L., & Smith, T. (2019, March 19). Of Ecosystems and Economies: Re-Connecting Economics with Reality. *Real-World Economics Review* (87), 212–229. http://www.paecon.net/PAEReview/issue87/SpashSmith87.pdf

Stern, N. (2006, October). *The Stern Review on the Economics of Climate Change*, Commissioned by Her Majesty's Government of the United Kingdom.

CHAPTER 6

The Wrong Climate Debate?

The public debate on global warming and climate policy can at times be contentious and emotional. Some groups argue about certain factual and scientific issues in particular. Certain others stress the point that we should be focused on finding the best way forward in climate policy, and others still point to the misinformation in digital media or the contradictions of inadequate climate policy in, for example, Germany and France, where the governments of both countries would not have reached their respective climate targets for 2020 in normal circumstances. These are admittedly all important factors to consider, but one could argue that the entire climate debate thus so far has been misdirected as little in the way of consideration, and discussion has addressed the crucial aspect that climate protection policy requires accelerated structural change in Europe, Asia, North America and other regions of the world—but that at the same time, economic inequality is likely to increase in almost all countries. This increasing inequality is a major political risk in many countries and should help to increase and amplify populist voices. On the other hand, this inequality and populist politics could push climate protection policy to the back of the political agenda in many countries thus making the global cooperation policy that is actually necessary much more difficult to achieve.

Therefore, certain questions of inequality should be included in the theoretical and practical political debate on the response to climate change—for first time, this has been done in the present study. Otherwise one cannot really be successful in protecting the climate. Since there is only one global climate as an international collective good, questions of international cooperation are also essential. Due to the populist Trump administration in the US, which withdrew the country from the UN Paris Climate Agreement of 2015, there is a large gap. Resistance to the acceptance of key analytical findings in the field of climate research—one cannot attach any real importance to a fringe opposition minority among the scientific community which will always exist—may also be considerable in many industrialized countries among millions of people, for example, among the owners of diesel cars, who in Germany are no longer allowed to drive their vehicles into certain cities if they are equipped with "older" engine technology (where "older" can means cars which are only three years old). No diesel owner likes to hear the news that he is now sitting in the "wrong" type of car and would have to spend a lot of money to buy a new car.

For some, there is an obvious internal psychological solution to the conflict, which simply means resigning oneself to accepting the idea that man-made climate change may not exist after all, and if the president of the US has doubts, then I can also have doubts. However, first Donald Trump is not a scientist, but a trained contractor—he knows a lot about concrete mixes, real estate projects and using Twitter, but he does not have any expertise in climate matters. His entire administration is clearly understaffed in many economic and ecological areas, and his cynicism is occasionally a signal in itself: for example, by appointing a coal lobbyist to head the US' Environmental Protection Agency. This is simply audacious, and for the US also a clear misstep as biased leaders ("political top managers") with no competence in the relevant field of work have never done anything sensible in terms of exercising authority to influence policy in the world of politics or within a company. We are all surely familiar from occasional experiences in one's own environment the annoyance that comes with dealing with incompetent, unqualified professionals, and one knows it from amusing films or plays, at which the audience can only laugh at a combination of important tasks and incompetence which leads to amusing entanglements and a worsening situation. In real life however, promoting unqualified people into positions of significant power are not amusing; it naturally contradicts the principle of meritocracy and also the principle of administrative competence, which economically leading states generally observe.

In order to solve the climate problem, a sensible scientific analysis and sufficient, reliable political cooperation are called for. The climate challenge can initially be traced back to global warming—but also to some other indicators; measurement results over decades and indeed centuries, since about 1850, leave little doubt about the overall trend: the problem is there, and it is getting more serious with every passing decade. The climate issue can be counteracted, apart from politically organized interventions in economic and consumption patterns, via the innovation dynamics which exist in industrialized and emerging countries; some of this is entirely coincidental on the one hand, while on the other hand some of these dynamics are intentional in the area of "green innovation dynamics", namely innovations which are designed from the outset to be climate protection-promoting. If you think of new methods of concrete production or steel production that save energy, lower costs and cause fewer emissions, then you have both the cost-cutting aspects that many other producers will try to emulate but also of course the second side of the coin is a reduction of CO_2 emissions. In the consumer sector, individuals can also contribute to climate protection through their behavior: those who, for example, choose to eat less beef a week than in the past will reduce demand for beef and thus reduce the number of cows and cattle herds. This means lower resource requirements and lower methane emissions caused by the cow's digestive processes, which are particularly harmful to the climate.

The farmers concerned will then keep fewer cattle and probably invest more in poultry or pig farming. Since there are over seven billion people in the world, almost everyone can make some seemingly small personal adjustment for climate protection. Billions or millions of individual contributions then often stand for a large global effect. However, what will be a major economic and political challenge in climate protection is the resulting increase in income inequality. Climate protection does not directly cause much in the way of inequality *between* countries, that is, an increase in per capita income disparities between the North and South of the global economy; however with income inequality increasing *within* almost all developed and emerging countries, in the form of an increased wage advantage for skilled workers, climate protection could certainly make it worse. In any case, this wage advantage will increase in the longer term for two reasons (see Jaumotte et al., 2008)—and climate protection policy will intensify the trend (in ways which I have stressed here):

- There is a distorting effect worldwide in terms of labor demand (i.e., in terms of skilled workers relative to unskilled workers) in favor of skilled workers: more and more information and communication technology—ICT—is being used in companies and public authorities, so that, as a result of ICT, the demand for qualified workers is structurally increasing in the private and public sectors; it cannot be ruled out that one day ICT applications may be so standardized and simple that computers of all kinds can be used well even without much education/training, but that may take decades until this important point for unskilled workers is reached (by the 1920s, electric motors had been standardized and simplified to such an extent that in the US the wage premiums of qualified workers fell, having been high for workers familiar with the technology previously).
- Due to financial globalization, which brings declining real interest rates for borrowers worldwide, those who already have assets—which are suitable to be used as collateral for an additional mortgage or bank loan—or a relatively good income have an advantage; in the latter case, one can save up equity and then get a desired real estate or acquisition loan from the bank at a very favorable interest rate. The unskilled, on the other hand, on average have low incomes, often too little to save much in the way of equity, and then of course one cannot hope to profit directly from cheaper loans to improve financial security.
- According to the Stolper-Samuelson theorem, the increasing global demand for emission-reducing products that are important for climate protection—as a rule, they are skill intensive to manufacture—means that the relative wages of the highly skilled will rise. In principle, this means that more climate protection also produces more economic inequality in the sense mentioned. If, however, the wages of unskilled workers fall relatively, politicians will increasingly have to consider whether it might be possible to generate additional income through a higher taxation of qualified workers so that slightly higher transfer payments can be made in favor of low-skilled or unskilled workers; this should be feasible in Germany, for example, if one considers that the proportion of unskilled workers in all employees is between 10 and 20 percent (depending on estimates). However, this approach would be much more difficult in France, Italy or the US, where the proportion of unskilled workers is significantly higher.

However, it would probably be better if the share of unskilled workers could be reduced.
- In the case of increasing inequality, state-funded—and also private—activities for more further training would be very appropriate. The state spends practically nothing on continuing education in the US and UK, in Switzerland (which almost always enjoys full employment) about 0.2 percent of the gross domestic product in this way, in Germany the relevant figure is 0.25 percent and in Denmark it is a good 0.5 percent of GDP. The fact that Italy and France, as well as the US, have problems with their education systems—in that a high proportion of children seemingly do not learn what one might consider basic educational or intellectual skills such as reading and arithmetic correctly—is obvious according to the graph below. It is also clear that more expenditure for education and further training cannot be obtained free of charge. It might be possible to use a small part of CO_2 tax revenues to set up additional further qualification programs for unskilled workers. It is known from Dutch studies (see Fouarge et al., 2013) that the return on further education of skilled and unskilled workers is roughly the same, but that the motivation for further training is significantly weaker among unskilled workers than among more highly qualified workers. Without a special motivation program for more further training, especially for the unskilled and low-skilled, resolving the issues associated with climate change will not be probably achieved. For if the income differences within all industrialized countries and emerging markets increase again significantly as a result of climate protection policy, this will also generate domestic political resistance to further climate protection measures, especially among low-income earners. To bring the earth back into a sustainable equilibrium and at the same time to maintain the social and political balance is the dual task of an intelligent climate protection policy. So not only do we need reasonable prices for CO_2 emissions through certificate trading systems or CO_2 taxes and, of course, better support for research and development, but we also need a well-thought-out training policy; in Germany, the latter is in part a political field of action at both the federal and state levels, but it is often also a matter of trade unions and co-determination agencies, which could, for example, seek to secure further training programs for their members within the framework of collective bargaining agreements (the IG Metall trade union has done some pioneering

work in Germany here, and one could also count thousands of committed small- and medium-sized enterprises which are active in this area, as well as many large companies—apparently with Bosch as an exception in some plants—which even lack basic training or apprenticing activities).
- Whether economic and climate policymakers can discuss, design and implement sensible measures depends on many things. An important role is played by the scientific advisory boards of the various relevant ministries, which are to provide scientifically sound analyses on the basis of which policymakers can then select alternative courses of action for which political majorities must be found. Among the influential advisory councils in the climate and environmental sector is the German Advisory Council on Global Change (WGBU), which has published a number of important reports and studies—which in 2019, however, attracted attention for a rather ideologically driven "report" on the digital future (German Advisory Council on Global Change (2019)); in addition, there is the German Advisory Council on the Environment (SRU), and the German Council of Economic Experts is influential.

The proportion of workers with very low qualifications is relatively high in Italy, Spain, France, the US, Ireland, Poland and the UK, as the proportion is over 25 percent (in Italy, the share is over 35 percent). This is why qualification requirements are particularly important in these countries; Germany is not in a much better position. As can be seen from Norway, the Slovak Republic, the Netherlands, Finland and Japan, improvements in the education system should make it possible to reduce the proportion of the very low skilled to around 15 percent (Fig. 6.1). In any case, the decades of innovation and modernization need to protect the climate and counteract global warming will be accompanied by an increased demand for qualified workers. The immigration laws of many OECD countries are already being updated to account for such developments.

Some climate policymakers clearly think little about the side effects of more climate protection and more green innovations, respectively, and thus could suddenly face considerable social resistance related to the sidetrack of major climate policy discussed here, namely, the issue of economic inequality—and then climate protection policy in general could get bogged down politically. In the US, at any rate, there are major problems in the area of inequality, as the lower half of income earners experienced a

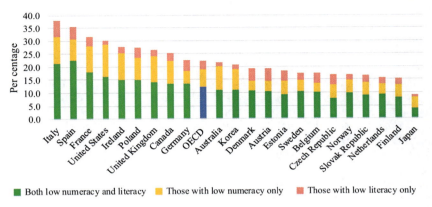

Fig. 6.1 Percentage of under-qualified workers (low literacy or numeracy skills, or both) in selected OECD countries. *Note: The term working-age adults refers to all adults aged 16–65. Data are from the year 2012. Low skilled are defined as those who are below level 2 on either literacy or numeracy according to the Survey of Adult Skills of the OECD Programme for the International Assessment of Adult Competencies (PIAAC). Low-skilled adults struggle with basic quantitative reasoning or have difficulty with simple written information. Data for Belgium refers to Flanders only. Data for the UK are calculated as the population-weighted average of England and Northern Ireland. The OECD aggregate is calculated as an unweighted average of 22 OECD countries (with the data for England and Northern Ireland combined by population weights) that participated in the first round of the Survey of Adult Skills.* (Source: Own representation of data from OECD (2017), Fig. 38, p. 51)

massive decline in the income share between 1991 and 2014 (from 21 percent to just 13 percent), a decline much greater than was seen, for example, in Western Europe during the same period.

A promising climate protection policy therefore also needs an expanded policy mix with which it should intervene to shape or control the North America-Europe-Asia triangle—or the agenda at the G20 level. The fact that a new communication policy should also be used to involve and inform a highly fragmented public is an additional consideration. It will not be easy, but it seems at least possible to implement a sensible sequencing of policy actions with a coherent mix to address interrelated issues.

References

Fouarge, D., Schils, T., & De Grip, A. (2013). Why Do Low-Educated Workers Invest Less in Further Training? *Applied Economics, 45*(18), 2587–2601.

German Advisory Council on Global Change. (2019). *Towards Our Common Digital Future*, WBGU: Berlin. Retrieved September 6, 2021, from https://issuu.com/wbgu/docs/wbgu_hg2019_en?fr=sM2QyYzU1OTI4OA

Jaumotte, F., Lall, S., & Papageorgiou, C. (2008). *Rising Income Inequality: Technology, or Trade and Financial Globalization* (IMF Working Paper WP/08/185). International Monetary Fund: Washington DC.

OECD. (2017, October). *OECD Economic Survey: United Kingdom.* Retrieved 15 October, 2021, from https://www.oecd-ilibrary.org/docserver/eco_surveys-gbr-2017-en.pdf?expires=1635959459&id=id&accname=ocid177160&checksum=0C3FFFC40D106393388A2D2CE7D01B66

PART II

What Could Policymakers, Business and Consumers Achieve?

CHAPTER 7

Climate Protection in the EU: Instruments and International Cooperation Aspects

The European Union has (along with some non-EU participants) established a CO_2 certificate trading system which covers the energy sector and energy-intensive industry, that is, for about half of production in the countries covered. The controversy over Ursula von der Leyen's candidacy for the position of President of the European Commission was in part a signal from the European Parliament that environmental and climate issues should not be to the foreground in the elections despite the strengthened position of Green parties across the EU and in the European Parliament itself. This in turn should only serve to reduce the tendency of the EU27 countries (plus UK and others) to cooperate actively in the field of climate protection. Various relevant policy alternatives, possibly also to be implemented as a package, are listed below (see Fig. 7.1):

- An expansion of CO_2 certificate trading can take place only for a subgroup of countries, for example, for the countries of the Eurozone; at the margin, possibly also only for Germany and France (unless one simply wants to realize a national emissions certificate trading).
- A possible approach could also be that EU countries and, for example, Japan, the Republic of Korea and some other countries agree on broader integration in the sense of joining their certificate trading systems in a certain way, which would in any case lead to lower costs

© The Author(s), under exclusive license to Springer Nature Switzerland AG 2022
P. J.J. Welfens, *Global Climate Change Policy*, Sustainable Development Goals Series,
https://doi.org/10.1007/978-3-030-94594-7_7

Fig. 7.1 Starting points for a national climate policy and complementary policy approaches. (Source: Own representation)

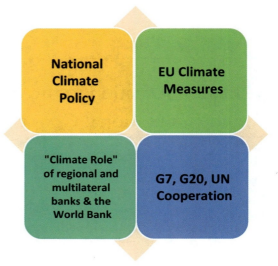

in terms of climate protection for the participating countries and industries – provided that volume targets are set in advance.
- A possible problem with the expansion and internationalization of emissions certificate trading is that the volatility of the certificate price, and thus also of share indices in the participating countries, could increase which would result in an increase in the risk premium for investments and innovation projects: a higher volatility of the certificate price can result from transfer effects of wider financial market volatility to the volatility of the emissions certificate price, for example, if companies or banks buy certificates speculatively within the framework of theoretical portfolio investment models. However, the opposite can also happen, since one could also expect greater liquidity in the expanded certificate markets – in the course of integrated certificate trading systems – so that the volatility of emission certificates decreases. This, in turn, could lead to lower share price volatility if the capitalization of surplus certificates in listed companies is viewed from a fundamental valuation perspective. Further empirical analysis is required here in the literature.
- The economic adjustment pressure of expanded certificate trading can presumably be reduced in countries if increasing numbers of

climate-friendly innovation projects are promoted at the same time – here, as is well known, there is a double positive externality in corresponding innovation projects, since on the one hand research promotion can be justified to a certain extent by the level of positive externality in innovation projects (the social marginal benefit of green innovations is higher than the private marginal benefit for the respective researching companies); and on the other hand, with innovation projects that promote climate protection, a reduction in climate damage effects can be expected through the application of such corresponding innovations, which of course indirectly reduces the price buoyancy of emission certificates and therefore lowers the costs of climate protection via emission reduction.

It is therefore necessary to examine how the volatility of emission certificate prices in the EU has developed over time and how this fluctuation intensity of CO_2 certificate prices is related to the fluctuation intensity of share prices in financial markets.

EU Objectives, Climate Policy Conception and Climate Protection Problems

The EU has set itself the target of reducing CO_2 emissions by 20 percent by 2020 compared to 1990 levels. This target will probably be achieved, as the figure was already −21 percent in 2018 (EUROSTAT, 2020); the target for 2030 is −40 percent, with 1990 again being the reference year. The EU achieves emission reduction targets through two conceptual elements of climate policy:

- In the emissions trading sectors (i.e., the energy sector and industry), which covers circa 45 percent of CO_2 emissions, there is an emissions certificate trading system that provides incentives for companies to reduce emissions and innovate accordingly via a CO_2 certificate market price. Firms which invest in such innovations then often have a surplus of certificates that can be sold in the EU certificate market.
- Outside the emissions trading sector, there are special measures ("Effort-Sharing Decisions") for individual sectors, which have 2005 as the reference year and have been reducing emissions through

national measures or EU-wide targets since 2013: for example, in the case of consumption reduction targets for the car fleet produced by automotive companies. Targets are set until 2030. From an economic point of view, this approach makes little sense and is relatively inefficient—it becomes, for example, visible in an unnecessary increase in the price of cars where the cost of reducing emissions by one ton of CO_2 is enormously expensive compared with other sectors. It would be much better to expand the emissions trading sector—following the example of California—to cover 85 percent of CO_2 emissions across the EU; presumably even 90 percent coverage could also be feasible. In any case, emissions certificate trading is a very target-oriented, simple and efficient, that is, cost-effective, system: The state specifies by how much the annual CO_2 quantity is to be reduced; however, this is a critically important figure with a view to the target year of 2050 in terms of climate neutrality (interpreted here as -90 percent in the emissions level compared with 1990). The rest must be made up by the companies affected by certificate trading through the purchase and sale of emission certificates, whereby most companies will also focus on CO_2-reducing innovations. A corresponding market price is formed via the price mechanism on the market, which also indicates how high the cost of avoiding one (additional) metric ton of CO_2 is. In 2019, the price of certificates traded in the EU was around €27 per metric ton of CO_2. Thus, when the European Commission imposes fuel consumption reduction targets on car manufacturers because of climate protection, the costs of which amount to €150 per metric ton of CO_2 reduced, this is inefficient: car drivers ultimately pay the costs through unnecessarily high car price increases. It is also unclear what to do with agriculture, which is very strongly organized in lobbying terms and which represents 1 percent of EU value added, but 10 percent of emissions. In principle, cattle farming would have to be made more expensive through a penalty tax, since cows emit large amounts of methane during digestion, with one unit of methane being 25 times as harmful to the climate as one unit of CO_2. With a CO_2 tax for agriculture, cattle farming would be less rewarding, and the incentive to identify feed with lower methane emissions from cows would be high. The European Commission, probably in response to pressure from EU member states, has been pursuing a climate policy that makes little sense since 2013 (embedded in the so-called EU growth strategy), as no attempt to expand CO_2 certificate trading coverage has been undertaken. Since 2015, California has shown that an 85 percent coverage of CO_2 emissions can be implemented without a hitch, and the price of a CO_2 certificate in California in 2018/2019 was lower than in the EU. As soon as the EU has really expanded the trade in certificates to cover 85 or 90 percent of emissions, almost all existing sectoral policy interventions can be dropped. There will then be a positive real income effect for almost all households, as efficient policies will replace the previously relatively inefficient ones. The transport sector in the EU should definitely be included in certificate trading within the next few years. Conventional gasoline will then become more expensive, while electricity should actually become cheaper if technical progress in renewable energies worldwide continues at the speed seen in the decade after 2008. When electricity becomes cheaper, there is a "rebound effect" in vehicles, machines and equipment that use electricity. Rebound means a certain rocking chair effect: if, for example, electricity becomes cheaper, then it is more worthwhile for companies to use electricity-powered machines or electricity-based Internet services than before. Then the electricity consumption rises again a little.

In terms of its trade policy, it seems the European Union has thus far paid little heed to climate protection targets. The EU-Mercosur free trade agreement of 2019 (which is yet to be ratified) can be subject to valid criticism as it provides Brazil, Argentina and other Mercosur countries with great incentives to increase meat production and, in particular, beef exports in the future. This, however, creates increased incentives for slash-and-burn logging in the Amazon basis region, a development in which neither the majority of people in Brazil nor the EU have a long-term interest. In any case, it would be sensible to carefully incorporate climate protection aspects into future free trade negotiations. It goes without saying that it is politically and psychologically inappropriate for the EU to play a quasi-colonial role against Brazil when it comes to protecting the Amazon forest. It would be better to involve the leading global forest countries – almost all in the G20 – in supporting a global forest conservation project. It probably sounds a little abstract but what the Netherlands has been doing exemplarily since the seventeenth century in its regionally cooperative polder model for flood protection, the G20+ countries should achieve from 2025 onward in the context of global forest and climate protection.

It is important that there is no short-term intervention due to the policies of individual countries, but that there is a long-term concept, which can be further developed, together, over time. G20 countries could also push ahead with joint research, for example, on passive real estate for administrative purposes. Newly constructed administrative or government buildings should be at least passive buildings, possibly even negative energy buildings via solar power production. To this end, it would certainly be easy to develop useful working groups and promote model projects at an EU and OECD level, as well as at G20 level.

Reference

EUROSTAT. (2020). *Greenhouse Gas Emission Statistics – Emission Inventories.* Retrieved March 15, 2021, from https://ec.europa.eu/eurostat/statistics-explained/index.php/Greenhouse_gas_emission_statistics

Traditional politics has become accustomed in some fields to making promises to the electorate without actually delivering corresponding results over the period concerned. This is certainly a problem in global climate policy to the extent that the G20 countries at least, as relevant major players, must necessarily be mobilized in order for significant improvements to be made in climate protection. In terms of national targets and national policy results, however, it is of course noticeable if interim targets—for example, for 2020, 2030—are clearly missed by individual countries or not achieved by the EU as a whole. In the age of the Internet, however, politics must expect massive digitally networked criticism, at least at the national level, when politicians make big promises and then realize only big mistakes, especially when it comes to the climate issue, which is very important for young people. Any government that promises two million electric cars on the road by 2020 (as the federal government in Germany did) and only manages to see around 100,000 electric vehicles on Germany's streets can quickly run into serious credibility problems. Such problems mean that the government's announcement policy will be less effective. Any underachievement of climate protection goals undermines the credibility of politics as a whole; therefore, an increase in political credibility issues can lead to a systemic economic crisis due to a lack of reduced political effectiveness. It is also true here that climate policy is not just about climate policy but has broader implications.

German Advisory Council on the Environment; Electricity Surcharges Too High

In the annual report of the German Advisory Council on the Environment, it is pointed out that there is no consistent CO_2 pricing for electricity, diesel, petrol and natural gas. However, in the case of petrol and diesel, it can at least be argued that mineral oil taxes indirectly serve to finance the road system in Germany. If, however, in the area of mobility through electric cars, e-buses and e-trucks, the aforementioned energy sources all become close substitutes, then the very different CO_2 burdens of the respective energy sources represent a problem that leads to inefficiencies. In any case, with a CO_2 price of €181 per metric ton of CO_2, the electricity (of households) seems to be taxed too highly, namely much higher than diesel, petrol and natural gas. The electricity surcharge is close to the damage costs of one metric ton of CO_2 estimated by the Federal Environment

Agency, which is even more contradictory since the other CO_2 prices are far from the relevant order of magnitude. However, it should also be noted that with reasonable innovation support for CO_2 reductions, the (marginal) social cost of carbon should decrease significantly. The German Advisory Council on the Environment (2019, p. 202) writes (translation by PJJW):

> *Pricing is not consistently oriented towards energy content and CO_2 emissions: At 13.6 ct/kWh (2018), the energy-related burden on electricity is significantly higher than on fuels (petrol 9.8 ct/kWh and diesel 6.8 ct/kWh) and heating fuels in the heating sector (light heating oil 1.7 ct/kWh and natural gas 1.5 ct/kWh) (ibid., p. 217). Moreover, with regard to the CO_2 emissions resulting from energy consumption, there is no uniform burden on the various energy sources: heating fuels are again by far the least polluting. The impact on electricity is around 181 €/t CO_2, on petrol 276 €/t and on diesel 177 €/t. Fuel oil and natural gas, on the other hand, have a very low burden of around 23 and around 27 €/t respectively.* (ibid., p. 218)

> *This leads to economic inefficiencies and distortions in the energy system, especially in the wake of increasing sector coupling. Thus, the current energy taxation hardly provides any incentives for a flexible and energy-efficient use of renewable electricity in the heating sector (ibid., p. 219). In view of the climate targets of the Paris Climate Agreement, the European and German energy and climate targets, the corresponding tight remaining emission budgets and the still relatively extensive reserves of fossil fuels, it is not to be expected that the necessary incentives and energy price signals will emanate from the market. It is therefore necessary for the state to play more of a steering role.*

German Advisory Council on the Environment: New Council for Intergenerational Justice

In a special report issued at the end of June 2019, the German Advisory Council on the Environment called for the establishment of a new Council for Intergenerational Justice by the German federal government, which would be elected for 12 years by the German lower house (Bundestag) and the upper house (Bundesrat) in equal parts, and which would have particular expertise in the areas of environmental, social and economic policy. This new council should have the power to veto proposed legislation for a maximum of three months—but Lamia Messari-Becker,

Professor of Building Technology and Structural Building Physics, University of Siegen, and member of the Council, is against such a weakening of parliament. This reservation cannot, however, be read in the summary of the expert opinion. In the *Frankfurter Allgemeine Zeitung* newspaper (Pennekamp, 2019) it was argued that Messari-Becker's objection can only be read in the long version, where it is stated that the content of the dissenting opinion was "presented for the first time to the regret of the other members of the Council in the course of the final vote on the expert opinion" and could therefore no longer be debated in the Council, but only noted. Prof. Messari-Becker contradicted this claim in a statement (translation PJJW): "The Council's account is untrue… I expressed my concerns about the content of the proposal at Council meetings and raised the relevant points clearly and critically". The Council also calls for the Ministry of the Environment to be given more power to initiate legislation outside its remit, for example, in the areas of agriculture and transport. In addition, the Federal Environment Minister should in the future have the right to delay draft laws by way of a suspensive veto in the cabinet—thus far, only the Federal Finance Minister has such a veto.

WHICH INSTRUMENTS FOR CO_2 REDUCTION ARE EFFICIENT?

In principle, the instruments for reducing CO_2 emissions that can be considered here are the framework conditions which can be established by the state, such as setting a target for car fleet consumption and thus also for CO_2 emissions by car manufacturers; or stipulating that emission quantities for a particular region or a country or indeed several countries—for example, the EU countries together—are to meet a specific target and from this basis of allocating certificates on the one hand and auctioning excess certificates on the other to certain industrial sectors (as an example), the total emission quantity and how high the price per metric ton of CO_2 should be is determined. Or the government sets a CO_2 tax, that is, about €50 per metric ton of CO_2 for sectors 1–3 (whatever that might mean in practice), or the state commits to promoting climate-friendly technologies and products. What are the advantages and disadvantages of alternative instruments?

- A CO_2 certificate trading system is indeed an accurate instrument, as the emission quantity can be precisely determined in advance. Companies from different countries in the EU (and participating partners) can trade CO_2 certificates with each other—this is efficient and leads to the desired emission quantity (implemented as an upper limit) being realized at the lowest possible cost. Therefore, this approach also keeps job losses due to cost disadvantages within acceptable limits; job losses are most likely to occur in the tradable goods sector, which is why many export sectors in the EU were initially generously granted a certain stock of "free" allowances during the first trading period of the certificates. Since certificate prices can fluctuate strongly over time, the certificate price is likely to have only a minor effect on innovation; if the certificate price fluctuates strongly, companies will be uncertain whether undertaking CO_2-reducing innovation projects is worthwhile or not. A global certificate trade would be particularly efficient.
- A CO_2 tax has the disadvantage that it may end up being technical, complicated and therefore expensive to implement; moreover, it is unclear how a meaningful "tax price structure" can be obtained internationally, for example, in the EU, or indeed on a worldwide basis. The example of the CO_2 tax in Sweden shows, however, that such a tax can be implemented at relatively low cost for relatively large companies or importers.
- Implementing certain restrictions or limits is a costly instrument, especially since the state or economic policy actors cannot know what the (marginal) avoidance costs of an instrument such as a petrol or diesel consumption cap for the fleets (i.e., the weighted mix of all car models sold) sold by automobile manufacturers are. The fact that the state is resorting to such an inefficient instrument at all—see the US and EU—likely only serves to illustrate just how great the fear of politicians is when it comes to the power of the concentrated car lobby: in many EU countries, the car industry stands for large numbers of jobs—and thus voter votes—and the scale of donations from car manufacturers to various political parties also should not be ignored. Thus, before the car industry is effectively and efficiently confronted by policymakers proposing to implement a CO_2 tax or to extend the CO_2 certificate trading system to include the transport sector, politicians first seek a kind of quiet compromise with the car industry. The compromise reached becomes a kind of innovation

target from the politicians, because the innovation dynamics of the products, that is, new cars, must be sufficiently high to achieve the targets set by the politicians. As the diesel scandal at Volkswagen and other German car manufacturers has shown, there are also absurd incentives for some manufacturers to ultimately try to undermine even the "soft" guidelines by attempting to defraud them.
- The promotion of innovation in terms of climate-friendly product innovations and process innovations—that is, new production processes—is certainly worth serious consideration: innovation promotion should be as high as the positive external innovation effects (i.e., the transfer effects from innovation services sector i to other sectors $j = 1, 2,...N$) in other sectors. An optimal promotion of innovation will want to compensate for the difference between the social (global) marginal utility of a green innovation and the private utility of users of resulting green R&D outputs through a corresponding subsidy. The extent to which targeted "green innovations" or climate-friendly projects should be supported by companies in research and development is not easy to determine: a scientific analysis is needed to determine how large and far-reaching—geographically speaking—the positive effects of innovation are in general. Furthermore, it should be examined whether there are any special features of climate-friendly innovation projects compared to innovations more generally which would require a differentiated approach.

It is somewhat unclear to what extent German and EU innovation funding is sufficiently well positioned in terms of the type of scientific analysis suggested here. International transfers of new technologies also take place via new products being traded across borders on the one hand and via multinational companies and their active subsidiaries abroad on the other. Austria is an example of an EU country that has increasingly attracted foreign investors to strengthen its research and growth dynamics in particular (Dachs, 2019).

CO_2 Tax Debate

The CO_2 tax debate goes back to the 1980s at least by which time a large share of the scientific world had come to understand that raising the global average temperature by burning fossil fuels creates a serious climate problem. Thus, anyone who produces energy intensively in, say, an industrialized or emerging country—and does not use hydropower or geothermal energy to generate electricity—indirectly creates a problem not just in the home country but in all other countries too. This is because the combustion of fossil fuels, for energy for the purposes of electricity generation or transport/mobility for example, releases CO_2 which can in part be absorbed on Earth by plants and forests, but which for the most part is released into the atmospheric layers thereby contributing to global warming, ultimately creating a global climate problem. Achieving better climate protection within a few decades, or even the reduction of CO_2 emissions from the current global average of 4 metric tons of CO_2 per capita to almost 0 by the end of the century, is a major undertaking; important interim targets have to be achieved by say 2020, 2030 and 2040, but great efforts are needed to achieve the necessary emission reduction targets. This is bad news for almost all producers around the world and especially for the relatively poor countries that want to engage in economic catching-up through industrialization. How can emission reductions be achieved at the lowest possible cost in Germany, France, the UK, the US, China, India, Japan and other countries?

In principle, adequate climate protection can be achieved if all countries, or at least all large countries, produce electricity on the basis of renewable energies and if the transport sector and housing industries would also be (largely) free of CO_2 emissions. Some particular problems remain, such as the agricultural sector—where beef cattle and dairy herds produce large amounts of methane, which is also particularly harmful to the climate (a unit of methane corresponds to several times as much CO_2 in terms of the global warming effect; this indirectly raises questions of diet, nutrition and lifestyle going forward). Moreover, global warming could lead to rising methane levels as that gas is released from softening and thawing permafrost soils in northerly regions. Therefore, beyond a certain point, global warming could even accelerate. On the question of incentives for savings with regard to CO_2 and similar gases, quantitative targets in conjunction with emission certificates and corresponding certificate trading are important tools. The EU has played a pioneering role in this respect, while still providing a certain number of free certificates to sectors heavily exposed to international competition. The result is a certificate price that should provide an incentive to reduce CO_2 emissions. In the EU approach, overly ambitious national savings targets set by policymakers are usually not particularly sensible, since the effect of an EU-wide reduction target is that other countries in the EU will have correspondingly higher CO_2 emissions. One exception, up to a certain level of support, is state-guaranteed feed-in tariffs for scale-intensive technologies for renewable energies in particular solar power plants—but partly also relating to wind power plants—for example, public support in Germany, Italy, Spain, France, the US and so on, because if there are static and dynamic mass production advantages, such advantages result in the world market price for such plants falling, and thus all countries of the world can invest in and build such plants more easily and cheaply than before. As far as the incentive effects of large solar and wind power plants are concerned, fixed, guaranteed feed-in tariffs are a considerable problem. The tender models practiced in Germany since 2017 are better, with the bidder having the lowest subsidy requirement being awarded the contract. Since then, offshore wind power plants have been able to be established without any subsidy from the state at all. The difference between the market value of the electricity produced and all feed-in tariffs paid by the state is considerable. The latter are fixed for many years and should have been reduced by the state earlier for each new plant. In 2015, feed-in tariffs in Germany amounted to €27 billion, the market value of electricity to about €7 billion, leaving a €20 billion shortfall required to be met by subsidies. This is a large amount that could possibly be justified on the grounds of innovation effects and the level of CO_2 emissions avoided. If the policy had been well thought out, however, the same effect would probably have been achieved with two-thirds of the subsidy amount. CO_2 emissions in Germany's energy sector fell from 466 million metric tons in 1990 to 343 million metric tons in 2016, with renewable energies playing a major role in the 123 million metric ton decline. Assuming that the damage of one metric ton of CO_2 amounts to €180 per ton, the value of this reduction in CO_2 emissions is €22 billion. Since part of the decline in CO_2 emissions comes from efficiency improvements in fossil fuel combustion—presumably up to a quarter—a promotion of renewable energies amounting to three-quarters of €22 billion would have been appropriate: up to €16.5 billion would have been adequate, thus the excess promotion amounted to circa €5.5 billion. Part of this overfunding can probably be justified if one also considers an increased use of economies of scale in solar and wind energy as well as national and international innovation transfer effects in terms of the corresponding product innovations. Nevertheless, the problem of overfunding remains—taxpayers' money has certainly been wasted.

In 2016 in Germany, the German Council of Economic Experts had the following to say on climate protection issues (German Council of Economic Experts, 2016, p. 431):

> *At the Paris climate summit, 195 countries signed on to ambitious climate targets and agreed to reach net zero emissions ("emissions neutrality") in all sectors in all countries by the end of the century. This presents confirmation of Germany's own endeavours to switch to a sustainable energy supply system. However, it also highlights that if an energy transition (Energiewende) chiefly aimed at mitigating the effects of climate change is to deliver meaningful results it will need more than the actions of one country alone. Without the introduction of a global emissions trading system or a global carbon tax a credible and economically efficient strategy to actually deliver on the agreed global goals would be missing.*
>
> *This global strategy would be credible, as the binding effect of participating in a global system would be far stronger than mere promises to reach national emission targets. and it would be economically efficient, as opposed to separate courses of action, it can leverage the advantages of the international division of labour in emissions abatement. To dismiss such a strategy and instead have a situation where each country takes separate steps to pursue national or even smaller-scale regional emission targets would be a waste of economic resources. For the climate summit in Paris to actually serve as the starting point for the introduction of global emissions trading, the distribution problem associated with the initial allocation of the number of permits would need to be resolved through negotiation.*
>
> *German energy and climate policy, in contrast, has so far concentrated on Germany's own energy transition. It is based on the "2010 Energy Concept", and on the Energy Transition Package adopted following the Fukushima nuclear disaster, which formulates a variety of targets at different levels to be achieved by the year 2050. at this stage, however, it seems likely that most of these targets will be missed, particularly the primary target of reducing greenhouse gas (GHG) emissions by 40 % in the year 2020 compared with the levels of the reference year 1990.*
>
> *The Federal Government responded to this foreseeable failure to meet targets in a centrally planned manner with a host of action programmes and plans containing over 100 individual measures, which will inevitably raise the cost of the energy transition. Instead of this kind of fine-tuning, more emphasis should be placed on the international dimension of the energy transition in the years ahead, coupled with a clear commitment on the part of the Federal Government to the EU-ETS as the guiding instrument. In particular, efforts should be made to extend emissions trading to all transport sectors, private households and to the industries which are currently exempted, rendering national support instruments and numerous subsidies superfluous.*

This early criticism of the climate policy of previous federal governments by the German Council of Economic Experts indeed contains some good and valid points. If climate protection is to be achieved in the short term, then it would only be wise to look for reform paths in the reduction of emissions which minimize costs when it comes to global climate protection—a global good, a global risk in the case of CO_2 emissions. In view of the high costs involved in a complicated project that was to be completed within a few decades, it would certainly be very sensible to avoid unnecessary cost increases. Anyone in Germany who unnecessarily spends about €5 billion annually—that is, over and above what would actually be required—on climate protection due to an inadequate climate policy reform design is essentially wasting vast amounts of money. According to the Federal Minister of Labor and Social Affairs, Hubertus Heil, such an amount would be just enough to pay the necessary basic pension. In principle, an expansion of emissions trading in the EU would be desirable, as would more international or global cooperation. But since June 2016—the year of the above cited German Council of Economic Experts analysis—the conditions for international cooperation have deteriorated considerably; June 23 that year saw a majority in favor of EU withdrawal in a referendum in the UK, which ultimately resulted in an important and large EU country leaving the European Union after more than 45 years of membership. This does not bode well for multilateralism and international cooperation with an emphasis on the important role of international organizations (the EU itself is one such organization). This perspective became even more valid in the wake of the inauguration of Donald Trump, who rejected multilateralism and, strangely enough, considered his private opinion on climate developments to be more important than that of hundreds of US and other "climate scientists" (e.g., experts from diverse fields such as physics, meteorology, biology, economics and oceanography) with experience in relevant research. If the largest Western economy, the US—with a share of about 17 percent of world income in 2015, the year the Paris Agreement was signed—would withdraw from efficient, market economy approaches to climate policy, the prospects for successful climate protection will deteriorate considerably. If the US turns the clock back on environmental and climate protection because of political populism, it will be difficult to stop a dramatic climatic development. This is because the US will not only fail as a player in climate protection—apart from a few individual states with their own programs, such as California—but will certainly also have a negative impact on many other countries. This was already seen in Brazil in 2018 with the election there of the new populist President Jair Bolsonaro. This is not only concerning when one considers the reduction of CO_2 emissions, but also for Brazil's huge forests, which serve as carbon sinks for such emissions and are of great importance for global climate protection. It does not take much imagination to see that if Brazil does not achieve its climate protection goals in 2040 or 2050 and continues a policy of (at best) ambivalence toward environmental degradation and destruction, very serious international conflicts could arise—including new scenarios for military conflict. Such scenarios must be avoided from the outset, and therefore reliable global cooperation in climate protection is of ongoing importance. Thus, one can see how dangerous a Trumpian policy approach is, in terms of weakening or undermining the starting points for international cooperation with many countries—from Iran to Russia, Mexico, China and the EU. Incidentally, it is a very unamerican policy for a president not to want to know anything about the findings of the scientific community.

From an economic point of view, there are good reasons to expand the emissions allowance trading system, which covers only 45 percent of emissions in the EU, and to engage in more cooperation internationally in this particular trade (e.g., with China, California and the Republic of Korea). However, the fact that international policy cooperation seems to be becoming difficult, at least temporarily, CO_2 taxes should also be increasingly considered as a complement to emissions trading. This does not exclude the possibility of new and intensified cooperation in terms of international economic policy, for example, in joint innovation promotion approaches among OECD countries and beyond. If there is insufficient cooperation in emissions certificate trading, CO_2 taxes and climate-friendly innovation promotion, national or EU-wide adaptation measures will have to be considered in the face of a pressing question: how best to cope with exceeding the 2-degree target (or indeed the 1.5-degree target)?

Since only part of value added is covered by certificate trading, it is also necessary to consider supplementary measures for a CO_2 tax, which would cover the remaining sectors. Here, one could introduce a CO_2 tax nationally or in cooperation with other countries. In addition, innovation funding to reduce CO_2 emissions is conceivable; as a bureaucratic instrument, also particular requirements to be met by firms or private households. Finally, there are also forest planting programs—as forests are carbon sinks, that is, they absorb more carbon than they emit. Despite all the focus on the climate protection problem, one cannot overlook that there are other important policy areas, such as species protection, where the UN expressed clear concern on the basis of scientific analyses in 2019.

The 1997 Kyoto Agreement referred to certain possibilities for industrialized countries to achieve emission reduction targets through offsetting measures in developing countries, which would of course require cooperation agreements. The 2015 UN Paris Agreement (successor to the Kyoto Protocol) stipulates that the 195 signatory states should be able to demonstrate a CO_2-neutral economy by the end of the twenty-first century. If it is not possible to achieve economic activity without CO_2 emissions in one country, compensation measures abroad would also be permissible.

Many relevant parties, scientists and politicians have contributed to the debate on a CO_2 tax. If one wants to investigate the complex question of how high a CO_2 tax should be and what effects would arise—possibly also in connection with CO_2 emission certificate trading—one needs to look at countries with many years of CO_2 tax experience, at the relevant technical literature and at macro models which include a CO_2 tax. Considering the experiences available in Europe, one could thus look at Switzerland, the UK and France (as well as Sweden and Austria), among others, as the Scientific Service of the German Bundestag has done—under the heading "Debate on the state of affairs" (Research Services of the Bundestag, 2018). It is striking, however, that the Research Services practically ignored the relevant specialist literature, that is, it did not do at all what a parliamentary research service should do. Instead, the report makes strong reference to proposals from think tanks and non-governmental organizations that have made a name for themselves in the field of ecological tax reform, but only with a partial analysis that does not offer the German Bundestag a comprehensive and appropriate perspective on the economic and ecological effects of a CO_2 tax. The non-governmental organizations mentioned are the *Forum Sozial-ökologische Marktwirtschaft* (also known as Green Budget Germany) and *CO2-Abgabe e.V.*, which are both listed as references with studies from 2017 (which are useful analyses for partial aspects of the CO_2 tax, but which lack any broader modeling). If the German Bundestag deals with such an important issue as the CO_2 tax on such a thin analytical basis, there is a danger that the introduction of such a tax in Germany will be seriously misguided. Since many countries around the world look to Germany in the matter of a CO_2 tax debate, this weak foundation to the study of the research service is a double problem.

The analysis of the German parliamentary research service therefore largely ignores essential aspects of such an important project as a CO_2 tax and indeed completely ignores them in others:

- What are the effects in terms of CO_2 reduction? After all, the study of the Research Service of the German Bundestag assumes a possible revenue of about €8 billion per year, which would be about 0.25 percent of the gross domestic product. With regard to the possible steering effects that reduce CO_2 volumes and therefore also the CO_2 tax base, it is pointed out that CO_2 tax revenues could rather be just under €5 billion. The additional tax effects (think of effects such as income tax, corporate income tax and value added tax) or reductions in total social revenues could, however, be close to zero for the total revenues of the state, taking into account negative production effects in the context of the CO_2 tax: namely if real gross domestic product were to fall by around €15 billion. A general tax rate—excluding CO_2 taxes—of around 20 percent would reduce tax revenue by €3 billion and social security contributions by another €3 billion (based on a social security contribution rate of around 20 percent). In any case, the overall macroeconomic effects, and also the overall revenue effects, for the state must be taken into account. All this does not exclude the possibility that the majority of the CO_2 tax revenue will be ultimately be returned to the citizens in some form by the state.
- The absolutely necessary accelerated reduction of CO_2 intensities in production and consumption—a significant part of car traffic is down to private consumption and is CO_2 intensive—should be reliably achieved. However, without more "green" or CO_2-reducing innovation dynamics (product innovations on the one hand and process innovations on the other), the emission reduction targets set by the federal government for 2030 will not be achieved. The lack of a focus on the innovation dimension appears to be a major shortcoming of the study.
- What were the international implications of France's CO_2 tax—a relatively large country in the EU? Or indeed what international effects did the minimum level for the CO_2 emission certificate price have in the UK?
- What are the effects of a CO_2 tax on the labor market, employment levels, current account, national budget and price levels?

- If one wants to examine various meaningful options for Germany—also within the framework of a German European Council Presidency, for example—questions of EU cooperation on the one hand and questions of G20 cooperation on the CO_2 tax or other taxes on the other are also to be addressed.

One of the many interesting studies in this area of the specialist literature is a Dutch-based modeling of the introduction of a CO_2 tax of €50 per metric ton (Kearney, 2018). Among other things, the effects on exports and export prices as well as the medium-term development of real incomes and employment are considered, and the fiscal use of tax revenues generated is also discussed: additional tax revenues are used to either reduce the government deficit or reduce social contributions, or corporate tax rates are reduced. Three scenarios are considered, namely a national solo effort to introduce a national CO_2 tax, a coordinated CO_2 tax introduction in Northern European countries (excluding Ireland and the UK) or the introduction of an EU-wide CO_2 tax. At 1.5 percent, the increase in export prices is highest in the case of an EU-wide CO_2 tax, although the deterioration of the Netherland's international competitiveness is relatively small in this case. After five years, the decline in real income is no more than 0.5 percent in the worst case. If social security contributions are reduced, consumption and real estate prices increase, which in turn leads to only a slight dampening of the real gross domestic product in the modified NiGEM model used in the analysis. The case constellations mentioned are also likely to be relatively important for Germany. The income dampening effects resulting from the export dampening effects could be somewhat lower than in the case of the Netherlands as Germany's export ratio is lower than that of the Netherlands. In addition, the German economy, as one of the world's leading countries in the export of machinery and equipment (note, the demand for CO_2-optimized machinery will increase throughout Europe with the introduction of an EU-wide CO_2 tax), is likely to benefit, as exports from the mechanical engineering sector will rise in the medium term. However, it should also be borne in mind that the shortage of skilled workers in mechanical engineering could be a barrier here from the sectoral employment side.

A CO_2 tax is best introduced in a sensible way:

1. In cooperation with other national economies, such as via the EU or the European Economic Area (EU plus Liechtenstein, Iceland and Norway), as well as Switzerland.
2. A CO_2 tax should be increased in real terms over several years following a pre-determined and publicized path. The economy needs reliable orientation.
3. At least in the longer term, a CO_2 tax should not be far removed from the price of emission certificates, as otherwise there would be considerable inefficiencies in climate protection policy; a CO_2 tax in the Eurozone is also recommended, which could—at least to a small extent—be used to fund more joint research in the Eurozone aimed at promoting climate protection.
4. In particular, the EU itself should cooperate with ASEAN and other regional integration areas (such as Mercosur and ECOWAS) on climate protection policy.

The major share of CO_2 tax revenues generated should, however, be returned to the citizens. In international cooperation beyond the EU, one would be well advised to grant poorer countries a lower CO_2 tax rate for at least a decade than rates applicable in rich OECD countries.

References

Dachs, B. (2019). Techno-Globalisierung als Motor des Aufholprozesses in österreichischen Innovationssystem [transl. PJJW: Technoglobalization as a Driver of Catching-Up in the Austrian Innovation System]. In P. J. J. Welfens (Ed.), *EU-Strukturwandel, Leitmärkte und Technoglobalisierung*. De Gruyter.

German Advisory Council on the Environment. (2019). *Demokratisch regieren in ökologischen Grenzen – Zur Legitimation von Umweltpolitik* [transl. PJJW: Democratic Government Within Environmental Limits – On the Legitimation of Environmental Policy]. Special Report June 2019, Berlin.

German Council of Economic Experts. (2016, November). *Time for Reforms*. Annual Report 2016/17, Berlin. https://www.sachverstaendigenrat-wirtschaft.de/en/publications/annual-reports/previous-annual-reports/annual-report-201617.html

Kearney, I. (2018, September 13). *The Macroeconomic Effects of a Carbon Tax in the Netherlands*. Retrieved 31 August, 2019, from https://www.dnb.nl/media/ac2prbq0/appendix3-macroeconomic-scenarios.pdf

Pennekamp, J. (2019, June 27). Regierungsberater: Mehr Macht für das Umweltministerium, Veto-Recht für Umweltministerium und Generationenrat [transl. PJJW: Government Advisor: More Power for the Environment Ministry, Veto Right for Environment Ministry and Generation Council]. *Frankfurter Allgemeine Zeitung*, FAZ Online Edition https://www.faz.net/aktuell/wirtschaft/regierungsberater-mehr-macht-fuer-das-umweltministerium-16257225.html

Research Services of the Bundestag. (2018b). Die CO2-*Abgabe in der Schweiz, Frankreich und Großbritannien Mögliche Modelle einer CO2-Abgabe für Deutschland* [transl. PJJW: The CO2 Tax in Switzerland, France and the UK, Possible models of a CO2 tax for Germany]. German Bundestag, WD 8–3000-027/18, April 2018.

CHAPTER 9

Modernization of the Energy Industry and National Interests

A key element of the climate protection debate is the modernization of the energy sector, which contributed around 40 percent to CO_2 emissions in industrialized countries over a long period of time. The energy sector, on the other hand, is dominated by large multinationals, some of which are trying to grow from their core business of fossil fuels into the field of renewable energies. How CO_2 emissions can be reduced within a few decades is basically clear—instead of an economy dependent on fossil fuel energy, a renewable energy economy (incorporating hydro, solar, wind and geothermal power among others) is needed; if necessary, nuclear power plants, too, provided that inherent safety can be achieved in the manner of reactor construction, so that a mega-accident can be effectively ruled out due to the design. However, nuclear power plants also have ecological weak points as water cooling is required. In July 2019, the Gronau nuclear power plant in Germany had to be taken off the grid at short notice because the source of cooling water—a local river—could not be used due to the record heat and drought-like conditions—extreme weather for Germany, which is presumably related to climate change. In France, two nuclear power plants had to be decommissioned for similar reasons. Low water levels in rivers and overheated water, which can occur during an extended period of summer heat, are therefore also a risk in the operation of nuclear power plants. In the EU, France could be particularly vulnerable here.

© The Author(s), under exclusive license to Springer Nature Switzerland AG 2022
P. J.J. Welfens, *Global Climate Change Policy*, Sustainable Development Goals Series,
https://doi.org/10.1007/978-3-030-94594-7_9

The fact that coal and oil deposits are to be abandoned will not please the main producing countries in this area, namely China, India, the US, Australia, Indonesia, Russia and South Africa as well as Germany; it is doubtful whether it will be possible to develop a safe carbon capture and storage process to allow to continue to exploit such deposits. The main producers of oil are the US, Saudi Arabia, Russia, Canada, Iran, Iraq, China, the United Arab Emirates, Kuwait, Brazil, Venezuela and Mexico, and here, too, there is likely to be strong resistance to abandoning the previously extremely valuable oil fields, especially since, with the exception of the US and Brazil, these countries tend to have very high levels of government revenues derived from oil production. In addition, thousands of highly paid jobs can be given to the friends of ruling politicians if necessary. With regard to CO_2, gas is cheaper than coal or oil; moreover it is a good substitute for both; gas power plants can be fired up within minutes and will therefore be irreplaceable for decades in terms of the electricity supply in places or during phases with little or no wind; until perhaps one day one has developed inexpensive mega-batteries to overcome such challenges. Russia, Iran, Nigeria, the US and the Arab countries are the main gas-producing countries on the supply side. This is not, as with oil, a perfect world market, but instead is characterized by regional offers on the basis of pipeline networks, with some regional price differences. However, with the increasing levels of liquefied natural gas (LNG) being transported by ship, the gas market is becoming increasingly global and inter-regional price convergence may soon be foreseeable. The main gas-producing countries are the US, Russia, Iran, Canada, China, Qatar, Australia, Norway, Saudi Arabia, Algeria, Turkmenistan and Egypt. These countries could benefit from the switch from coal or oil to gas operations in the power plant sector and from increasing numbers of gas-powered ships, trucks and buses in the context of climate protection. Some of the main oil-producing countries are not gas-producing countries and will therefore hardly actively support more climate protection which may disadvantage themselves. A similar logic applies to the coal-producing countries (see Tables 9.1, 9.2 and 9.3).

For economic and political reasons, the US under President Trump pushed for a significant increase in liquified natural gas (LNG) exports. NATO allies in particular faced pressure to buy US LNG—despite its being about 10 percent more expensive than gas from pipelines—rather than natural gas from Russia. So far, oil has mainly been used for the mobility of cars, trucks, buses, ships and aircraft. In principle, gas or

Table 9.1 The main natural gas-producing countries in the world, on the basis of proven reserves

Largest natural gas producers by country (top 12 ranked by production in 2019; plus selected countries in italics), in billions of cubic meters (bcm)	2019	2010	2000	1990
US[c]	951	604	544	507
Russia[c]	740	657	573	629
Iran[a]	240	144	59	23
Canada[a]	183	156	182	109
China[c]	175	96	27	15
Qatar	173	121	24	6
Australia[b]	139	53	33	20
Norway[a]	118	110	53	28
Saudi Arabia[c]	98	73	38	24
Algeria[a]	90	85	59	23
Turkmenistan	83	–	47	85
Egypt	70	57	18	8
Indonesia[b]	*66*	*86*	*70*	*48*
Uzbekistan	*60*	*60*	*56*	*41*
UK[a]	*40*	*58*	*115*	*50*
The Netherlands	*34*	*90*	*73*	*76*
France	*0*	*1*	*2*	*3*

[a]Also major gas and oil producer
[b]Also major gas and coal producer
[c]Major gas, oil and coal producer

Source: Own presentation; Global Energy Statistical Yearbook 2020
https://yearbook.enerdata.net/natural-gas/world-natural-gas-production-statistics.html

electricity—ideally from renewable energies—could replace oil here. Gas and coal are important for power generation, with coal and nuclear usually covering the base load, while peak loads are served by gas or pumped storage power plants. The restructuring of the energy sector is a lengthy and expensive process, and the capital input per worker in this sector is very high. Therefore, a restructuring of the energy industry means that part of the capital stock has to be written off, which means a loss of value for the shares of corresponding companies. One can also ask who, conversely, will benefit from the energy revolution and the decarbonization of the economy (where decarbonization means severely limiting or eliminating CO_2-intensive production or switching to new production processes without significant CO_2 emissions): innovative mechanical engineering producers,

Table 9.2 The main oil-producing countries in the world

Largest crude oil producers by country	In MT 2019	2010	2000	1990
US	745	334	353	413
Russia	560	504	322	524
Saudi Arabia	545	461	436	342
Canada	268	164	125	92
Iraq	232	117	129	104
China	195	204	163	138
United Arab Emirates	183	134	121	92
Brazil	146	107	64	33
Kuwait	144	123	105	46
Iran	137	214	199	164
Nigeria	99	127	115	88
Mexico	94	145	169	151
Norway	*79*	*100*	*161*	*82*
Venezuela	*58*	*159*	*174*	*115*
UK	*52*	*63*	*126*	*92*
France	*1*	*1*	*2*	*3*

Source: Own presentation; Global Energy Statistical Yearbook 2020
https://yearbook.enerdata.net/crude-oil/world-production-statitistics.html

important players in the digital economy—which will have to be called upon for decarbonization—and the solar and wind energy companies as well as manufacturers of machines for water power generation and geo-thermal energy will benefit. From an EU perspective, the solar power markets and the wind power markets are particularly important lead markets (Korus, 2019).

The worldwide share of renewable energy in electricity consumption was around 24 percent in the years 2015–2017 and has increased only slightly (according to IRENA). By region, Asia was clearly the largest producer of electricity from renewable sources in 2018 (with 2643 terawatt hours (TWh)), followed by Europe with 1298 TWh and North America with 1226 TWh. At 794 TWh, the figures for South America were relatively small; the same applies to Africa, where the figure was just 160 TWh. In absolute terms, China, the US, Brazil, Canada India and Germany plus Russia, Japan, Norway and Italy lead the field in terms of renewable energy locations in 2018 (see Figs. 9.1, 9.2 and 9.3).

A look at the global wind distribution shows the different regional opportunities for electricity generation from wind. North America and

Table 9.3 The main coal- and lignite-producing countries in the world

Largest coal and lignite producers by country (top 12 ranked by production in 2019; plus selected countries in italics), in MT	2019	2010	2000	1990
China	3692	3316	1355	1040
India	745	570	336	225
US	640	996	972	934
Indonesia	585	325	79	10
Australia	500	436	307	205
Russia	425	300	242	377
South Africa	264	255	224	175
Germany	132	184	205	434
Kazakhstan	117	111	77	131
Poland	112	133	163	215
Turkey	84	73	63	47
Colombia	83	74	38	21
Canada	*52*	*68*	*69*	*68*
Czechia	*41*	*55*	*65*	*101*
Ukraine	*27*	*58*	*63*	*159*
Romania	*22*	*31*	*29*	*38*
France	*0*	*0*	*4*	*14*

Source: Own presentation; Global Energy Statistical Yearbook 2020
https://yearbook.enerdata.net/coal-lignite/coal-production-data.html

parts of South America are clearly favored (Fig. 9.4). The daily high winds in Patagonia, the southern regions of Chile and Argentina are so strong that enough electricity could be produced there for the whole of Latin America. However, this would require high initial investments, first in wind farms and, second, in the power lines that would transport the electricity generated northward to the consumers. Here, one can note that there is already a large Chinese wind farm project in Patagonia.

There is no guarantee that the owners of the electricity grids in the north would allow new electricity suppliers from wind farms in Patagonia to use their grids. Often the grid owners are also themselves electricity producers, and if they allowed new suppliers (i.e., new power plants) to use their grids, electricity prices and thus the profits of their own power plants would fall. Here, the state with its competition policy is called upon to follow the electricity sector models of the UK or Poland (in the case of Poland, this author was personally involved in the development of the electricity sector after 1991 with my colleague George Yarrow from Oxford University as part of an EU project): there is a national agency overseeing the

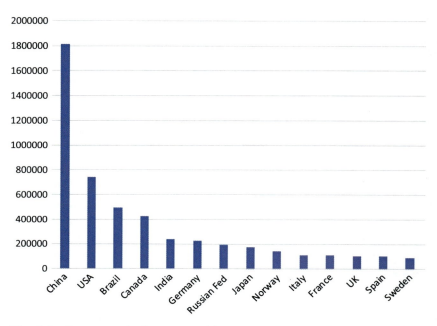

Fig. 9.1 Power supply from renewable energies, 2018 (GWh). (Source: Own representation of data available from IRENA (2021), Renewable Energy Capacity Statistics 2021, International Renewable Energy Agency (IRENA), Abu Dhabi)

state-owned electricity grid, whereby independent private or state-owned power plants feed their electricity into this grid in a competitive procedure. If such a sectoral structure is not ensured within the framework of state regulation, high monopoly prices for line use combined with high electricity generation prices will result in high electricity prices, which will slow down industrial production. However, if you have a competitive model with the separation of grid operation and electricity generation, then you can take electricity from suppliers possibly far away—especially wind, solar or water power. There is more cheap electricity from renewable energy sources, government price regulation of grid use ensures quasi-competitive prices for line use and thus there is relatively cheap electricity. The demand for green electricity will then increase, and that is exactly what is desired in the sense of both prosperity and indeed climate protection.

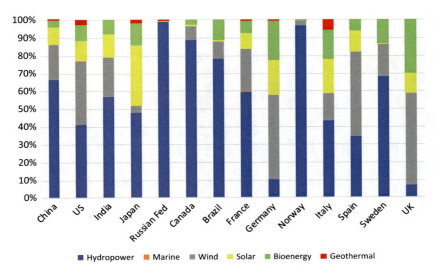

Fig. 9.2 Electricity generated from renewable energy sources (by type in percent), 2018. (Source: Own presentation of data available from IRENA Renewable Energy Statistics 2020, International Renewable Energy Agency (IRENA), Abu Dhabi)

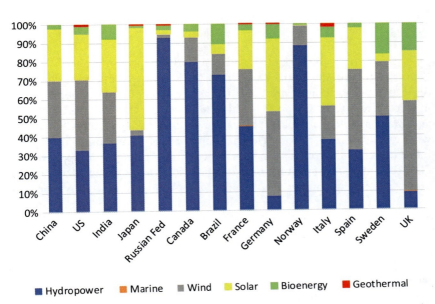

Fig. 9.3 Electricity capacities from renewable energy sources (by type in percent), 2020. (Source: Own presentation of data available from IRENA Renewable Capacity Statistics 2021, International Renewable Energy Agency (IRENA), Abu Dhabi)

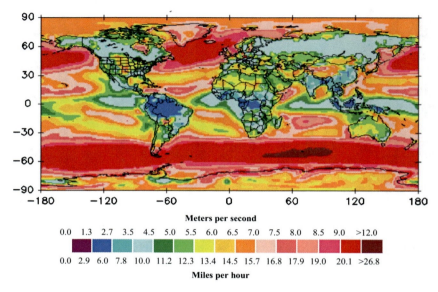

Fig. 9.4 The global distribution of wind energy intensity. (Source: NASA (2004), NASA Surface Meteorology and Solar Energy: Methodology, 12/16/04, p. 47)

Argentina is a G20 country, and it would be appropriate for all G20 countries to submit annual reports on the state of competition in their respective electricity industries and indeed the extent of international trade in electricity. In this way, one could at least see to what extent Argentina and Brazil are blocking market access for green electricity from Chile or to what extent Brazil is making electricity imports from Argentina and Chile more difficult. Of course, the same type of reporting should apply to all G20 countries. It is apparent that South Africa could also be a large wind power-producing country if you look at the NASA wind intensity map. In this respect, there are also geographical advantages for Japan and Russia, as well as Western Europe and the US in terms of wind power generation in the north of the world economy.

The largest solar power producers in the world are located in China, the US, Japan and Europe; in terms of wind energy the ranking goes Europe, Japan, the US and China (according to IRENA statistics). It is noteworthy that the list of leading producing countries of solar power systems is not identical with that of the main producers of solar power in the world. International trade disruptions will therefore make the production of solar power more expensive, and the same applies to wind-based power generation.

It is foreseeable that nuclear power plants will continue to be built in certain countries; China, Russia, the US, the UK and France are important producers of nuclear power, but according to President Macron of France, the proportion of power generated by nuclear plants in France at least is expected to decline in the longer term and fall below 50 percent. If significantly more wind energy generation capability is built up, there will be a regional energy transmission problem and thus the need to build new power lines. This in turn often provokes resistance from citizens who on the one hand demand electricity from renewable sources, but who—as is frequently evidenced in Germany—do not want to see new above-ground or underground power lines being constructed on the other. In Germany, for example, wind power from the north needs to be routed to the industrial and residential centers in the south of the country. When energy flows are financed through the Renewable Energy Levy in Germany, this results in some strange shadow transfer payments between regions or federal states.

> **Box 9.1: North Rhine-Westphalia Is Severely Disadvantaged by the Financing Mode for Renewable Energies**
> The most populous state in Germany is North Rhine-Westphalia (NRW), whose population of 17 million is about the same as the Netherlands. In Germany, the 16 federal states are integrated into an inter-regional redistribution system for tax revenues: federal states with high per capita revenues should support federal states with low per capita revenues through transfers. In addition to the official inter-regional redistribution system, there is also a widely unknown system of redistribution, which arises via the electricity bill or the regionally unequal distribution of renewable energies. Under the Renewable Energy Sources Act, private households pay a surcharge on the electricity price to promote renewable energies (e.g., to finance the guaranteed feed-in tariffs for operators of solar or wind power plants, whereby the majority of wind power plants are in the northern federal states, namely Schleswig-Holstein and Lower Saxony).

(continued)

(continued)

It is not only NRW's own policies that are weighing on North Rhine-Westphalia's growth dynamics—with old structural problems in parts of the Ruhr region coming on top of that. On the contrary, there are external negative impulses for NRW: above all, the unbalanced Renewable Energy Sources Act of 2009—with two amendments—which in fact mean a kind of second shadow state financial compensation concerning NRW via electricity prices or the electricity bills of private households and feed-in tariffs for producers of renewable electricity in other states: the order of magnitude in 2014/2015 was about 0.5 percent of NRW's gross domestic product—or €3 billion a year—and the trend over time was further upward. For NRW, the amounts paid out in this way on household electricity bills have increased over the years. For several years, Bavaria enjoyed a net financial inflow, but switched to a net payer position in 2014, while the federal state of Schleswig-Holstein has a considerable net inflow position (Menges & Untiedt, 2016). The cumulative amount flowing out of NRW via the extra costs on electricity bills paid by households in the period 2010–2014 was around €9.5 billion, which corresponds to a per capita payment of €500 to other federal states. Assuming 3.5 billion NRW-related payments via household electricity bills for 2015–2017, the total sum for 2010–2017 could come to about €20 billion, which corresponds to more than €1000 per capita.

NRW has a clear net payment position among the federal states. It cannot be ruled out that some of the de facto redistribution funds from other federal states will flow back to NRW via various channels (e.g., if the firms E.ON and RWE operate wind farms as electricity producers in northern Germany, but this feedback factor is likely to be low). Thus, this shadow state financial equalization II could rise to almost 1 percent of NRW's gross domestic product by 2020, since Baden-Württemberg will change from being a net contributing state to being a net recipient state in the course of the rapid expansion of renewable energies, and thus households in NRW will see an even greater reduction in terms of purchasing power. For years, state policy at the federal level should have been to oppose this rather

(*continued*)

> (continued)
> unfair redistribution mechanism via private household electricity bills, an effect which was originally not an intended outcome on the part legislators. For NRW, the reduction of purchasing power of households means weakening demand and the associated reduction in investment and growth. The inclusion of the electricity price-based disguised fiscal equalization system in the normal fiscal equalization system or a meaningful credit model is required here.

While nuclear power is to be phased out in Germany in 2022, coal-fired power generation will be phased out only by 2038. In any case, these are major changes which have been decreed by the state, and it is not yet quite clear whether the decisions are reasonable from the point of view of climate policy; it would perhaps be better to phase out coal-fired power generation by 2030, but let the nuclear power plants, which are favorable from the point of view of climate policy, run until 2040. At least in terms of climate policy, nuclear power plants can be classified as cheap because they have almost no CO_2 emissions. However, they have other major risks, and a major accident such as what occurred in Fukushima, Japan, has shown how enormous the cost of a major accident at a nuclear power plant could be. The fact that nuclear power plants in Germany only have to have liability insurance for a miserable €2.5 billion shows a silent, enormous subsidy, without which nuclear power would never have been competitive in Europe in the twentieth century.

This subsidization of nuclear power, in turn, has enormously hampered the expansion of renewable energies. In Germany, the state had to pump €10–20 billion of hidden subsidies into the electricity system over many years by increasing electricity prices for private households (via the Renewable Energy Levy), for example, in order to achieve the breakthrough of renewable energies. Is the subsidization of renewable energies by private households or the Renewable Energy Levy appropriate, or is it too high?

The restructuring of the current CO_2-intensive economy, including the housing and transport sectors, is a gigantic historic task: what are the main and side effects of steps toward a more climate-friendly economic structure; new products and new production processes will create millions of new jobs while at the same time, millions of old jobs will be lost—what is the net effect on employment, real income and net exports as well as the government budget? By how much will life expectancy increase, and which countries will be winners and losers in the world economy? What degree of global coordination is necessary for timely and strong climate protection, how can sufficient international coordination be promoted and which international organizations can play an important role in this?

In the modern Internet society, there is a tendency for millions of households to worry about problems which are not really pressing. In the US, for example, survey respondents completely overestimate the extent of globalization in the US—across all fields cited by respondents. In Europe, on the other hand, respondents in other surveys clearly overestimate unemployment rates in different countries by a factor of 2 or even 3. However, if the unemployment rate is clearly overestimated, then people tend to worry more about employment and job security where such worries should not play so big a role; even in Switzerland, the unemployment rate is overestimated by a factor of about 2. Those who struggle internally and politically with mainly imaginary problems often do not have enough energy left to successfully tackle the really important problem areas. Where does this misperception actually come from in the US or Europe?

Can Subsidies for Renewable Energies and Nuclear Power Be Justified?

Private households pay a good 6 cents per kilowatt hour of electricity; over the course of one year, this renewable energy surcharge to finance the guaranteed feed-in prices for solar and wind power producers, among others, raises about €20 billion, while the market price of the electricity generated was about €2 billion in 2018. Economists would only advocate a subsidy of €18 billion per year if there were positive externalities worth €18 billion—possibly in the form of damage from increased electricity production from fossil fuel sources being avoided. Germany's Federal Environment Agency (or *Umwelt Bundesamt—UBA*) estimates the damage caused by CO_2 emissions for 2016 at about €160 billion; since the electricity sector accounts for about one-third of CO_2 emissions, and about 32 percent of the electricity came from renewable sources in that year, the CO_2 emissions avoided through the renewable energy generation amount to about 10 percent of €160 billion, that is, €16 billion. A subsidy of €18 billion for renewables is roughly to be expected. One can argue that the Environment Agency's figure of €180 in damages per ton of CO_2 is implausibly high. If one assumes say rather €60 of damages per ton of CO_2, then the renewable energy subsidy is unreasonable.

This applies even if one argues that the fact that solar and wind power plants in Germany are heavily subsidized on the world market has led to falling prices for these plants—via static and dynamic mass production advantages. One could argue that the rapid installation of solar and wind power plants in China, India, the US and other countries has led to positive external effects internationally, since a reduction in CO_2 emissions of one metric ton in China, for example, leads to a reduction in damages in Germany of around €1.8 per metric ton: here it is assumed that Germany represents 1 percent of the world's population, and therefore a CO_2 emission reduction of one metric ton in China—with a population-based unit of sharing the global resulting damage or benefit sharing—means that the damage in Germany (€180 per metric ton of CO_2 according to the Federal Environment Agency) is reduced by 1 percent. Whether such a back-of-the-envelope attribution could be considered sensible is open to discussion.

The issue of subsidizing forms of energy is also relevant to nuclear power, for example, as can be seen. The accident at the medium-sized nuclear plant in Fukushima is likely to have cost a good $200 billion—a large share of this burden was borne by the state—that is, the Japanese taxpayers. A nuclear disaster near a major German city would have costs that could exceed the gross domestic product of almost €3500 billion (in 2018). Politicians in Germany have not dealt appropriately with the risk pricing of nuclear power plants in Germany; according to German law, nuclear power plants are to be insured with a liability insurance sum of €2.5 billion. The situation is akin to driving a car but only having to insure the fenders; every normal individual would recognize such a scenario as absurd, yet that is essentially how we behave with respect to nuclear power plants. Measured against the normal risks to be insured, the liability for nuclear plants amounts to hidden subsidies for such operations in Germany and many other OECD countries (on this debate, see Hennicke & Welfens, 2012). Moreover, there is in fact no normal market-wide comprehensive liability insurance policy for nuclear plant operators to purchase—not even the largest insurance companies could find reinsurers, and therefore the nuclear power plants are simply not marketable when risk costs are included. In 2022, this will end in Germany, which means large writedowns on capital in the nuclear power plant energy industry.

If you take a look at Japan, there is no end to the unreasonable approach even post-Fukushima. Nuclear reactors in Japan have gone back online, and not even the nuclear power plants on the Pacific side of the main Japanese islands, which are particularly risky in terms of the tsunami risk, have been permanently shut down. As far as the Fukushima accident is concerned, one can acknowledge Japan's luck in misfortune: that a US cruise ship filled with American tourists was not coincidentally located in the sea around the nuclear power plant accident site; if US tourists had been radioactively contaminated, US courts likely could and would have imposed hundreds of millions of dollars in compensation per person in verdicts against the Fukushima operator (think of the Monsanto lawsuits in the US against the weed-killer Roundup, which under certain conditions must probably be regarded as carcinogenic). It is also noteworthy to recall that a container ship from Japan was refused entry to the port of the university city of Xiamen in China 20 days after the Fukushima catastrophe because the radioactivity levels were deemed too high.

Climate Protection Is More Than Climate Protection Policy

Young people in dozens of countries are very concerned about the issue of global warming, and several thousand scientists find this concern quite appropriate in terms of the overall orientation: politics in leading industrialized countries—perhaps also in emerging economies—achieves too little, too many targets have been set, which have not been reached. Originally, the German government wanted to have two million electric vehicles on the road by 2020, then the target was reduced to one million in 2016, and this target also seems strangely unattainable; hardly 100,000 are to be expected to be driving on Germany's streets. Senior politicians in Berlin can be grateful that at least the federal company Deutsche Post, in conjunction with innovative scientists and entrepreneurs from the RWTH Aachen University, has provided for several thousand electric parcel distribution vehicles or "street scooters". Developments in the federal government's own vehicle fleet look modest; not even 10 percent of the vehicles were electric by the end of 2018, although there are many top range German and foreign vehicle brands represented.

German suppliers of electric buses are lagging far behind international competitors, and the whole issue of electromobility looks like resulting in significant job losses, especially since complex car parts such as the previous transmission are no longer needed in an electric car. Leading politicians delivered the Paris Climate Agreement in 2015, but initial optimism only lasted until the beginning of 2017, when a new kind of imbalance arose: the second largest CO_2 emitter and historically the largest of all—if you look at cumulated CO_2 emissions—the US, withdrew from the Paris Agreement under populist President Trump.

In a rather bizarre and incompetent line of argumentation, Trump has said that there is no man-made global warming and that the "climate problem" was in fact devised by China in order to weaken the US in international competition; Trump, the skilled contractor, thus openly contradicted thousands of leading US scientists and many thousands of climate researchers and experts (including physicists, meteorologists, geologists and oceanographers) across the world. There is little to be said for that. The Fridays for Future demonstrations, which students in Europe and other parts of the world—led by the Swedish Greta Thunberg—have held since 2018, may be considered somewhat exaggerated. Yet at least the overall direction of thought is correct, and of course it is obvious that young people would indeed worry about their future. Some of them are probably also concerned that in many countries climate protection policy promises a great many things, but often delivers only token gestures.

In the US, more and more people are driving energy-hungry SUVs, that is, thirsty and resource-intensive off-road vehicles. As they are not thoroughly regulated by politicians because they fall under the category of trucks, the design, production and marketing fantasies of the large US car companies and also of the Japanese and German manufacturers producing in the US have focused to some extent on producing these mega-cars. This is an irresponsible situation. Why do you need huge, off-road vehicles when living in large US cities or towns, or even seven- or nine-seater minibuses for small families? The taxation of cars by weight is an idea worth considering.

In Japan, there are rather few large cars because of the many narrow streets in Japanese urban areas, and Japanese environmental policy also has some approaches—such as the "top runner program"—which ensures a rapid diffusion of environmentally friendly innovations as all companies have to adopt the innovations of the leading companies within a relatively short period of time. In the days of Prussia, there were similar approaches to machines: the Prussian government paid entrepreneurs a purchase subsidy for new machines—which were mostly coming from England in those days—if the entrepreneur concerned demonstrated and explained the respective machine to a minimum number of other entrepreneurs. Today, is it certain that a sufficient level of green innovation will be available and that a rapid diffusion of such innovations will take place in Asia and Europe as well as in other regions of the world?

It is possible that very many climate-friendly innovations are currently being developed by companies in North America, Europe, Asia and other regions, but the (sometimes chaotic) dynamics of international political relations or even important national political systems are such that there is no reasonable, effective and efficient international cooperation. Could it even be possible that there will soon be a critical number of populist politicians around the world who, for a lack of competence and motivated by neo-nationalism and their rejection of multilateralism—including the role of international organizations—effectively prevent reasonable international cooperation on climate protection? For certain, sometimes strange reasons, the national policy debate may also focus politicians' attention and energy on sham problems—with the result that there is not enough political energy left in the area of climate protection to get the ball of actually urgently required laws, regulations and information rolling. There is indeed no shortage of such problems, as will be shown. For example, US citizens greatly overestimate the extent of globalization, which leads to fears in terms of globalization and multilateralism, while people in Europe overestimated the unemployment rate by more than double in 2018. This means, of course, that voters—and thus politicians—will focus their activities very strongly on apparent issues, while the extent of the very real climate problem, for example, may be underestimated. It is also strange to find that the world's leading car manufacturers, such as those in Germany, have only a modest ambition to reduce fossil energy consumption and the CO_2 emissions of cars and trucks.

Some of the possible delays and problems related to climate-friendly innovation policy are not yet on the political radar: such as the question of how increased global demand for climate-friendly products will affect structural change and income inequality in Germany and other countries. It can be regarded as quite impossible that an increasing demand for climate-friendly products in industrialized and emerging countries will—without meaningful flanking measures as shown here—lead to a stable social and political future. Rather, a significant increase in global demand for such products will lead to an increased demand for qualified, skilled workers and thus also to a rising ratio of the wages of skilled workers to those of unskilled workers: income inequality is thus increasing in almost all countries of the world, beyond the already emerging inequality trends in income due to technology disparities. How can climate-friendly progress, a limitation of income inequality in industrialized and emerging countries *and* sufficient international policy cooperation be achieved at the same time? How can companies be persuaded to view climate-friendly product and process innovations as welcome challenges rather than looking for ways to avoid meeting new efficiency and emission reduction requirements?

CO_2 reduction incentives exist in Germany, and the EU, above all in the form of CO_2 certificates, which companies generally have to buy at a market price as a "right to pollute". At barely €27 per ton of CO_2 in 2019, the certificate pricing was significantly below the €180 of damages per ton of CO_2 emissions, which the German Federal Environment Agency estimated. From an economic point of view, a CO_2 tax should reflect the amount of CO_2 damage. The Federal Environment Agency's estimate is controversial, but politicians have so far been somewhat carefree, although the price difference of €180 and €27 per ton of CO_2 in certificate trading is enormous. Moreover, in view of the manageable progress made in reducing CO_2 emissions in the period between 1990 and 2016, Germany will by 2030 have to achieve emission reduction rates three times as high as during the first mentioned period. This looks like a difficult task, and one can only start to see that the government in Berlin, and policymakers at an EU level, is beginning to take appropriate steps to reach the targets for 2040 and 2050. The later one begins to undertake serious reforms, the more pressing, hectic and misguided the adjustment activities will become in the decade from 2040 to 2050.

At first glance, it is difficult to comprehend that the diesel emission scams came from Germany of all places and that the state did not take quick and decisive action against the companies concerned, such as Volkswagen, Audi and Porsche. At a second glance, one comes to recognize the role of leading car companies as huge and influential lobbyists. The fact that center-of-the-road, mainstream parties could perhaps be digging their own electoral graves by essentially looking the other way and ignoring such issues became apparent to some extent in Germany, among other places, at the European Parliament elections in May 2019.

Without a comprehensive and analytical understanding of the problem areas in the field of economic-ecological policy, there will be no real progress and little chance of success. This study can, of course, make only a modest, yet hopefully important, critical contribution. The present study is characterized by a combination of approaches from Europe, North America, Latin America and Asia, and for the first time, new perspectives for climate-friendly housing and transport policies in certain areas are presented. The incentives in industrialized countries, including Germany, to date are not very effective in terms of achieving efficient progress toward a climate-friendly future. From the point of view developed here, it is also about a meaningful combination of various contributions to climate protection and the affordability of such progress—this is a task for economists and certainly important when one considers the social acceptance of climate policies in Western market economies. An exaggerated climate policy without broad social acceptance would simply be a springboard for the expansion of even more populism in Western countries and other regions of the world than had already become apparent by 2019. Populists in Western countries deny that there is an important climate protection problem and that man-made influences play a role in global warming. Populists are often quite expert on seductive rhetoric, empty promises and wishful thinking. One can expect science to first record and analyze the facts, then point out the various alternative solutions to problems identified—but it will be for politicians to finally decide which alternative it regards as most effective and capable of winning majority support.

REFERENCES

Hennicke, P., & Welfens, P. J. J. (2012). *Energiewende nach Fukushima: Deutscher Sonderweg oder weltweites Vorbild?* [transl. PJJW: Energy Turnaround after Fukushima: A Special Path for Germany or a Worldwide Role Model?]. oekom Verlag.

Korus, A. (2019). Erneuerbare Energien und Leitmärkte in der EU und Deutschland [transl. PJJW: Renewable Energies and Lead Markets in the EU and Germany]. In Welfens, P. J. J. (Ed.), *EU-Strukturwandel, Leitmärkte und Techno-Globalisierung* [transl. PJJW: EU Structural Change, Lead Markets and Technoglobalisation]. De Gruyter.

Menges, R., & Untiedt, G. (2016). Ökostromförderung in Schleswig-Holstein: Empirische Analyse der regionalen Verteilungswirkungen der EEG-Zahlungsströme, [transl. PJJW: Green Power Promotion in Schleswig-Holstein: An Empirical Analysis of the Regional Distribution Effects of EEG Cash Flows], Study on behalf of KSH-Gesellschaft für Energie- und Klimaschutz Schleswig-Holstein GmbH. Kiel, GEFRA.

CHAPTER 10

Climate Protection Policy: 2019 Special Report of the German Council of Economic Experts

The special report of the German Council of Economic Experts "Towards a New Climate Policy" (German Council of Economic Experts, 2019) stresses that globally uniform CO_2 certificate prices and an expansion of CO_2 emission certificate coverage beyond industry and the energy sector would be useful approaches. At its core, the Council of Economic Experts considers alternative measures intended to reduce emissions, such as CO_2 emission certificates and a CO_2 tax. A CO_2 tax outside the sectors that work with CO_2 emission certificates is regarded as a temporary but pragmatic climate protection solution, although it is not clear here how strong an effect a CO_2 tax (in those areas not covered by certificate trading) would have in the direction of reducing CO_2 emissions by providing an impetus for households and the sectors concerned. In the medium and long term, an expansion of the areas covered by CO_2 emission certificate trading in the EU would be preferable. In principle, one can agree with this, and many of the passages in the report are indeed easy to read for economists. Germany should not be a lonely pioneer in climate protection, but rather a role model encouraging others to adopt a similar position. Nevertheless, a whole series of critical points can be noted about this important report, some of which are fundamental in nature:

© The Author(s), under exclusive license to Springer Nature Switzerland AG 2022
P. J.J. Welfens, *Global Climate Change Policy*, Sustainable Development Goals Series, https://doi.org/10.1007/978-3-030-94594-7_10

- Questions of climate-friendly innovation policy are only marginally considered—in the latter part of the analysis even though, from an economic logic point of view, climate-friendly innovations should be regarded as a fundamentally important problem-solving option and, moreover, within the government (in Germany as in most OECD and G20 countries) ministries other than that concerned with the environment are responsible for research funding.
- CO_2 certificate prices fluctuate quite considerably, and listed energy and industrial companies with surplus certificates—which have to be accounted for according to the applicable rules—therefore experience fluctuations in share prices via fluctuations in certificate prices, whereby the increased volatility of share prices is likely to have a negative influence on investments and innovations; however, this aspect must also be taken into consideration when comparing the policy options of CO_2 certificates or stable and predictably rising CO_2 tax rates.
- Options for the technical cooling (read: geoengineering) of the atmosphere are practically not discussed at all, which means a considerable narrowing of the analysis. There are a number of methods that have already been investigated in DFG (*Deutsche Forschungsgemeinschaft*—the German Research Foundation) projects involving a range of natural scientists and economists.
- The increase in income inequality in industrialized and emerging countries as a result of increased climate protection policy is not addressed. Although the Council points out that low-carbon production is generally capital intensive, low-carbon products and production processes are above all relatively skill intensive, so that the demand for qualified, skilled labor will increase relative to the demand for unskilled and the wage premium in favor of the skilled will thus increase. Increasing income inequality can, however, become a stumbling block in the transformation to a climate-friendly society. If the general demand for climate-friendly products increases in the OECD countries and in China plus the ASEAN countries—they are skill intensive in manufacturing—then the price of these products will rise and therefore the remuneration of the relatively intensively used production factors will increase: this is skilled work and often also capital. It is necessary to find an answer to the resulting aggravated inequality problem, which comes at the expense of the unskilled and the low skilled.

- The capital market prospects for climate protection are hardly mentioned, although it is precisely the financing of better, more climate-friendly infrastructure and a different, more climate-conscious orientation of investors both nationally and internationally that is important. In this context, the role of multilateral banks including the World Bank should also be addressed, banks which—at the suggestion of Germany or other European countries—could co-finance climate protection projects abroad or in important partner countries. Germany—as with France, the UK etc.—is a member of the World Bank, the Asian Development Bank and the "Eastern Europe Bank", the European Bank for Reconstruction and Development. Questions of insurance coverage for different sources of energy are also not addressed, although nuclear power receives enormous indirect subsidies with a statutory minimum of just €2.5 billion in terms of liability insurance in Germany. No insurance company in the world would be prepared to insure against a nuclear accident with an expected loss of approx. €5000 billion, or 1.5 times the annual gross domestic product of Germany, at a price that would still leave nuclear energy on the market (Hennicke & Welfens, 2012).
- The Council's report points out that it would be desirable for Germany to exert greater influence at the international negotiating table. Yet there are unfortunately no further considerations in this regard; although in view of the fact that Germany represents circa 3 percent of global CO_2 emissions, and the EU only about 10 percent, the question of a climate policy globalization strategy is very important from both a German and an EU perspective. One conceivable approach would be for the EU and China to integrate to some extent their CO_2 emissions trading systems while at the same time intensifying research cooperation in areas of climate protection—possibly with expansion options to include ASEAN countries, Mercosur countries or NAFTA countries or, in the absence of national approaches, individual US states as well as Canadian provinces and territories. Reference has already been made to the need to involve regional development banks and the World Bank; Berlin and leading EU countries have so far lacked a strategy here.
- The German government has an enormous credibility problem with the younger generations when it comes to climate protection, as the Fridays for Future protests spearheaded by schoolchildren in Germany show; it also has this problem to a certain extent among a

broader section of the population. Any government (or grand coalition) that announces a target of one million electric vehicles by 2020 and then ends up with 100,000 has either too little understanding of target-setting or is simply incompetent in some areas. It is hard to conceive that a government with a visible and major reputation or competence problem at home can, despite a significant international negotiating weight, have a serious impact.

- The investigation of the German Council of Economic Experts is quite simply incomprehensible to a large part of the public: a single descriptive graph with individual fields of action is presented—alongside various graphs with time series or comparative bar charts. The aim of the Council, however, is to promote public debate. In a phase in which certain sections of society completely reject academic, scientific or economic analyses of climate change—as apparently large sections of support particularly of right-wing populist parties do—or, as with the relevant youth-led groups, are close to an internal panic, it would be very important to have a balanced and well-founded study of the possibilities for action in climate protection policy in a widely understandable and accessible format. The rudimentary summary is only superficially helpful in this respect; an explanatory YouTube video, for example, is missing.

Role of Multilateral Development Banks in Energy and Transport Transformation

In its 2017 Annual Report, the European Bank for Reconstruction and Development (EBRD) focused on environmental policy and sustainability issues, while the EBRD actually co-financed numerous projects in Eastern European EU countries (EBRD, 2017). It is important in this context that the EBRD projects generally also support efficiency gains and often innovation projects and, in some cases, also research or innovation projects that would have climate-friendly effects if implemented in the economy. If one asks oneself who should help to push climate protection-friendly innovation projects, one thinks initially about innovative firms on the one hand, but capital markets and, in this context, the multilateral development banks are also important players: from the EBRD via the Inter-American Development Bank to the African Development Bank and the Asian Development Bank, as well as the younger Asian Infrastructure Investment Bank (AIIB) based in Beijing, and the World Bank; in terms of

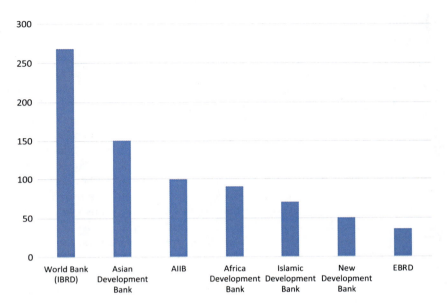

Fig. 10.1 Equity (subscribed capital) of multilateral development banks and the World Bank (in billions of US$, 2017). (Source: Own calculations and presentation according to published, publicly available data from the relevant banks for 2017)

equity capital, the latter two are also the largest (see Fig. 10.1).Thus, there are considerable opportunities worldwide to co-finance the long-term modernization requirements in the energy and transport sectors through multilateral banks. There are also enormous opportunities for the EU countries represented in these banks to set the course for more climate protection policy worldwide, including outside of Europe. The relevant EU countries would have to form a meaningful and coherent group on this issue—also involving the European Commission—and develop a corresponding consensus strategy. Here, we will see what role the new president of the European Commission can and wants to play.

Cost Aspects of Energy System Transformation

In a report of the German Academies of Sciences (within the framework of the project "Energy Systems of the Future" (ESYS)), a number of important findings on the topic of efficient climate protection were developed. The summary of Pittel and Henning (2019) stresses the following points:

- If CO_2 neutrality is to be achieved in Germany by 2050, adjustment costs will arise in the form of investments, the import of sources of energy, maintenance and operating costs for plants and the domestic production of certain energy sources: the difference between the climate protection scenario and the current development path (a "business-as-usual" scenario) is the cost of the energy system transformation, which can be described as cumulative total systemic costs; in a broader perspective, beyond the energy sector, other sectors of the economy can also be included, and finally, in a comprehensive approach the so-called external costs of CO_2 emissions can also be included. These are essentially the consequential costs of climate change, for example, as recorded in the Stern Report. Pittel and Henning (2019) estimate the cost of one metric ton of CO_2 emitted at between €40 and €350 for the global economy. The external costs of Germany's greenhouse gas emissions in 2018 are therefore in the range of €35–300 billion. That is, one must admit, a wide range of values.
- On the basis of model calculations, the cumulative systemic additional costs for an energy system transformation by 2050 amount to between €500 billion and a good €3000 billion. This corresponds to about 0.04 percent to 2.5 percent of Germany's gross domestic product in 2019. Rather lower costs will result if, for example, the electricity market is better integrated within the EU, for example, through the expansion of interconnectors in the cross-border electricity transmission network.
- The expected CO_2 avoidance costs result from considering the systemic additional costs and the CO_2 emissions avoided. In the favorable case, the net amount is about €60 per metric ton of CO_2, and in unfavorable cases up to €400 per metric ton.
- The existing levy system in Germany—as the special report of the German Council of Economic Experts points out—can be characterized as being unsystematic and overly complicated. Petrol and diesel are charged at around €60 per metric ton, whereas heating with crude oil for private households incurs a cost of just €8 per metric ton of CO_2. Electricity, in turn, is subject to a total charge of around €200 per metric ton in the form of an electricity tax, emission

certificates and the Renewable Energy Levy. If, however, electricity from renewable energies is in the future to be used more sensibly than currently in the transport sector and in heat generation, then the artificially high electricity price burdens must absolutely be reduced. If by 2021, more than 50 percent of electricity comes from renewable sources, it would be odd to artificially increase the cost of consuming relatively climate- and environmentally friendly electricity.

All in all, the CO_2 burden resulting from a conversion of the economic system into a climate-friendly new system is within manageable limits: with about 10 metric tons of CO_2 per capita in emissions and a CO_2 price of €50 per metric ton, this results in a burden of €500 per year. Since, however, the CO_2 emissions decrease over time as a result of climate protection policies, the burden per year also decreases. In Sweden, an annual reduction in CO_2 emissions of 1 percent was achieved between 1991 and 2017 through a combination of emission certificates and a CO_2 tax. However, such a reduction path is still far too small if CO_2 climate neutrality is to be achieved in Germany and the EU by 2050.

References

EBRD. (2017). *Sustainability Report*. European Bank for Reconstruction and Development.

German Council of Economic Experts. (2019, July). *Setting Out for a New Climate Policy*, Special Report. Berlin. Retrieved 1 September, 2019, from https://www.sachverstaendigenrat-wirtschaft.de/fileadmin/dateiablage/gutachten/sg2019/sg_2019_en.pdf

Hennicke, P., & Welfens, P. J. J. (2012). *Energiewende nach Fukushima: Deutscher Sonderweg oder weltweites Vorbild?* [Transl.: Energy Transition After Fukushima: A Special Path for Germany or a Worldwide Role Model]. oekom Verlag.

Pittel, K., & Henning, H. M. (2019, July 12). Klimapolitik: Energiewende erfolgreich steuern, Was uns die Energiewende wirklich kosten wird [transl. PJJW: Climate Policy: Successfully Managing the Energy System Transformation, What the Energy System Transformation Will Really Cost Us]. *Frankfurter Allgemeine Zeitung*, FAZ Online Edition. Retrieved July 22, 2019, from https://www.faz.net/aktuell/wirtschaft/klimapolitik-energiewende-erfolgreich-steuern-16280130.html

CHAPTER 11

Failures in Carbon Certificates and Emissions Trading Systems?

From an economic point of view, the trading of carbon certificates on markets such as the EU Emissions Trading System is the cheapest method of achieving climate protection: improvements in terms of global warming abatement at the lowest possible cost. It is necessary to define the scope of relevant emissions trading systems, which comprises a modest 45 percent in the EU ETS—namely the energy sector plus industry—but which reaches 85 percent coverage in California. In California, free certificates were allocated to energy suppliers (100 percent), and in the EU such allocations were for the most part made to companies in the export sector. Emissions trading that is of an insufficient dimension, as in the EU (cf. Fig. 11.1), is seriously flawed. Why should California be able to achieve 85 percent coverage, while the EU misses out on the possible coverage of a further 40 percent of emissions? Other means may then be used to make up the shortfall—if at all—and these are in any case more expensive than the adjustment costs involved in emissions certificate trading; the EU weakens its own growth dynamic through an undersized ETS.

One important question in certificate trading concerns the effects of a minimum price. Burmeister and Peterson (2017) have developed a model for Germany and the EU that suggests a minimum price of CO_2 emissions of around €37 per metric ton could be helpful. For the EU, and also for other certificate trading areas, this is an important question that should be examined more closely. The certificate price sends a signal to investors,

© The Author(s), under exclusive license to Springer Nature Switzerland AG 2022
P. J.J. Welfens, *Global Climate Change Policy*, Sustainable Development Goals Series,
https://doi.org/10.1007/978-3-030-94594-7_11

249

EU Emissions Trading System (EU ETS)

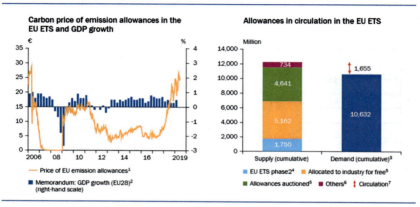

Fig. 11.1 EU Emissions Trading System (EU ETS). (Source: German Council of Economic Experts (2019), Setting out for a new climate policy, Special Report 2019, Chart 7, p. 36)

and, of course, the emission certificates held also form part of a company's balance sheet, so fluctuations in the certificate price will affect the company's net asset position.

It is important to note that the allocation of about 20 percent of the stock of certificates in the form of free certificates allocated to companies to account for certain corporate issues achieves profit neutrality (Bushnell et al., 2013). Thus, if the state really would issue 100 percent of certificates free of charge to companies, this would be a major economic policy error as it would artificially increase corporate profits: it is effectively a redistribution in favor of capital, as a factor of production, and the owners of the corresponding enterprises. However, this cannot be the purpose of climate protection policy; it is not intended to turn a blind eye to a redistribution from labor to capital.

A certain problem with certificate trading in the EU, as well as in the US federal state of California, is the sometimes very high volatility of certificate prices. From an economic perspective, the certificate price should represent the (marginal) cost of reducing CO_2 emissions by one unit.

However, it is quite implausible to assume that one day this marginal cost is $8 per metric ton and the next day it is $15. Emissions certificates have of course become part of broader financial markets, whose temporarily high fluctuation intensity is apparently also transferred to emissions certificate trading. The efficiency of the certificate trading system is impaired by the price fluctuations and volatility. Therefore, the link between financial market developments and the certificate market remains to be investigated. Apart from this aspect, from an economic point of view, there should be no reservations about the crucial role of such certificate trading. One could certainly consider whether better regulation of the certificate trading system and financial markets in general could bring more stability and efficiency to both fields.

The certificate price in California in March 2018 was around $15 per metric ton, in the EU more than €20, that is, more than $22. This is an indication that California has lower CO_2 reduction costs than the EU. The integration of the EU ETS with that of California—or indeed with other countries—would therefore bring advantages. EU-California integration would bring about a reduction in the price of CO_2 certificates in the EU, reducing adjustment costs; but the overall EU plus California adjustment would not be reduced if a common ceiling in terms of emissions is set. Such an integration, with a view to climate protection policy, is desirable in the medium term, so the EU should consider with some urgency to start corresponding talks with California, but also with the Republic of Korea and the relevant regions there, as well as with China.

The empirical analysis of De Haas and Popov (2019) has shown that countries with well-developed stock markets—and otherwise comparable economic indicators—have lower per capita emissions. There are two important analysis results:

- Equity markets exert pressure on investment spending in favor of sectors with a relatively low CO_2 emission intensity, as the authors deduce from sectoral analyses.
- Moreover, green/sustainability-oriented patent dynamics in CO_2 emission-intensive industries are increasing in the context of a stock market deepening.

As a consequence, one can conclude that financial market modernization in Europe and other regions of the world can therefore be important for more growth and better developments in the field of emissions; here, one can discern the apparent lack of appropriate course-setting in the Eurozone, whereas the US and UK are known to have a stronger stock market orientation of the financial markets.

By way of a sensible regulatory and policy approach, and promoting the holding of equities and a share culture among savers, the state can provide critical impulses with regard to wealth accumulation and climate protection.

Climate change, or more precisely the associated extreme weather events, endangers life and property in regions affected by such extreme conditions. By examining the case of New York and Hurricane Sandy, which hit the US on 26 October 2012, Rehse et al. (2019) find that real estate certificates from disaster regions were traded relatively little and that the differences between purchase and sale prices were high: extreme weather—or the climate change on which such weather depends—leads to less liquidity on real estate markets. According to this, the economic demand for money would have to increase in order to maintain the desired overall level of liquidity. This reaction on the part of portfolio investors would then likely lead to a dampening of the macroeconomic price level. This is only one aspect of the connection between climate development—as well as climate policy—and financial market dynamics.

There are sectors in the EU that are part of the EU Emissions Trading System. Then again, there are also additional state interventions intended to reduce CO_2 emissions in various ways through special political projects. An excessive level of government interventions designed to reduce CO_2 emissions in sectors already subject to emissions trading can actually serve to weaken the market signals from the certificate market and ultimately to create price volatility on the certificate markets, effectively undermining what should be a very powerful mechanism to reduce CO_2 emissions across the economy. In a contribution to the literature on emissions trading, Borenstein et al. (2019) point out—with a view to California—that government interventions outside the framework of the respective emissions trading system and uncertainty about emission levels in a state without an emissions trading system will lead to a significant propensity for either very low or very high certificate prices: this means that—and this should also apply to the EU ETS—a considerable instability of certificate prices can occur, partly due to additional interventions by the state. With regard to the EU, and Germany in particular, one can point here to the enormous extra intervention of the so-called German Coal Commission, which is apparently supported by parts of the federal government in Berlin in ignorance of the relevant contributions to the specialist literature. The allowance system can bring about different equilibrium points as a market equilibrium—namely, one equilibrium point at a very high price, one equilibrium point at a very low price and one equilibrium point at a normal price. If policymakers proceed with radical additional interventions which prevent the certificate trading market from finding a normal mean price level as a point of equilibrium, the certificate market can potentially see volatile fluctuation back and forth between phases of very high and phases of very low prices (technically speaking, no internal equilibrium position is reached). The market signals for a climate-friendly innovation dynamic would then de facto be confusing and weak, and the social usefulness of the entire certificate trading system, which can achieve CO_2 reduction at minimum cost, would be undermined and possibly completely negated. From a political point of view, additional interventions of the state in the certificate market should therefore be wisely limited—and not simply undertaken for good headlines and viral Internet publicity campaigns, which may bring extra sympathy or political support for a few days, but which would undermine the certificate market in the longer term. It needs to be examined whether the UK certificate market—which has a minimum price for emissions certificates—was more stable than other EU submarkets. Of course, the state can create an instrument by means of a reserve tranche of emissions certificates that could be used to help prevent or cushion extreme increases or falls in certificate prices. Such a reserve emissions certificate tranche available in California and in the EU should stabilize market expectations upward outside periods of crisis.

The German Council of Economic Experts (2019) has published some interesting considerations on the issue of the free allocation of allowances to companies (paragraphs 59–62), which also show, however, that the distribution aspects of favoring companies with a large free allocation of emission certificates are not recognized, even though 5162 million metric tons were allocated free of charge in the first half of 2009. Neither the paper of Bushnell et al. (2013) nor the literature cited therein is referenced by the Council in its report; only paragraph 189, referring to De Bruyn et al. (2016), refers to the fact that companies may even generate additional profits by participating in certificate trading.

The Council writes (2019, points 60 and 61, p. 35):

> *All certificates were originally allocated to companies free of charge. Since 2013, however, electricity producers have not received any more free certificates, although exemptions apply to some less affluent member states. A total of 57 %*

of all emissions allowances issued during the third trading period (2013–2020) are auctioned. Auctions of new allowances (primary market) and trading in certificates (secondary market) currently take place mainly on the European Energy Exchange (EEX) and the Intercontinental Exchange (ICE), with only small volumes being traded in the secondary market on other exchanges or over the counter (OTC). Almost daily auctions are intended to ensure that these are seamlessly integrated into the market and that the prices achieved in auctions are consistent with the level of prices in exchange trading.

Since the second trading period (2008–2012) it has been possible to transfer unused allowances to the following period. Transactions in certificates are booked to an account held with the EU emissions trading register (Union Register), which is operated by the European Commission. All actors involved in the EU ETS, which include banks and trading houses, possess such an account. For Germany these accounts are administered by the German Emissions Trading Authority (DEHSt).

Prices in the EU ETS have repeatedly fallen sharply since 2005. In addition to the free allocation of certificates during the first two trading periods (2005–2012), severe economic downturns such as the recession of 2008/09 and the related decline in industrial production are likely to have exerted strong downward pressure on prices. Furthermore, companies were able to use international credits to meet their commitments under the EU ETS. Unused allowances have been transferred to Phase III (2013–2020). Given the accelerated expansion of renewable energy in countries such as Germany, this situation created a large surplus of certificates in the EU ETS, so the price of certificates remained below €10 per tonne of CO_2 for some time.

The enormous quantities of emissions certificates allocated for free indicate that the EU Emissions Trading System has in fact had a significant redistributive effect in favor of the large companies that have received significant amounts of free allowances. Finally, one of the most important questions remaining concerns how climate protection policy affects macroeconomic development. In essence, this question can be answered only if at least one energy sector and an emissions certificate market are integrated into existing macro models. This would make such models more complicated, but the simulations which could be developed using the new, expanded models would certainly be more interesting for the worlds of business and politics and indeed society at large. It would be easier to understand the adaptation processes which are to be expected—and how national or international policy can then influence them.

References

Borenstein, S., Bushnell, J., Wolak, F., & Zaragoza-Watkins, M. (2019). Expecting the Unexpected: Emissions Uncertainty and Environmental Market Design. *American Economic Review, 109*(11), 3953–3977. https://doi.org/10.1257/aer.20161218

Burmeister, J., & Peterson, S. (2017). *National Climate Policies in Times of the European Union Emission Trading System (EU ETS)* (Kiel Working Paper No. 2052). Institute for World Economics.

Bushnell, J. B., Chong, H., & Mansur, E. T. (2013). Profiting from Regulation: Evidence from the European Carbon Market. *American Economic Journal: Economic Policy, 5*, 78–106. https://doi.org/10.1257/pol.5.4.78

De Bruyn, S., Schep, E., & Cherif, S. (2016). *Calculation of Additional Profits of Sectors and Firms from the EU ETS*. Report 7.H44, CE DELFT – Committed to the Environment, Delft.

De Haas, R., & Popov, A. (2019). *Finance and Carbon Emissions* (ECB Working Paper Series, No 2318). European Central Bank: Frankfurt am Main. https://www.ecb.europa.eu/pub/pdf/scpwps/ecb.wp2318~44719344e8.en.pdf

German Council of Economic Experts. (2019). *Setting Out for a New Climate Policy*. Special Report July 2019: Berlin. Retrieved 1 September, 2019, from https://www.sachverstaendigenrat-wirtschaft.de/fileadmin/dateiablage/gutachten/sg2019/sg_2019_en.pdf

Rehse, D., Riordan, R., Rottke, N., & Zietz, J. (2019). The Effects of Uncertainty on Market Liquidity: Evidence from Hurricane Sandy. *Journal of Financial Economics, 134*(2), 318–332. https://doi.org/10.1016/j.jfineco.2019.04.006

CHAPTER 12

Macroeconomic Aspects of CO_2 Pricing

The effects of the pricing of CO_2 emissions on growth, employment and income distribution can be investigated in intertemporal equilibrium models. In principle, CO_2 prices cause the (marginal) costs of companies to rise. If a CO_2 tax is introduced, there will be considerable revenue generated for public coffers unless the revenue from the CO_2 tax is largely returned to the taxpayers in some form of transfer payments or tax reductions elsewhere. Therefore, investments will decline to the extent that capital—that is, machinery and equipment—and energy use are considered complementary. Some studies relating to the US and the Netherlands put the resulting decline in long-term real income at 0.1 percentage points of real income.

Of course, for such simulation results it is essential how the revenues from CO_2 taxes or certificate auctions are used by the state. With regard to the Netherlands, it can be stated that a revenue-neutral complementary reduction in corporation tax or income tax counteracts the production-dampening effect of CO_2 pricing (Hebbink et al., 2018); with a reduction in income tax, the net effect on real income development is even positive. There are other studies showing greater expansion effects from a reduction in corporate tax rates (Jorgenson & Wilcoxen 1993; Cogan et al., 2013; Goulder & Hafstead, 2013).

The problems associated with macroeconomic modeling are, however, somewhat more complicated than is often presented in the usual approaches, and the cobbling together of CO_2 taxes and emissions certificate trading is often not convincing. Certificate trading is more efficient, and in a two-country macro model with the "countries" of EU and China, one can expect that:

- Emissions certificate trading in the EU, initially expanding to cover 70 percent of emissions, and a parallel certificate trading system in China—with increased EU support for innovation—will result in low growth losses for the EU and China, with a loss of growth in China naturally having a negative feedback effect on the EU.
- If, at the same time, both certificate trading systems are integrated—after an expansion at national level (preferably to achieve a coverage of 85 percent of emissions)—the growth losses for the EU and China will be lower than in the case before. One problem with regard to China—and India—is that the issue of CO_2 certificate trading has not been widely discussed at G20 summits so far. The EU or even leading EU countries such as Germany, France or Italy could well try to advance this issue at the G20 summits in the future.
- Moreover, if a CO_2 tax is introduced for 25–30 percent of residual emissions, one-fifth of which is used to promote innovation in the EU and one-fifth used likewise in China—with the remaining four-fifths of CO_2 tax revenues returned to private households—the combined EU+China economic area is unlikely to suffer from growth dampening.
- The modeling becomes more complicated when looking at the tripolar EU-US-China, where of course continued US-China trade conflicts lead to a real income dampening effect in both China and the EU.
- A difficult question concerns the role of international technology transfer and—associated with it—the role of direct investment by multinational companies abroad. If US and EU companies in China could have 100 percent ownership of subsidiaries in climate-relevant sectors, then international technology transfer to China will be faster and more comprehensive than under the conditions of the rather limited ownership of subsidiaries in China. The question of the framework conditions for direct investments by multinationals, which are essential carriers of global innovation dynamics, should not be overlooked.

- From the point of view of the Western OECD countries, a considerable disadvantage in terms of climate protection dynamics is that Japan still does not have a national, comprehensive emissions trading scheme. It is quite incomprehensible that in the EU-Japan free trade negotiations of 2018, the issue of the rapid expansion of Japanese certificate trading from the two pilot regions (Tokyo and Saitama) to the whole of Japan would have played no role. Nevertheless, it is still good that there is an EU-Japan free trade agreement at all.
- If numerous large countries introduce CO_2 pricing, the demand for fossil fuel energies will decline; this will probably be accompanied by an increasing demand for real capital. The world's leading exporters of machinery and equipment, that is, Germany, Republic of Korea, Japan, the US, France, Italy, the Netherlands and Switzerland, should benefit from this; effects on the current account positions of these and other countries are to be expected in the medium term, and therefore also real exchange rate effects. A real appreciation of the Euro, Japanese Yen and US dollar is conceivable. Moreover, the demand for qualified workers is increasing in virtually all countries, which increases the wage premium or advantage of this group of workers over the relatively unskilled.
- As companies move closer to climate neutrality worldwide, they will ask themselves how the market value of the certificates they hold in their balance sheets will develop. There is a kind of "end-phase problem" here, as many companies will be tempted to place their remaining certificates in bulk onto the market in the final phase, shortly before climate neutrality is achieved. This could lead to sharp price reductions for CO_2 certificates and high price volatility for certificates, either in individual certificate trading regions or, in the case of integrated global certificate markets, to global price volatility, which in turn could also disrupt the world's stock markets. This could lead to negative wealth effects and a global recession. It would be worth considering providing for a standardized depreciation option for emission certificates in the national taxation regulations, whereby companies would have to decide on a certain date for the following decade whether they would like to write off the emission certificates evenly on a straight-line basis; or whether they would like to use a market valuation method. In any event, there are negative tax revenue effects in terms of corporate income taxes, which could be spread over a decade.

- The International Monetary Fund (IMF) could be called in to help poorer countries, which at the same time often have balance of payments problems, in the phase of a global slowdown in growth. The OECD and the G20 could also develop special growth initiatives to support transformation in the final phase, with the G20 Brisbane Summit of 2014 serving as a model at which the G20 countries committed to increasing real economic growth by 2 percent by 2019—compared to the normal growth path, with the OECD offering to help model various policy options for the participating countries, but also to identify and document the progress made by the G20 countries in meeting their targets.

Since Asia accounts for 60 percent of the world's population and most of the economic growth in the twenty-first century will probably take place in Asia, the relevant regional development banks Asian Development Bank (ADB) and Asian Infrastructure Investment Bank (AIIB)—with a seat in Beijing and geared to financing the new "Silk Road"—will play a major role in a phase of intensified climate protection policy. Here, it would be desirable for these regional banks to also provide support for initiatives to introduce emissions trading systems. Since the Asian Development Bank is dominated by Japan—and the US is also a large shareholder—the ADB could provide little impetus in this direction, at least not until Japan has itself implemented a national emissions trading system. As China's economic interests are the mainstay behind the AIIB, one can expect that the implementation of a national Chinese emissions trading system in 2021 (albeit a less ambitious scheme than previously assumed—covering only thermal power generation which is responsible for about 40 percent of emissions) will also encourage the promotion of similar systems in other Asian countries or in Eastern Europe. After all, the Silk Road stretches as far as Eastern Europe and ultimately also to Western Europe (including non-EU countries).

How Much Does Global Climate Neutrality Cost?

The annual emission of carbon dioxide in the world in 2017 was 36 billion tons, by 2050 or so this will at times have reached up to 48 billion tons per year. If not only the EU, Republic of Korea, China, California plus Quebec and Japan (with two prefectures), but at least all of the G20 countries would have a certificate trade covering 90 percent of the emissions by around 2030, then the following approximate calculations can be made—if the global certificate price (possibly an average of the various certificate prices) amounts to €40 per metric ton and the G20 countries accounted for 90 percent of the global emissions:

- Since a certificate price of €40 per metric ton also corresponds to the (marginal) costs—under certain assumptions also to the average costs—of eliminating one metric ton of CO_2 emitted, the aforementioned figures would result in an annual cost for 72 percent climate protection neutrality of €1382.4 billion, which corresponds to about $1500 billion. It is assumed that 48 billion metric tons of CO_2 emissions will be reached in 2030, which is likely to be too optimistic in the absence of an effective global climate policy. With a global national product of about $100,000 billion (2030), this amounts to about 1.5 percent of this world income. If one wants to achieve 95 percent climate neutrality, the order of magnitude is likely to reach about 3 percent of world income in 2030. If the world economy reached an annual real economic growth rate of 3 percent, one would in fact have to be content with 1.5 percent if one assumes climate neutrality of about 75 percent. This means for an average household that the annual income—here set low at €30,000—does not increase by €900 per year (without CO_2 reduction costs) but instead by €450. If you have an annual income of €60,000 (as in many industrialized countries), the income would not increase by €1800 but instead by €900. This is a considerable dampening of income, but not an intolerable one. If one fails to reduce CO_2 emissions to the extent described above, from the point of view of most households one would have another problem, which is also extremely costly: insurance companies would increase insurance premiums for buildings worldwide, which would cause rents or property costs to rise accordingly and would mean asset losses—especially for households that have real estate in regions for which insurance companies no longer offer insurance at all due to the increased risk of flooding and storms. If climate protection progress is insufficient, floods and extreme weather events will occur more frequently, leading to significant asset value losses due to real estate being destroyed and probably also to an increased number of fatalities and injured. Between 2030 and 2050, one would have to come with further steps toward 90 percent climatic neutrality. Technical progress, especially progress in emissions reductions, will be decisive for the long-term burden of climate protection policy. If this rate of progress is high, global CO_2 emissions in 2040 could be only 20 billion metric tons, and the price would not necessarily have to be significantly higher than €40 per metric ton (calculated at constant prices). The emission costs would thus only be at about 0.5 percent of world income, and by 2050 they could have fallen proportionally to about 0.3 percent of world income.

- If there were an integrated global CO_2 certificate market by around 2030, countries like India, Russia and probably also the US could be exporters of CO_2 certificates, while Japan, China and the EU could import certificates. The question of whether the structural current account deficit ratios of major countries in the world economy would change will have to be considered. If the US were to be a net exporter of CO_2 certificates, the US current account position would improve, and a real appreciation of the dollar would be expected. A net export position of the US in CO_2 certificates can be expected if the whole of the US follows, for example, California; relatively early and CO_2-efficient innovations from California and other US states are implemented relatively quickly across the whole of the US.
- It must be assumed that global emissions will decline in the longer term during the 2030s and 2040s. This is particularly the case when emissions trading systems require an annual reduction in the volume of the emissions cap of -5 percent, -6 percent or even -7 percent. If CO_2-reducing innovations have been strongly promoted until 2030 and 2040—in the respective preceding decade—then reductions in the order of magnitude of -6 percent or -7 percent per year should definitely be feasible. However, it will not be possible to create such orders of magnitude without a significantly increased global promotion of innovation in this area—including more basic research. If in 2045 only 10 metric gigatons of CO_2 are to be emitted and the CO_2 certificate price (in 2020 prices) is possibly €100 or €150 per metric ton, then in such a scenario it is indeed foreseeable that the costs of a further reduction of one metric ton of CO_2 emissions are indeed relatively high.
- Assuming a significantly higher emissions certificate price of €80 per metric ton in 2030, then 72 percent climate neutrality would cost 3 percent of the world income, that is, also 3 percent of the average per capita income. However, an approximate climate neutrality of 72

percent should not be a bad scenario at all. Global afforestation measures and the artificial lowering of the temperature of the atmosphere can increase climate neutrality to circa 90 percent—which science considers necessary—with manageable costs.

- The level of CO_2 abatement costs naturally depends to a large extent on the innovation dynamics of the relevant technologies—given the degree to which CO_2 emissions are covered: the extent of sustainability innovations (Erdem, 2015) and the corresponding state support for such innovations are important, as are the framework conditions for national and international diffusion of new technologies. If climate protection mitigating innovations can be quickly diffused internationally, to which the activities of multinational companies and the Internet, among other things, contribute, this will also contribute to lowering the global average costs of CO_2 reduction. International trade conflicts are certainly detrimental to such diffusion effects; for this reason, a Trumpian trade conflict policy is also a problem of climate policy.

There are further one-off adjustment costs, since, for example, replacement capacities have to be created for electricity generation (based on renewable energies), additional power lines and large batteries have to be installed and energy-related building refurbishment costs and additional infrastructure costs (such as installing overhead power line systems for hybrid trucks) must also be necessarily incurred. However, this should not account for more than 0.1–0.3 percent of the gross domestic product over 30 years; in modern economies this will be seen as part of the normal structural change which economies undergo, and in return one should see a more stable climate with fewer risks for all. Nevertheless, achieving comprehensive climate protection means the end of the current comfort zone, as the global economy will or must adapt over three decades in a row. This is very unusual, especially since increased international cooperation is also required, especially from Western industrialized countries with countries in Asia—but perhaps the most difficult part of the EU's cooperation will indeed not be with Asia, but with the US. If populists were in power in Europe or in the White House in the US for a longer period of time, there would be not only further trade conflicts but also climate protection conflicts. At least one can hope that international cooperation should not be a problem at the level of cooperation between scientists from all over the world. It is also conceivable that, as the climate problem worsens, the share of populist parties in Western countries will fall again at a certain point.

Therefore, there is little to speak for a great sense of pessimism in Europe or the world, at least if one assumes that there is sufficient international willingness to cooperate among the G20 countries, and among all countries. Future populist administrations in the US in the long run would be a global climate protection problem; a populist Indian government that rejects comprehensive climate protection measures would certainly also be one. In any case, the EU countries and allied international actors (possibly the EU27 plus the UK, Japan, Republic of Korea, California, Canada, etc.) should bear in mind that it would not be wise to set up climate protection programs that would inadvertently only serve to strengthen populism nationally and internationally for a lack of meaningful accompanying measures. However, one must also warn against naive assumptions:

- Reaching 90 percent climate neutrality for the global economy by 2050 is not possible unless all G20 countries have introduced comprehensive emissions trading systems by 2030.
- It would be a serious global problem if the US would again have a populist president who would withdraw the US from international cooperate measures such as the Paris Climate Agreement under President Trump. For some perspective, one can recall that the former mayor of New York, Michael Bloomberg, founded an initiative called We Are Still In and brought on board more than 2500 top managers and the mayors and administrations of dozens of cities across the US to engage in CO_2 reduction measures, which should enable half of the original US pledge at the 2015 Paris Climate Summit to be fulfilled (Hsu & Weinfurter, 2018). President Trump's dismantling of the previous Obama administration's environmental regulations seriously undermined the basis for US contributions to climate protection in the longer term, possibly apart from the contributions of California and the RGGI—another regional CO_2 certificates trading pact in the northeast of the US. President Trump is thus likely to have weakened the innovative strength of the US economy in the longer term and thus indirectly increased the US current account deficit, which could further weaken the dollar. How quickly and effectively President Biden can counteract years of Trump's policies remains to be seen.

It is therefore essential that climate protection policy, including emissions trading systems, should be developed in a way that is easy for the entire electorate to understand or be presented by the government. In Germany, the Merkel governments have not really delivered on this point. In 2019 it is apparently still completely unclear to school pupils and students in Germany that protests and "occupy" movements in the Rhenish lignite mining area with the aim of prematurely shutting down coal-fired power plants do little to help the climate—since the energy sector together with industry is already part of the EU ETS (with an EU-wide annual cap for the emissions quantities of the energy sector plus industry)—as this shows that pupils, students and apparently also many teachers do not know or do not understand the EU ETS which has applied since 2005. Voters cannot really be reproached, simply because the German government and the EU have for almost two decades not really bothered to explain the benefits of the innovative EU ETS. Such systems have also worked well in the past, for example, in the reduction of sulfur emissions in the US and Europe.

REFERENCES

Cogan, J. F., Taylor, J. B., Wieland, V., & Wolters, M. H. (2013). Fiscal Consolidation Strategy. *Journal of Economic Dynamics and Control, 37*(2), 404–421. https://doi.org/10.1016/j.jedc.2012.10.004

Erdem, D. (2015). *Foreign Direct Investments, Innovation Dynamics and Energy Efficiency.* Verlag Dr. Kovač.

Goulder, L. H., & Hafstead, M. A. C. (2013). *Tax Reform and Environmental Policy: Options for Recycling Revenue from a Tax on Carbon dioxide* (Discussion Paper RFF DP 13–31). Resources for the Future: Washington, DC.

Hebbink, G., et al. (2018). *The Price of Transition: An Analysis of the Economic Implications of Carbon Taxing.* DNB Occasional Studies 1608, Netherlands Central Bank, Research Department.

Hsu, A., & Weinfurter, A. (2018, September 24). All Climate Politics Is Local. *Foreign Affairs.* Online Edition https://www.foreignaffairs.com/articles/united-states/2018-09-24/all-climate-politics-local

Jorgenson, D. W., & Wilcoxen, P. J. (1993). Reducing US Carbon Emissions: An Econometric General Equilibrium Assessment. *Resource and Energy Economics, 15*(1), 7–25. https://doi.org/10.1016/0928-7655(93)90016-N

CHAPTER 13

Financial Market Aspects of CO_2 Certificate Trading in the European Union

How does the emissions certificate trade in the European Union affect production volumes and the profits of participating companies? Such as energy producers and industrial companies? The certificate trade ultimately leads to a certificate price that influences the production costs of the companies concerned: the higher the certificate price for one metric ton of CO_2 emitted, the higher the costs of the companies involved; to consider just one sector, say the production of steel, the question arises as to how certificate trading affects the cost curve of the competing companies, and how the new sales price or the equilibrium price on the goods market (i.e., the steel market) develops.

Using an "event study" methodology, Bushnell et al. (2013) have investigated how the certificate price affects the companies integrated in the EU Emissions Trading System (i.e., the energy sector and industry) on the basis of the sudden strong fall of the CO_2 certificate price, which occurred at the end of April 2006. In the previous year, the value of the certificates held by companies according to the market price still amounted to around €60 billion; the price collapse at the end of April 2006 reduced the value of the emission certificates held by €28 billion. For 552 companies listed on the European stock exchange, the authors examine the effects of the effective halving of the price of certificates at the end of April 2006, looking at companies from the electricity sector and industry, usually companies with a high share of sales in the EU. On the one hand, the

© The Author(s), under exclusive license to Springer Nature Switzerland AG 2022
P. J.J. Welfens, *Global Climate Change Policy*, Sustainable Development Goals Series,
https://doi.org/10.1007/978-3-030-94594-7_13

unit production costs of industrial companies and power generation companies fell, but on the other hand sales also fell and the effect on sales was stronger than on costs. As a result, corporate returns fell, which caused share prices to fall. The corollary would indicate that rising certificate prices are therefore likely to lead to rising share prices. The introduction of an emission allowance system has therefore had no negative economic impact on the EU as a whole. As a result, negative economic effects are hardly to be expected in other industrialized countries either.

There are a number of simulation studies to determine the effects of an emissions trading system for the US and the EU (Bovenberg & Goulder, 2001; Goulder et al., 2010; Burtraw & Palmer, 2008; Smale et al., 2006), which work with the assumption of Cournot competition, that is, an oligopoly in which a small number of suppliers set their production volumes in relation to their competitors: the main finding is that the inclusion of companies in an emissions trading system leaves the profit situation unchanged if approximately 20 percent of the volume of emissions is linked to free certificate allocations by the state. Therefore, the often much more generous allocations of free emission certificates to companies in the energy sector or in the exporting industrial sector in the EU are to be classified as effectively a state redistribution in favor of capital owners or shareholders; in this context, large EU "gifts" in the form of free emissions allowances have also been made to US shareholders in view of the high direct investment holdings of US investors in companies in the EU. One cannot call such an EU policy wise; it would be advisable—as is often the case—for the European Commission to obtain better advice on economic policy (and also to rely on leading economists from Europe and the US). It cannot be the task of the European Commission to unnecessarily increase wealth and income disparities in the EU; the fact that EU member state governments do not noticeably address these aspects also shows a worrying lack of knowledge among governments at the national policy level. It is somewhat strange that in the Republic of Korea, too, free emission certificates were given away in large quantities—up to over 90 percent of certificates—to power plants and industrial companies in the first phases of trading. These actions of essentially gifting permission to emit via free allocations of certificates in key regions of the global economy are likely to have contributed in some way to the long-term rise in share prices since 2005 (with an interruption for some years due to the Great Recession of 2008–2010). This is a dynamic of the world economy that has not yet been addressed.

It should be pointed out that the linkages shown by Rehse et al. (2019) for the US may also apply to the European Union. Accordingly, extreme weather regions will suffer from a reduced liquidity of real estate financial market products (e.g., so-called REITs or Real Estate Investment Trusts). It will be interesting from the perspective of the European Central Bank and national banking supervisors as well as the European Systemic Risk Board (ESRB) to take a closer look at these interrelationships.

References

Bovenberg, L. A., & Goulder, L. H. (2001). Neutralizing the Adverse Industry Impacts of CO_2 Abatement Policies: What Does It Cost? In C. Carraro & G. E. Metcalf (Eds.), *Behavioral and Distributional Effects of Environmental Policy* (pp. 45–85). University of Chicago Press.

Burtraw, D., & Palmer, K. L. (2008). Compensation Rules for Climate Policy in the Electricity Sector. *Journal of Policy Analysis and Management, 27*(4), 819–847. https://doi.org/10.1002/pam.20378

Bushnell, J. B., Chong, H., & Mansur, E. T. (2013). Profiting from Regulation: Evidence from the European Carbon Market. *American Economic Journal: Economic Policy, 5*, 78–106. https://doi.org/10.1257/pol.5.4.78

Goulder, L. H., Hafstead, M. A. C., & Dworsky, M. (2010). Impacts of Alternative Emissions Allowance Allocation Methods Under a Federal Cap-and-trade Program. *Journal of Environmental Economics and Management, 60*(3), 161–181. https://doi.org/10.1016/j.jeem.2010.06.002

Rehse, D., Riordan, R., Rottke, N., & Zietz, J. (2019). The Effects of Uncertainty on Market Liquidity: Evidence from Hurricane Sandy. *Journal of Financial Economics, 134*(2), 318–332. https://doi.org/10.1016/j.jfineco.2019.04.006

Smale, R., Hartley, M., Hepburn, C., Ward, J., & Grubb, M. (2006). The Impact of CO_2 Emissions Trading on Firm Profits and Market Prices. *Climate Policy, 6*, 31–48. https://doi.org/10.1080/14693062.2006.9685587

CHAPTER 14

The Housing and Transport Sectors

In Germany, different sectors are responsible for different levels of CO_2 emissions in 2016: 343 million metric tons of CO_2 emissions in the energy sector, 188 million metric tons in industry, 166 million metric tons in transport, 130 million metric tons in building and construction, 72 million metric tons in agriculture and 10 million metric tons in other sectors. In the areas of buildings and industry, the declines of 1.8 percent per year and 1.6 percent per year, respectively, were relatively high during the period from 1990 to 2016, but significantly higher declines per year would be necessary between 2016 and 2030 in order to achieve the 56 percent decline in terms of the 1990 benchmark by 2030 as desired under the federal government's climate protection plan. Since the total CO_2 emissions in Germany in 2016 amounted to 909 million metric tons and the shares of energy, industry, transport and buildings were 37.7, 20.7, 18.3 and 14.3 percent respectively, it is foreseeable that special efforts will indeed be necessary in these four areas as well as in agriculture until 2030 and indeed further until 2050 to meet the relevant targets.

It is clear that without new approaches and higher efficiency in reducing CO_2 emissions, such targets can hardly be achieved and that the cost burden—with a view to foreseeable rent increases, for example—is hardly socially bearable. An important initiative in the housing industry would therefore be a series of model projects concerning "climate-neutral cheap buildings" (with a view to the inexpensive but ubiquitous classic IKEA

© The Author(s), under exclusive license to Springer Nature Switzerland AG 2022
P. J.J. Welfens, *Global Climate Change Policy*, Sustainable Development Goals Series,
https://doi.org/10.1007/978-3-030-94594-7_14

bookshelf, one needs a "Billy" model house/apartment for everyone, so to speak).

In the UK, the Climate Change Commission, which advises the government and parliament, has proposed that the country become climate-neutral by 2050. This does mean that all CO_2 emissions are simply to be reduced to zero by the middle of the century, but that the UK also wants to credit CO_2 compensation measures which are financed by the British government, for example, in developing countries, against emissions. Such measures include, for example, the planting of forests. Prime Minister Theresa May declared in June 2019 that the UK, a pioneering industrial country, also wanted to become a global pioneer in climate protection with a net zero CO_2 target in 2050. Between 2007 and 2018, CO_2 emissions in the UK fell by as much as 30 percent.

Among the important sectors not covered by the tradable emission certificates in Germany are the housing industry and the transport sector, where private households and individuals are largely responsible for emissions. According to a key points paper of late summer 2019, the German government plans to provide incentives for CO_2 savings by means of a kind of step-by-step CO_2 tax, starting at €10 per metric ton in 2021 and increasing until 2025, after which a national CO_2 certificate trading scheme will be developed. In addition, tax incentives to promote the energy-related modernization of real estate are to be enacted. Launching the CO_2 tax at just €10 per metric ton seems strangely low, since the price of an emissions certificate in 2018/2019 was already around €25 per metric ton. Methodologically, the kind of stepwise progression of the tax is probably difficult to enshrine in law. The federal government in Berlin apparently wants to return additional revenues back to households through a small reduction in electricity prices and an increase in the commuter tax allowance. The problem remains that citizens would not receive a clear annual reimbursement—as, for example, in Switzerland—as a visible, tangible direct reimbursement—which psychologically would increase support for the measure. It is incomprehensible why the buildings and construction sector does not already start with certificate trading in 2020, in view of the model cases of California (since 2015) and Tokyo (since 2010). The debate on climate policy in Germany suffers from the fact that the international community hardly seems to look around for useful policy approaches in use elsewhere. This is not a sensible approach and creates unnecessarily expensive climate policy in countries which try to "reinvent the wheel".

In Germany, the majority of people live in rented apartments, so that real estate companies are particularly challenged here. It would be important for the legislator here to set clever incentives. Since climate-friendly, CO_2-reducing conversion measures cannot be implemented at zero cost, new meaningful government incentives for sensible action by housing associations and real estate owners would have to be considered; corresponding laws are necessary here. In the case of real estate companies, such laws would have to bring about a departure from the traditional principle that the landlord—at least up to a certain limit—can simply pass the cost of any renovations on to the tenants. With a view to a sensible climate policy, the core problems are as follows:

- Real estate companies and housing associations have very few incentives to try and find the cheapest possible measure to reduce CO_2 emissions from dwellings. This is because housing associations can also achieve a reduction of CO_2 emissions through relatively expensive and inefficient emission reduction measures or conversion costs: as the costs are passed on 100 percent to the tenants. That's not a smart or sustainable situation.
- Within the framework of a concept for sensible climate policy reform, certain housing quality or standard categories would have to be defined at municipal level (e.g., based on property standard V to very high property standard I), whereby the typical costs of a standardized, efficient CO_2 reduction measure would have to be determined by an independent committee of experts: for each category of property quality or standard. Then the legislator would have to specify that the cost of such efficient modernization measures to reduce CO_2 emissions can be passed on by the landlord or property owner to the renter, and only such measures. The cost of inefficient, that is, overpriced, modernization measures could only be apportioned to renters up to the amount corresponding to an efficient modernization measure; in addition, there would be a discount of 20 percent to set incentives. Only in this way would there be an incentive for housing companies to focus on efficient CO_2 emission reduction measures. This would at the same time be an impulse to limit rent increases. The German federal government could support municipal pilot projects here and also promote special projects in the capital Berlin. Moreover, telecommunications regulation has had good experience with the concept of efficient service provision in other

contexts (Deutsche Telekom AG, as a provider with market power, had to make the "last mile" of its lines available to competing providers in fixed network customer access not simply on a cost basis but on the basis of the costs of efficient service provision; this was and is a clever incentive regulation in the Telecommunications Act). It is also conceivable that, with a view to determining the profits of large housing construction companies, only the costs of the efficient provision of services can be included in the profit and loss account.

- Insofar as the state itself builds or has built new housing in the social housing sector, inexpensive and, in the long-term, sustainable construction approaches are essential. In Europe, the so-called passive house innovations in Austria are also among the interesting showcase projects. Austria is indeed a leading country in the field of passive houses, but national as well as federal building regulations in other countries are barriers which are extremely obstructive to the diffusion of passive houses across the EU; that is, the already existing and proven innovation steps in passive house construction in Austria—whereby zero CO_2 emissions arise (or such homes are even emissions negative, as far as self-generated electricity from renewable energies is fed back into the public grid)—can only be realized with great difficulty over the border to Germany and in other EU countries. This is an untenable situation, which also makes the construction of passive houses across the EU unnecessarily expensive. This is a particularly strange situation as well as being economic and political nonsense, since some of the progress in passive house development in Austria was achieved with research funding from the EU (Dachs & Budde, 2019).
- Modern house concepts with certain passive house standards have also been developed in Germany and other EU countries. All new administrative, school and university buildings from 2025 onward in Germany—in the longer term in all G20 countries—should comply with such effective passive house standards. Solar power generation for third parties should be offset up to 10 percent against the 100 percent passive house standard (i.e., a 90 percent passive house standard would then be sufficient for the building itself; an effective passive house standard is defined here as being the degree of passive house standard plus the proportion of solar power generation for third parties converted into passive house equivalence standard). This gives more flexibility in building and provides sensible incentives.

Instead of solar power generation, other forms of renewable energy could also be realized. It is likely to become particularly important that modern passive house concepts are implemented in the social housing sector and that the state makes a contribution to ensuring that rents do not simply rise sharply in the course of climate protection policy. If the cost of electricity falls or if the yields from electricity sales to third parties reduce the rent burden, the proposed effective passive house approach offers an important socio-political advantage.

- Similar incentive problems exist in the transport sector as in the housing industry. There are few meaningful incentive structures. Here, one would have to demand that on the one hand certain fixed costs with regard to automobility are covered by a motor vehicle tax and, on the other hand, petrol, diesel and natural gas as well as hydrogen should be taxed according to their CO_2 emission intensities. This would probably result in slightly higher gas, diesel and gasoline prices—on a transitional basis it would be possible to reduce the motor vehicle tax on private vehicles for at least a period of five to ten years, and it could even become negative for a time in principle, which would mean subsidizing those vehicle types that are particularly relevant to climate protection and innovation.
- All airlines would be required by law to levy a CO_2 tax on airline ticket prices. Since the CO_2 tax on aviation fuel would probably be different in the EU than in many Asian countries or in Canada or the US, for example, at least for reasons of transparency, the invoice for airline tickets should have to show how high the CO_2 tax on the relevant flight is compared to the OECD average for air traffic; that would be a new information policy. Intra-European tickets are likely to increase in price by €10 to €20, which seems politically feasible with the gradual introduction of a CO_2 tax on air traffic. However, the policy should also regularly and clearly explain the measures being taken and the benefits for all. For countries in other regions of the world that do not provide air traffic with reasonable incentives to save energy through a CO_2 tax, this new information policy—which could also be communicated via the Internet—creates long-term pressure to also introduce CO_2 pricing in air traffic. The private CO_2 compensation measures which can be bought on the Internet would have to be more differentiated and preferably also state certified. In spring 2019, for example, a carbon compensation instrument for an

open-jaw flight itinerary from Düsseldorf to Washington, DC, and return from New York to Düsseldorf (between Washington, DC, and New York there was an ecologically sensible train journey) could not be bought on the Atmosfair website (whereas for a straightforward return flight it was possible). In any case, it should in future be ensured, first, that airlines regularly offer a compensation option when buying tickets directly and, second, that the development trends in terms of CO_2 compensation instruments for flights are made increasingly visible on the Internet over time. Publication requirements would make sense here with regard to airlines, and the same could of course also apply to the cruise industry. However, long-term CO_2 emission reduction measures, especially in air and sea traffic, would be better than simple CO_2 offsetting. As far as passenger shipping is concerned, 2023 will possibly see an international regulatory improvement for new ships, which will then restrict the combustion of heavy fuel oil, which is the most commonly used, and which is sulfur and NOX intensive as well as CO_2 intensive. However, the International Maritime Organization (IMO), the responsible body at an international level, will not necessarily have developed a sensible solution to this problem by 2023. Cruise ships in particular are facing serious problems as a result of increasing anti-cruise ship protests in public—including blockades of the port exits of certain ships—in Europe, and in the longer term, presumably such protests will also occur in the US. Cruise holidays are widely perceived as a luxury by the general public, but why cruise ships use the dirtiest diesel available on the market as their primary source of fuel is hard to understand. Some shipping companies have begun to use gas turbines as the propulsion system of new ships, and the conversion of the propulsion systems of existing ships is also conceivable. Increases in transport costs resulting from such measures, especially in the area of freight transport, are certainly bearable as they would have to be spread over huge transport volumes. It remains to be seen how the US will behave at the IMO in the corresponding reform discussions, although the election of President Biden assuages some fears here. The German Bundestag has commissioned the parliamentary Research Services of the Bundestag (2018) to carry out a study on ship emissions which is very informative. It also becomes clear that the time horizon of 2023 is relatively late for the IMO, and a signaling of measures is urgently desirable. In the context of the European

Union's Council Presidency in the second half of 2020, Germany could possibly have generated European pressure—subsequently also Portugal as a successor country to the Council Presidency—to persuade the IMO to bring forward the conversion point to 2021 or mid-2022. However, the corona pandemic and response largely dominated the policy agenda.

In the end, one may classify the climate problem as part of a much larger challenge. The climate issue is a subfield of the larger environmental protection problem, which also includes issues such as plastic waste, the pollution of drinking water and the extinction of species of flora and fauna. However, one should try to take a focused and structured approach and not try to solve all the world's problems at the same time.

REFERENCES

Dachs, B., & Budde, B. (2019). Fallstudie Nachhaltiges Bauen und Lead Markets in Österreich. In Welfens, P. J. J. (Ed.), *EU-Strukturwandel, Leitmärkte und Techno-Globalisierung* [transl. PJJW: A Case Study in Sustainable Building and Lead Markets in Austria. In Welfens, P. J. J. (Ed.), *EU Structural Change, Lead Markets and Technoglobalisation*]. De Gruyter.

Research Services of the Bundestag. (2018). Maßnahmen zur Minderung von Emissionen in der Schifffahrt – Alternative Kraftstoffe und Antriebe, Sachstand [transl. PJJW: Measures to Reduce Emissions from Shipping, Alternative Fuels and Propulsion Systems, State of Play], German Bundestag, WD 8–3000-032/18, May 2018.

CHAPTER 15

A CO_2 Tax as a Sensible Climate Policy Instrument

In Germany, as in certain other EU countries, there is an ongoing somewhat confused debate about the introduction of a CO_2 tax. Some politicians reject a "new" tax: they do not want to be associated with the introduction of another tax, and they claim that there has to be a better climate protection instrument. However, the situation is not that simple and in any case is not about an increase in the overall tax burden in the long run at all. Even if one could think instead of the expansion of the coverage of CO_2 certificate trading in Europe from about 45 percent of emissions to 95 percent, this could be complicated and would probably not make sense if the certificate price were to fall to just a few euros—according to IMF figures from 2019, the average global emissions certificate price was just $2 per metric ton of CO_2.

Incidentally, a CO_2 tax is essentially revenue-neutral, since the state is rather more interested in the steering effect rather than revenue generation, that is, other taxes would be reduced in a compensatory way, possibly more so for low-income households than for high-income households. A simple CO_2 tax can have a targeted effect and provide considerable incentives for both carbon savings and environmentally friendly innovations. Sweden, for example, has had a CO_2 tax since 1991, and this tax, together with Sweden's participation in the EU's Emissions Trading System, reduced emissions by 26 percent by 2017. At the same time, real income in Sweden rose by about 76 percent. If other countries succeed in reducing CO_2 emissions reliably and over a longer period by 1 percent per year, this would be a good global starting point for achieving sustainable climate protection in the medium and long term.

In Sweden, the CO_2 tax faced by companies was initially much lower than that on households, but by 2018 the level of the tax for companies had been raised to the higher value for private households. The CO_2 tax was not levied in a complicated way on every individual household, but indirectly, for example, by taxing import companies or wholesalers—so the tax collection costs were low. Moreover, the Swedish government has returned CO_2 tax revenues to taxpayers by reducing other taxes. It is also conceivable that at times the additional revenues may be used to increase "green innovation support"; here, society can expect a kind of double dividend from more environmentally friendly innovation support, namely intra- or intersectoral innovation transfer effects, with the result that environmental damage is ultimately reduced not just directly via lower emissions but also indirectly by deploying environmentally friendly innovations. Here too, however, as a rule CO_2 tax revenue should be fully offset via tax cuts elsewhere. The CO_2 tax therefore need not simply be about a tax increase, and this must be communicated effectively if the politicians want a citizen-friendly, credible strategy.

Switzerland also has a CO_2 tax for which a maximum value has been set, and at the same time another mechanism is anchored in the legislation: if CO_2 emissions fall too slowly compared to a target reference path, the CO_2 tax increases automatically. The politically prescribed maximum value of CHF120 (that is 120 Swiss francs) per metric ton of CO_2 is intended to create strategic planning security for companies. For this reason, the CO_2 tax in Switzerland also has considerable innovation and steering effects. As in Sweden, the CO_2 tax in Switzerland is paid back to private households; unlike in Sweden here it is done directly by check from the statutory health insurance; since the amount to be repaid is the same for all, the reverse side of the CO_2 tax revenue repayment appears to be part of social policy. What is economically decisive is that the relative price for CO_2 emissions rises and leads to emission-reducing behaviors. One could note that in France it was precisely the intention of the Macron government to increase diesel tax for environmental reasons combined with the removal of the initially planned compensating tax refund from the proposed legislation during parliamentary deliberations that provoked the so-called yellow vest (or *Gilets jaunes*) protests which rocked France during 2018 and 2019.

In German legislative practice, at least three ministries would need to be involved in a proposed climate-improving CO_2 tax policy, which does not make things very easy: the Federal Ministry of the Environment, the Federal Ministry of Finance and the Federal Ministry of Economic Affairs, the latter if there is to be a temporary increase in funding for environmentally friendly, green innovations. However, this combination should ultimately also be politically viable. If all Eurozone countries were to introduce CO_2 taxation at the same time, at least cross-border green innovation projects in the Eurozone could also be pushed forward simultaneously; probably a good option to win over countries such as Spain and Italy to CO_2 taxation, whereby a parallel expansion of electricity interconnectors at the borders of the EU and the Eurozone countries could lead to more international trade in electricity—above all from renewable energies— which could help Germany and Austria to temporarily avoid negative electricity prices. At the same time, coordinated and better funded battery storage investments could take place across the EU; negative electricity prices mean a tacit demand for storage capacities, which can be expanded relatively cheaply in the near future as soon as the second life battery phase begins, that is, the recycling phase of original batteries, such as those purchased from local transport authorities or other e-bus operators. With major advances in battery technology and investments in electricity storage projects, further elements of a climate-friendly electricity system could be mentioned. Comprehensive innovation-oriented procurement programs for e-buses in Germany and Europe are desirable, with the research ministries of all EU countries likely to be involved in this; EU innovation funding is also desirable. A comparison of e-bus mobility in Europe and China shows important findings for the starting points of an economic policy in this area (Welfens et al., 2018).

A major additional benefit within the framework of CO_2 emissions trading can be achieved—without much in the way of further costs—if the EU Emissions Trading System could be combined with CO_2 emissions trading in China and North America (especially California and its Canadian partner provinces of Quebec and (formerly) Ontario). This would bring considerable global efficiency gains in the context of international price convergence. The major international differences to date, for example, in CO_2 emission certificate prices (see Table 15.1), mean economic-ecological inefficiencies as well as differences between the price of an emissions certificate and the price of metric ton of CO_2 emitted in terms of a CO_2 tax. EU countries should set up a mechanism to prevent the two prices from

Table 15.1 CO_2 pricing in selected countries, 2018

Country/Region	Year of launch	Price 2018, US$/tonne CO_2	Degree of coverage, % Climate gases
CO_2 Taxes			
Chile	2017	5	39
Colombia	2017	6	40
Denmark	1992	29	40
Finland	1990	77	38
France	2014	55	37
Iceland	2010	36	50
Ireland	2010	25	48
Japan	2012	3	68
Mexico	2014	1–3	47
Norway	1991	56	63
Portugal	2015	8	29
South Africa	2019	10	10
Sweden	1991	139	40
Switzerland	2008	101	35
ETS[a]			
California	2012	15	85
China	expected 2020	N/a	N/a
EU	2005	16	45
Kazakhstan	2013	2	50
Korea	2015	21	68
New Zealand	2008	15	52
RGGI	2009	4	21
CO_2 minimum price			
Canada	2016	8	70
United Kingdom	2013	25	24

Source: IMF (2019), Fiscal Policies for Paris Climate Strategies—from Principle to Practice, IMF Policy Paper, May 2019, International Monetary Fund: Washington, DC, p. 11. Note: The Chinese national ETS launched in 2021

[a]Emissions Trading System; N/a = cannot be specified

drifting apart within each country and between OECD countries. It is astonishing that international CO_2 emission certificate prices also vary between countries over time; international differences in real incomes seem to play only a limited role (see Table 15.2 and Appendix 2). The global average price of 2018 for CO_2 emission certificates of $2 per metric ton quoted by the IMF (2019) is certainly insufficient to provide

Table 15.2 Key figures in international comparison, 2019 (ranked by gross domestic product)

Country	GDP, PPP (Constant 2017 Intl $), 2019	GDP per capita, 2019	CO_2 per capita, 2019	Price CO_2/ metric ton, 2018	Hours worked, 2019	Import ratio, 2019	Export ratio, 2019
China	22,492,450,166,615	16,092	7.096			17.34	18.50
US	20,524,945,253,654	62,530	16.06		1779	14.58	11.73
EU	19,799,809,964,722	44,237	6.555	16		43.64	47.15
India	9,155,083,977,020	6700	1.915			21.14	18.41
Japan	5,244,855,837,846	41,539	8.724	3	1644	18.29	18.52
Germany	4,457,045,052,845	53,639	8.405		1386	41.10	46.89
Russia	3,956,044,247,175	27,395	11.506		1965	20.76	28.31
Indonesia	3,196,682,696,485	11,812	2.282			18.90	18.41
UK	3,111,520,331,967	46,554	5.477	25	1538	32.68	31.60
Brazil	3,092,216,664,772	14,652	2.207			14.65	14.32
France	3,082,298,498,955	45,966	4.971	55	1505	32.75	31.77
Italy	2,549,656,994,037	42,281	5.567		1718	28.45	31.50
Mexico	2,513,408,575,238	19,701	3.437	1–3	2137	39.08	38.83
Turkey	2,352,635,791,884	28,199	4.856			29.94	32.74
Korea, Rep.	2,208,960,970,715	42,719	11.933	21	1967	37.05	39.95
Canada	1,831,547,833,141	48,720	15.414	8	1670	33.33	31.64
Saudi Arabia	1,609,323,719,894	46,962	16.988			27.61	36.05
Australia	1,254,476,578,633	49,456	16.308		1712	21.60	24.11
Argentina	991,523,444,188	22,064	3.996			15.19	17.44
South Africa	730,913,368,015	12,482	8.173	10		29.35	29.85

GDP gross domestic product, export and import ratio (export and import relative to GDP), G20 countries

Source: Own presentation of data available from World Bank, OECD Database, World Bank, IMF, Eurostat

reasonable incentives for adaptation and innovation. A minimum CO_2 price for certificates—around $25 per metric ton in the UK—is worth considering. From the investor's perspective, this represents an important lower limit for emission-reducing incentives. It is also important from the point of view of foreign investors that medium- and long-term CO_2 price developments can be (at least roughly) estimated.

In addition, at least three other aspects are very important:

- With regard to air transport, care must be taken to encourage the purchase of CO_2 offsetting products by private travelers and to include such purchases in statistical recording and economic policy assessment. In Germany, for example, if you want to make an expense claim for a US business trip, it proves almost impossible to claim back the cost of the CO_2 offset certificate purchased as a "valid expense"—on the part of the federal and state authorities, however, such accounting should be encouraged or the legislative prerequisites should be enacted.
- Since, according to the World Values Survey, environmental preferences expressed by citizens diverge internationally, some attention should be paid to research on this issue. Public opinion regarding the apparent conflict regarding economic growth, on the one hand, and environmental protection on the other reflects both citizens' personal preferences, attitudes toward climate change and protection and external influences. Public opinion, in turn, determines the social-political room to maneuver on the part of policymakers considering, for example, introducing or expanding climate-friendly measures (Drews et al., 2018). However, one can note that the idea that there is necessarily a trade-off between economic growth and environmentally friendly, pro-climate policy is contested in the literature (Den Butter & Verbruggen, 1994), and any such trade-off is indeed not always tied to the respective country's economic development (Grossman & Krueger, 1995; Dasgupta et al., 2002). Policies aimed at environmental protection, and sustainable development more generally, might indeed promote economic growth and vice versa. As discussed previously in the present analysis, improvements in terms of productivity in the long run could be realized if climate-friendly policies—such as those proposed herein—create incentives for innovation (Kozluk & Zipperer, 2014). All too often, environmental protection and economic growth are portrayed as being in conflict with one another, see, for example, the "degrowth" debate. Increasing economic activity in terms of consumption or production is seen as being inevitably harmful to the environment and by extension the climate. Meanwhile, by others, policies seen to be climate-neutral or environmentally friendly are considered to have a negative impact on growth. In the short to medium term, policies aimed at achieving climate neutrality such as environmental or carbon taxes and emissions trading systems such as used in the EU, California

and, more recently, China, as well as technology-based standards and regulations on firms impose an additional production-related cost and limit the range of profitable technologies available to industry for production (Kozluk & Zipperer, 2014). On the basis of the World Values Survey, it is possible to model how individuals in different countries, and possibly within countries, regard a conflict between objectives such as more environmental protection or climate-neutral policies on the one hand and more economic growth on the other (Udalov, 2019; Udalov & Welfens, 2021). Here, there are identifiable differences between the high-income groups and the low-income groups. One hypothesis is that such differences are reflective of a so-called Environmental Kuznets Curve (EKC), whereby beyond a critical peak, the willingness to act in more environmentally friendly manner or support climate-neutral policies is more clearly related to certain key variables. With regard to the effect of income—that is, how beyond a certain per capita income level, individual preferences for climate-neutral policies increase—this is explained in the literature on the basis of three main hypotheses: the post-material hypothesis of Inglehart (1971, 1997), whereby voters will tend to exhibit more post-materialistic attitudes and be more willing to provide political support to more environmentally friendly and climate-neutral policies when their own socio-economic security rises. The related affluence hypothesis (Franzen & Vogl, 2013) according to which concern with environmental degradation and climate change is closely correlated with both the wealth of the nation as a whole and per capita income, respectively—indicating that on the one hand the wealthier strata within societies may be more likely to support CO_2-reducing measures, and on the other than wealthier countries would lead the agenda. On the other hand, the globalization hypothesis would argue that concern about climate change is not dependent on the level of national wealth or post-materialist values (Dunlap & York, 2008). According to this hypothesis, public support for climate protection policies is not limited to the wealthy, or wealthy nations, but actually represents a global phenomenon shared by the less wealthy strata and less wealthy countries including in the Global South. Indeed, the disadvantaged groups and societies often disproportionately bear the burden of climate change.

- Furthermore, private CO_2 reduction innovations should be promoted digitally, read via the Internet, by setting up a global networking platform (Udalov & Welfens, 2021).
- Finally, one of the options proposed in the important report is that—with reference to the Albedo effect—communication networks should be promoted worldwide so that the roofs of houses, cars, trucks and trains could be more easily painted white or with light colors where possible. This would not cause much in the way of additional costs, if any, but would help the climate in a simple and reliable way.

The analysis shows considerable potential for optimizing climate policy in Germany, Europe and worldwide.

References

Dasgupta, S., Laplante, B., Wang, H., & Wheeler, D. (2002). Confronting the Environmental Kuznets Curve. *The Journal of Economic Perspectives, 16*(1), 147–116. https://doi.org/10.1257/0895330027157

Den Butter, F. A. G., & Verbruggen, H. (1994). Measuring the Trade-Off between Economic Growth and a Clean Environment. *Environmental and Resource Economics, 4*(2), 187–208. https://doi.org/10.1007/BF00692203

Drews, S., Antal, M., & Van Den Bergh, J. C. J. M. (2018). Challenges in Assessing Public Opinion on Economic Growth Versus Environment: Considering European and US Data. *Ecological Economics, 146*, 265–272. https://doi.org/10.1016/j.ecolecon.2017.11.006

Dunlap, R. E., & York, R. (2008). The Globalization of Environmental Concern and the Limits of the Postmaterialist Values Explanation: Evidence from Four Multinational Surveys. *The Sociological Quarterly, 49*(3), 529–563. https://doi.org/10.1111/j.1533-8525.2008.00127.x

Franzen, A., & Vogl, D. (2013). Acquiescence and the Willingness to Pay for Environmental Protection: A Comparison of the ISSP, WVS, and EVS. *Social Science Quarterly, 94*(3), 637–659. https://doi.org/10.1111/j.1540-6237.2012.00903.x

Grossman, G. M., & Krueger, A. B. (1995). Economic Growth and the Environment. *Quarterly Journal of Economics, 110*, 353–377. https://doi.org/10.2307/2118443

IMF. (2019, May). *Fiscal Policies for Paris Climate Strategies – From Principle to Practice* (IMF Policy Paper). International Monetary Fund. https://www.imf.org/~/media/Files/Publications/PP/2019/PPEA2019010.ashx

Inglehart, R. (1971). The Silent Revolution in Europe: Intergenerational Change in Post-Industrial Societies. *American Political Science Review, 65*, 991–1017. https://doi.org/10.2307/1953494

Inglehart, R. (1997). *Modernization and Postmodernization: Cultural, Economic and Political Change in 43 Societies.* Princeton University Press.

Kozluk, T., & Zipperer, V. (2014). Environmental Policies and Productivity Growth – A Critical Review of Empirical Findings. *OECD Journal: Economic Studies, 1,* 155–185. https://doi.org/10.1787/eco_studies-2014-5jz2drqml75j

Udalov, V. (2019). *Behavioural Economics of Climate Change – New Empirical Perspectives* (SpringerBriefs in Climate Studies). Springer.

Udalov, V., & Welfens, P. J. J. (2021). Digital and Competing Information Sources: Impact on Environmental Concern und Prospects for Cooperation. *International Economics and Economic Policy, 18,* 631–660. https://doi.org/10.1007/s10368-021-00503-8

Welfens, P. J. J., Yu, N., Hanrahan, D., Schmülling, B., & Fechtner, H. (2018). *Electrical Bus Mobility in the EU and China: Technological, Ecological and Economic Policy Perspectives* (EIIW Discussion Paper No. 255). https://uni-w.de/0nfih

PART III

Multilateralism as a Solution to the Climate Problem

CHAPTER 16

International Perspectives

The issue of climate protection has led to numerous protest movements springing up across Europe and indeed worldwide. In the spring of 2019, protests by the rather radical "Extinction Rebellion" group in the UK resulted in a national press response. Parliament in Westminster declared "a climate emergency"—without defining exactly what such an emergency might mean. Nevertheless, it is clear that concerns about climate change are growing in the UK and in many other countries.

It is unclear whether policymakers in Europe and other regions of the world will adopt timely measures for comprehensive climate protection, and whether science will provide a sufficient number of people with the information, facts and understandable analyses that in time to inform a critical and intensive global climate debate. One has to come to terms with the fact that climate protection policy will not always be the focus of people's attention anyway: with every economic recession, income and employment interests are likely to take top spots in terms of the concern of individuals. It is only during an economic upswing that many people become interested in issues such as regional integration or (international) climate protection. Without adequate and timely climate protection, however, considerable international economic crises can occur. For this reason, the temporary suppression of climate protection policy as a pressing issue on the part of the electorate is above all a reflection of traditional thinking—a linear historical understanding of the problem of economic development.

Information Deficits as a Particular Challenge

The contradictory nature of global economic policy is a problem when it comes to sustainability and climate protection: annual global subsidies for fossil fuels amount to about 6 percent of world income. Yet the ability of countries to reduce or remove these subsidies—in the face of tough lobbying interests—is apparently quite low. It is also quite strange that one will hear or see practically no discussion of the aforementioned subsidy figure on news or current affairs programs in Germany or the European Union. The competence of the publicly funded TV newsrooms in the field of climate protection in Germany is certainly limited; with the exception of some infrequent interesting and compact environmental protection programs or reports, little can be seen on German TV channels or ARTE (a Franco-German TV station) as well as the BBC and other well-known TV channels on climate protection topics apart from sporadic reports on glaciers melting—and, in Germany, the occasional interviews with the climate researcher Mojib Latif. A broad, balanced coverage of climate issues on TV is certainly lacking. There is much to be done to a achieve an in-depth and differentiated presentation of the various aspects of climate policy (in a broader sense). It would probably make sense for different groups of scientists to be able to develop their own TV platforms and Internet-based streaming channels. Climate protection issues could certainly be only one part of a broad knowledge TV approach, with many widely understandable contributions from the world of science a welcome development.

TV programs which explain the role and scope of emissions trading in the EU and globally are virtually non-existent. There is an enormous lack of information here. Not even the websites via which one can offset the CO_2 emissions of flights are known to more than 10 percent of the population in Germany. This is actually a hardly credible weakness given the reach of digital networks and the Internet as a whole. The functioning of the emissions trading systems in Germany and other EU countries is likely to be unclear to 80 percent of the population—and this level of knowledge is likely to be similarly bad in other countries that also have such a system. It is quite astonishing and also alarming that possibly the most important and effective instrument for survival on the planet in the twenty-first century is completely unknown to the vast majority of the population.

Revenues from CO_2 taxes and certificate trading, or the government sale of emission certificates, are also likely to become a major issue. That only revenues are easily generated here, which the state can then let flow directly back to citizens, is probably a wishful thinking. At any rate, one could look at the revenue situation of the federal government in Berlin as an example: the potential government revenue effects are interesting. With about 900 million tons of CO_2 emissions in Germany in 2019 alone and an assumed price of €40 per metric ton of CO_2, this would result in revenues of €36 billion; that would be about 10 percent of the federal budget. However, the certificate price in 2017/2018 was only just over €20 per metric ton, and just 45 percent of emissions are covered by the EU certificate trading scheme; if the state gives away a share of the certificates in free allocations, this will also reduce revenues. In any case, if CO_2 emissions are covered more broadly by certificate trading and CO_2 taxes, the state can expect considerable revenues—10 percent of such revenues in terms of the total budget of the federal government is a significant amount. New questions would also be conceivable, namely to what extent the CO_2 tax revenue mentioned above and the proceeds from certificate trading should not flow at least in part into EU coffers. After all, EU certificate trading has thus far been organized at the EU level, and the EU indeed suffers from structural underfinancing. It is likely that the EU will also play a more important role in international organizations in the medium and long term, which will increase the financial needs of the EU further—or even the Eurozone.

New International Facts and Perspectives

In August 2019, the World Trade Organization (WTO) and the United Nations Environment Programme (UNEP) presented an important new report on the role of world trade in environmental and climate protection, which highlights a number of important points (WTO/UNEP, 2019):

- If it were possible to significantly reduce fisheries subsidies worldwide—and the EU is also conspicuously inactive in this respect—an increase in global fisheries profits from $3 billion to $86 billion could be achieved in the longer term: however, first, it must be made possible for fishing companies and communities to reduce the overfishing of important stocks. In the medium term, fishing for certain fish species will first have to decline before it can increase sustainably once stocks recover.

- In 2018, two-thirds of new investments in the global electricity sector related to renewable energies.
- By 2016, the share of electricity from renewable sources had risen to 11 percent. This share is, admittedly, still quite modest. It must be borne in mind that new coal-fired power plants built and brought online in 2020 will normally still be producing electricity in 2050. Whether this is a manageable or a major problem for the climate depends, among other things, on how modern these power plants operate in terms of efficiency.
- The prices for solar cells in 2018 had fallen to just one-quarter of the respective prices in 2009 and are expected to fall again by 67 percent by 2040. Onshore wind turbines have fallen in price by 30 percent over the period from 2009 to 2018 and are expected to fall again by 47 percent by 2040. It should also be added that the price reduction potential of offshore wind turbines—which are relatively large when operated at sea—is likely to be even higher than for onshore wind power generation. Existing import tariffs for wind turbines should be reduced to zero so that renewable energies can increase their market share in electricity generation worldwide. The ambition of former US President Trump to increase coal production and coal-fired power generation in the US is unsustainable and indeed incompatible with the long-term interests of the people of the US and the world economy. Market access restrictions for wind turbines are visible as non-tariff barriers in Japan: China's wind turbine producers have achieved significant market shares in the US, but are virtually not present on the Japanese market at all. There, domestic producers such as Mitsubishi are apparently being shielded from foreign competition by politicians; this makes little sense for Japan or for global climate protection. Free trade can, however, also bring climate policy-relevant problems, for example, when in Brazil large areas of virgin forest are cut down in order to raise more cattle—with large cattle exports to Europe, the US and Asia; or to cultivate maize, whereby the maize is then exported worldwide as animal feed. If a metric ton of harvested corn is indirectly associated with CO_2 emissions—in other words, the lower CO_2 absorption by the trees felled to clear fields—a negative value would have to be added to the export value of a metric ton of corn (according to Germany's Federal Environment Agency, the cost of the damage of a metric ton of CO_2 is €180); if a metric ton of corn was harvested on the basis of one-

tenth of a metric ton of CO_2 production, then €18 would have to be deducted from the normal market value of approximately €150. The question arises as to how much of the corn harvest will be lost in Brazil if the "internalized market price" falls to €132—Brazil should actually introduce a CO_2 tax or an emissions certificate system for 85–95 percent of its emissions: the EU should address this issue with Brazil and other countries within the framework of an EU-Mercosur Free Trade Agreement. Ultimately, every consumer around the world will have to ask herself the question: how indispensable is a high level of beef consumption for me? Here, modern agri-food developments could be helpful, creating meat without the need for animal husbandry.

- An important question from the point of view of the G20 countries, and ultimately of all the countries of the world, concerns how to reach an agreement on the conservation of Brazil's rainforests and Russia's boreal forests. Certainly, there is a certain pride in the natural environment of every country of the world, a pride which may also protect native forests from large deforestation. However, Brazil and Russia and some other countries may be of strategic global interest when it comes to absorbing CO_2 through the sheer extent of forested areas in those countries.
- The growth rate of the patents in OECD countries for clean forms of energy has risen to 9 percent per year over 1999–2014, while in the other areas the growth rate has been 6 percent per year in the industrialized countries. Of course, patents outside the area of clean forms of energy should also be seen as an impetus for greater sustainability and climate protection. Schumpeterian innovation dynamic in the form of green patents can hardly be emphasized enough as a key to more climate protection. It still remains to be seen whether it might be possible to convert CO_2 emissions to a greater extent into useful oil replacement products for the chemical industry. Such technologies (e.g., Covestro), which already exist to some extent and are currently used in a pioneering way, could help to alleviate the CO_2 emission problem in the medium term.
- It can be observed that regional free trade agreements also increasingly include environmental aspects. In 1997, it was 8 percent, and by 2017/2018 it was about 16 percent. Integrating climate protection aspects sensibly into regional free trade agreements will remain a major challenge for decades to come. It is not easy to negotiate

contradictory free trade agreements here. Of course, as populism spreads, there is a danger that existing free trade agreements may be dissolved and new trade conflicts arise—as seen, for example, between Japan and the Republic of Korea in 2019.

- Moreover, it should be noted that a reduction in the price of environmentally friendly products as a result of technological progress is—in the longer term—leading to increased demand for such products in terms of quantity, which has a dampening effect on the positive environmental progress associated with these products (the so-called rebound or take-back effect). Nevertheless, modeling of the use of environmentally friendly ICT technologies shows that Germany has a positive macroeconomic production effect on the one hand while, on the other hand, emissions of climate gases are falling (Welfens & Lutz, 2012).

One can see from these figures that, of course, a global perspective is indispensable for the goal of global climate neutrality by 2050 and that many individual approaches have to be considered within a broad package. Pragmatically speaking, this means that at least the G20 countries should be in the focus of the analysis and political cooperation should be considered accordingly. It is well known that international cooperation can function successfully in the context of smaller groups of countries; historical examples include the International Commission for the Protection of the Rhine with the six partner countries Austria, Switzerland, Liechtenstein, Germany, France, the Netherlands plus the European Economic Community (which was founded in 1950), or the Danube Commission—founded as early as 1848—(initially comprising a group of 7 countries), which in 2019 now has 11 partner countries that also have common interests through the river itself: unimpeded navigation and relatively clean water, especially for drinking water abstraction.

The more similar the per capita incomes—measured by purchasing power parity—of the countries in an international organization, the more likely it is that there will be scope to find acceptable compromises or consensus positions. Relatively compact organizations, for example, including certain industrialized countries, would therefore have to work well together: the G7 was a good example here at least until the populist President Trump took office in 2017. The G5/G7, which has been successful since the 1970s, was also weakened by Trump considerably in 2018/2019. President Trump's policy pattern emphasized bilateralism, which was supposed to bring advantages for the US, and protectionism, which the former US president—wrongly in the long run—also hoped would bring special US advantages. In addition, Trump stands for authoritarian politics that wants to gain support with emotionalized arguments and informal networks but does not rely on well-founded arguments and serious public discussion. By failing to ratify the Trans-Pacific Trade Agreement, Trump—with a negative stroke of the pen—withheld US cooperation with 11 partner countries in the Pacific region and forced Japan into adopting an unexpected leadership role with regard to the agreement. Such self-destruction of America's role in regional leadership as happened during the Trump presidency was not seen since the nineteenth century. Moreover, Trump tried to override the US' economically sensible recovery in terms of high current account deficits with an aggressive trade policy, including a massive increase in arms exports: if the import values are much higher than the export values, then the US will incur more debt abroad in the long run. Trump has indeed given some impetus for the US to sell more US agricultural products, liquefied natural gas and defense exports around the world. However, tax incentives would also be necessary to encourage private households to save more. There is hardly anything to be seen of such measures with President Trump.

If oil were no longer particularly important as a form of energy for mobility, there would be some relief in a number of regional conflicts and in terms of the safety of maritime transport routes. Here, as in the case of the Strait of Hormuz, for example, conflict over free and unrestricted passage of shipping is frequently an issue; in other words, the secure transport of oil to and from the West and Japan as well as the Republic of Korea, which have so far been very important economically, is also at stake. However, such conflicts can also emerge once again—perhaps with slight geographical variation—if liquefied natural gas transports become increasingly important for the global energy supply in the coming decades. The major losers in a global phase-out of coal would include countries such as Australia, India, China, Russia and the US. The problem should, however, be manageable if the countries concerned invest more in further training for the workforce and regional programs to cushion the effects of structural change (although such spending is almost zero in the case of the US).

Incidentally, solar power generation also has a security policy perspective. The Desertec project, which was envisaged by Germany at the beginning of the twenty-first century—whereby many solar farms would be developed in North Africa which would eventually also export electricity to the EU—has failed for the time being because of internal issues, such as civil war terrorism creating a difficult security situation in some North African countries. The Desertec Foundation, founded by Gerhard Knies and others in Munich, initially hoped that large solar investments in North Africa would generate a great deal of solar power: a 300 km² area of solar panels located in the Sahara should be sufficient to generate 17 percent of the EU's electricity in 2050 from the Desertec project alone; in addition, new power cables had to be laid through the Mediterranean Sea. The Desertec Foundation wanted to promote their project together with the Club of Rome and also collaborated with the Desertec Industrial Initiative (Dii). However, this initiative with various commercial partners plus banks and the foundation was at loggerheads, one of the questions being whether the intended solar power systems should not cover the needs of around 400 million people in North Africa first, and another being whether profitable projects in North Africa and Saudi Arabia would be possible at all due to the new investment risks which emerged after the beginning of the Arab Spring. The Dii ultimately disbanded, leaving an advisory board with Innogy from Germany, ACWA Power from Saudi Arabia and the State Grid Corporation of China.

Indeed, in Saudi Arabia, Tunisia and some other countries in North Africa, other large solar power projects are still being promoted, with new solar plants having the same capacity as a nuclear power plant. In the longer term, the idea of exporting electricity to Europe will probably be picked up once again. It is clear that the oil-rich OPEC members would not be a winning group in a global exit from oil, although some of the main oil-producing countries are also gas-producing countries. Yet the Desertec project itself shows that there are also great investment opportunities for the often technologically ambitious OPEC countries in the field of renewable energies. China is very active in various energy projects in Africa; India, on the other hand, makes little use of its strong solar power know-how in the form of African solar projects. The EU and India could actually work well together on this in future.

It is not too difficult to calculate how far CO_2 emissions would have to fall in the long term in order to achieve a climate-neutral world economy by 2050. It will have to be assumed that global CO_2 emissions will continue to rise initially, possibly until 2030, as relatively poor countries such as India and China claim that their industrialization and thus fossil energy consumption will continue to expand for the time being; 60 percent of the world's population live in Asia, and most of the real global economic growth (since the 1990s) also comes from Asia. Meanwhile, Western industrialized countries and Japan are expected to reduce their CO_2 emissions significantly. Global emissions would have to fall a few years before 2030, and CO_2 emissions from all G20 countries would also have to fall. This could, however, be possible only if the West and Japan were to share some of their climate-improving technologies with other G20 countries, at a rather symbolic nominal price. For example, the EU could offer India a free trade agreement with favorable conditions if India's government would significantly accelerate the expansion of renewable energies in India and carry out a joint solar technology expansion project with the EU in Africa. All G20 countries should commit themselves to the goal that international air tickets (outside the EU area, where intra-EU flights are already part of the EU's Emissions Trading System) should always be offered bundled together with a compensation option—with a separate price indication—on the Internet and on all digital platforms. This should not be difficult to realize; however, it should be linked with only valid, certified providers of CO_2 compensation (e.g., Atmosfair). The same should apply to journeys on international cruise ships. A G20 CO_2 certificate area could also be defined here immediately as a community system, which would help to keep CO_2 certificate prices low: this reflects the fact that the most favorable ways of reducing CO_2 emissions globally are found in shipping.

Institutional Innovation: A New Climate Neutrality Organization Under the Auspices of the G20

If one wants to reduce emissions from a per capita emission of 5 metric tons per capita per year on average for the world economy to just under 1 metric ton per capita in 2050, the global target would be around 9 metric gigatons of CO_2 in 2050. Reforestation measures and measures to cool the Earth would then have to effectively reduce emissions to less than 5 metric gigatons of CO_2 in 2050. This is not just a fanciful thinking but in fact quite a realistic scenario. Fundamentally, you need to begin with a world map that shows the starting position for each region and the intermediate target value five years later. It would make sense to set up a climate neutrality secretariat under the G20 umbrella—perhaps with its seat in Rio de Janeiro as the location (or at least another a city in Brazil, as the country is strategically important for successful global cooperation)—to provide input for G20 policy in terms of analysis, innovation promotion, benchmarking and technology transfer. Such a G20 climate neutrality organization could set a decisive course for timely progress on global climate protection. Given its global scope and urgent task, this organization should be expected to have several thousand employees and an annual budget equivalent to about one-third of that of the World Bank.

Negative Scenario

However, it is by no means certain that international cooperation will enjoy sufficient success. One possible scenario is that the US and some other G20 countries would ignore the CO_2 reduction targets and continue to achieve sustained national growth with rising CO_2 emissions after 2030, while the majority of other G20 countries would reduce CO_2 emissions. The 1.5-degree target, which the UN Climate Commission said would be very important in 2019 for stabilizing the climate and achieving climate neutrality by 2050, would then not be achieved. We may even fail to meet the 2-degree target, leading to a dangerous tipping point in global climate dynamics, since the world's food supply, for example, can no longer be guaranteed in the face of rising global temperatures. Serious malnourishment and associated health problems in large parts of the world would be added as new challenges for the international community, and on top of that, there could be more than 60 million climate refugees pushing toward North America and Europe. The coastal regions of North America and the EU suffer from regular flooding, and such events would increasingly be caused by the melting of the polar ice cap, until new barriers on the coasts have been completed at gigantic costs after a decade or more. Poor countries such as Bangladesh and Indonesia will not be able to afford the cost of such huge coastal defenses; Japan will have to shut down all nuclear power plants on the Pacific side of its main islands as the dangers of a new Fukushima-type nuclear accident will be far too great.

Of course, in Japan one could have considered as early as in the late twentieth century that because of the dangers of tsunamis in particular on the Pacific side of its main islands that nuclear power plants have no business being there and that permission for all nuclear power plants should only have been granted to plants constructed on the northwest side of Japan's main islands facing the Republic of Korea and China. It is obvious that the climate protection issue could lead to completely new economic, social and military conflicts in the world. If the US would enter an age characterized by structural populism—that is, further CO_2 increases on the part of the US for a decade and more (despite the exemplary CO_2 reductions achieved in California and some other networked US regions or city networks)—then it is clear that NATO, too, will ultimately break down, as it is hard to imagine that if the main values of the European partner countries and the US drift apart in the longer term, NATO would continue to hold as a defense alliance. It is completely unclear whether the international institutions that have grown over many decades will still be able to act by 2030 or 2040. Incidentally, it is also hardly conceivable that even a UK that is geared toward climate neutrality in 2050 could continue to be a loyal ally and partner of a US that is geared toward populism in the longer term.

In 2019, there was widespread fear that the G7 summit—organized in France by President Macron—would end for the first time without a prepared and agreed summit declaration, not least because of the differences of opinion between the US and France in the field of climate policy and Brazil in particular (Macron blamed President Trump for the US withdrawal from the Paris Climate Agreement). With such uncertainty, one can imagine that the ability of the West to cooperate could be severely damaged for years due to disagreements in the field of climate protection policy. The global warming problem could become an internal and external field of conflict between Europe, the US and many countries in Asia, Africa and Latin America—and the Fridays for Future movement could continue to spread globally. Australia, as with other G20 countries with a poorly effective emissions balance, could lose much of its reputation and institutional capital in the medium term. In a 2019 report on the Australian Carbon Footprint, the Australian Conversation Foundation showed that on the one hand the government argued that production in the country represents only 1.4 percent of global CO_2 emissions. However, if you also consider Australia's high coal and gas exports, which go primarily to Asia, then Australia actually accounts for 5 percent of global emissions. If we look at the medium-term development until 2030, Australia—including coal and gas exports—will already effectively account for 13 percent of global emissions (Parra et al., 2019).

In Australia and other important coal-, oil- and gas-exporting countries, the interests of foreign investors are also at stake, notably interests such as those of a large Indian multinational which is active in the coal mining sector in Australia. Once huge new coal mines have been opened—which involves investments worth billions—investors will certainly not want to close such mines again within a decade without massive resistance—and compensation claims. The fact that a conservative government in Australia has pursued a policy that is not very climate friendly raises a number of critical questions and ultimately also creates new international conflicts. The government in Australia could take the position that the country, within its national autonomy, can decide for itself how much coal and gas it wants to extract and export. This view can, however, be considered critically, as Australia's government is indeed fully aware that very high coal and gas exports are actually undermining climate protection worldwide. Nor is there much evidence that Australia's government has invested a particularly large amount of research funding in renewable energies.

The re-elected Australian government's decision in 2019 to set the course for concessions for new coal mines is therefore highly questionable. The serious concerns of billions of people in the West about adequate climate protection will potentially turn Australia's coal and gas exports into an international political conflict in the longer term. Such international conflicts should be tackled through international organizations.

We must be aware that investments in coal mines, oil and gas fields and power stations represent high capital costs and that these issues will have to be debated in meaningful discussion forums such as the OECD, G20 and the UN. Incidentally, huge capital investments cannot simply be shut down from one day to the next, as massive compensation payments would always have to be made. It therefore always makes sense to achieve a gradual, market-based phase-out of CO_2-intensive production through appropriately high CO_2 taxes or a sufficiently high price for CO_2 emission certificates.

Social Prospects

In many industrialized and emerging countries, climate protection is a policy area that emotionalizes and, of course, mobilizes various interest and lobby groups. The actions of one such group, Environmental Action Germany (*Deutsche Umwelthilfe*), may occasionally raise doubts as to what exactly their main interest is. In the summer of 2019, this organization won a court victory over a ban on private New Year's Eve fireworks displays in 38 major cities, arguing that such displays cause a critical fine dust problem. But one could also view it differently, namely that a legally and fiscally privileged institution set out to reduce a once-a-year event which provides entertainment and increases people's joie de vivre—winning new donations from certain other groups due to the extremely high profile of the case. It is doubtful whether parliaments should allow such business models to continue. If society's optimism, future orientation, the innovative strength of the workforce and entrepreneurship are to be combated by influential organizations, then there is probably little chance of reaching sustainable and successful climate protection policy action. Never before in history has a large group of people in a pessimistic and combative mood—resenting interference from environmental groups—developed and advanced a sensible project for the future viability of the next generation. Moreover, it cannot be ruled out that in parts of Europe and other regions of the world the path toward an eco-dictatorship will be taken. This is not the solution. For long-term climate neutrality, democracy, climate protection, a market economy and the rule of law are needed in equal measure—and a basic optimism on the part of society and policymakers. Reasonable signals from capital markets must be added.

It would be helpful in terms of the desirable taxation of fossil fuels in the medium term if large Western investor groups and funds no longer invested directly or indirectly in fossil fuel projects. Norway's sovereign wealth fund has already given important signals in this direction; gas production could probably be considered acceptable for a number of years to come, provided that natural gas replaces oil and coal with their higher specific CO_2 emissions. Whether it will be possible to quickly find a way to ensure secure CO_2 capture and storage, which would probably prolong the ecological-economic lifetime of oil and gas, remains to be seen. An unruly, unstructured discussion via organizations such as Fridays for Future and in the public sphere of the world's regions will be of little use in quickly finding convincing solutions to problems. Instead, relying on more technological progress and on more reliable international cooperation is likely to be the most important prospect on the journey toward global climate neutrality by 2050.

References

Parra, P. Y., Hare, B., Fuentes Hutfilter, U., & Roming, N. (2019, July). *Evaluating the Significance of Australia's Global Fossil Fuel Carbon Footprint.* Report Prepared by Climate Analytics for the Australian Conservation Foundation (ACF).

Welfens, P. J. J., & Lutz, C. (2012). Green ICT Dynamics: Key Issues and Findings for Germany. *Mineral Economics, 24*(2), 155–163. https://doi.org/10.1007/s13563-012-0017-x

WTO/UNEP. (2019). *Making Trade Work for the Environment, Prosperity and Resilience*. World Trade Organization. https://www.wto.org/english/res_e/publications_e/unereport2018_e.pdf

CHAPTER 17

G20 Problems in Climate Protection Policy

There have been a significant number of international organizations only since the end of the Second World War. The first such organizations were, however, established in the 1860s and 1870s, when the standardization of telegraphy and mail as well as units of measurement (such as meters, kilograms) and the question of international patent protection in the new industrialized societies of Western countries were at stake. The International Court of Justice was created in 1899, partly on foot of an initiative of Russia, which was hoping to curb the arms race at the international level. International organizations were, however, missing in the run-up to the First World War; only after this war was the League of Nations founded; and only after the Second World War were more international organizations founded, this time with the active participation of the US. The more recent G20 group is likely to become particularly important in terms of climate protection policy.

The G20 can be seen as an ideal group of countries for such a purpose as they represent the world economy in a manageable framework: 81 percent of the world's gross domestic product (Table 17.1), almost 80 percent of global CO_2 emissions and 60 percent of the world's population. The G20 has been active since the end of 2008, and in November of that year it was clear that the older G7 group of countries was too small to stabilize the global economy in view of the impending collapse of—particularly—Western financial markets—following the bankruptcy of the US

© The Author(s), under exclusive license to Springer Nature Switzerland AG 2022
P. J.J. Welfens, *Global Climate Change Policy*, Sustainable Development Goals Series,
https://doi.org/10.1007/978-3-030-94594-7_17

Table 17.1 G20 countries: gross domestic product (in purchasing power parity (PPP)), 2019[a]

Country	2019 GDP in PPP (millions current intl. $)
China	23,487,797,982,261
US	21,433,226,000,000
European Union	20,786,860,685,064
India	9,560,219,601,244
Japan	5,345,808,049,899
Germany	4,644,165,657,909
Russian Federation	4,315,442,962,881
Indonesia	3,338,143,991,973
France	3,320,558,731,410
UK	3,240,510,715,194
Brazil	3,229,055,074,104
Italy	2,677,117,877,149
Mexico	2,608,649,754,477
Turkey	2,279,166,087,282
Korea, Rep.	2,209,423,793,035
Canada	1,898,869,931,236
Saudi Arabia	1,680,540,365,364
Australia	1,324,171,341,810
Argentina	1,035,400,864,701
South Africa	763,258,133,432

Source: Own presentation, data from the World Bank https://data.worldbank.org/indicator/ny.gdp.mktp.pp.cd

[a]Note: Data on GDP for 2019 or most recent available year

bank Lehman Brothers. There were certainly better opportunities within the larger G20 group, which includes India, China, Indonesia, Russia, Saudi Arabia and Brazil, to develop and coordinate measures aimed at limiting the effects of the Transatlantic Banking Crisis. Since then, the G20 summits have dealt with new international issues once a year; among other things, they have decided to reduce energy subsidies, which is a problem above all in developing and OPEC countries—but also in Germany. In terms of country composition, the G20 is of course much more heterogeneous than the G7/G8 group, which makes it more difficult to reach a consensus or even compromise position. Moreover, in the long term, differences in per capita income could narrow as relatively poorer countries catch up over time with the US and other Western countries plus Japan. However, it is not only economic differences that present a barrier to consensus; ideological differences can also play an important role.

Particularly during the term of President Trump in the US, ideological differences played a negative role within the G20; US populism, which also stands for nationalism and protectionism, undermines the G20. If, however, the major international organizations of the world economy were to disintegrate, international political chaos and declining economic growth would threaten. It is not only important from a Western and Japanese point of view that there are forums for dialogue of leading politicians on international topics (some years ago, I myself participated along with Horst Siebert, I.W. Kiel, from the German side providing expert testimony at an InterAction Council Meeting in Paris on the topic of globalization; the InterAction Council is an organization which brings together a group of former heads of government to meet and discuss pressing issues).

The 20 large countries, which met at the G20 World Economic Summit in Osaka at the end of June 2019, clearly had enormous difficulty in agreeing a common position in the areas of trade liberalization or free trade—here efforts were hampered by the US-China trade conflict—and climate protection policy.

It is not only the US, China, Japan and the EU that are important for the G20. If Brazil under President Bolsonaro, elected in 2018 on a political platform similar to that of former US President Trump, should continue with the idea of clearing ever larger areas of rainforest, it would be a disaster for global climate protection: the rainforest areas in Brazil and the huge forests of Russia act as carbon sinks absorbing massive quantities of CO_2 from the atmosphere. However, the expected conclusion of a free trade agreement which was reached in principle between Mercosur (including Brazil, Chile, Paraguay, Uruguay, Argentina—suspended from membership is Venezuela) and the EU in 2019 could at least prevent Brazilian President Bolsonaro from taking a consistently pro-Trump position. The EU as a customs union has a potential strategic global partner in Mercosur, as the Mercosur country club is also a customs union; at least for the time being, this means that there are still common, that is, uniform, external tariff rates vis-à-vis third countries—and free trade within the integration club.

With regard to the European Union, it must also be emphasized that this is a customs union in which there is not only duty-free trade between EU countries, but also a community external tariff vis-à-vis third countries. It is something rare, indeed remarkable, that in the case of the EU—and Mercosur—national policymakers have transferred competence for foreign tariffs and trade policy to a supranational institution (in Brussels: the European Commission). To share political sovereignty with others in a field of action in order to better assert trade interests together in the end than if each individual had tried it alone, that is the idea of a supranational approach. Indeed, it should be convincing, but Brexit shows that this was probably not the case at least in the UK. Part of the problem is that EU integration has rarely been included in the school curriculum as an issue. Where the population lacks an understanding of the fundamental connection between regional economic and political cooperation, regional integration projects can disintegrate once again. The example shows that if climate protection policy is not properly explained, if the mechanisms of the EU Emissions Trading System, for example, are not discussed in school lessons, then one should not indulge in the technocratic hope that intelligent institutions, such as the certificate market, will continue to exist and do much good in the long term.

In principle, one could expect regional integration clubs to cooperate well with one another, such as EU-ASEAN or EU-Mercosur. This is indeed partly the case, but this area of international cooperation could be expanded, and joint efforts in climate protection should have been an important field of cooperation since 2000—that is, since the Kyoto Climate Summit. But the EU-Mercosur Free Trade Agreement of 2019 already shows that climate protection is not really seen as a big, crucial issue at that level; this same criticism can be leveled at the EU-Japan Free Trade Agreement of 2018.

The G20 countries have tackled a number of environmental issues over the years. For example, the countries agreed to reduce high subsidies in the energy sector, including of fossil fuels, in some G20 developing countries. The issue of plastic waste in the oceans and the need for more recycling have already been addressed within the G20. The summit press releases often contain attention-grabbing announcements, but promised projects often fall short of the rhetoric and theory in practice. The G20 Brisbane Summit was a certain exception to this rule when the participating countries pledged to deliver 2 percent more economic growth by 2018 than would be expected under the normal economic expansion path;

the OECD was included as an advisory and monitoring organization for the achievement of the objectives. This gave the objective a certain gravitas.

If the G20 fails in the medium term due to all kinds of climate policy disputes at the summit, then it will be almost impossible to achieve and adhere to the 2 °C target of the Paris Climate Agreement, for the G20 summit usually has an important function—in this manageable "small group" there is mutual pressure to participate in reforms and to engage in major international projects. If, on the other hand, certain climate protection projects are attempted only or first via the United Nations, the corresponding much large relevant country networks are overly complicated, and the incentive for individual countries to free-ride is much higher than with the G20.

Of course, there is more than just the politically relevant international pressure to reform. Countries with a high use of coal in power generation, such as China and India, are likely to move more toward more renewable energies in the medium term; otherwise air quality levels in the two countries' conurbations will deteriorate unbearably and rapidly. For China, modernization reforms are obvious, since the Chinese economy is characterized by a high number of patents for both solar panel and wind power plant, equipment and machinery, and is also a major global producer in both areas. Japan, the EU and the US are also committed countries in these areas.

CHAPTER 18

Global EIIW-Vita Sustainability Indicator and Green Bonds: Opportunities and Problems

The sustainability orientation of countries, companies and projects is important from the point of view of the capital markets and climate policy. For investors, liquidity, profitability—both positive—and risk (negative) are on the assessment checklist for all financial products. If many more sustainability-oriented bonds are issued by the European Investment Bank, the World Bank or other issuers from 2020 onward, liquidity will improve. It remains to be seen whether the expectations of many investors and some experts are correct, namely that green bonds are less volatile in price—that is, less risky than standard bonds—and at least as profitable as traditional bonds. Studies at ETH Zürich provide some empirical evidence in this direction for the EU, while there is less evidence of such a connection for the US. Further considerations on the EIIW-vita indicator presented here reflect key parts of the EIIW Discussion Paper No. 231 (Welfens & Debes, 2018), which essentially aims at recording the sustainability of the economic development of countries.

If all countries strive for sustainable economic development, then global economic development will be sustainable; sustainability here is understood to mean that future generations will have the chance to achieve a standard of living similar to that of the present generation. Climate policy aspects are doubly represented in the EIIW-Vita Sustainability Indicator, as the share of renewable energies is one pillar of the three-pillar indicator. In addition, the "green international competitiveness" of countries is determined, with the

© The Author(s), under exclusive license to Springer Nature Switzerland AG 2022
P. J.J. Welfens, *Global Climate Change Policy*, Sustainable Development Goals Series,
https://doi.org/10.1007/978-3-030-94594-7_18

index standardized between -1 and +1. The indicator is also based on the savings rate—in a broad World Bank definition—since savings are the basis for the accumulation of capital (read: machinery and equipment) and of human capital (via investment in education); in addition, there is the aspect of preserving natural capital or, in many countries, the opposite—namely the exploitation of natural resources. The "total capital" as the basis of current prosperity may not be preserved for future generations if the real savings rate is too low or falls. It is probably no coincidence that the real savings rate (as defined by the World Bank) in Greece, Portugal and Spain had already deteriorated significantly a few years before the Euro Crisis. Whether the real savings rate here has the quality of an early growth indicator remains to be examined. The better the value of a country in the EIIW-Vita Sustainability Indicator, the more interesting the country in question becomes from the point of view of investors with a sustainability orientation.

Sustainability as a Task

Sustainability is an important dimension of economic activity in all countries of the world, especially with regard to climate change, which was once again on the international agenda as a political topic at the UN Climate Change Conference (COP23) in Bonn in 2017. However, it became clear at that conference for the first time that the US—somewhat isolated internationally under President Trump—no longer wanted to participate in cooperative climate policy and would realize its exit from the global Paris Climate Agreement. The Trump administration did not see the greenhouse problem or global warming as a problem which is essentially man-made, but—according to Trump's tweets—rather as an obstacle to US growth imposed by various actors (including China). The analysis of the vast majority of climate researchers in the US, Europe and worldwide continues to speak against this view. How this intra-US contradiction can be resolved in the longer term remains to be seen. As the second largest economy in the world—measured by gross domestic product at purchasing power parities—the US continues to be important for significant progress in international climate policy. How sustainability can be meaningfully captured using existing measurement concepts remains a challenge.

From an economic point of view, it is initially a matter of maintaining the substance of the production apparatus, which presupposes a corresponding savings rate; the reduction of greenhouse gases through a high share of renewable energies must also be considered, as well as the extent of environmentally friendly innovation dynamics, as can be seen in particular in sectoral export specialization. The EIIW-Vita Sustainability Indicator focuses in particular on these analytical pillars, whereby Schumpeter's perspective on innovation is also important as an impulse for problem-solving possibilities in trading partner countries. A country that has a high relative competitiveness in environmentally friendly goods will have a high international market share in these products and help solve problems abroad. At the same time, one can expect a leading export country in this field to also use the excellent export products in its own home market.

National policymakers and investors are looking for indicator concepts that capture the degree of sustainable orientation and environmentally friendly technological progress—for example, as the basis for country-specific investment strategies or in search of best practice and benchmarking. In addition to the many highly complex indicators, some of which arbitrarily combine more than 100 individual indicators, there are very few indicators that meet the OECD requirements for such composite indicators while also being theoretically sound and at the same time statistically feasible for the majority of countries. The EIIW-Vita Sustainability Indicator is a tool which has been available for many years and which, in addition to environmental aspects, also takes into account international competitiveness perspectives which for economic policymakers and investors is important. By taking the real savings rate—according to the World Bank—as a partial indicator (here, a number of additions are made to the savings rate from the national accounts, namely education expenditure is included, natural resource extraction is deducted as a quasi-capital consumption and damage caused by particulate matter emissions is reflected), the economic idea of preserving the substance of the capital stock as a basis for sustainable economic activity is directly expressed—future generations should have at least as high a standard of living as the current generation. The partial indicator of the share of renewable energies is also considered: if this indicator rises, the sustainability situation improves as global warming tends to be limited. Finally, the relative share or the national position value for environmentally friendly goods is considered—a relative improvement of the "green export position" stands for an environmentally friendly contribution to problem-solving in other countries, whereby it can be assumed that countries with strong exports can generally also successfully sell the corresponding products on the domestic market—which can also be a lead market.

Since an improvement in the international export position of environmentally friendly products is usually associated with corresponding upstream innovation activities, this indicator dimension reflects an innovation perspective. An important dimension of economic activity in an open economy is international competitiveness, as expressed in the relative specialization of countries or of the firms based there. International competitiveness refers to the relative sectoral export-import ratio in a given sector—in the sub-sector of tradable goods. In the course of international competition, companies, or the country under consideration, specialize in the production of such goods in particular where the country in question has a competitive advantage. The concept of Revealed Comparative Advantage (RCA) relies on the comparison of the sectoral export-import relation with regard to the overall export-import relation. Alternatively, one can look at the ratio of sectoral exports (in sector i) relative to total exports of a country and divide this ratio by the corresponding sectoral world exports (i.e., in sector i) relative to total exports in the world; if this ratio is multiplied by the sectoral exports of the country under consideration, one obtains a modified RCA for sector i.

The indicator, which indicates "green international competitiveness" (later also called the Green RCA indicator) and is composed of the relative share of "green" exports in the total export volume, is calculated by the EIIW on the basis of a list of products classified as environmentally friendly by the OECD. It is calculated from the ratio of the "green" exports of the respective country to the total exports of the country in question in relation to how this value looks together for the 123 countries recorded in the Global Sustainability Indicator, multiplied by the green export volume of the respective country.

> **Sectoral International "Green Competitive Advantage" (RCA): Calculation Approach**
> In the case of Germany, one could write:
>
> $$\frac{\left(\frac{German\ Green\ Exports}{German\ Total\ Exports}\right)}{\left(\frac{World\ Green\ Exports}{World\ Total\ Exports}\right)} * German\ Green\ Exports = Green\ RCA\ Indicator.$$

(continued)

> (continued)
> However, since the EIIW-Vita Global Sustainability Indicator is composed of the mean of three indicators, all of which lie between −1 and +1, the formula is modified so that the results lie within this value range with the help of the hyperbolic tangent.
> The modified formula can be written as:
>
> $$MRCA_{c,j} = tanhyp\left[\ln\left(\frac{X_{c,j}}{\sum_{j=1}^{n} X_{c,j}}\right) - \ln\left(\frac{X_{I,j}}{\sum_{j=1}^{n} X_{I,j}}\right)\right]$$
>
> The list of products used for this indicator can be found in the book *Towards Global Sustainability* by Welfens et al. (2015).
> Source: Welfens & Debes, 2018

Here you can see the results of the last update (Table 18.1). They show, starting from the top 10 and bottom 10 placed countries in the RCA ranking of 2015, the placement of these countries in 2000 with the absolute and relative changes since then.

At first glance, very little fluctuation can be seen over time (apart from a few exceptions mentioned separately). In the 15-year observation period presented here, it can be seen that countries that did poorly in 2000 were very likely to do so again in 2015. Although the absolute worst values have improved somewhat over the last 15 years (+0.04 points), the absolute best values of the two periods under consideration have also improved (+0.04).

The leading group of ten countries is even more consistent than the bottom group. Exceptions in the RCA indicator ranking are France (+105 places to the tenth place), the UK (+110 places to the ninth place) and China (+127 places to the second place). However, a look at the absolute values puts the performance of two countries into perspective, as they are based only on a very small increase in the absolute score. The UK owes its top 10 ranking in 2015 to an increase of almost +0.06 points to 0.03 points, while France improved by +0.05 points to 0.03 points over the same period. There are very many countries that lie between the −0.05 to

Table 18.1 Top and bottom 10 RCA ranking countries (leading countries 2015: green field; comparison with results from 2000)

Country	RCA Ranking	2000	Ranking	2015	Change	Comparison
Germany	2	0.70732064	1	0.95120817	1	0.24388753
China	129	-0.05422317	2	0.48314901	127	0.53737218
Italy	4	0.26478718	3	0.30370979	1	0.03892261
Japan	1	0.91144181	4	0.24871461	-3	-0.6627272
Mexico	5	0.10790259	5	0.16448695	0	0.05658436
Austria	9	0.01363652	6	0.04517463	3	0.03153811
Belgium	10	0.01201023	7	0.04213901	3	0.03012878
Hungary	17	-0.00608793	8	0.03733938	9	0.04342731
United Kingdom	119	-0.02500984	9	0.03401491	110	0.05902475
France	115	-0.01870704	10	0.03285886	105	0.0515659
Luxembourg	112	-0.01684421	134	-0.0238867	-22	-0.00704249
Philippines	114	-0.01832516	135	-0.02481197	-21	-0.00648681
Canada	143	-0.08429353	136	-0.0323785	7	0.05191503
Indonesia	122	-0.0286378	137	-0.03266894	-15	-0.00403115
Australia	124	-0.0331318	138	-0.03347561	-14	-0.00034382
Spain	130	-0.0561603	139	-0.03439802	-9	0.02176228
Russia	128	-0.04572129	140	-0.04113308	-12	0.00458821
Singapore	131	-0.05880113	141	-0.0439934	-10	0.01480773
Ireland	126	-0.03828724	142	-0.0442691	-16	-0.00598186
India	120	-0.02505041	143	-0.04879183	-23	-0.02374142

Source: Own representation

+0.05 values and that can be left behind with even a very small increase in absolute values.

If you look up the table from these very frequently occurring values, values quickly begin to thin out, and at the higher end of the top 10 ratings, values are very different in absolute figures. Even the top group is obviously not homogeneous, here visible as a graph showing the absolute values of the RCA indicator from 2015 of the top 10 (Fig. 18.1).

The most obvious change in the top 10 is in China's position. An absolute improvement of +0.53 in the last 15 years has raised China to the second place. What is the reason for this increase?

Let us take a few individual products out of the RCA indicator where China has dramatically increased its exports. China has been able to increase its export of mineral water (Commodity Code (CC)) 220110 eleven-fold since 2012 to US$33 million in 2015. This trend continued in

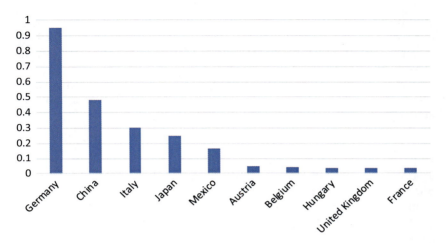

Fig. 18.1 Top 10 countries ranked by RCA indicator, 2015. (Source: Own representation)

2016 with exports of $62 million. This corresponded to a total volume of 284 million liters of water in 2016. The export of CC 283524 (phosphates, phosphites and hypophosphites) has tripled since 2009 to $125 million. In 2016, however, this figure fell again by $6 million. CC 283536 (polyphosphates) also experienced a very strong increase; exports rose from $37 million in 2010 to $114 million in 2015.

The export of household goods CC 392490 (tableware, kitchenware or household goods (made of plastic)) also tripled to $3.33 billion. This figure also fell in 2016 to $2.87 billion, although the absolute volume in kilograms continued to rise. China also exported other plastic products (CC 392690) worth $10 billion in 2015. In 2009, the figure was "just" $3 billion. Here, the value of exported goods stagnated in 2016 compared with 2015, even though China was able to increase the weight of exported goods by about 6 percent compared to the previous year.

The export of technical products such as pumps or centrifuges for liquids (CC 841990) has also doubled in the last five years to $1.2 billion. The export of machines, for example, for metal treatment, but also with other individual functions (CC 847989) more than doubled in the six years prior to 2015 from $95 million to $210 million. The same applies to the export of supplier goods for craftsmen, such as taps, valves, tanks or drums, pressure reducers or thermostat-controlled valves (CC 848180), which doubled to $10 billion. It is worth noting that in 2016, the sum of these export goods weighed only one-third of the total export goods of 2012, but nevertheless brought a result which was $2 billion higher than in 2012.

Thus, no single "green" product can be found that China is increasingly exporting; for China, the rise seems to be more a cross-industry development.

G20

A look at the positions of the G20 countries in the Green RCA indicator shows large differences (Fig. 18.2). Both the best and the worst placed country in the Green RCA indicator are members of the G20. India occupied last place in 2015. Seven G20 countries are in the top 15 (rankings in green) and seven G20 countries are among the worst performing 12 (rankings in red).

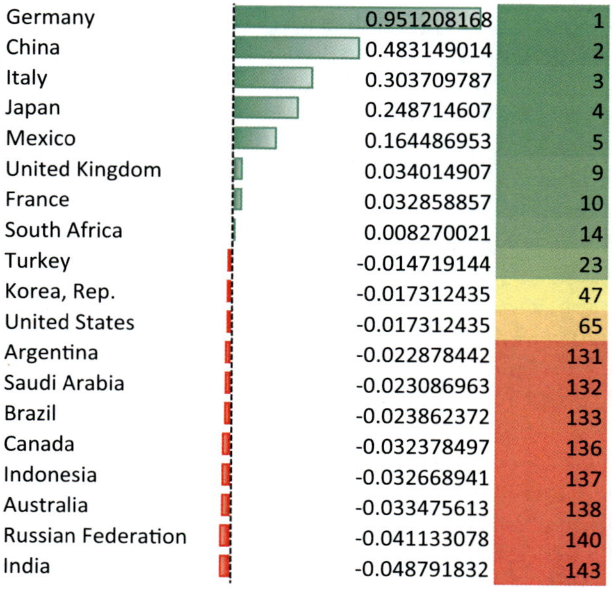

Country	Value	Rank
Germany	0.951208168	1
China	0.483149014	2
Italy	0.303709787	3
Japan	0.248714607	4
Mexico	0.164486953	5
United Kingdom	0.034014907	9
France	0.032858857	10
South Africa	0.008270021	14
Turkey	-0.014719144	23
Korea, Rep.	-0.017312435	47
United States	-0.017312435	65
Argentina	-0.022878442	131
Saudi Arabia	-0.023086963	132
Brazil	-0.023862372	133
Canada	-0.032378497	136
Indonesia	-0.032668941	137
Australia	-0.033475613	138
Russian Federation	-0.041133078	140
India	-0.048791832	143

Fig. 18.2 RCA indicator for environmentally friendly products, G20 countries in 2015. (Source: Own representation)

EIIW-Vita Global Sustainability Indicator: OECD-Compatible Approach

All sub-indicators are in the value range −1 to +1 for each country and can be combined as a sub-indicator or as an overall indicator to form a "global" indicator sustainability value. The overall indicator can be calculated for each country for which data are available—missing data for individual years are calculated by the EIIW by interpolation. The EIIW-Vita Global Sustainability Indicator is, unlike many other composite sustainability indicators from the technical literature, compatible with the OECD guidelines for such a composite indicator. This is crucially important because only indicator constructions which meet these guidelines provide consistent investor and policy signals. How the weighting of the sub-indicators is realized (e.g., politically determined weighting, weighing scheme determined by the investors or weighting determined on the basis of factor analysis or survey values) is not discussed further here.

The overall indicator, which consists of one-third each of the indicators for (1) Environmentally friendly ("green") exports, (2) Indicator for sustainable energy production and (3) Real savings rate, contains the results just presented, while at the same time it can also provide a larger overview of the development of the individual countries in terms of sustainability than any one of the three individual indicators alone could.

The countries that performed particularly well in the 2008 ranking were also in the top group of 2015. Germany, Nepal and Norway were able to grow by a small margin in absolute terms, while Namibia fell back somewhat. Tajikistan, Ethiopia and Paraguay have also improved. The newcomers to the top of the table are Iceland and Costa Rica.

Just as the top group was able to improve a little bit, the countries taking the places at the bottom of the table have deteriorated a lot. There is also a higher volatility at the bottom of the rankings compared to the top group, with five new countries among the bottom ten compared to the ranking 2008. Sadly, newcomers among the worst performing ten countries compared to 2008 are St. Vincent and the Grenadines, Republic of the Congo, Benin, Tunisia and Ukraine. The position of Trinidad and Tobago has slightly deteriorated compared to 2008, but the strong deterioration compared to the 2011 ranking is striking indeed. This is a visible outlier within the final group.

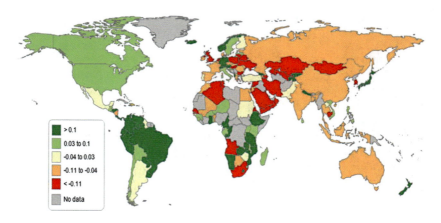

Fig. 18.3 World sustainability indicator positions, 2000 (green = leading). (Source: Welfens et al. (2015), toward global sustainability. Issues, new indicators and economic policy, p. 131)

If we now move on to the 15-year period under review, these developments will become even more visible. A world map of the overall indicator from 2000 can be seen here (Fig. 18.3).

This results in long-term changes in the top and bottom groups (Table 18.2).

In the last 15 years, the top group was able to improve its performance slightly in absolute terms, while Germany, with an absolute increase of 0.15 points in the overall indicator, was able to move ahead of 20 countries which were ahead of it at the bottom of the rankings, thus improving from the 21st to 1st place. Nepal has been in the top 3 since 2000, Costa Rica and Paraguay have also placed in the top 10 for 15 years.

Against this background, Japan has seen a very interesting development: in the year 2000, the nation took the second place with an absolute score of 0.225 points but fell 62 places by 2015 (-0.22 in absolute terms to a score of 0).

At this point, special attention should be paid to China. China was at a level of -0.05 in 2000, which at that time corresponded almost exactly to the average of all countries included in this indicator and thus to the world average. That was resulted in China taking 80th place. By 2015, China had improved by almost 0.25 points in absolute terms and ranked 12th in 2015. By comparison, the winner of the 2015 ranking, Germany, finished with 0.29 points in absolute terms, only 0.09 points higher than China.

Table 18.2 Long-term changes in ranking in the top and bottom groupings

Long-term changes in the EIIW-Vita Global Sustainability Indicator

	2000		2005		2010		2015	
Top 10								
1	Namibia	0.2340	Namibia	0.2654	Nepal	0.2907	Germany	0.2937
2	Japan	0.2250	Nepal	0.2631	Germany	0.2630	Nepal	0.2837
3	Nepal	0.2229	Germany	0.2411	Ethiopia	0.2292	Norway	0.2402
4	Costa Rica	0.2167	Norway	0.2339	Namibia	0.2275	Tajikistan	0.2370
5	Albania	0.2143	Costa Rica	0.2282	Norway	0.2192	Namibia	0.2282
6	Norway	0.2140	Paraguay	0.2209	Costa Rica	0.2189	Paraguay	0.2136
7	Iceland	0.2135	Albania	0.2096	Zambia	0.2056	Ethiopia	0.2089
8	Paraguay	0.2114	Iceland	0.2095	Paraguay	0.2026	Mozambique	0.2082
9	Mozambique	0.2054	Ethiopia	0.1900	Albania	0.1973	Iceland	0.2052
10	Ethiopia	0.1985	Georgia	0.1873	China	0.1956	Costa Rica	0.2007
Bottom 10								
134	Trinidad and Tobago	-0.1317	Uzbekistan	-0.1325	Ireland	-0.1467	Zimbabwe	-0.0591
135	Saudi Arabia	-0.1392	Lebanon	-0.1326	Poland	-0.1470	Vietnam	-0.0576
136	Bahrain	-0.1410	Trinidad and Tobago	-0.1400	Canada	-0.1523	Zambia	-0.0566
137	Lebanon	-0.1501	Syria	-0.1515	Kyrgyzstan	-0.1549	Yemen	-0.0581
138	Oman	-0.1513	Eritrea	-0.1544	Vanuatu	-0.1555	Venezuela	-0.0513
139	Brunei Darussalam	-0.1602	Brunei Darussalam	-0.1661	Mongolia	-0.1722	Uzbekistan	-0.0419
140	Eritrea	-0.1607	Oman	-0.1722	Sudan	-0.1770	Uruguay	-0.0464
141	Azerbaijan	-0.1697	Kazakhstan	-0.1737	Latvia	-0.1783	Vanuatu	-0.0424
142	Angola	-0.1937	Solomon Islands	-0.1749	Oman	-0.1794	Ukraine	-0.0356
143	Yemen	-0.2016	Yemen	-0.2358	Saudi Arabia	-0.2028	US	0.0294

Source: Own calculations

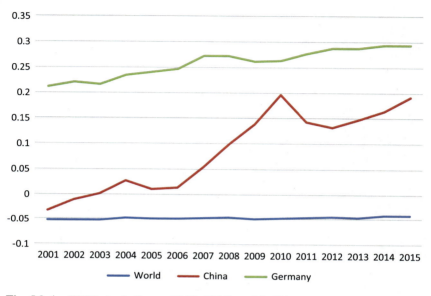

Fig. 18.4 EIIW-vita indicator 2000–2015 world, China and Germany. (Source: Based on Welfens and Debes (2018), Fig. 4, p. 8)

China's very good development can also be seen in comparison with Germany and the world average (Fig. 18.4).

China's strong development could already be seen from the Green RCA indicator. The placement of two top 10 nations and two bottom 10 countries in the remaining two sub-indicators is interesting in comparison to China (Table 18.3).

In the net savings indicator, China ranked third, similar to its performance in the Green RCA indicator (international competitiveness in environmentally friendly goods). In the renewable energy indicator, China finished only in 83rd place. A similar phenomenon, albeit not so pronounced, is also evident in Germany. Here, too, the renewable energies indicator ranking is the weakest of the three. In the case of Germany, it is also visible that Germany owes its top ranking almost exclusively to the Green RCA partial indicator, with the almost perfect absolute value mentioned above. Norway, which was also among the top 3 in the 2015 ranking of the overall EIIW-Vita Global Sustainability Indicator, shows a specifically different behavior in sub-indicators. The worst rating here comes from the Green RCA indicator.

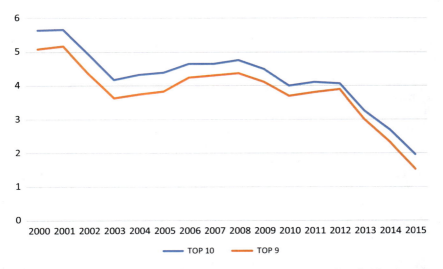

Fig. 18.5 Development of the yield in ten-year government bonds (for the top 10 and top 9 sustainable countries according to the RCA indicator). (Source: Based on Welfens and Debes (2018), Fig. 5, p. 14)

Table 18.3 Comparison of "savings indicator", "renewables indicator" and "RCA indicator/green international competitiveness" (rankings in color)

Country	Savings indicator	Rank	Share of renewable energies	Rank	International green competitiveness	Rank
China	0.25777206	3	-0.166286326	83	0.48314901	2
Germany	0.05582001	44	-0.125950928	76	0.95120817	1
Norway	0.12916926	13	0.612060122	9	-0.02077765	127
Trinidad and Tobago	-0.33903209	141	-0.366697498	142	-0.01731244	64
United States	-0.00913849	80	-0.241445099	99	-0.01731244	65

Source: Own calculations

POLICY PERSPECTIVES

The fact that large countries such as China, the US, the EU—and especially Germany, France, Italy and the UK—play an important role in global sustainability cannot be overlooked. China in particular, as a dynamic growth and technology country, has a special role to play here, initially as a polluter and/or the largest emitter of climate-damaging gases in the context of rapidly increasing production and consumption, but also as an increasingly important producer and exporter of environmentally friendly technologies. The decoupling of economic growth from emissions and greenhouse gas growth cannot be achieved in the long term without more environmentally friendly technology development. This technology development could be examined in detail in its components—such as product innovations and process innovations—and also start-up dynamics in the field of environmentally friendly products, which is also relevant here.

There is an obvious rivalry among the leading companies for innovations relevant to environmental and climate protection, as can be seen from the international patent statistics. However, there is also a measure of technological globalization, which means the international distribution of innovation dynamics in multinational companies—that is, networked research within corporate groups and thus knowledge generation and bundling across borders—and the innovation dynamics driven by individual companies or multinationals from different countries in cooperation with each other. This technological globalization (see Jungmittag, 2017; Dachs, 2017), which progressed significantly among OECD countries until about 2005, has slowed down since then—possibly because certain technology fields have been "exhausted" or because the penetration of new suppliers from China and other countries has reduced the expected returns on internationalized research and development. If the relationship between process and product innovations is taken as a kind of measure of the maturity of technology fields, then it is also possible to estimate the extent of green innovation dynamics with a view to corresponding indicators, at least for EU countries—where both types of innovation are covered by statistical surveys. Since new markets are primarily developed through product innovations and cost-reducing process innovations, and then become increasingly important in the advanced market process, the relationship between process and product innovations can generally be taken as an indicator of market maturity. Among all technological fields in the EU, the field of information and communication technology (ICT) continues to be characterized by relatively high product innovation dynamics, which in turn is very important for the level of technological progress and productivity growth in the medium term. This makes it all the more important to focus more strongly on approaches in the area of digital sustainability. It is important to consider existing industrial initiatives—such as those of the leading telecom companies in OECD countries—and, at the same time, the research priorities of industrialized and emerging countries in the area of basic research on information and communications technologies. Industry 4.0 addresses important new fields of research funding in Germany—but also in other countries such as China—and the European Commission also intends to set funding priorities here. Of course, this can provide significant impulses for environmentally friendly international competitiveness in the future. Since first-mover advantages (advantages of pioneering companies) of a quite considerable nature exist in some ICT fields—often only a handful of companies account for over 90 percent of the market share—the emphasis on diffusion dynamics, which is so important in the old, traditional "industrial world", is likely to lose importance over innovation dynamics in the narrower sense.

Survey results on demand preferences for environmentally friendly goods can also be regarded as strategically important (Udalov et al., 2017; Udalov & Welfens, 2021). Due to the establishment of a national emissions trading system in China—following the completion of the pilot phase with certain Chinese cities and regions (Welfens et al., 2017)—the prospects for improving air quality in China will improve significantly from 2021. China, unlike the US under President Trump, is committed to abiding by the UN's Paris Climate Agreement. It is conceivable that, in the decade following 2020, emissions trading will also take place between China and Europe as well as parts of the US (where some federal states already participate independently in a system of tradable emissions certificates) and Canada (Quebec as a region is especially active here). It makes little sense to increase the price of emission rights in isolation, which the European Commission is planning for the European Union, if the price differences between say the EU and China diverge greatly. In the longer term, global emissions trading can be expected to make a positive contribution to climate protection, with an efficient system having a globally uniform price. In a transitional phase, China will use its new emissions trading system to first adjust the existing regional price differences within the country and include all regions in the ETS—the incentive effects for efficient structural change will become apparent in China after a few years.

The fact that some regions of China stand (incidentally) for emission-intensive primary products from other regions of China within the framework of domestic Chinese trade has been investigated in the literature (Du, 2017), and this could lead to domestic compensation payments at the expense of emission-intensive regions with emission-intensive primary product production. The import of energy- and emission-efficient intermediate products and machines is likely to increase temporarily, which in turn offers good opportunities for countries with international competitive advantages in environmentally friendly products: there are opportunities for Germany here, for example, in the context of Industry 4.0. As China has increasingly specialized in such products since around 2010, partly due to the increasing production of solar and wind power plants and energy-efficient plant and machinery, China will be able to increasingly develop these specialization advantages nationally and internationally in the context of structural change. An analysis of the various policy options in China's environmental policy shows that the taxation of emissions and emissions trading systems can indeed bring significant progress (Parry et al., 2016).

Among the G20 countries which should greatly develop their potential in the field of environmentally friendly products is India, where an appropriate innovation policy appears to be lacking. However, it can be argued that the expansion of the digital software sector offers an approach to developing an international leadership position in sustainable ICT dynamics. However, targeted incentives for innovation have so far been lacking, and Indian telecom companies have yet to participate in global green industrial projects in the area of information and communications technology. More research cooperation between the EU, the US, China and India could be a G20 impulse for further global sustainability progress. It should also be pointed out that increased support for start-ups, for example, in the case of green ICT, can be a national and international impulse for modernization that has been underexploited to date. As far as patent dynamics are concerned, the relationship between product innovations and process innovations provides information on the maturity of the technology cycle—a high relationship between product and process innovations speaks for an early cycle. Data on this are available at an EU level through the Community Innovation Surveys. There is a need for further and more broad research in this area.

Sustainability-Oriented EIIW-Vita Government Bond Portfolio

If, from the perspective of a sustainability-oriented investor, one had invested in long-term government securities over the years from 2000 to 2015—with Laos and Trinidad and Tobago being omitted due to data problems—and focusing on the top 10 sustainability indicator countries, one would have seen the following yield development (see Table 18.4):

Table 18.4 EIIW-Vita Global Sustainability Indicator-based sample government bond portfolio 2000–2015 (SABIS strategy; EIIW calculations), ten-year government bonds of the most successful ten countries of the RCA indicator

Country	2000		2001		2002		2003		2004		2005		2006		2007	
Japan	1.74	Germany	4.80	Germany	4.78	Germany	4.07	Germany	4.04	Germany	3.35	Germany	3.76	Germany	4.22	Germany
Germany	5.26	Japan	1.32	Japan	1.26	Japan	1.00	Japan	1.49	Japan	1.35	Japan	1.74	Japan	1.67	Japan
US	6.03	US	5.02	US	4.61	Italy	4.30	Italy	4.26	Italy	3.56	Italy	4.05	Italy	4.49	Italy
Italy	5.58	Italy	5.19	Italy	5.03	US	4.02	US	4.27	US	4.29	US	4.79	US	4.63	US
Mexico	10.76	Mexico	10.13	Mexico	10.13	Mexico	8.98	Mexico	9.54	Mexico	9.42	Mexico	8.39	Mexico	7.79	Mexico
Switzerland	3.93	Denmark	5.09	Denmark	5.06	Denmark	4.31	Denmark	4.30	Denmark	3.40	Czechia	3.80	Czechia	4.05	China
Denmark	5.66	Switzerland	3.38	Czechia	4.88	Czechia	4.12	Czechia	4.82	Austria	3.39	Austria	3.80	Austria	4.30	Czechia
Austria	5.56	Belgium	5.13	Switzerland	3.20	Switzerland	2.66	Switzerland	2.74	Mexico	9.42	Hungary	7.12	Hungary	4.30	Austria
Belgium	5.59	Austria	5.08	Sweden	5.30	France	4.13	Austria	4.13	Czechia	3.54	Korea, Rep.	5.15	Hungary	6.74	Hungary
Czechia	6.31	South Africa	11.41	Austria	4.96	Austria	4.14	France	3.64	Switzerland	2.10	Denmark	3.81	Denmark	4.29	Denmark
Excl. Mexico	*5.64*		*5.65*		*4.92*		*4.17*		*4.32*		*4.38*		*4.64*		*4.65*	
	5.07		*5.16*		*4.34*		*3.64*		*3.74*		*3.82*		*4.22*		*4.30*	
Variance	*5.01*		*8.82*		*4.86*		*3.95*		*4.28*		*7.72*		*3.57*		*2.68*	
Standard deviation	2.24		2.97		2.20		1.99		2.07		2.78		1.89		1.64	

	2008		2009		2010		2011		2012		2013		2014		2015	
Germany	3.98	Germany	3.22	Germany	2.74	Germany	2.61	Germany	1.50	Germany	1.57	Germany	1.16	Germany	0.50	Germany
Japan	1.47	Japan	1.33	Japan	1.15	Japan	1.10	Japan	0.84	China	3.85	China	4.13	China	3.36	China
Italy	4.68	Italy	4.31	China	3.50	China	3.86	China	3.49	Italy	4.32	Italy	2.89	Italy	1.71	Italy
China	3.91	China	3.37	Italy	4.04	Italy	5.42	Italy	5.49	Japan	0.69	Japan	0.52	Japan	0.35	Japan
US	3.67	US	3.26	US	3.21	Mexico	2.79	Mexico	5.60	Mexico	5.68	Mexico	6.01	Mexico	5.93	Mexico
Mexico	8.31	Mexico	7.96	Mexico	6.90	Belgium	6.67	Belgium	3.00	Belgium	2.41	France	1.67	Austria	0.75	Austria
Czechia	4.63	Hungary	4.84	Hungary	7.28	France	7.64	France	2.54	France	2.20	Belgium	1.71	Belgium	0.84	Belgium
Austria	4.36	Czechia	3.59	Netherlands	3.88	Hungary	2.99	Austria	7.89	Austria	2.01	Austria	1.49	Hungary	3.43	Hungary

(*continued*)

Table 18.4 (continued)

Hungary	8.24	Hungary	9.12	Denmark	2.93	Czechia	3.71	South Africa	7.90	Hungary	5.92	Hungary	4.81	UK	1.90
Denmark	4.28	Austria	3.94	Korea, Rep.	4.42	Korea, Rep.	4.20	Austria	2.37	Poland	4.03	UK	2.57	France	0.84
	4.75		4.49		4.01		4.10		4.06		3.27		2.70		*1.96*
Excl. Mexico	*4.36*		*4.11*		*3.68*		*3.81*		*3.89*		*3.00*		*2.33*		*1.52*
Variance	4.28		5.46		3.46		3.92		6.38		3.10		*3.13*		*3.18*
Standard deviation	2.07		2.34		1.86		1.98		2.53		1.76		*1.77*		*1.78*

Note: Data from OECD (as of 20.12.2017); data for China from https://investing.com/rates-bonds/china-10-year-bond-yield-historical-data; for Mexico: Federal Reserve Bank St. Louis; EIIW-vita indicator top 10 (excluding Trinidad and Tobago and Lao PDR)

Source: Own calculations. The interest rate trend for the top 10 and top 9 countries in the table is shown here (Fig. 18.5) as a trend over time

the temporal yield development for the modified top 10 list in the portfolio is assumed to be one-tenth of the investment sum per country, while a top 9 line (excluding Mexico) is shown to address the problems of high exchange rate fluctuations in Mexico. The actual return from the perspective of a US investor would be determined only after adjustment for the changes in bilateral exchange rates, and naturally the portfolio return would look different again from the perspective of a Eurozone investor, that is, an investor from Germany or France, since here too the bilateral exchange rate changes would still have to be taken into account. However, since all nine countries considered were low-inflation countries in the period under review, the nine-country interest rate development can certainly be regarded as a meaningful presentation for an international sustainability-oriented investor.

If one assumes that economic policy is interested in improving the respective national sustainability position—as measured by the EIIW-Vita Global Sustainability Indicator—when competing for votes on the one hand, while on the other hand sustainability-oriented investment funds or investment strategies can provide environmentally friendly impulses via the capital market, then two important dimensions of a positive effect (national and global) of the EIIW-Vita Global Sustainability Indicator can be identified. The indicator can therefore provide substantial global sustainability impulses: broad and rapid implementation is crucial here.

The country weighting could also be done from the investor's perspective with regard to the value of countries' share in global income; furthermore, from a portfolio theory perspective, the volatility of country interest rates—or exchange rates—would have to be considered; interest rate variance can be regarded as an appropriate risk measure.

Since the transatlantic banking crisis, sustainability bonds have played a certain role in the bond market. The idea of many investors is that financing long-term projects which promote environmental quality will yield higher or more stable returns than traditional bonds. Projects or companies wishing to place such bonds on the market usually have a corresponding "green rating"—for example, from the New York Stock Exchange or Dow Jones. In Europe, Luxembourg has become an important financial center for green bonds. The European Investment Bank issued its first green bond in 2007, listed in Luxembourg. In the medium term, green bonds will increasingly be listed in Luxembourg, meanwhile the World Bank intends to add another 174 sustainability-oriented bonds.

The portfolio volume of green bonds in Luxembourg is likely to reach €200 billion in the medium term. However, that would be less than 2 percent of the bond volume needed to achieve the transformation to a sustainable, climate-neutral world. Luxembourg's Finance Minister Pierre Gramegna, who will have to replace a maturing Luxembourg bond with a new one in 2020, also plans to issue a green government bond. The Netherlands, which is an active fund trading center in the Eurozone, has also issued green government bonds, with Luxembourg and the Netherlands both having top ratings of AAA, that is, almost zero risk, rated by the leading rating agencies. What exactly a green bond should be, however, is somewhat unclear as long as there is no widely accepted catalog of criteria for it in either the political or business sphere. In France, for example, nuclear energy is regarded as climate-neutral, whereas the German government does not consider it to be sustainable due to the problem of the final storage of waste materials.

The Swiss federal government (Federal Office for the Environment, 2018, p. 23) has expressed the expectation that the Swiss financial markets will contribute to climate-friendly development on a voluntary basis. The Swiss federal government writes (transl. PJJW): "Other countries, such as France and Sweden, have already issued obligations or recommendations on the disclosure of climate-related financial risks in order to encourage an adjustment of investment behavior".

In Germany, the federal government in Berlin and some state governments have indicated that certain state investment funds—such as savings funds for civil servant pensions—will no longer be invested in stocks of companies which linked with damage to the environment. The Swiss Central Bank, which manages large currency reserves—including foreign equities—has apparently begun to reduce its investments in climate-damaging sectors proportionately in 2018. The same applies to Norway's sovereign wealth funds. Investment in gas production projects will still likely be regarded as (relatively) environmentally friendly for a number of years to come, as the specific CO_2 emissions are, for example, much lower than for coal and oil.

Countries with a worsening sustainability indicator over time may experience lower capital inflows and higher capital outflows, resulting in higher real interest rates in the medium term and thus lower economic growth. Here, Brazil is a country that is pursuing a questionable policy under President Jair Bolsonaro, a populist: under his leadership the Amazon forest is to be cleared more intensively so that the agricultural sector can expand. This forest is very important for the global climate. Some European countries, led by Norway, are contributing to an Amazon fund that is committed to rainforest conservation in Brazil, providing significant amounts of investment. When the Brazilian institute INPE, based on a satellite-based early warning system, reported in August 2019 that the area deforested in the Amazon in July was four times larger than in the same period of the previous year (namely 2254 square kilometers(!)), the head of the INPE, Ricardo Galvao, was dismissed from his post by President Bolsonaro. President Bolsonaro obviously doubts the satellite data as well as the hypothesis of climate change. Like many populists in the West, Bolsonaro stands for wishful thinking when it comes to environmental degradation and climate change. This is problematic for a rational economic policy in the area of climate protection policy. Therefore, addressing the problem of populism is a necessary political and scientific task for a better climate protection policy. It is a task for science insofar as empirical and economic policy research is fact based, that is, offers a natural basis for argumentation against political of any kind.

References

Dachs, B. (2017). *Techno-Globalization as the Engine of the Catching-up Process in the Austrian Innovation System* (EIIW Discussion Paper No. 222). https://uni-w.de/n3s70

Du, H. (2017). *Mapping Carbon Emissions Embodied in Inter-Regional Trade of China*. Presentation at the EIIW in Wuppertal at 8th of November 2017.

Federal Office for the Environment. (2018). *Switzerland's Climate policy – Implementation of the Paris Convention. Environment Information 2018*. Bern.

Jungmittag, A. (2017). *Techno-Globalization* (EIIW Discussion Paper No. 221). https://uni-w.de/0wdse

Parry, I., Shang, B., Wingender, P., Vernon, N., & Narasimhan, T. (2016). *Climate Mitigation in China: Which Policies are Most Effective?* (IMF Working Paper WP/16/148). International Monetary Fund.

Udalov, V., Perret, J. K., & Vasseur, V. (2017). Environmental Motivations Behind Individual's Energy Efficiency Investments and Daily Energy Saving Behaviour: Evidence from Germany, the Netherlands and Belgium. *International Economics and Economic Policy, 14*(3), 481–499. https://doi.org/10.1007/s10368-017-0381-7

Udalov, V., & Welfens, P. J. J. (2021). Digital and Competing Information Sources: Impact on Environmental Concern und Prospects for Cooperation.

International Economics and Economic Policy, 18, 631–660. https://doi.org/10.1007/s10368-021-00503-8

Welfens, P. J. J., & Debes, C. (2018). *Global Sustainability 2017: Results of the EIIW-vita Sustainability Indicator* (EIIW Discussion Paper No. 231). https://uni-w.de/0o0hg

Welfens, P. J. J., Perret, J. K., Yushkova, E., & Irawan, T. (2015). *Towards Global Sustainability: Issues, New Indicators and Economic Policy*. Springer.

Welfens, P. J. J., Yu, N., Hanrahan, D., & Geng, Y. (2017). The ETS in China and Europe: Dynamics, Policy Options and Global Sustainability Perspectives. *International Economics and Economic Policy, 14*(3), 517–535. https://doi.org/10.1007/s10368-017-0392-4

CHAPTER 19

Weaknesses of the EU Emissions Trading System and Prospects of Linking Emissions Trading Systems and Further Development of the WTO

The EU Emissions Trading System has developed relatively well over time, and among other things, the EU has clearly inspired other countries and regions—such as China and California—to adopt the same approach. However, the weaknesses of the EU system include in particular the following points:

1. The EU Emissions Trading System could have been extended to more than the initial coverage of 45 percent of emissions a long time ago; within a few years California had gradually reached a share of 85 percent in 2015. Under the new von der Leyen Commission, both broadening and new international cooperation approaches are conceivable for the EU.
2. The annual percentage reduction of the upper emission limit is too low to even come close to achieving a reduction of 90 percent of the 1990 CO_2 level by 2050;—5 percent from 2025 would be an order of magnitude that would appear both sensible and feasible; the CO_2 certificate price would then rise to around €40 per metric ton. The more climate-friendly innovation projects that are successful or expected in the medium term, the lower the price buoyancy in the CO_2 certificate market would be. It will therefore be unreasonable

© The Author(s), under exclusive license to Springer Nature Switzerland AG 2022
P. J. J. Welfens, *Global Climate Change Policy*, Sustainable Development Goals Series,
https://doi.org/10.1007/978-3-030-94594-7_19

to wait a long time for innovation policy to increase its expenditure—and also to block new priorities for climate-friendly research and development projects.
3. The targeted 40 percent allocation of free EU CO_2 allowances for the period 2021–2030 is far too high; it creates significant redistributive effects in favor of capital (a figure of about 20 percent could be considered neutral). The expected auction revenues from certificates sold on the part of the state are €250–330 billion in the fourth trading period of 2021–2030. These are high amounts, of which at least a quarter could be invested in more national and supranational climate protection innovation projects. Another quarter could possibly become a new own resources pillar for the EU or the Eurozone—an amount of €7–8 billion is manageable and could be used for climate-friendly, cross-border infrastructure projects.
4. The research projects developed on the European side to analyze the EU Emissions Trading System sometimes read strangely, namely too uncritical and lacking in proposals to improve emissions trading in the EU; one example of this is the study "Exploring the EU ETS Beyond 2020" (I4CE/ENERDATA, 2015; in the COPEC Research Program—the study does offer interesting insights into many individual points). However, one can also expect little in the way of critical analysis if the financing—as in the case of the study mentioned—is provided via private companies from France, the French government and the EU. A mixture of such clients is rarely conducive to the quality of research output, as there is no clear responsibility on the project award side. Without a critical analysis, however, the EU Emissions Trading System cannot be further developed in a meaningful way.
5. The EU itself and its member states apparently see parts of the EU ETS as a kind of isolated regional project. That approach is inappropriate. There would be enormous additional benefits if the various CO_2 certificate trading systems that exist worldwide were integrated and common rules and principles were established. The EU should take the initiative here, as there is a current lack of any course-setting for such an integration of emissions trading systems.

Although the issue of CO_2 leakage is addressed—for example, in the above study—the fact that CO_2 pricing in the EU leads to the relocation of CO_2-intensive production steps and the production of CO_2-intensive manufactured goods to other countries is analytically part of a larger challenge. One conceivable option here would be EU countervailing duties (Transport & Environment and the Trade Justice Network, 2017; special taxes are also proposed here for certain direct investment projects in the field of fossil energies, which could, however, lead to international uncontrolled growth), which in many cases would be problematic with regard to the rules of the World Trade Organization and would presumably lead to new transatlantic EU-US conflicts. At the very least, it is necessary to do more research into questions of countervailing import duties and to consider whether it would not be possible to introduce a simple principle at the World Trade Organization: industrialized and emerging countries that cover at least 60 percent of their emissions with emission certificate trading systems and have at least a 3 percent annual reduction in the upper emission limit can export without facing CO_2 compensation duties. This would be a good incentive for many countries to introduce emission certificate trading systems, and it would also create enormous opportunities for the long-term global cost-reducing networking of emission certificate systems. Each individual WTO country would be free to decide which sectors should fall below the 60 percent limit, so that the flexibility desired by certain countries would be ensured. Of course, it cannot be ruled out that OECD countries, for example, would introduce the requirements for ETS for trading partners with protectionist policies, but here one could counteract with new test procedures at the World Trade Organization. Since the G7 and G20 countries already want to push the WTO in the direction of reform, this is a good time to include climate protection issues here. It could be assumed that the US under President Trump would cause particular difficulties here, but under President Biden there is perhaps an opportunity for progress. The EU, for its part, has good opportunities within the framework of its network of trade agreements with over 70 countries to take up the linkages between emissions trading systems and free trade mentioned here within the framework of a network policy. It would also be interesting to incorporate the climate protection aspects mentioned here within the framework of the QUEST macro model, so that policymakers could gain a broad impression of the expected economic effects of alternative policy measures or scenarios by means of appropriate economic and growth policy simulation analyses.

Since climate protection is a very important global public good, it will probably be necessary to link this policy area as consistently as possible with the World Trade Organization. It is, after all, remarkable that it has been quite a long time since the WTO itself has really analyzed the links between trade and environmental protection (WTO, 1999).

It appears, therefore, that the WTO itself has had a gap in its analytical perspective for a number of years. One can still hope that internal and external research will be able to close this gap relatively quickly. Further similar research projects are also needed within other international organizations. Although the International Monetary Fund's analysis (IMF, 2019) is useful in many fields, there is a partial lack of a meaningful systematic approach, and it is also inappropriate to mix emission certificate price models and CO_2 tax rates in such a relatively crude way.

In any case, major challenges remain for further international research, and, of course, the pioneering studies that have been carried out thus far are indeed very useful. Some of the new ideas and approaches for problem-solving have been further developed and presented here that they may promote international and national debates and be an impulse for effective sustainable solutions.

An International Climate Certificate Fund (ICCF)

Policymakers in the EU, as in other countries, are keen to ensure that the development of emission certificate prices is not subject to very strong fluctuations or volatility and certainly that there are no very strong short-term price increases; such developments could also have an impact on other financial markets. However, the EU must also be criticized for this as the reduction path in the emission ceiling for EU ETS in 2021–2030 is too modest in view of the annual emission reduction of 2.2 percent, which will be required in order to avoid a very strong price increase in 2031–2050—with the target of climate neutrality in 2050. However, it is up to the EU to set up a kind of certificate intervention fund that can have a price dampening effect by issuing new certificates in the event of imminent price peaks (this would temporarily weaken climate protection, but hopefully for good reason in the medium and longer term). Such an intervention authority should be supported by experts, whereby the purchase of certificates by such an intervening fund should also be considered in the case of very *low* prices. Based on the work of such an intervention fund, expected lower and upper price limits would emerge, which would help guide companies' investment decisions. From a political point of view, it is at any rate possible to keep the risk of short-term price spikes low, which is of course very important in the case of an increase in the coverage of

CO_2 emissions or the expansion of emission certificates. Moreover, the example of certificate trading in Tokyo has shown that considerable annual reductions in emissions of commercial real estate are also possible.

The question of maximum price limits—and possibly also of minimum price limits—will, however, arise even more strongly if an international integration of certificates trading areas is undertaken, for example, between the EU, California, China and the Republic of Korea. The establishment of an International Climate Certificate Fund (ICCF) by the participating countries is recommended. Such an ICCF would intervene according to certain principles and should help to avoid extreme price peaks as well as phases of very low prices for CO_2 emission certificates. Obviously, one would have to decide on the statutes, budget and location of such an intervention authority. The establishment of such an ICCF should increase the political courage of policymakers in participating countries to introduce a fairly large share of their respective CO_2 emissions into the (integrated) certificate trading system.

This is, in turn, very important in order to realize an efficient path toward achieving climate neutrality. Germany, France and other EU countries should develop common policy initiatives for an ICCF in this area. The net costs for the participating countries should remain within reasonable limits in the longer term. It must be clear that ICCF will also be able to partly finance itself by issuing its own bonds on international capital markets. If sufficient institutional modernization is carried out quickly, energetically and with sufficient international networking, it will indeed be possible—without any serious problems—to achieve climate neutrality by 2050. It is obvious that the G20 countries should be careful to maintain good relations among themselves if this is to be successful.

References

I4CE/ENERDATA. (2015, November). *Exploring the EU ETS Beyond 2020*. COPEC Research Program: The Co-ordination of EU Policies on Energy and CO_2 with the EU ETS by 2030, a First Assessment of the EU Commission's Proposal for Phase IV of the EU ETS (2021–2030), Institute for Climate Economics/Enerdata.

IMF. (2019, May). *Fiscal Policies for Paris Climate Strategies – From Principle to Practice* (IMF Policy Paper). International Monetary Fund. https://www.imf.org/~/media/Files/Publications/PP/2019/PPEA2019010.ashx

Transport & Environment and Trade Justice Network (2017, November). *Can Trade and Investment Policy Support Ambitious Climate Action?* https://www.transportenvironment.org/sites/te/files/publications/2017_11_trade_and_climate_report_final.pdf

WTO. (1999). *Trade and Environment, Special Studies 4*. World Trade Organization. https://www.wto.org/english/tratop_e/envir_e/environment.pdf

PART IV

Concepts and Practical Fields for More Sustainability

CHAPTER 20

Climate Policy Problems: The Concept of a Sustainable Social Market Economy

The conversion of economic systems toward production and consumption with very low CO_2 emissions is a major challenge. This transformation is to be carried out after two centuries of industrialization, which until about 1980 faced no critical demands from science with regard to the combustion of fossil fuels or the use of coal/coke in the steel industry. If an economy without carbon is indeed to emerge and function, this would be a very demanding but historic task. The creativity required to mobilize the innovation dynamics of people and companies will be a major challenge in all countries of the world economy; in the field of environmentally friendly innovation dynamics, international competition is already effective in many areas, and in the EU meaningful approaches to an environmentally friendly industrial policy can be developed (Walz, 2015). The economic framework conditions must therefore be changed appropriately so that the incentives run in the direction of CO_2-light production and consumption. Regular international benchmarking can boost the ambition of economic policymakers, where new instruments will need continually to be explored and considered.

It is remarkable that Brazil and Canada are among the leaders in terms of renewable energy among the G20 countries and of course that many countries around the world have made great progress in renewable energy within just two decades. If the demand for wind and solar power rises simultaneously in many countries of the world, this will make it easier to

© The Author(s), under exclusive license to Springer Nature Switzerland AG 2022
P. J.J. Welfens, *Global Climate Change Policy*, Sustainable Development Goals Series, https://doi.org/10.1007/978-3-030-94594-7_20

make optimum use of mass production advantages for wind and solar systems. If the investment costs of wind and solar power fall under the variable costs of coal-fired power generation, soon no new coal-fired power plants will be built. Energy production is regarded as a long-term course-setting process as the capital intensity of such production is high.

When a social market economy transitions toward climate neutrality, the result should be a sustainable social market economy. This means that productivity and economic growth remain high and that the state can finance some redistributive and social policies, and that environmental quality is high and CO_2 emissions very low in the long run. This means an increase in the quality of life and health of citizens, as well as a higher life expectancy, developments which of course will also lead to associated challenges for social systems.

In view of the ongoing climate problems—that is, the threat of global warming above the +2 degree target by 2050 compared with the start of industrialization around 1850—the political spheres and the economies in Germany, the EU and the G20 countries are coming under greater pressure. Naturally also because of the foreseeable missing of certain targets in Germany and other countries as well as because of the international Fridays for Future student protest movement. In the debate on the introduction of CO_2 taxes, Germany's federal government is three decades behind Sweden and a decade behind Switzerland.

Since CO_2 emissions trading—a good instrument in itself—only covers 45 percent of emissions in Germany, a much greater share of production and thus emissions will likely have to be covered by expanded certificates trading; for the rest, the CO_2 tax option must be adopted quickly (in parts of the German government, there was no desire to entertain any discussions about such a tax before the European Parliament elections of 2019). However, following the Green Party's impressive gains in voter shares in these elections, the grand coalition was frightened enough to consider the economically sensible option of a CO_2 tax in parts of the economy. It remains to be seen whether climate protection policy will be sufficiently (even optimally) structured as a combination of certificate trading and a CO_2 tax and whether the G20 perspectives will be emphasized. The discussion thus far overlooks some important points in the overall complex of climate and economic policy: structural change and the dynamics of inequality are the key words.

While environmental politicians like to call for a more committed climate policy, the additional economic aspects of increased climate protection are strangely ignored. The main point is easy to understand, namely that a structural change toward more climate-friendly, that is, low-emission, products increases the demand for qualified, skilled workers—the only exception to this rule is probably the field of electromobility as electric vehicles are easier to produce than gasoline or diesel vehicles due to the nature of their construction, for example, without complex transmissions. It can be assumed that the introduction of CO_2 taxes in Germany and other EU countries will give a boost to the demand for climate-friendly goods and that the relative price of such goods will therefore rise. The consequence for skilled workers, according to the well-known economic Stolper-Samuelson theorem, is that their relative wage rate—compared to unskilled workers—increases. Since the production of low-emission products is relatively skill intensive, an even larger shortage of skilled workers will emerge in Germany and other EU countries than has been seen before, while at the same time, the economic inequality in Western Europe is further increased as a result. The wage advantage of the skilled workers will increase, which will enable populists to gain more votes among the unskilled and low-skilled part of the workforce in the future. Expecting a sensible climate policy in the case of broad political destabilization would be absurd.

The politicians in the centrist parties would therefore be well advised to implement a genuine dual strategy and to take the educational (skills) challenge at least as seriously as climate policy. Stronger incentives for education and (re-)training are needed. Unskilled workers in particular should be encouraged to invest in further education. Interestingly, study results from the Netherlands show that the educational return for skilled and unskilled workers is about the same. However, unskilled workers are on average less motivated to undertake further training than qualified workers. This challenge is likely to apply to all G20 countries.

The political system in Germany calls on both the federal government and the state governments—in dialogue with employers' associations and trade unions—to set a better course for more continuous professional development and training, especially for the unskilled. Trust in this field in some federal states will not be very high, since they seem to be clearly overburdened with the task of doing their homework with regard to their own universities or planning when it comes to teacher training. If, for example, North Rhine-Westphalia, Germany's most populous state, is lacking 7000 teachers in 2019, this is a shocking figure that does little to create trust in the ministries responsible.

The German and global surge in demand for climate-friendly products will be substantial if one follows the findings of the German Economic Institute (*Institut der deutschen Wirtschaft*) with its findings for Germany. If the 1990–2016 reduction in emissions is taken as a reference point, Germany would have to achieve triple the reduction in CO_2 emissions in 2016–2030 in view of the targets which have been set for 2030. This may well succeed with a massive structural change in favor of low-emission products and production processes but would be inextricably linked with a sharp increase in the wage ratio of skilled workers. The challenge for policymakers to tackle the (re-)training issue is therefore considerable. The easiest way for Germany and the EU27 to attract more skilled workers into the country, in addition to a smarter general immigration policy and new incentives for further training, is to attract EU citizens from the UK, which is plagued by Brexit, through a clear relocation initiative. These can generally be considered to be qualified employees, and of the more than 2.5 million EU workers in the UK, around one million could probably be brought to Germany, France, the Netherlands and so on, with committed policies. However, this immigration policy—here following another international trade theorem (namely, the Rybczynski theorem)—also means that the production of skill-intensive goods will continue to rise. The necessary offensive to promote and support further training therefore remains indispensable even then.

It is sometimes astonishing how little economic policy in Western Europe incorporates key standard economic doctrines. This is to the detriment of Germany and the EU and ultimately of a solution to the global climate problem.

It goes without saying that the vast majority of CO_2 tax revenues should be recycled back to private households. If, for five years, one was to take one-fifth of the additional revenue in order to support more "green innovation research funding" in Germany and the EU, this would be reasonable, as this would achieve a double internalization for some time: first, the internalization of positive knowledge transfer effects can be expected from innovation funding. Private incentives for innovation are thus meaningfully promoted. The additional social benefit of private innovation—which can be national or international—is adequately remunerated, and one can expect an optimal intensity of innovation. Second, it can be expected from the exploitation of climate-friendly innovations that further damage to the climate will be limited or even avoided more quickly than previously hoped—estimated to amount to 10–15 percent of world income in the

Stern Report with a weak climate policy. In other words, the two-degree limitation target will be achieved more reliably in the long term. CO_2 tax revenues, which are partly used for funding innovative CO_2 reduction projects, thus has a double advantage: harmful CO_2 emissions are reduced by increasing the price of CO_2-intensive production, while the increased funding of "climate protection innovations" creates additional innovation benefits in an area that is important for long-term ecological-economic stability.

After all, it has become clear in the discussion so far on climate policy and the CO_2 tax option that at least Sweden and Switzerland should be followed to the extent that there should be an emphasis on poorer households in terms of recycled revenues via tax refunds. However, if you really want to do it well, part of the repayments should be made in the form of a training voucher for the low-skilled. By "nudging" the low-skilled toward the right activity, namely further training, government would create a good and clever signal of a sustainable social market economy in Western Europe, which is essential in the new global competition of systems. Climate protection policy and a changed social and fiscal policy must be combined in a meaningful way.

It remains to be seen whether the new European Commission under President Ursula von der Leyen will take up the CO_2 tax issue in a reasonable way. There is a great opportunity for Europe to work with China on CO_2 emissions trading in the near future. China will have a national emissions trading scheme from 2021, and there is also scope to include California, which has been active in cross-border trading with the Canadian provinces of Ontario and Quebec. An international adjustment of CO_2 certificate prices would promote global efficiency and would therefore bring about cost-minimized progress in terms of climate stabilization. More global sustainable market economy approaches are necessary and sensible here. If President Biden leads the US back to the table, it would be a US policy success that also promises to undo the US backlog in terms of green innovation which occurred under Trump.

Moreover, the average global price of CO_2 certificates in 2018 was much too low at €1.8 per metric ton of CO_2. In the EU, the certificate price at the beginning of 2019 was around €25 per metric ton. A sensible CO_2 tax would be close to the certificate price and initially lower for the firms than for households, following the example of Sweden. If politicians in the EU and elsewhere do not raise certificate prices significantly—by reducing the volume of certificates in circulation—some governments in the West will probably run the risk of being ousted by Fridays for Future-style movements.

Without a novel policy mix, climate progress and politico-economic stability will not be achieved. At the same time, politicians should point out more strongly than in the past just how low unemployment rates are in the EU and also in Switzerland; in all EU countries—just as in Switzerland—they are overestimated by more than twice the true level by respondents to surveys. Worrying about imaginary problems distracts most people from developing successful solutions to the really important problem areas in good time. Incidentally, political misguided debates do not make much sense either, but are instead a waste of rather scarce political design and consensus capital. A new digital information policy from governments is also rather urgently needed in social networks.

More climate-friendly economic growth is an important goal of economic policy in Germany and other countries. The Stability and Growth Law should be amended to this end at all costs; and in Germany, too, the objective of a balanced balance of payments, which has been questionable since the establishment of the Eurozone, should also be adjusted—it would essentially have to be applied to the Eurozone. Greater cooperation in EU tax issues could be appropriate in the area of CO_2 tax policy; approaches to more international cooperation in tax policy which were discussed at the G20 summit of finance ministers and central bank governors in June 2019 would also be useful in this context. With the German European Council Presidency in the second half of 2020, German tax and economic policy would have had a unique opportunity to set smart national, EU and global accents were it not for the corona pandemic. The Renewable Energy Levy on households which drives the electricity price higher could be reduced. Lower electricity prices already by 2023 with over 50 percent green electricity generation should increase the demand for climate-friendly energy.

A sustainable social market economy in the EU is an important new concept that consistently combines market-driven growth, climate policy, social equity and international policy cooperation. Since climate protection concerns a global public good, the social market economy in the twenty-first century must be seen even more so than before in terms of global markets and policies. In relation to the EU, G7 and G20 summits, Germany can provide important impetus in the fields of tax, climate and growth policy, in further training policy and in Eurozone reforms. In 2019, environmental tax revenues in Estonia, the Netherlands, Slovenia, Denmark, Latvia and Italy amounted to almost 3.5 percent of gross

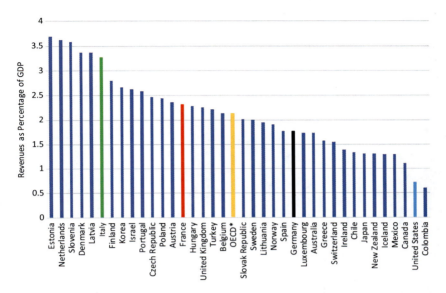

Fig. 20.1 Environmental tax revenues as a percentage of gross domestic product, 2019. (Source: Own presentation; OECDStat "Environmentally-related tax revenue", annual revenue 2019 or latest available, https://stats.oecd.org/Index.aspx?DataSetCode=ENV_ENVPOLICY)

domestic product; in France the corresponding figure was 2.3 and in Germany only 1.8 percent (Fig. 20.1).

Higher environmental taxes and emission certificate prices make sense in Germany in particular, while other taxes—also on investors and on the benefits of further training or middle incomes—must be reduced significantly. It is important to promote more sustainability-oriented capital market products globally, whereby climate-friendly infrastructure and battery-related projects are also important and useful for planning a modern, new economic policy.

Reference

Walz, R. (2015). Green Industrial Policy. In M. Mazzucato, M. Cimoli, G. Dosi, J. Stiglitz, M. Landesmann, M. Pianta, R. Walz, & T. Page (Forum), Which Industrial Policy Does Europe Need? *Intereconomics, 50*(3), 120–155. https://doi.org/10.1007/s10272-015-0535-1

CHAPTER 21

Economic Policy Consequences: Innovation, Mobility Policy and Global Cooperation

First of all, it makes sense for the state to promote proven innovations in the field of climate protection. This should also be the thoughtful approach of the European Commission. EU member states are also called upon to face up to the challenges, and international cooperation is essential both regionally and globally. It could also be worth considering that innovators—following the example of Elon Musk of the US electric car manufacturer Tesla—disclose sustainability-relevant patents for worldwide use in some fields, whereby a certain degree of reciprocity would have to be found in North America-Europe-Asia. The question of the global diffusion of green innovations will be very important, so that special activities on the part of the UN or the G20 could also be developed in this area.

Moreover, while promoting innovation dynamics in the field of sustainability, an international treaty would be necessary to ensure the maintenance and, if necessary, further afforestation of the world's largest forests, which are important as carbon sinks. This is likely to be a difficult challenge, as strategic behavior by certain countries can play a negative role. The G20 could be a relevant starting point here. However, it can hardly be assumed that substantial positive results can be achieved as long as the US would be governed by a populist president with a focus on nationalism, bilateralism and protectionism. This poses difficult challenges for the EU; in the case of Brexit, there will probably also be disputes between the EU27 and the UK over important G20 issues, as the US under President

© The Author(s), under exclusive license to Springer Nature Switzerland AG 2022
P. J.J. Welfens, *Global Climate Change Policy*, Sustainable Development Goals Series,
https://doi.org/10.1007/978-3-030-94594-7_21

Trump certainly tried to put pressure on the UK to further weaken the EU, while President Biden will reverse this course to a large extent. Since Brexit has been completed, the EU is economically weakened and its global negotiating weight is also weakened. Moreover, it will not be especially easy to specifically promote more green innovation dynamics, since it is often not foreseeable at the outset that climate-protection-relevant product and process innovations will occur in the promotion of innovation or within certain projects.

The question arises as to how an increased climate- and environmentally friendly innovation dynamic can be strategically promoted—possibly as part of a generally improved promotion of innovation overall. Here, the study by Bell et al. (2019) for the US should be noted. On the one hand, the study shows strong income concentration effects among US innovators; on the other hand, it illustrates a rather low significance of low income tax rates and a large role for innovation role models—possibly a form of innovation-promoting mentoring program would be advisable to take advantage of these findings—even in adolescence. The results for the US are likely also be relevant for other OECD countries, but this and the applicability in emerging countries still needs to be investigated.

As far as the promotion of innovation is concerned, it can be concluded on the basis of the aforementioned new, weighty study from the US (Bell et al., 2019) that tax rates are not decisively important for a high innovation dynamic—at least on the basis of US studies. Instead, it depends on good innovation role models and, if necessary, state-supported innovator mentoring programs; if this is transferred to Europe (where necessary, with certain reservations concerning transferability), corresponding conclusions can also be drawn regarding the promotion of innovation dynamics in the EU and in Germany. If climate-friendly innovation dynamics are to be promoted, successful projects should be clearly communicated, and an appropriate mentoring program should be established—especially for young people in the EU—in conjunction with cluster approaches, lead market projects and benchmarking. It is probably obvious that one will have to have some patience to await medium- and long-term innovation successes here. It cannot be ruled out that a playful introduction to science and innovation for children through a "junior university"—such as that exists in Wuppertal in Germany—could bear fruit here. The analysis presented herein shows considerable possibilities for optimizing tax and climate policy in Germany, Europe and worldwide.

Digitalization and Consumption

In its study Consumption 4.0—How Digitalization Changes Consumption (*Konsum 4.0—Wie Digitalisierung den Konsum verändert*), the German Federal Environment Agency has no clear conclusions to offer on the question of how digitalization is changing consumption (Federal Environment Agency, 2018). For example, increasing levels of orders over the Internet result in increasing numbers of delivery trips—including those for returns—while, at the same time, the corresponding trips of the consumer to shopping malls, towns and cities for shopping are no longer necessary. If the professionalized, logistic supply chains in the Internet society are better than the substituted purchases by consumers in the city (i.e., purchases in bricks and mortar stores), one can argue that digitalization could make consumption more environmentally friendly in this respect. Reading digital newspapers save the paper, ink and energy involved in publishing printed newspapers, which in itself is a positive environmental effect in terms of resource savings, but the mass of information designed for consumption purposes is constantly increasing and the Internet itself is power intensive. This means that a significant environmental all-clear is only given if a very high percentage (100 percent in the long term) of electricity is generated from renewable sources. One new problem may be the spontaneous shopping stimulated by Internet-based advertising, which could induce households to shop more than usual. It remains to be seen whether households will really buy more in volume terms in the end, because the budget restriction of the household also applies in the digital economy and society. In the digital world economy, as in the old economy, private households cannot spend more on consumption plus savings plus tax payments than their income.

It is conceivable that more environmental awareness will emerge in the digital world, since the Internet—possibly also encompassing "green apps"—can and will be used specifically for the diffusion of environmentally friendly knowledge and behaviors. As young people in particular are active on the Internet, including as "influencers", it is important to press ahead with corresponding analyses. In addition, changes in people's attitudes toward the environment and climate protection also need to be investigated further, with the World Values Survey providing numerous new international insights here.

It cannot be ruled out that the effective price of Internet purchases will fall on average compared to purchases in the analog world, as in the analog world the respective VAT/sales tax rate on the corresponding consumer goods could be enforced more strongly by the state than in the digital consumer world. In any case, it has been shown that a number of problems arise in the enforcement of sales taxes and VAT in the digital economy (Goolsbee, 2000; Jones & Basu, 2002; Agrawal & Fox, 2017). If the relative price of consumer goods falls as a result, the consumption rate will rise and the savings rate will fall, leading to a drop in the level of the growth path of per capita real income in a standard growth model extended to include VAT aspects. This, in turn, would result in a long-term reduction in per capita emissions, provided that energy consumption is proportional to gross domestic product. The German Environment Agency did not consider this topic in its study, although of course long-term environmental and consumer issues should always be analyzed in a growth model. The research methods mentioned by the Federal Environment Agency, on the other hand, do not indicate any extended growth models.

As a conclusion, the Agency writes in its study (Federal Environment Agency, 2018, pp. 78–79; translation PJJW):

> *What are the consumer effects of the extra time we will have in the digital world? The discussion on instant shopping has clearly shown that a key effect of digitalization is to avoid less valued, more disruptive activities or to significantly reduce time spent on such activities. This immediately raises the question of how the extra time will be used. The additional time available can flow into more working hours or be used for leisure activities. Additional income generated from extra work could, via increased consumption, lead to additional environmental pollution. Depending on their nature, additional leisure activities can also have a direct and negative impact on the environment. At the same time, digitalization is creating various new leisure opportunities that have relatively little impact on the environment. So here the question immediately follows: what will leisure activities look like in the future?*
>
> *How far will the possibilities of consumer influence go? And to what extent can they also be used for environmental policy? As has been shown, the digitalization of consumption opens up considerable new possibilities for influencing consumers. It needs to be clarified to what extent private consumers are willing to accept extensive consumer influence from the various providers in the long term. Of course, this question goes far beyond environmental policy aspects, but it does play an important role in the context of the conception of a sustainable consumption policy.*
>
> *Similarly of great importance is the question of the extent to which environmental policy in turn can and would like to use the newly emerging channels*

for information, but also for influencing consumers, in order to promote sustainable consumption. A special aspect is the use of "influencers" to communicate the issue of sustainable consumption. It would also be relevant to examine the extent to which such an influence could lead to a social or cultural shift towards more sustainable consumption. There is also a concrete and current need for research into the extent to which product evaluations and placements on platforms such as Amazon, Ebay, etc. have a positive or negative impact on the sustainability of consumption. The influence of these platforms, the resulting environmental impacts and possible starting points for environmental policy need to be examined here.

Core research questions: Which factors determine the acceptance limits when influencing via the Internet? Can these be influenced by environmental policy? What is the scope for environmental policy? What concrete starting points can environmental policy employ to use existing ways of influencing consumers themselves to promote sustainable consumption? To what extent are sustainable products and sustainable consumption hampered by the current rating systems of the relevant major platforms? Implementation possibilities: A study of developments in the field of consumer influence, with a focus on environmental policy approaches. Workshop on acceptance issues with potential green "influencers" and other experts.

To what extent will a digital "Green Advisor" be possible and feasible in the future? This question follows on from the previous one. Various other aspects play a role in answering the question, e.g. under which conditions such an instrument can be developed and introduced with a view to success and how a "Green Advisor" would have to be institutionally positioned/secured. In order to ensure that such an instrument can place itself permanently on the market, it is necessary to know the success factors in advance. The technological developments on which such an instrument would be based would also need to be further analyzed. The extensive consulting services of this tool along the entire customer journey require complex and comprehensive digitized processes that require a thorough investigation of their implementation possibilities in detail. Consideration should also be given to how the independence of such an instrument can be guaranteed in the long term. Such an approach would certainly be valuable as a counterbalance to increasing commercial customer influence and would provide important links for environmental policy.

Core research questions: Which aspects of Green Apps have been interesting or successful so far? How can these aspects be bundled (technical/institutional etc.)? What are the ongoing developments in the field of Green Apps? How can they be bundled?

One can point out here that there are important initiatives for environmentally friendly information and communication technologies (ICTs) on the part of the world's major telecommunications companies. However, there is no effective G20 working group in this field. Since the state is the majority or minority shareholder in telecommunications companies in many countries, this would indeed be an important starting point for climate-friendly ICT dynamics, and the International Telecommunications Union (ITU) as an international organization active in this field, with its own sustainability competence, should also be mobilized more strongly. In the field of rail transport, where the state is an important player in many EU countries and other regions of the world—where the debate on climate protection often makes positive reference to the low CO_2 emissions of rail transport—the state is also called upon to act. A simple request for people to travel more by rail, however, will hardly be considered a good contribution to climate protection in Germany, as the rail system in Germany is often dysfunctional with significant delays or canceled trains many days. In Switzerland, rail travel is punctual and a reliable method of mobility, but in Germany the reality is quite different.

Aspects of Japan's Emissions Trading System and Global Certificate Market Integration

The city of Tokyo and the neighboring prefecture of Saitama have set up regional certificate trading systems in 2010 and 2011, respectively, with Saitama providing for voluntary participation by companies (Arimura, 2018). The two emissions trading systems were integrated in 2011. In Tokyo, the cooperation of large companies and also of companies with large buildings is mandatory, whereby the initial allotment of certificates was free of charge. Industrial companies and owners and managers of large buildings must reduce their respective emissions according to annual emission reduction targets. If the requirements are not met, penalties are due. The annual reduction in emissions required in the first trading period was -8 percent for commercial real estate and 6 percent for industrial plants in relation to a reference year. This not only creates pressure on industry to deploy energy-saving technologies, but also creates an incentive for users of large properties to optimize their use of heat, which usually goes hand in hand with CO_2 emissions. The establishment of a national certificate system in Japan has so far failed because of resistance from industry—so far only a low CO_2 tax has been introduced, which can hardly be attributed a noticeable effect.

Since the emissions certificate price in Japan (Tokyo and Saitama Prefecture) is relatively high, one can consider an integration of the certificate system with that in China, the EU and possibly the US, which from Japan's perspective points to a reduction of the certificate price in an internationally integrated semi-global system. Japanese firms could then buy CO_2 certificates cheaply, for example, in China. Financial investors are not permitted to trade certificates in Japan for the time being. Instead, bilateral transactions between companies are envisaged. There are also fears regarding increased fluctuation margins with regard to certificate trading in the Republic Korea and the EU (Kim, 2014).

If national certificate systems are interconnected (e.g., EU, US, Canada, China, Japan—with a uniform certificate price), simulation analyses according to Takeda et al. (2015) show an estimated welfare gain for Japan of 0.4 percent of national income. As the (marginal) CO_2 abatement costs for Japan—estimated at $380 per metric ton in another model (Akimoto et al., 2015)—are significantly higher than in the EU at $60–68—the following can be assumed: the welfare gain of a global certificate system for the EU would be lower than in the case of Japan, presumably about 0.2 percent of national income. With an estimated gross domestic product of €20 trillion in 2030, that would be €40 billion. In fact, the welfare gains of Japan and the EU are likely to be somewhat higher than indicated here, as a positive EU income effect through global certificate market integration, for example, has a positive international transfer effect on real incomes in Japan, China, the US and Canada. This has a positive rebound effect on the EU. Similar considerations apply to Japan. For Japan, therefore, 0.6 percent of real income could be a welfare gain, and for the EU 0.3–0.4 percent in terms of a long-term income gain through global certificates market integration. That would be €60 to €80 billion, or up to €150 per capita in the EU. The global welfare gains from G20+ certificate trading are likely to be in the order of €400 billion worldwide. These efficiency gains can potentially be offset by additional financial market risks that could arise or newly emerging risks in the absence of regulation of global financial markets. It is therefore advisable to emphasize here that the certificate systems of the G20+ countries (i.e., G20 plus Nigeria) should be integrated and that (1) the EU, Japan, China and other countries should set the course for this; and (2) the participating countries should implement cooperation in the area of financial market regulation. If both challenges are not overcome, a global integration of the certificate markets could ultimately cause a negative welfare effect. Of course, such an outcome should be avoided. Since the EU and Japan have already signed a free trade agreement in 2019, it would make sense to add a treaty on the integration of certificate trading systems. However, it would be desirable if Japan were to set up a national CO_2 certificates trading market beforehand. This cooperation should be opened to integration with markets in other G20 countries creating a global certificate trading system in the medium term; of course, the question of cooperation in financial market regulation should be considered in the context of such an integration of certificate trading markets. This brings the issue of cooperation between financial market and banking supervisors at an international level into the focus of climate protection policy analysis.

References

Agrawal, D. R., & Fox, W. F. (2017). Taxes in an e-commerce Generation. *International Tax and Public Finance, 24*(5), 903–926. https://doi.org/10.1007/s10797-016-9422-3

Akimoto, K., Tehrani, B., Sano, F., Oda, J., Kainuma, M., Masui, T., & Oshiro, K. (2015). *MILES (Modelling and Informing Low Emissions Strategies)*. Project—Japan Policy Paper: A Joint Analysis of Japan's INDC.

Arimura, T. (2018). *The Potential of Carbon Market Linkage Between Japan and China, Carbon Market Cooperation in Northeast Asia*. Asia Society Policy Institute.

Bell, A., Chetty, R., Javarel, X., Petkova, N., & Van Reenan, J. (2019). Do Tax Cuts Produce More Einsteins? The Impacts of Financial Incentives Versus Exposure to Innovation on the Supply of Inventors, Joseph A. Schumpeter Lecture 2017. *Journal of the European Economic Association, 17*(3), 651–677. https://doi.org/10.1093/jeea/jvz013

Federal Environment Agency. (2018). *Konsum 4.0: Wie Digitalisierung den Konsum verändert* [transl. PJJW: Consumption 4.0: How Digitalization Is Changing Consumption]. Federal Environment Agency. https://www.umweltbundesamt.de/sites/default/files/medien/1410/publikationen/fach-broschuere_konsum_4.0_barrierefrei_190322.pdf

Goolsbee, A. (2000). In a World Without Borders: The Impact of Taxes on Internet Commerce, *Quarterly Journal of Economics, 115*(2), 561–576. https://www.jstor.org/stable/2587003

Jones, R., & Basu, S. (2002). Taxation of Electronic Commerce: A Developing Problem. *International Review of Law, Computers & Technology, 16*(1), 35–51. https://doi.org/10.1080/13600860220136093

Kim, E. S. (2014). Imagining Future Korean Carbon Markets: Coproduction of Carbon Markets, Product Markets and the Government. *Journal of*

Environmental Policy & Planning, 16, 459–477. https://doi.org/10.108 0/1523908X.2013.865510

Takeda, S., Arimura, T., Sugino, M. (2015, March). *Labor Market Distortions and Welfare-Decreasing International Emissions Trading* (WINPEC Working Paper Series No. E1422). www.waseda.jp/fpse/winpec/assets/uploads/2015/06/ No.E1422Takeda_Arimura_Sugino.pdf

CHAPTER 22

Mobility Policy

The Problems Surrounding Rail Policy in Germany and Other Countries

In many countries, transport accounts for 10–15 percent of CO_2 emissions. In Germany and other EU countries, rail transport is considered to be environmentally friendly, so rail transport actually has a strategic role to play in climate protection. However, does the railway deliver what it is supposed to and claimed to? What would it take to get the service quality of the punctual Swiss operator SBB in European Union countries? High-speed trains in many countries of the world are an important part of the existing infrastructure. If trains run 100 percent on electricity generated by renewable sources, then rail travel is indeed a very environmentally friendly mode of transport. In addition to long-distance travel, however, local rail transport must also be considered. Good networking, high levels of punctuality and good service—including functioning customer toilets—are indispensable from the traveler's point of view. Railway systems are complex, and they function to differing degrees of success. In China and the EU, as well as in Russia, there are well-developed rail systems. In Germany, rail passenger transport is regarded as successful, yet in the day-to-day reality, considerable weaknesses can be identified—in addition to the many certain advantages that exist.

© The Author(s), under exclusive license to Springer Nature Switzerland AG 2022
P. J.J. Welfens, *Global Climate Change Policy*, Sustainable Development Goals Series,
https://doi.org/10.1007/978-3-030-94594-7_22

The German rail operator Deutsche Bahn AG is part of the public transport system, and with a climate-friendly reorientation of passenger transport, rail transport could play an important role for millions of people in Germany. However, rail services in many instances are actually getting worse and worse in terms of punctuality and quality or remain at the same sub-standard levels. Germany's rail system is much worse than that of exemplary Switzerland. The smaller network in Switzerland may be easier to manage than the larger one in Germany, but only a slightly higher delay frequency could be explained in this way. While in 2017 in Switzerland only about 3 percent of customers were delayed by more than three minutes late in terms of their scheduled arrival times, the figures for Deutsche Bahn AG are likely to be just under 20 percent.

In any case, the punctuality statistics in Germany do not even record trains which were canceled in a reasonable way, meaning they are not included in the late train statistics. Under these circumstances, railway cannot be a preferred means of transport for many millions of people dependent on trains, for example, for commuting to work. In regional transport, canceled trains, frequently disorientating announcements on the platforms of major stations (such as one recent memorable experience in Cologne, for example, regarding a train which should have departed for Krefeld according to the timetable from platform 9, the display first showed the train would be delayed, then that it would subsequently depart from platform 8, an automated announcement over the PA system then informed that it would actually depart from platform 7—all train passengers waiting now on platform 7 were subsequently directed to return to platform 9, again by automated announcement; this is an unacceptable imposition particularly for mothers or parents with small children or the disabled making train travel a miserable experience; another example was that on 23 June 2018 the train to Cologne-Bonn Airport was simply canceled with no notice that anything was amiss), are commonly occurring challenges.

It seems unacceptable that the railways are frequently affected by strikes—routes to and from regional and international airports are not excluded from such strike action. Key parts of the rail system should be organized on the basis of civil servants, then one has at least high reliability in crucial railway routes. It is up to legislators to also guarantee 100 percent reliability for rail connections to airports.

Railway Problems in Germany

As millions of everyday rail users can confirm, Deutsche Bahn AG is a poorly managed company in the passenger transport sector. For many years, no daily punctuality statistics have been published on a regular basis; the rail freight sector, which is supposed to take a larger share of freight transport in competition with the road network, is also in a sad state in many areas. One entrepreneur from the Westerwald, who sent clay to the Netherlands by rail for processing, reported that sometimes too few wagons were provided by Deutsche Bahn, sometimes none at all. At some point, the result of such poor management resulted in the aforementioned entrepreneur switching from rail to road transport with a heavy heart; the environmentally friendly railway had derailed itself in terms of its competition with HGV transport.

Due to the frequent and considerable delays of German InterCity Express (ICE) trains on the transit route through Switzerland to northern Italy, the Swiss firm SBB has a replacement high-speed train waiting in Basel to step in should the train from Germany not appear on time so that the timetable in Switzerland does suffer disruption. Of course, there are always force majeure events affecting rail travel which inevitably lead to delays or cancellations, but the fact that the train delay statistics of Deutsche Bahn AG are so much worse than those of the Swiss SBB should speak volumes and ultimately be unacceptable.

French high-speed trains only take passengers who have a reservation, in German ICEs this is not the case—even without a reservation, one can still board the train. On some days, this leads to overcrowding and indeed chaotic conditions, especially when a train, which is intended to be composed of X number of wagons starts its journey with less than the advertised number of carriages from Munich, Cologne, Berlin, Hamburg or Leipzig main station. The rail company obviously does not care too much about such problems. As a train passenger, you also have no right to a refund of the ticket price if you have to travel standing in a completely overcrowded train. Compared to the Swiss SBB, Deutsche Bahn AG is certainly underfunded, but even where it could deliver, the quality is simply too poor and appears to be worsening over time. Politicians want to attract more and more people to the environmentally friendly railways; however, as things stand, this is an impossible and unacceptable policy—which is also exposed to the prospect of significant errors and accidents, partly because of the unsafe overcrowding in trains at certain stations (e.g., in Cologne, Hanover, Berlin). Under the headline "Railways must compensate more and more", the *Frankfurter Allgemeine Zeitung* newspaper reported on 5 August 2019 that late payments to rail customers had doubled to €55 million since 2014. The damage caused by the delays of the Deutsche Bahn AG—including damage not compensated in regional traffic—amounts to several billion euros. In 2018, 75 percent of ICE and IC trains were "on time", that is less than six minutes late. There are about 150 million long-distance train passengers each year, and according to DB figures 3500 trains a year were canceled altogether just in the area of long-distance traffic. The federal government in Berlin would have to provide Deutsche Bahn with more, better and safer (financial) resources in order to enable it to make a better offer to customers.

After a delay of 60 minutes you are entitled to a 25 percent refund of the ticket price according to EU regulations (for long-distance transport), and after 120 minutes you are entitled to a 50 percent refund, whereby the refund procedure is extremely complicated. In Germany, the railways have a total of 2.5 billion travelers per year—the majority in local transport, and one can assume, for the purposes of a rough calculation, that every second traveler is one hour late per year, and the value of one hour is set at €20. The negative value added by rail in this case would therefore be €25 billion or about €20 billion if one wants to allocate one-fifth of the delay to external providers on the DB rail network. Passenger and freight rail transport generate €44 billion in turnover for Deutsche Bahn AG; whether the net value added in passenger transport is positive remains to be clarified. Customer satisfaction surveys are rarely carried out. As in Spain, high-speed trains could be fenced in over long distances for safety reasons. The punctuality rate in long-distance traffic could be the same as in Japan or Switzerland, if the management of the railways were to be overhauled and more investment made in the rail network. When it comes to rail usage, it cannot just be a question of how environmentally friendly the railways are or whether they use 100 percent of electricity generated from renewable sources, but rail travel also includes the goal of getting from A to B safely and—at least usually—on time. One can only warn politicians that should they plan on expanding rail traffic without sensible structural changes and sufficient investment, it just wouldn't be a sustainable policy.

If the railways are indeed to play a central role in modern transport solutions, then a return to the railways staffed by civil servants in key areas must be investigated: at least in the entire infrastructure sector. In addition, the law would have to ensure that airport connections in particular could not be impacted by strike actions. It should also be mentioned that during my time as a university lecturer at the University of Münster, my colleague Prof. Ewers, active in research and teaching in the field of transport economics, was able to award a prize for the best final theses in the transport and railway sector, thanks to a donation from Deutsche Bahn AG. The corresponding award-winning works were then forwarded to the Deutsche Bahn AG for further consideration. It was later reported to me that a certain university graduate of a German university later began a job at the Deutsche Bahn and was assigned an office: on the first day at his new job, he opened a cupboard in the office and found a large stack of unopened mail from the University of Münster—with all the award-winning theses from Münster. This may be a bad coincidence, and Deutsche Bahn AG will have to be allowed to present its own view to the German public on quality and productivity issues; it is currently clear that Deutsche Bahn AG is in a crisis situation and is lacking any recognizable and convincing modernization strategy. It would certainly be very sensible for the EU to present comparative statistics on a regular basis on the railway undertakings of all EU countries and also to set reasonable EU-wide standards in the field of high-speed trains in particular.

Electric Cars as a Systemic Problem in Germany and Europe

The state is an important player in mobility and not only because public investment in infrastructure appears to play a major role in almost every country in the world. As a local actor, as a commune, town or city, the state as an institution is of course occasionally just as important as the national political perspective when it comes to climate protection. As far as cities are concerned, one needs to think only of the problem of electric buses, which in 2019 already accounted for a good third of public bus transport in the Dutch province of Limburg (i.e., around Maastricht, where there are 95 electric buses, with plans for 260 by 2026), but which account for barely 1 percent of buses in most other EU cities. China has a city (Shenzhen, with circa 13 million inhabitants) in which there are over 12,000 electric buses on the road. If the buses of the Ruhrbahn local transport company in Essen/Mühlheim, in Germany, were e-buses, then according to Ebusplan, a consulting firm based in Aachen, this would mean at least 25,500 tons less carbon dioxide, 9.5 tons less nitrogen oxide and 200 kgs less particulate matter (Kohlstadt, 2019).

The conversion of a bus fleet in a large city, however, requires local political decisions, must also be accompanied by a high level of investment, requires the existence of larger bus depots and, of course, also requires investment in loading infrastructure. In some European and Asian cities, there are existing bus services powered via overhead lines; such systems could have a new future if the electricity would come from renewable energy sources, and reasonable modernization concepts are developed. The expansion of renewable energies in the electricity sector to 80 percent by 2040 will not be possible in Germany and many other countries without an expansion of wind energy plus network line expansion; the resistance to line expansion in many regions is considerable, and farmers in Germany receive high compensation for the laying of underground cables (one can note that the electricity companies concerned do not negotiate prices with individual farmers affected, but rather with the German Farmers' Association, which could be classified as a somewhat odd situation under antitrust law). Moreover, the EU continues to lack electricity export and import opportunities because of insufficient investment in the electricity grid at the borders of many countries. In California, there are bus fleets that use natural gas, as well as e-bus fleets which are charged using inductive technology—that is, wirelessly. In the area of individual transport, the transition to e-cars is a particular challenge in Europe—this will be the focus of further discussion.

The German government wanted to have one million electric cars on the road in 2020, but the actual number will be just about 100,000 such cars, 100,000 electric cars from a stock of circa 46 million cars. This is a target deviation of 90 percent, which can only be described as an embarrassment for parts of the federal government and certainly also a huge disappointment in terms of climate policy. With state-funded purchase premiums of €2000, the incentives for e-vehicles have so far been low (the alleged €2000 additional purchase premiums from the manufacturers do not mean anything, because the car manufacturers usually simply increase the prices beforehand by €2000—why the legislator has devised such a nonsensical approach as that of a purchase premium paid by the car industry remains unfathomable). There is no apparent meaningful idea in large parts of the government of what a systemic change to electric mobility both means and demands. In many offices of government, it has not yet been realized that one has to leave the old comfort zone in order to protect the climate. The opinion of a senior official in the Ministry of Finance in Berlin in 2018 that in a troubled world economy, the best course of action for Germany is to leave everything as it was stands for a dangerous illusion. There is no reason to panic, but to simply continue on traditional paths presents a real risk for society, and the world. If we want to preserve the world, we all have to change; and many processes, products and institutions have to change.

Electromobility with the Merkel governments in Germany is as if the US had announced a moon landing but had instead landed on Mars. How can the situation of a misleading and misdirected policy and sub-standard levels of innovation arise in one of the world's leading automotive and innovation centers? The answer to this lies in the sometimes grim transport and economic policy of the so-called *GroKo* (the grand coalition of center-right and center-left parties in Germany), the transitory blocking of the market to some car manufacturers via the German Association of the Automotive Industry (VDA) and the lack of political understanding of electromobility as a systemic challenge—especially when it comes to a system change at a federal state level. In the case of a systemic change, at least the initial conversion phase is not suitable for serving as a parade ground for achievements by federalist small states. Rather, for a period of four or five years, it would be important to tackle the systemic change efficiently together and to promote the possible and necessary mass production advantages of electric cars—including battery production—by boosting e-car sales and thus making electric cars inexpensive at the same time. There are hardly any mass production advantages in the car industry under 100,000 units, and the total number of e-cars accumulated over five years at this level shows a dangerous scaling problem.

The case of Germany, with its large and innovative automotive industry, is a useful example to study in Europe. The fact that some car bosses want to sell large, luxury plug-in electric cars at a sales price above €50,000—with good return for the auto manufacturer—is, in the early twenty-first century with the challenge of climate change, a naive and thoughtless dream; a better proposal to significantly hamper Germany as a rival could not have been concocted in Beijing. e-Cars can initially show their strength in urban traffic, and e-cars with a price tag of less than €30,000 can do exceptionally well, but in this mid-price segment only Renault and Nissan, as well as Korean suppliers, have electric cars on offer in Germany in 2019. The two largest German bus manufacturers have sleepwalked past the subject of electromobility entirely. Those cities in Germany that want to use e-buses need to mainly import buses from Belgium, the Netherlands, Poland, Sweden and China.

Battery prices for electric cars have fallen much faster than traditional car manufacturers in Germany had expected. Electric cars and the needed e-charging stations are still missing on German streets. The construction initiative for charging points considered by the political VDA at a summit in June 2019 is far too large scale and would lead to a huge number of loss-making charging points and thus to an unjustifiable need for subsidies. At the same time, it has become obvious that the institutional setting for e-charging stations is such that Federal Regulatory Authorities hardly have any influence in terms of imposing price transparency requirements and price regulations, respectively. The price variance for e-charging across regions in Germany in early 2021 was enormous, and there is no reliable information flow from e-charging stations to electric cars—so that a driver eager to recharge their car's battery at station X might travel to the charging point only to find out that charging station is not working on that day. There is a market power problem in the traditional electricity sector in Germany, and such regional market power, sometimes reinforced by regional or local government ownership, has negative impulses for the development of e-mobility in Germany. The higher charging prices and charging risk (e.g., not finding a charging station which works), the lower the willingness of consumers—and firms—to invest in e-mobility.

The nightmare of electric car buyers, running out of power somewhere with no access to a recharging infrastructure or suitable outlet, cannot be countered from an economic point of view by simply rolling-out an oversized number of expensive charging stations; a reasonable dimension to the charging station network is of course important, but more important would be a drone-based emergency charging express from car driver networks or other special organizations or even car manufacturers themselves, whereby a standardized spare battery for all car brands should be provided. Such a drone-based breakdown service should not have to be used more often than traditional cars when battery or fuel problems prompt a call to the breakdown services. The federal government in Berlin should propose such a breakdown service at EU level during its European Council presidency as a standard throughout the EU.

When already undergoing a systemic change, one could try at least one additional policy in Germany: a generous max speed limit of 160 km per hour on motorways—limited to an initial trial period of five years—would be well worth considering. From the point of view of accident research, this would be a blessing for motorists—namely, lower injury and death rates in car traffic collisions—and it would make superfluous the peculiar comments in car test magazines of the type "the car X was marked down in the test due to its low maximum speed of 180 km/h". The test was carried out at the same time as the car was being tested. For ambitious, hobby racing drivers, a Nürburgring II can be built, possibly in the very south of Germany, where there is nothing comparable for sunny weekends.

For a long time, the German government has remained inactive in the field of the standardization of charging processes, including from a billing point of view, although the topic of systemic change—as with changing from driving on the left to the right side of the road—demands decisive standardization as a government-driven task. The fact that there are no especially high fines for drivers of diesel and petrol vehicles that park in front of and block e-charging points is a serious mistake; the lack of cameras on charging stations, necessary to deter and if necessary sanction blockade parkers, is also incomprehensible. All this in fact shows the unwillingness of German transport policymakers to take the issue of e-mobility seriously. The Minister of Transport probably wants to do BMW and Audi a favor with his traditionalist approach, but it is only a disservice, as the systemic change—which will be inevitable—seems to be put on the long finger and discouraged.

By combining each charging station with a camera, one could certainly increase the respect for such e-charging stations among drivers. The fact that politicians themselves have not massively switched over to electric cars for their own ministerial cars and fleets is another political mistake, especially in Berlin. It would have been a good idea for the federal government to initiate an e-mobility project in which, for example, IKEA—or another well-recognized chain—in combination with an electric car leasing package or an electric car trial purchase, would promote future mobility concepts nationwide using the amplifying signal of its own brand. If electric cars come across as being almost exclusively luxury cars, the traditional car manufacturers in Europe cannot be quickly converted to the goal of developing climate-friendly products, certainly not in Germany. The Fridays for Future student protest movement has rightly asked why the government had promised one million e-cars for 2020 and can only achieve a miserable 10 percent of this target. Why should one believe the "GroKo" in announcing further targets for 2030, when the credibility of important ministries in Berlin has already fallen to low levels having missed previous targets? Those who are concerned about mobility, who point out that only

40 percent of electricity comes from renewable energy sources, do not really have a good, sustainable argument, as the share could be close to 50 percent by 2020 and 70 percent by 2025.

The German government's mobility policy suffers from further conceptual shortcomings. If you want more climate-friendly mobility, you cannot possibly want to continue the course with Deutsche Bahn AG given its propensity for delays, cancellations and defective trains. Management of DB should be outsourced to the Swiss Federal Railway company for a few years as a supply contract—or another company that promises, under acceptance of a possible penalty payment, to approximately realize the SBB's effective low delay rates, namely 3 percent for passenger traffic. Due to the larger German network, which is more complex to manage than that of Switzerland, one could also live with a 7 percent delay rate. At least not with the effective delay rate of at least about 15 percent, as claimed by Deutsche Bahn. The call for people to use more local public transport is in part an unreasonable demand if one is to use a breakdown-prone, and often poor information policy, service provider such as the Deutsche Bahn.

If Germany's auto manufacturers do not follow VW boss Diess' approach of quickly producing cheap electric cars and of course also electric buses or at least gas-powered buses—as they have long been used in California—then one of the most important traditional German industrial sectors could soon face a dramatic shrinking process. Thus far, it is only thanks to the logistical and production errors of Elon Musk and Tesla and its factories in the US and China that Germany's traditional auto companies still have good market opportunities for conventional vehicles and e-cars. The automotive industry, which accounts for 4 percent of value added and which represents a significantly higher contribution to gross domestic product with multiplier effects, will not survive as a leading sector in Germany if parts of the automotive sector continue to hope to be able to continue with tricks to massage emission values or strategy of stonewalling on the production of small- and middle-range e-cars for the years to come.

In the end, the question that remains in the present study concerns the conclusions which can be derived from the description and analysis of the global economy with regard to the challenge of climate protection in the twenty-first century. The next section provides some answers to this question, and it will be possible to say that the very important points can indeed be summarized in just a few pages (and in one illustration). In following this approach, one has to break with all conservative thought structures, do what is reasonable in many countries simultaneously and, if possible, in a coordinated way, and only then can one achieve the goal of climate neutrality by 2050.

Reference

Kohlstadt, M. (2019, August 12). Grüne fordern mehr Tempo bei Ausbau der E-Bus-Flotte in NRW [transl. PJJW: Greens Demand a Faster Expansion of the E-Bus Fleet in NRW], *Westdeutsche Allgemeine Zeitung*. WAZ Online Edition. Retrieved 29 March, 2021, from https://www.waz.de/politik/landespolitik/gruene-fordern-mehr-tempo-bei-ausbau-der-e-bus-flotte-in-nrw-id226746875.html

CHAPTER 23

Conclusion: International Cooperation and the Climate Protection Concept

The G20 still has little to show in terms of its own innovative climate protection initiatives. Despite that, the G20 format has indeed already been realized for a meeting of the relevant environment ministers. The massive global subsidies for fossil fuels (as of 2017) were not reduced at the 2019 conference in Japan. Germany's Federal Ministry for the Environment in Berlin writes on its website (https://www.bmu.de/themen/nachhaltigkeit-internationales/int-umweltpolitik/g7-und-g20/g20/, last accessed on 6 September 2019; transl. PJJW):

> On 15 and 16 June 2019, the first joint meeting of energy and environment ministers in a G20 format took place in Karuizawa (Japan). The environment and energy ministers of the G20 countries adopted a communiqué on climate protection, energy system transformation, marine waste and resource efficiency. In the Joint Final Declaration, all G20 countries except the US reaffirm their commitment to the implementation of the Paris Convention on Climate Change. In addition, a joint "G20 Action Agenda" on climate adaptation was adopted. Moreover, all G20 countries agreed on a common strategy to combat marine litter, including the better monitoring of plastic and other waste inputs and improved knowledge sharing on waste disposal and recycling.
>
> The Environment and Energy Ministers' Meeting will be followed on 28 and 29 June 2019 by the G20 Summit of Heads of State and Government in Osaka, Japan. As expected, the heads of state and government focused on cli-

mate protection alongside trade and economic policy issues. In addition, the summit also dealt, amongst other things, with marine litter, in particular through plastics, and with questions of resource efficiency.

One can hardly claim that the G20 countries already have a demonstrable, realistic approach to climate protection policy—and the US under President Trump was on the sidelines of the 2019 summits anyway. For the G20 summit in Japan there were the usual policy briefings, that is, short studies on certain policy issues, including on climate protection, with a particular emphasis on infrastructure projects and various financing approaches (including green bonds, that is, government bonds to finance environmental projects). However, a critical stocktaking and analysis of global climate policy was lacking, although UNEP submits annual reports on the "CO_2 climate improvement gaps" (or carbon gap), which repeatedly reveal significant structural problems on a global scale (see UNEP, 2018).

An Innovative Path to Global Climate Neutrality

Climate protection policy has become a major challenge for Germany, the EU and the global economy. A number of court rulings handed down during 2021 have also become important, such as a ruling in the Netherlands against the multinational energy company Shell, which is required by the court decision to make greater efforts to reduce CO_2 emissions in the medium term than management had planned thus far. In Germany, the issue of climate protection policy, which is important for the economy, society and politics, is the subject of a controversial debate, most recently because of the ruling by the Federal Constitutional Court in Karlsruhe on the need to revise Germany's Climate Protection Act: in April 2021, the court called on the government to adopt a stricter and more concrete climate policy, also for the period after 2030, with a view to future civil liberties of the younger generations. In response, the German government has drafted an amendment to the law: a 65 percent CO_2 emission reduction by 2030—instead of the 55 percent previously planned—and then an 88 percent reduction by 2040 as a new interim target, in each case compared to the 1990 baseline. After the amendment to the law is passed, a new, earlier, target date of 2045 for achieving climate neutrality will apply in Germany—instead of the 2050 timeline as applied previously. In essence, this means that production and consumption can be realized

23 CONCLUSION: INTERNATIONAL COOPERATION AND THE CLIMATE...

in 2045 without net emissions of climate gases such as CO_2 or methane; residual amounts would have to be compensated for by extra afforestation and other CO_2 absorption measures.

Incidentally, the German government has set CO_2 tax rates for the transport and residential/real estate sectors that will rise in stages and are to lead to national emissions trading in the medium term, perhaps also to expanded CO_2 certificate trading at the European Union level, where emissions from industry and commerce have been covered up to now. A CO_2 tax rate that is pre-programmed to increase stepwise over time makes sense in the area of emissions taxation in the household sector, since the strong price fluctuations over time that occur in CO_2 certificate trading are unacceptable for private households: in the event of a strong short-term price increase, heating bills could double within a year (see Fig. 23.1). Companies, on the other hand, are used to coping with strong price and cost fluctuations over time. The following figure shows that in the EU's

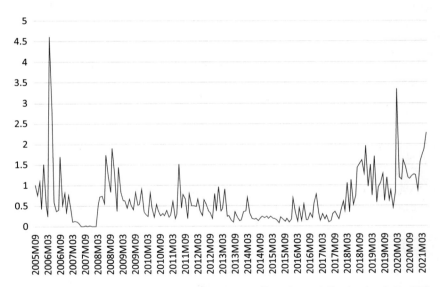

Fig. 23.1 The monthly fluctuation intensity (based on daily data) of the EU CO_2 allowance trading price between September 2005 and May 2021. (Source: Own representation of EIIW calculations based on data from Ice Futures Europe. Note: this graphic shows the monthly standard deviation of the EU ETS CO_2 price in euro (first beginning future nearby settlement price) calculated using daily data)

ETS CO_2 allowance trading, significant allowance price fluctuations (monthly standard deviations based on daily data) occur occasionally. The analysis of Welfens and Celebi (2020) shows that the CO_2 certificate price development is causally influenced—in the sense of so-called Granger causality—by share price developments in the EU.

For a good 80 percent of CO_2 emissions, a CO_2 certificate trading system is feasible and preferable to a CO_2 tax, also because of the possibilities of integrating EU CO_2 certificate trading with the CO_2 certificate trading systems of other countries: in this way, the goal of climate neutrality by 2050 (or earlier) is achieved at minimal cost through certificate trading regulated by the G20 countries. The G20 countries would have to specify the annual CO_2 reduction—ideally for the G20 region as a whole—while the companies would provide an optimal adjustment through their certificate sale or certificate purchase decisions: including the necessary emission-reducing innovations. This is much more efficient or better than, for example, the government formulating sectoral emission reduction targets for sector A (cars) or B (construction) from above. If, for example, cars account for 20 percent of emissions, and residential/commercial real estate for 30 percent, it makes no sense at all for the government to stipulate that sector B must achieve greater emission reductions than sector A; what is relevant from an economic and climate policy point of view is how high the CO_2 avoidance costs are in each of the two sectors—in the case of possible innovation projects. If the automotive industry had significantly lower abatement costs compared to the construction and real estate industries, one should focus more on CO_2 reductions in the automotive industry in terms of innovation. This is precisely what is achieved through CO_2 certificate trading.

What is important in allowance trading is that the government sets a reasonable annual reduction rate for the allowance trading area by 2050, that is, the rate by which the annual cap on the total volume of CO_2 for the sectors included declines. However, the EU's low 2021–2030 target of just − 2.2 percent per year is problematic, which arithmetically then requires a large annual jump to nearly − 9 percent in the two subsequent decades to be at 0 by 2050 in the relevant "dual sector" of industry and energy. Such a politically imposed jump would lead to economic instability, which must be avoided.

The European Commission, under President Ursula von der Leyen, has set out to introduce a border tax equalization levy in the future against countries without certificate trading or CO_2 taxes. In 2020, a manageable number of countries had CO_2 allowance trading systems: 16 percent of global CO_2 emissions were covered in this way involving countries that accounted for half of global production and one-third of the world's population, according to the International Carbon Action Partnership (ICAP, 2021, p. 26). It is also possible that the EU would join the US to form a transatlantic climate club to call for a CO_2 border tax offset levy, but the approach is not convincing as a strategy.

Such an offset levy can be used to protect one's own industry against foreign competition, which would result in an unfair competitive advantage without cost-based CO_2 emissions burdens. On the one hand, one can certainly argue this way, viewing climate protection as a global collective good—or world club good—to which each country should contribute its fair share. The political provision, internationally, of a global public good is difficult, since the incentives for free-riding are high: demanding climate neutrality as a country or government and hoping that other countries will commit themselves sufficiently to climate policy, while one wants to get away without one's own adjustments and innovations—possibly at high cost—in the borderline case.

However, if border adjustment levies are called for, they will be very difficult to design in a way that is compatible with World Trade Organization rules. Moreover, a reasonable calculation of the levy rate is difficult, and a number of important trading partners—such as India and presumably also China—could implement countermeasures against EU exports or US exports. At most, EU CO_2 offset taxes could be implemented temporarily on a few CO_2-emission-intensive foreign goods, such as aluminum, steel and cement, primarily as a means of creating pressure on partner countries to also develop CO_2 emission allowance trading systems.

It would be prudent for the EU to dispense with border adjustment levies in the medium term, provided that at the G20 one can reach a stage where all participating countries—as a group they account for 80 percent of global CO_2 emissions—initially launch CO_2 certificate trading in the industry sector or the energy sector by 2025 and have at least both sectors anchored in the CO_2 certificate trading system by 2030; this will then also lead to an internationally integrated G20 certificate trading system within three years. In the longer term, CO_2 emissions coverage in all G20 countries should be as high as that in California's allowance trading system, namely covering at least 80 percent of emissions. This would actually amount to achieving global climate neutrality efficiently by 2050. International certificate trading would bring enormous trade benefits. Just how important and advantageous the case of an international integration of emissions trading systems would be, for example, in the form initially of a transatlantic integrated certificate trading system, can be seen from the conceivable case of California's CO_2 certificate trading system being integrated with the EU ETS.

It is noteworthy, first, that California mimicked the EU approach in 2012, but has achieved nearly double the CO_2 emissions coverage since 2015: namely, nearly 85 percent instead of just under 45 percent in the EU. Nevertheless, second, CO_2 allowance trading in California has seen a lower CO_2 allowance in price than the EU's CO_2 allowance price in most years: in mid-May 2021, the EU was at €55 per metric ton of CO_2, while in California the price was about €18 per metric ton of CO_2 (see Fig. 23.2 for California, and Figs. 23.3 and 23.4 for the EU).

This means that, given the alternative for any company in California of innovating to reduce CO_2 by one ton as an investment and innovation

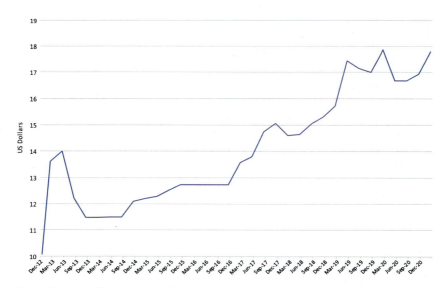

Fig. 23.2 California cap-and-trade current carbon auction settlement price in US dollars per metric ton, November 2012–February 2021. (Source: California air resources board, California Cap & Trade https://ww2.arb.ca.gov/our-work/programs/cap-and-trade-program/auction-information accessed 10.05.21)

23 CONCLUSION: INTERNATIONAL COOPERATION AND THE CLIMATE... 377

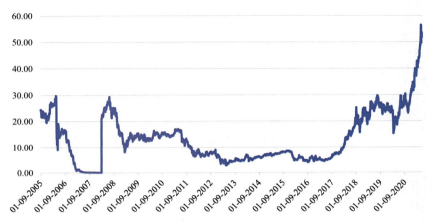

Fig. 23.3 EU CO_2 allowance price (forward price) in euro (€) per metric ton. (Source: Own representation of data available from ICE Futures Europe, IHS Markit)

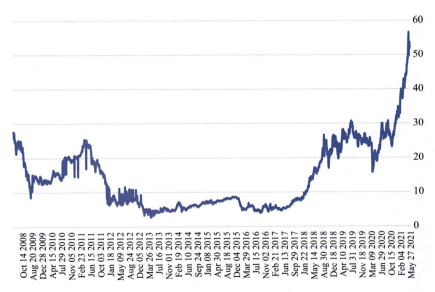

Fig. 23.4 EU CO_2 allowance prices: forward price at the year end (in euro [€] per metric ton). (Source: Own representation of data available from investing.com)

expense or else buying a CO_2 allowance at the market price, the CO_2 mitigation innovation cost in California is €18 per metric ton of CO_2. By the same logic, the corresponding cost in the EU is €55 per metric ton of CO_2, so CO_2 mitigation innovation costs in California appear to be much lower than in the EU. Apparently, it is relatively easier to implement CO_2 mitigation innovations in California's innovation-rich economy than in the EU. In terms of the international division of labor, it would only be sensible to integrate the CO_2 certificate trading systems of California and the EU and then arrive at a transatlantic common price of about €35 per metric ton CO_2: this would create a major incentive for innovative US companies to launch even more CO_2-saving innovation projects, while production costs would fall for companies in the EU—compared to the case of a pure EU allowance trading system with an EU allowance price some €20 higher per metric ton.

It does not matter to the climate where in the world most CO_2 savings and CO_2 reduction innovations initially take place; in the longer term, global competition will ensure that particularly effective CO_2-reducing California innovations will spread worldwide. Of course, at the end of the adaptation process, CO_2 emissions in the EU will also be zero in 2050.

If the previously separate allowance trading systems are merged into one integrated system, the US (as a whole) and California (in particular) stand to gain just as much as the EU. This is because the new transatlantic CO_2 community price of around €35 per metric ton will mean enormous cost relief for many companies in the EU and thus a stronger post-Corona economic upturn, along with more jobs. US companies from California, on the other hand, which sell surplus allowances to companies in the EU with allowance requirements, generate additional income or are motivated in advance to increase their innovation efforts to reduce CO_2 emissions. In this thought experiment, the US current account improves—thanks to the sale of US emission allowances to the Eurozone, the current account surplus of the Eurozone decreases. The EU, that is, Germany, France, Italy—and the UK—should therefore urgently press at the G7 summit for the US, Japan and Canada, all of which already have regional CO_2 certificate trading experience, to each launch a national CO_2 emissions trading scheme within two years. The EU should promote this with the incentive that this would take border adjustment levies off the table vis-à-vis the corresponding G7 partner countries.

This would enable the West to present a united front at the G20 summit, where the issue of emissions certificate trading systems should also be put on the agenda. Incidentally, it would be sensible if about half of the revenues generated via state auctions of CO_2 certificates were returned to private households—this would increase the acceptance of climate protection policy, especially among people with low incomes. The other half should be invested in increased research funding for climate-friendly "green" innovation projects. This would be in line with the economic logic of rewarding positive external effects of innovation funding, that is, the fact that the social return on such innovations is higher than from the perspective of the returns for the company implementing the research project. CO_2 certificate trading plus more innovation promotion could even stabilize the growth path in the North and South of the global economy. In view of the enormous benefits of CO_2 certificate trading, it is incomprehensible that the Biden administration did not give any signals in spring 2021 that the federal government would strongly encourage other US states to follow California's example and gradually introduce state-level CO_2 certificate trading (beyond California, there are only manageable approaches to CO_2 certificate trading in the New England states) as a first step toward a national system.

With an efficient G20 climate protection policy—with a one-time initial technology transfer from the US and EU to India and Brazil as a starting motivation—climate neutrality could be achieved at relatively low cost; less than 1 percent of world income would have to be spent for three decades, roughly, and the world would then have as a prosperity gain the avoidance of more and more extreme weather events that cost human lives and destroy assets—residential plus commercial real estate. The fact that the bill in terms of investments in dike reinforcement schemes and other flood protection measures can then also be lowered is also a plus. Of course, beyond the compact G20 group, in which negotiations can be conducted at relatively low transaction costs, the other countries of the UN would also have to be brought on board around 2030. A similar strategy has, however, already proven successful in the past with regard to the hole in the ozone layer and the reduction of CFC substances.

Moreover, analyses by UNEP (2021) in the Global Methane Assessment report show that in the short term it is particularly important for policy to focus on reducing methane, a particularly dangerous greenhouse gas. This gas, which has been accumulating significantly in the atmosphere for about a decade, is mainly produced by waste management, fossil fuel extraction and agriculture. If 45 percent of methane emissions worldwide can be reduced by 2030—that is 180 million metric tons of reduction per year—then 0.3 degrees of global warming can be avoided by the 2040s; in each year, there would be 255,000 fewer premature deaths worldwide, 775,000 fewer asthma-related hospitalizations and 73 billion fewer hours of work lost annually in the context of extreme weather conditions (for comparison, 60 billion hours is equivalent to the annual work volume in Germany). The UNEP has largely neglected the climate problem of methane emissions—avoiding a ton of methane emissions is 83 times more effective in terms of global warming than a ton of CO_2—for a relatively long time; after all, a clear report in 2021 has given an important impetus to the global climate policy debate.

Green Innovation Dynamics Are Key for the Path Toward Climate Neutrality

CO_2 pricing—in the form of taxes or CO_2 allowance pricing—will provide incentives for innovative companies with the ability to reduce CO_2 emissions, as well as other critical emissions, through innovation. Certain climate policy-related regulations could also be drivers of climate-friendly R&D, green innovations and climate-mitigation projects. One of the key challenges in terms of efficient R&D subsidization is that many climate-friendly R&D projects will generate international technology spillovers, while there is no easy approach available to internalize such positive external international effects. As the switch to climate neutrality is such a major transformation and climate neutrality is a global public good, there are indeed serious challenges here, and an international research project (e.g., under the auspices of the World Bank) which would monitor and measure international innovation spillovers can indeed be recommended here as a crucial policy element.

The global transformation of the economy toward a low-carbon system cannot be achieved in a world economy with a long-term rise of the population without large-scale process and product innovations. As regards climate change mitigation innovations, there is a rather limited number of OECD countries plus China which seem to be rather active in the area of green R&D and successful innovation projects. While about 40 countries are strongly active here in a Schumpeterian context, one may ask how other countries' firms and key sectors, respectively, could also be mobilized to focus more in terms of R&D and innovation on climate-friendly innovations. At the same time, the challenge of international and indeed global diffusion should not be underestimated. If the knowledge gap between innovator and the diffusion country is rather wide, no diffusion might happen at all. From this perspective, one may argue that it is not only high-tech green innovations which are desirable, but rather a broader portfolio of such innovations—including high-tech, medium-tech and sometimes even low-tech—and the respective R&D projects. The ability of firms in the Global South to leapfrog vis-á-vis crucial green technologies might be rather limited in reality, and even for the absorption of major innovations from the Global North, considerable R&D capital in the recipient economy will often be necessary. To the extent that the G20 is a key group of innovative countries in the world economy, it would be important to develop an outreach program as a kind of G20 diffusion and innovation policy cooperation project so that the above-mentioned problems could be adequately addressed.

As regards the broader dynamics of climate-mitigation patents and international diffusions, papers by Dechezleprêtre et al. (2011), Glachant et al. (2020) and Probst et al. (2021) have shown that international patents in this field are highly concentrated in a small group of countries, including the US, Germany, Japan, South Korea, France, the UK, Italy, Canada, China and Netherlands; the growth rate of such patents has not increased much after 2005—the year in which the EU adopted its Emissions Trading System. At the same time, North-South technology diffusion—according to the aforementioned research—is rather weak which may be considered to be a crucial impediment for effectively fighting global warming.

Growing North-South trade and intra-South trade could play a significant role in terms of green technology diffusion. However, other channels should be exploited as well. Development assistance programs of OECD countries should be adjusted in an adequate way, namely, to put much more of an emphasis on international green diffusion dynamics and on climate-friendly R&D projects than has been the case in the past. To the extent that a rather strong role of the stock market is useful as a driver of green patent growth (De Haas & Popov, 2019), a strengthening of capital markets and the stock markets, respectively, should also be considered. A broader role of stock markets should be embedded in a new framework of modernized economic systems which encourage broader long-term stock market investments (following the approach of, e.g., Sweden); this proposal has particular relevance in a situation where for more than a decade now bond interest rates have been very low and indeed could remain modest for quite some time.

WHAT CAN BE DONE?

Summarizing the analysis to date and drawing certain conclusions allows one to identify some areas of work in progress where more is needed and, indeed, a number of clear conclusions. The main finding is that a G20+ approach to a comprehensive, integrated CO_2 emissions trading system could work if such trading schemes were first implemented in all G20 countries, or at least in the G19Plus. The integration of certificate systems from different countries and regions will be reasonable only if the degree of emissions coverage is roughly the same in each case and if the annual percentage reductions in the annual CO_2 quantity cap are fairly similar as Tietenberg (2010) has pointed out in a paper titled "Cap-and-Trade: The Evolution of an Economic Idea". Before integrating certificate trading systems, one therefore needs a structural convergence phase of countries or regions that want certificate trade integration.

It is conceivable that the OECD G20 countries will initially integrate certificate trading systems and that India, Brazil, Russia and China plus Indonesia will implement a longer phase of convergence and cooperation. If there are ideological barriers here, the proposed areas of cooperation may have to be redefined. In principle, elements from the Kyoto Protocol on cooperation between the Global North and South can continue to be useful (e.g., the Clean Development Mechanism [CDM] and Joint Implementation; the latter means that an OECD country, e.g., active in a developing country—whereby both countries have official reduction targets under the Kyoto Protocol—finances a climate protection project in said developing country, which the industrialized OECD country can offset the effect against its emissions in order to meet CO_2 reduction targets; in the case of the CDM, it is similar to Joint Implementation, except that the developing country in question has no reduction commitment).

Before conclusions can be considered, it is still necessary to determine the contradictions which currently exist in some fields of climate protection policy, that is, which consistency requirements need to be (re)considered. This will show that there is indeed a need for further research and that achieving climate neutrality by 2050 is a massive challenge, but meeting that target is still feasible, with no more than 80 or 90 percent emission reduction targets compared to 1990, as the last 10 percent or so of emission reduction targets are likely to be enormously expensive. Supplementary measures for climate cooling and CO_2 storage plus other options for action can then achieve effective climate neutrality in a comprehensive sense. It is also clear that good intentions alone will not achieve anything and that a certain level of wisdom is needed in terms of the sequencing of national and international steps, as well as a risk management strategy that allows unexpected stumbling blocks or economic or political shocks experienced along the journey to be dealt with sensibly. Just as there has been a macroprudential analysis in the European Union since 2010, in which a specialized institution (the European Systemic Risk Board) tries to develop a picture of the overall risk situation vis-á-vis the economic system, and then makes proposals on how to sensibly limit said risks, it is reasonable to set up a similar authority in the area of global climate protection—an international climate protection watchdog.

Emission Certificates, Damage of One Metric Ton of CO_2, CO_2 Tax Rate and Innovation

The prices of emission certificates, the level of the CO_2 tax and the (marginal) costs of CO_2 reduction should actually follow a certain logic, whereby the price of emission certificates in Switzerland should also be the same as the price abroad:

- From a simple economic point of view, a certain problem arises from the logic of emissions trading. If the market price of a CO_2 certificate is €25 per metric ton in the EU (with 45 percent of emissions covered), this means that it is possible for an innovative company to avoid one metric ton of CO_2 at this price through innovation measures or certain investments. In California, the CO_2 certificate price is around €15 per metric ton. The international price differential will exist as long as the two certificate markets are not integrated. Integration is possible on the basis of appropriate policy decisions.
- In a market equilibrium, the certificate market price should be equal to the (marginal) damage of one metric ton of CO_2: here, Germany's Federal Environment Agency has said in a study that this damage amounts to €180 per metric ton in 2018; the Environment Agency study of 2013 "An estimation of environmental costs in the energy and transport sectors" gives CO_2 costs of €80 per metric ton in

2010, €145 in 2030 and €260 in 2050 as an average estimate, on the basis of estimated avoidance or damage costs. How high are the CO_2 damage costs in Switzerland, Austria, France or the US, and how high is the cost in India, China, Russia and other G20 countries? The price of €180 per metric ton of CO_2 appears to be relatively high for Germany in 2018. One can expect that the contradiction between the price of €25 per ton (EU ETS market price in 2019/2020) and cost of €180 per metric ton can be resolved. One might wonder what the price of allowances in the EU would be if 85 percent of emissions—or 90 percent of emissions—were covered in 2025.

- In 2018, the CO_2 tax in Switzerland was around €90 per metric ton. In Sweden, where the CO_2 tax has existed for a long time—longer than in Switzerland—it was around €110 per metric ton. If all certificate markets in all active countries were integrated, there would only be one certificate market and one price. EU companies would then apparently have an incentive to buy emission certificates in California. Thus, if one were to link the certificate trading markets of California and the EU, the common equilibrium price would probably be about €21 per metric ton; if the EU were to achieve 85 percent coverage of emissions, one would probably be more likely to reach €24 per metric ton. If, at the same time, the governments of EU countries and the state of California intensify their efforts to promote innovation in emission reduction technologies, saving one metric ton of CO_2 will become easier and cheaper for all companies. It is not easy to understand why Sweden as an EU country has such a high CO_2 tax—which is levied at the same rate on companies and households outside the combined energy and industry sector in 2019—when the certificate price is only €25 per metric ton.
- It would therefore make sense for Sweden to insist within the European Union that the level of emissions coverage of the EU ETS be doubled to 90 percent without delay. Then one can expect an increase in the CO_2 certificate price in the broader certificates trading area. Perhaps the certificate price will rise to €60 per metric ton, then one could possibly lower the CO_2 tax rate (in a smaller taxation sector).
- The certificate price will rise relatively quickly if the annual maximum quantity allowed is lowered at a higher speed; for example, not by 2.2 percent per year from 2021, but by about 5, 6 or even 7 percent.

- The puzzle of adaptation—the necessity of finding an optimal solution according to the equation: certificate price = the damage of another metric ton of CO_2—is solved as follows: one moves toward a degree of coverage of emissions of circa 85 percent in as many G20 countries as possible, whereby all certificates trading areas are integrated step by step according to an announced timetable. The G20 countries that do not have certificate trading systems are encouraged to develop such certificate systems as a matter of urgency. Since countries with broad certificate systems can be expected to develop relatively well, the credit ratings of these countries for government and corporate bonds are likely to be relatively good. These countries therefore receive larger inflows of capital from abroad. The currencies of the countries without certificate trading depreciate, which creates pressure in the non-certificate trading countries to also introduce certificate trading systems. The capital market therefore has an important function for progress toward a G20 certificates trading system. It is conceivable that the share price indices of countries with broad certificate trading will rise, especially if the innovation dynamics on the sales side causes prices to rise more strongly than on the costs side.
- As a rule, CO_2 certificates are traded between companies; in the case of Japan, trading of certificates by third parties, including banks and other financial market players, was initially expressly prohibited. Under certain conditions, one could allow wider certificate trading, and some countries will do so over time. Governments should take precautions to ensure that certificate trading does not become a plaything for wild, deregulated financial markets. Here, there is a task for financial market regulators and regulation with a view to certificate trading, which can probably do little if the broader financial markets are not regulated sensibly overall. Brexit and the Trumpian economic policy positions, both of which ushered in a new wave of deregulation, are damaging the prospects for global certificate trading. There is thus also a considerable contradiction in terms of UK climate protection policy, which has not yet been much discussed. If the US and UK allowed a broad unregulated trade in certificates, this would be a reason from the point of view of the EU and China not to integrate their own certificate markets with those of the US and UK (now as a non-EU country). The global economy does not need a new banking and financial market crisis—as was seen in 2008/2009.

- It obviously makes little sense to simply blindly follow the figure of €180 per metric ton as an estimate of the cost of damage caused by CO_2 from the Federal Environment Agency in Germany. The methodology behind this figure seems to be in need of improvement, as the relevant figure for Switzerland appears to be significantly lower (about €60 per metric ton), although the price level and per capita income in Switzerland—measured in purchasing power parities—are actually higher than in Germany. The main points for global progress toward climate neutrality are the arguments discussed herein: perseverance, pragmatism and transparency—scientific studies and debates must therefore be key parts of a sensible new G20 cooperation approach.
- It is worth considering whether CO_2 compensation taxes should be levied on imports from countries that do not have a CO_2 emissions trading system or CO_2 taxes. One should nevertheless be careful not to plunge the world's trading system into a series of serious conflicts with such a CO_2 compensation tax. Since 80 percent of CO_2 emissions originate from the G20+ countries (G20 countries—including all EU countries), this topic should be discussed meaningfully at the level of the G20, provided that the European Commission chief receives the corresponding negotiating mandate from EU member states.

If on the other hand you ignore the aforementioned connections, the costs of climate neutrality become unnecessarily high and perhaps you will then—and indeed therefore—not achieve climate neutrality in time. One could be too slow in the G20 group to stabilize the climate and world economic development efficiently and reliably. Of course, all the countries of the Paris Climate Agreement are called upon to participate in a reasonable way within the framework of the overall system. Further investigation is necessary to determine the amount of damage of one metric ton of CO_2. Trade, climate and distribution policies are three pillars of a historic bridge toward a new world of climate neutrality. If the G20 countries refuse to promote and engage in meaningful and sensible international cooperation, it will likely not be possible to achieve climate neutrality by 2050. As useful as the Internet is for presenting facts and disseminating scientific studies, it is likely intensifying a political problem: by favoring the channeling of millions of Internet and social media users into individual "echo chambers", where one appears to be surrounded by like-minded people who share one's own point of view, and by promoting a rude and impolite level of discourse from a very large number of users—and thus also a polarization of political positions—it becomes more and more difficult to reach a national political consensus in the offline world. Since a similar logic also applies internationally, it could result in international consensus finding being made more difficult. If the Internet promotes populism in particularly important countries, it indirectly undermines free trade and international cooperation. Populism is at heart nationalist and protectionist.

If one considers the climate protection challenge of making the global economy broadly climate-neutral by 2050, then it will be appropriate to have a clear fundament of thought with regard to some key relevant indicators:

- Real climate protection success is only possible if the G20+ countries—defined as the G20 including all EU countries (i.e., not only the large ones)—cooperate; the G20+ countries accounted for 81 percent of global greenhouse gas emissions, 80 percent of world income (calculated in purchasing power parities) and 63 percent of the world's population in 2017. It is worth pointing out here that the EU is represented at G20 meetings in the form of the president of the Commission. There is nothing against activating other signatory countries of the Paris Climate Agreement in the longer term, but for practical reasons, the focus should first be on G20+. This is a simpler and faster forum and can serve as a basis for other countries to gradually join in. The G20+ could also be extended to include the leaders of Mercosur, ASEAN and ECOWAS (in West Africa). This would then be "G25" in terms of the number of participants in the consultations, which still entails relatively low transaction costs and a low threat of free-rider problems.
- Climate-friendly mobility will be a major issue for many years to come. E-mobility will be part of a difficult transition. Electric cars have a limited range, without fast charging stations; charging to 80 percent of battery power takes a long time and at home a wall charging box is necessary, which can cost about €1500. As long as legislators fail to provide for new standards here and also grant tax advantages, there will be a confidence deficit on the part of potential buyers and, on top of that, a price problem. The e-car companies would also have to offer a guarantee for a replacement car battery of

less than €4000, so that this cost item, which is difficult to calculate in advance, remains manageable from the buyer's point of view; furthermore, a long guarantee for the first battery is necessary and the recycling of batteries (in so-called second-life approaches) would have to be largely regulated. The CO_2 burden of every car battery—concerning the production of the battery itself—is considerable, and the CO_2 advantage of e-cars will only emerge after about ten years of operation, as studies by the Fraunhofer Institute in Germany show. The testing of electric trucks in Germany on very short stretches of motorway of 5–6 km in length with overhead power lines are somewhat strange; hybrid trucks could in any case use such power lines on sections on motorways and run on diesel in other areas. However, e-mobility has additional advantages in connection with digital, comprehensive communication, since congestion times could be significantly reduced in the longer term through the Internet-based networking of all motor vehicles. However, the necessary investment in infrastructure is lacking in Germany. The focus in fiscal policy on a so-called black zero (a balanced federal budget) in times of sustained growth does not make sense; it was only through the Corona shock of 2020/2021 that the federal government's fiscal policy started to accept a considerable rise of the deficit-GDP ratio. There is a structural public underinvestment in Germany in the areas of transport, education and digital networks. The overly ambitious upper limit of a 0.35 percent deficit ratio for the state (including social security), which has been set in the Basic Law of Germany for several years, amounts to a long-term debt ratio of 23.3 percent at a trend growth rate of 1.5 percent of the real gross domestic product. This is astonishingly low and will worsen the creditworthiness of the Eurozone and thus increase the real interest rate of the Eurozone in the long term—initially in Germany's partner countries—curbing growth in the Eurozone 18 (i.e., the Eurozone excluding Germany) and thus also slowing Germany's economic growth. The German government wanted to show other EU countries how "good" you can be by being overly ambitious in limiting deficit quotas. This is a clear mistake, which is not helpful for climate protection either. There will be an unnecessary lack of funds for large climate-friendly infrastructure projects; for example, to build overhead power lines for trucks on the right-hand lane of motorways—assuming that this is an economic-ecological mobility model that is fit for the future.

The Fridays for Future movement will probably also have to raise and deal with such issues in the longer term. It remains to be seen whether it can do this competently.
- Achieving significant CO_2 emission reductions is notably difficult in some sectors. According to a study by the LBBW (Landesbank Baden-Württemberg, 2019), German industry will have major problems achieving its emission reduction targets for 2030. The level of CO_2 emissions fell from 283,000 metric tons in 1990 to 200,000 metric tons in 2018; the reduction in emissions was around 2.3 percent per year over the period 1990–2007. During the period of 2007–2017, an annual average reduction of 0.3 percent was achieved in CO_2 emissions from industry despite a strong rebound in emissions from 2012 to 2017, namely of +2 percent per year. A decrease of 1.7 percent per year—that is the annual reduction of the EU emissions ceiling in the energy and industry sectors—is seen as being relatively demanding for industry. It is therefore not easy to expect its performance to become significantly better, that is, to achieve the EU-wide reduction figure of -2.2 percent from 2021 (by 2030). However, if an annual 5 percent reduction in emissions becomes necessary, which is what is needed on average by 2050 in the EU to achieve a climate-neutral EU by 2050, then the vast majority of industrial companies will have to focus much more on the issue of CO_2 reduction. Of course, it could be that the mechanical engineering sector will achieve reductions below average, with other sectors above average. All this will be made easier if there are more CO_2-reducing innovative manufacturing processes or corresponding new products. If the industry's target of 140 million metric tons of CO_2 emissions in 2030 is to be reached, then carbon dioxide emissions will have to be reduced by an average of 2.6 percent each year; if one does not come close to -5 percent before 2030, then very high reduction percentages per year will tend to be needed between 2030 and 2050 to meet targets: this could yet become a crisis-ridden transformation process that was simply initiated too late in the day to have the intended effect.
- It is currently unclear how it would be possible to reach an order of magnitude of 5–6 percent in at least part of German industry—one of the international leaders in innovation dynamics. It could certainly help if the CO_2 emission certificate price could rise to €40 per metric ton in the short term and in the medium term to €60–80 per metric

ton, and if at the same time government support for climate-friendly innovations could be increased in OECD countries. Broad government intervention in the ETS market is not necessary, but to impose a nominal or relative minimum price over the medium term could indeed be useful for private investors.
- The goal of EU climate neutrality cannot be achieved by 2050 if efforts to reduce CO_2 emissions do not become much more ambitious before 2030 than is currently planned in the EU. Incidentally, as a kind of thought experiment, this will not work well within the framework of the market economy if more nuclear power plants are used. Nuclear power plants are not really a market-compliant form of electricity generation, as comprehensive liability insurance in the private insurance market is not available for such plants. From a market economy point of view, nuclear power plants cannot be safely integrated into a rational power supply for the time being. Why claims to the contrary—which do not show any consideration of insurance issues—appear again and again in the press is an interesting question. On 31 July 2019, there was even an editorial in a national newspaper in Germany in which the author presented the view that nuclear power plants should play a special role in a transition period to increase climate protection as part of a market-based climate protection approach. However, the important questions of adequate liability insurance for nuclear power plants are conveniently ignored—as if the minimum liability sum of just €2.5 billion is a significant figure, when one has to reckon with insurance losses of up to €6000 billion in the event of a major accident (for details, see Hennicke & Welfens, 2012). Nuclear power plants stand for the highest hidden subsidy for one form of energy in OECD countries, with mega-shadow subsidies that have deprived renewable energies of the metaphorical air and light needed to allow growth and a fair expansion in competition in the market economy over decades.
- The fundamental insight remains that with comprehensive emissions trading systems for the G20 countries, and a sufficient annual reduction in the emissions cap, it will be possible to reliably achieve the goal of climate neutrality across the world by 2050. However, the enormous challenge of including countries such as Indonesia, Brazil, Mexico, India, South Africa, Russia and Turkey in certificate trading must be faced. It is conceivable that the EU might initially seek to include Turkey, India and South Africa in the EU's certificate trade

umbrella; special free trade offers from the EU could be part of the coordination approach here. Australia, Argentina, Brazil, Indonesia and Mexico could possibly cooperate with Russia as a group of notable resource-producing countries in certificate trading. Of course, the countries in question will have to form a cooperation group themselves: common interests are necessary for this, and it is not ruled out, of course, that the US—under a populist president—might want to prevent the development of such groups due to Washington's own special interests. It also cannot be completely ruled out that the transformation to a climate-neutral world economy will fuel new fears among many social groups in many countries: of growing insecurity, of growing inequality, of ever-delayed policy approaches. Subjective perception and objective developments should not be allowed diverge widely, one might hope, and the scientific community has a great responsibility here. Another important challenge is comprehensibility. In the digital world, scientists should strive for more comprehensibility than before and avoid using many ever-changing and emerging abbreviations, buzzwords and foreign terms which often only serve to obstruct people's access to knowledge and an understanding of problems. Any form of democracy will appreciate the involvement of many people in the public debate; however, it is important to bring people with you with understandable and transparent studies and analyses when fundamental changes occur in society, politics and the economy. Creating large internationally integrated certificate trading systems will require a careful consideration of issues of sensible and consistent regulation (some issues here appear to be similar to those affecting traditional financial markets). From this perspective, it remains to be seen whether a global emissions trading system should actually be realized. In terms of risk control and stability prospects, it may be preferable to have several regionally integrated carbon markets.

- As far as the Fridays for Future movement is concerned, this climate lobby group has enjoyed high emotional momentum, while they stress that many thousands of scientists support the goals of the protest movement. Understandably, this spurs on the protesting student groups and gives rise to many new activities. There are certainly many interesting discussions and activities taking place. Yet one should also bear in mind that exaggeration rarely helps with climate protection and can in fact damage the cause itself. It would be good

if the many obviously clever minds in the Fridays for Future movement could take a look at the overall picture of the problem of climate protection; with the necessary broadening of horizons and some differentiation, there is much to be learned about cost-minimized climate protection through emissions trading. It remains a historical credit to the Fridays for Future movement that it has managed to mobilize and energize the oft insufficiently active climate protection policy in many countries. One can only wait to see if the Fridays for Future movement will also responsibly live up to its considerable power. Simply spreading panic and fear is not desirable; this has not really helped with real solutions to the problems.
- Another big challenge is the provision of good teaching material on the subject of sustainable change in schools. Here, there are a number of innovative approaches and materials that have also been tested in reality (see, e.g., Liedtke & Welfens, 2008).

Increased CO_2 reduction efforts are needed in the context of research and development in the energy sector, industry, transport and buildings, and agriculture in the EU and OECD countries, as well as in the context of the G20+. Mobilizing the G20 into a truly effective climate action grouping will be a major challenge, especially when students in all of the countries and scientists in almost all of the countries involved have a strong interest in increasing knowledge and engaging in problem-solving in terms of national and global climate protection. G20 city partnerships and G20 university cooperation agreements could be helpful here in advancing networked climate protection internationally. Not all networking has to take place at the high-level, official G20 policy meetings; at the level of citizens and civic society, important networking can also take place, building links and sharing knowledge from the bottom up. Little chance of timely global climate protection exists if many countries fall victim to populism.

A serious problem will arise in the G20 if important countries such as the US, Russia or India do not want to participate in a networked CO_2 emissions trading system. For some years, the biggest problem was the US, whose populism under President Trump can be explained by the long-term rise in income inequality in the US combined with a lack of state training budgets and a relatively inefficient health system—despite, of course, some world-famous institutions in the health sector—as well as insufficient income redistribution. The drivers of increasing income inequality, namely digitalization, financial globalization and China's export dynamics and technological catching-up process, are likely to continue; the globally intensified climate protection dynamics will then be added insofar as the wage premiums of qualified workers in the US (and many other countries) will increase. A fallback solution could, only to a limited extent, be a network of climate-friendly states and cities across the US. Germany's transatlantic political relations with the US were worse under President Trump than under the Carter presidency, when Chancellor Helmut Schmidt occasionally used the Friedrich Ebert Foundation in Washington, DC, as an unofficial channel to seek contacts and ways of reaching agreement with the administration. Since the Trump presidency, the US is facing a long road back from the sidelines, where it had moved on the world stage due to the enormous bloodletting of qualified advisors and ministers—men and women—which led to an increasingly poor quality of leadership and problem-solving; only in an economic stress situation in the US related to the Corona World Recession (Welfens, 2020a, b), and the growing death toll, did this lack of capable officials in high office become visible to the US public and lead to a clear loss of popularity for President Trump. Perhaps only in the medium term will increasing frequencies and extent of extreme weather events and floods in the US significantly reduce populism; perhaps the Fridays for Future movement will succeed in gaining a broad foothold in the US going forward. Greta Thunberg's exciting journey to New York by sailing yacht for a lecture at the UN attracted a lot of media attention in the US and become a visible starting point for a pro-climate protection youth movement in the US. Prior to the European meeting in Lausanne in the summer of 2019, an announcement was made on the group's website illustrating its growing importance and self-confidence—referring to representatives from as many as 37 countries attending the summit (Fridays for Future, 2019):

> The Fridays for Future movement is reaching an unprecedent scale with strikes all around the world. Over the last months, activists from all 6 continents brought a new light to the environmental issues that we are facing. As we are getting global and more complex, members from more than 37 countries have decided to meet for a one week meeting, the Summer Meeting in Lausanne Europe.

The Lausanne summit brought together circa 450 activists from at least 38 countries calling for climate justice and equality and limiting the global average temperature rise to 1.5 degrees Celsius from a benchmark at the beginning of the age of industrialization. According to the final declaration, one should listen also to the best climate researchers. In connection with the UN Climate Assembly in mid-September 2019, global demonstrations were held by school pupils and students. The Fridays for Future movement is indeed growing in size and influence.

With regard to economists and climate scientists, one can only hope that a meaningful distribution of roles will be maintained: as well-founded and impartial a body of scientific analysis as possible, which will advance the debate and politics worldwide—toward efficient and rational solutions. It will be seen whether individual scientists will even enter politics themselves and thereby try to advance rational climate policy. It would be unreasonable for scientists to bring their private political views into reports for governments or parliaments as normative perspectives. A responsible division of roles and labor is needed; otherwise climate protection policy could descend into political chaos.

The overall problem of global climate protection remains manageable, on the one hand, yet complicated, on the other. Climate neutrality cannot be achieved worldwide without international cooperation. A well-considered strategy and the use of previous successful market, technological and social approaches to CO_2 reduction remain indispensable—there is no cause for pessimism. The creativity of networked individuals, entrepreneurial innovation dynamics, including open innovation approaches, and the targeted mobilization of research and development in firms and research institutions must be taken into account.

If an internationally integrated emissions trading system were to be set up within the group of OECD countries, effective political control would be important. Since all OECD countries are democracies, the establishment of a special climate protection organization for countries with emissions trading systems is indeed a step worth considering, as well as an associated parliamentary institution and a kind of OECD Council of Ministers. Climate protection is an international, and ultimately a global, public good. It would be highly desirable to further develop the Western tradition of modern political thinking here and also to incorporate ideas from outside Europe; international climate protection should be safeguarded in a special way by an internationally representative democracy—this does not preclude the inclusion of international elements of referendums on certain issues in the era of the modern Internet. International democracy needs to be further developed in a meaningful way, and the question of global democracy as an institution—ultimately a form of parliament—needs to be considered in the longer term.

Modern democracy is about securing freedom and tying political power to the constitution and the law, in a representative democracy (see also Vorländer, 2019). The modern world of the twenty-first century is not ancient Athens or even an Italian or Swiss city that could organize local political decision-making by way of a citizens' assembly; the answer to the age-old question of how to organize democracy in a large country is probably—despite the Internet—still through some element of representative democracy for the G20 or an even larger group. In any case, the G20 would be manageable in terms of the number of countries involved. In this case, the West would also have to deal with large Asian countries in the long term and be cooperative, ready for a new level of multilateralism. This could also be an attempt to counter populism, which is not oriented toward international cooperation. Even an international climate "democracy" as a forum needs rules, a separation of powers and transparency in the exercise of power if it is to follow the ideas of Jefferson, Kant and Montesquieu. Of course, when it comes to climate protection, one expression from the historic US Constitution drafted in 1787—"We the People"—has a new international application if people from OECD countries or the G20 want to opt for democratic approaches to a common climate protection policy. It goes without saying that it is not only Western approaches which will shape a global layer of democratic accountability if China is added.

It would be important to win over in particular the five key players of the EU, California, China, Japan, Republic of Korea plus India for a combined emissions trading system; the CO_2 emissions certificate trade comprises a proportionate share of the national (or regional) emissions volume in 2020:

- EU: 45 percent (energy sector plus industry, relatively well-developed system, in operation since 2005)
- Republic of Korea: 68 percent (system is in an early phase, hardly any certificates issued via auctions by the state)
- Japan: approx. 20 percent in the two active prefectures
- China: 20 to 30 percent (energy sector only, with a step in 2021 toward a national system with greater coverage)
- California: 85 percent (well-developed system which includes Quebec (and previously also Ontario) in Canada)

- India: 0 percent (there is a regional pilot project on CO_2 certificate trading; there are several pilot projects on certificate trading for pollutants, including SO_2 and NOx)

One should try to gradually increase coverage to 85 percent for the first five actors mentioned and encourage India to establish such a system—in stages—by 2030 through regional pilot trials or a national project. The EU, Japan and the Republic of Korea could provide assistance directly or indirectly, with the Asian Development Bank also contributing loans and technical knowledge; technology transfers, temporary financial assistance and technical expertise from EU countries are also possible—the issue is important for the EU-India policy dialogue. It would be advisable for the EU27 to continue working with the UK, despite Brexit, in the field of CO_2 certificate trading and, if necessary, to support new projects jointly with India and other countries.

In areas that are not covered by certificate trading, a CO_2 tax is needed—presumably for about 15 percent of emissions. The annual reduction must become more demanding with regard to the maximum quantity (i.e., the cap): it would have to be close to 6 percent if one were to assume an emission level of 70 (1990 = 100) and be around 10 by 2050. One should avoid allocations of free certificates of considerably more than 20 percent of such certificates, as these bring considerable unnecessary redistribution effects to the benefit of capital. The integration of the certificate trading systems of different countries will certainly be difficult; it is essential that all G20 countries are on board, with India being a particularly important challenge—in India the coal lobby is also very strong. The expansion and integration of certificate trading systems must be complemented by a broader and better promotion of climate-friendly innovations. In addition, it is necessary to gradually expand a qualification policy for unskilled and low-skilled workers; otherwise income inequality could exceed critical values on the path to a climate-neutral society. If this triad of strategic aspects is realized, there is a good chance of achieving a climate-neutral global economy by 2050. The main aspects of the policy tasks are shown in (Fig. 23.5).

Even a supranational-global G20 "budget" is conceivable, whereby any kind of CO_2 tax to be implemented could possibly be decided in a global parliament, likewise decisions on the use of revenue generated from the sale of CO_2 certificates. There is a second policy area that is already global, namely the Internet. Adopting agreed rules for digital markets could be

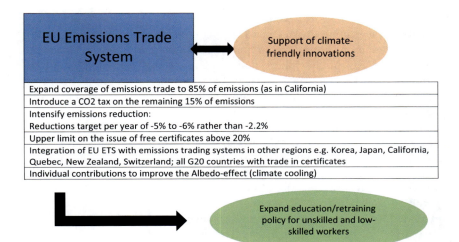

Fig. 23.5 Challenges: climate protection policy options. (Source: Own representation)

the task of a G20 parliament and an executive elected by said parliament, a sort of G20 Commission. One can well imagine that digital disarmament and arms control in the area of cyber warfare should also be among the topics of discussion. Debates on the Internet, including between citizens of all participating countries, would certainly be welcome. However, there should also be digital "communication standards", which should promote tolerance and politeness—in the matter itself, one can still exchange different arguments for positions both pro and contra. Democracy should not mean a form of political decision-making that Aristotle once foresaw namely the possibility of "mob rule", a form of raw and tyrannical rule in which it is not a single individual who rules but the whole of the electorate motivated by base emotions rather than reason. A digital form of mob rule in the age of the Internet cannot be ruled out, either nationally nor internationally for the time being—enabled to a certain extent by a rise of digital populism—but one could try to counter this with some kind of international constitution with some key rules. Since the majority of people in the twenty-first century live in Asia, a global level of democracy will reasonably contain important elements from Asian philosophical thinkers.

As far as international communication is concerned, it is quite unacceptable, for example, with regard to EU countries, that national, state-owned TV stations are marketed abroad for money; of course, this means that no pan-EU public sphere and discourse can emerge. It would be interesting for German viewers to be able to watch, for example, the news channels of other EU countries free of charge, and of course there should be a reciprocal approach for more freedom of information: in every EU country, one should be able to receive news programing broadcasts of other member states of the EU free of charge; if really appreciable costs arise for broadcasters to transmit abroad—hardly plausible in the Internet age—one should be able to purchase an EU-wide package of the public TV offerings from across the bloc at a reasonable cost or be able to subscribe to such a service for a low flat rate. This idea could certainly be extended to all publicly funded TV news programs worldwide. The Internet is global. It could be of great interest in terms of democratic decision-making in the West for voters and politicians to understand how political debates are conducted in Asian, African, Latin American or Australasian countries on climate protection and other issues. Naturally, it could be very interesting for people in non-European regions to understand at least to some extent the public debate and opinion-forming in the EU via more information and news TV formats.

It would therefore make sense not just to organize an international political struggle for global climate protection by 2050 while spreading panic in the Western world, but instead to develop a global democratic renewal—combined with an attempt to advance G20 debates on many levels and on many topics with the digital public. In these discussions, the contributions from many people and particularly from the younger generations are certainly of value. Admittedly, it is clear that countries that are committed to unilateralism are unlikely to participate in such a "G20 parliament" framework.

India as an Important Country in the G20 and for a Globally-Strengthened Climate Protection Policy

India is a very important country in terms of emissions trading in a global context—also as a G20 country. Almost 80 percent of India's electricity generation in 2018 was coal based, and half of the Indian rail's freight revenue is generated by transporting coal from coal-mining regions to the often-remote state-owned coal-fired power plants. The state at regional, national and local levels is a key promoter of coal-fired power generation, and the coal mines and coal-fired power plants are—in terms of lobbying—highly visible and well networked often providing local benefits such as road construction. The largest coal mine is state owned, and the coal-fired power plants are state owned. Still, head of government Prime Minister Narendra Modi clearly wants to focus on an expansion of solar power and wind power in the energy industry in the longer term (for more on this it is worth reading the article "India shows how hard it is to move beyond fossil fuels" The Economist (2018)).

The power grid in India is often overloaded, so that electricity from renewable sources stands for an additional stress factor on the grid. In some regions power outages are a common occurrence. With coal being the most CO_2-intensive fossil fuel energy source, an expansion of renewable energies has been taking place in India with high growth rates since 2010. India, forecast to be the world's most populous country by 2030, is a heavyweight in every respect, especially since growth rates of real national income and thus in core production of 4–8 percent per year are expected for decades to come.

If India continues to invest in new coal-fired power plants, those investments will be made in the expectation of returns for decades to come and that will lead to lobbying and create enormous political resistance to any comprehensive expansion of renewable energies—even if the costs of solar and wind energy per kilowatt of electricity are close to the variable costs of coal-fired electricity. India's energy policy has been to attempt to strategically strengthen the role of renewable energies since around 2010, and India indeed can point to some successes here, especially in solar energy (Niti Aayog, 2015).

In many discussions on climate issues, India has pointed out that countries such as the UK and Germany have been able to carry out their industrial economic development undisturbed since about 1850, while India is only now in a catching-up phase: it also has the right to growth and its own electricity industry. Thus, criticism by the West of the dominant coal-fired electricity sector in India is seen as "carbon imperialism". There is a very serious problem here, and with every new coal-fired power station in India, the problem is actually getting bigger. It would be important for the development of renewable energies if India could increasingly export solar power equipment and indeed entire plants, and possibly in the longer term also wind power plants. The political lobbying interests of the coal industry should be countered with something positive from a politico-economic point of view. The EU could cooperate with India to also facilitate better access to EU markets through a free trade agreement and to increase the expansion of renewable energy in Africa.

It should also be borne in mind that a reduction of coal-fired electricity in India will probably be accompanied by an expansion of nuclear power plants. Russia's nuclear power producer Rosatom, the leading exporter of nuclear power plants at the beginning of the twenty-first century, would be a major winner here. Some experts see nuclear power as a welcome CO_2-neutral contribution to more climate protection. However, this overlooks the issues of liability insurance for nuclear power plants. Those who build nuclear power plants rely on what is in fact a relatively risky form of electricity generation, one for which there is no comprehensive insurance policy available in the insurance market and which is therefore not reasonable according to market principles (not to mention ethical and defense aspects).

It is obviously not against prevailing law if the German government uses expert commissions to inform and steer policy, as was the case with the nuclear phase-out and the German Coal Commission. Such commissions, however, violate the spirit of representative democracy—all major political issues should be discussed, even controversially, in the public sphere and in parliament, so that a reasonable majority decision can be made in the competition of ideas and in the knowledge of relevant facts. The method used by the Merkel governments to "outsource" certain large controversial issues to such mega-commissions is perhaps—unintentionally—a quiet step toward the promotion of authoritarian political structures, even if the governments concerned apparently did not have any such intention. In the appendix there is a list showing the composition of the Ethics Committee at the time of the nuclear phase-out and of the Coal Committee. It should, after all, be possible to openly debate major issues—such as more climate protection—in the spirit of representative democracy and to further develop sensible approaches. Of course, it is convenient for politicians to allow decisions on major contentious issues to be made in mega-commissions by inviting a large number of experts and representatives of various social groups to form a mega-commission. Do we really want to promote this kind of weakening of democracy?

With regard to the contradictory nature of Germany's and the EU's climate protection policies, a final critical look must be taken at the

2020–2050 time window. By 2050, the EU wants to achieve climate neutrality, defined as a CO_2 emission level of 10 percent relative to 1990. Since the EU has set a reduction of the emissions cap of 2.2 percent per year for 2021–2030, the question arises of whether the target of 10 percent of emissions can be achieved by 2050 with this cap and with other meaningful reduction parameters for CO_2 emissions for 2030–2050. The answer is a clear no, and it is very difficult to understand what the relevant ministries of the Grand Coalition think, since this dangerous contradiction in terms of pre-programed policy is obvious to everyone, as the following figure—with a brief analysis—shows.

An Enormous Contradiction in the EU Adaptation Path in Climate Policy

The EU wants to reduce emissions by 43 percent by 2030 compared to 1990 (set at a baseline level of 100) and is well on the way, based on figures for 2020 (with an expected -27 percent). With climate neutrality to be achieved by 2050, this means that for the EU CO_2 emissions by 2050 should have fallen to 10 percent of 1990 levels. The EU still has no plausible adjustment path to meet this target on the basis of the establishment of an annual reduction of the EU emission limit by just 2.2 percent over the period from 2021 to 2030: if in 2030 one had actually reached -43 percent compared to 1990, the emission level would be 57. The logarithmic representation in (Fig. 23.6) shows various possible adjustment paths between 2030 and 2050, each with a uniform annual drop in the emissions cap: at -7 percent one would reach the desired level of 10 percent in 2054 (in continuous time terms, with discrete seasons such as those in the EU approach, about two more years are added); if one seriously aims for 2050 as the target point, one would have to implement a reduction of -8.3 percent annually. This would be very challenging even with a vigorous new innovation policy. This is based on the assumption that by 2025 at the latest the EU would have expanded its Emissions Trading System to cover 85 percent of emissions. In the new fields of transport, housing and agriculture, a reduction in emissions from 100 in 2025 to 15 in 2050 would require an annual reduction of 7.3 percent (with a target of 10—of more than 8 percent), which will certainly require special efforts. This could be particularly difficult to achieve in the housing sector, where there is a large inventory of real estate. Economically, it makes little sense to turn a

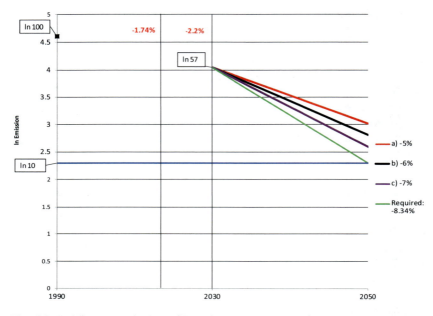

Fig. 23.6 The contradiction of EU plans on climate protection policy. (Source: Own representation)

residential house built in 1980 to the prevailing standards back then into a passive home to meet new standards.

These perspectives are very risky, from an economic point of view, for the EU countries which have adopted resolutions which are simply not ambitious enough; policymakers cannot possibly want to be forced into adopting shock-like adjustment paths later. If the tacit adaptation paths were not meant to be taken seriously at all, the EU's entire climate policy could be deemed untrustworthy. Without urgent policy adjustments by the EU or EU member countries, there is a very real threat that either an economic crisis or a political credibility crisis (or both) will occur.

In the middle of 2019, which saw a certificate price for CO_2 of approximately €27 per metric ton, many German, French, Dutch and so on companies had already bought the desired quantities of certificates in reserve for the years ahead—and in the knowledge of -2.2 percent as the annual reduction figure at the EU upper limit for 2021–2030—one can easily imagine what a transition to - 7 percent or even - 8 percent would mean for the years 2031–2050: namely, a very strong increase in emission certificate prices, probably at times to well over €100 per metric ton. This could act like a politically organized quasi oil price shock to the whole economy, leading to stagnation and a severe recession in the EU.

EU countries, however, still have the option of making the adjustment path less growth-dampening or less shock-like (accepting that no retroactive changes can be introduced): one could think of gradually increasing the annual upper limit reduction rate to 6 percent between 2022 and 2030, which would allow the target level 10 to be reached with a reduction rate just below 7 percent between 2031 and 2050. From 2024, however, 85 percent of CO_2 emissions in the area covered by the EU ETS should be included in the trading system, whereby one could roughly follow California's model of broader coverage—itself a system introduced based on the EU model of 2005. In order to avoid a sharp increase in the price of certificates to close to €100 per metric ton, the certificate markets of the EU and California (including the Canadian province of Quebec (and formerly also Ontario)) should be integrated from 2025 or 2026, and—if possible—a few years later also with the certificates trading market of China, which started in 2021 with a coverage of CO_2 emissions of a good 40 percent. The Republic of Korea, Switzerland and New Zealand also have certificate markets that should be included in the medium term in the interests of minimizing CO_2 reduction costs globally. It would also be desirable for all G20 countries to have established certificate trading systems by 2030, which could then be integrated with each other over time. The G20+ as a group—defined here as G20 including all EU countries—represents 80 percent of global emissions. For large integrated certificate trading markets, a certain amount of regulation is needed, which should be sensibly linked to broader financial market regulation. It is also worth noting that from an economic point of view the state should not issue more than 20 percent of the stock of certificates in the form of free allocations to companies, as otherwise the state would engage in redistribution in favor of capital.

If the proposed steps can be implemented and two-thirds of a CO_2 tax introduced to cover the circa 15 percent of emissions not covered by certificate trading (assuming coverage of 85 percent), climate neutrality can be achieved by 2050 without major economic disruption while a high, sustainable increase in global economic benefits can be achieved at the same time, since the threatening global loss of income of about 10 percent, as calculated in the Stern Report, can be avoided if the 2-degree limit (in terms of the increase of the global surface temperature on Earth) is exceeded (Stern, 2006).

How high will CO_2 prices be around 2030 or 2040? If one assumes that the certificate price P'' is calculated according to a simple formula in which the real per capita income (y) leads to an increase of the certificate price (i.e., a demand effect)—relative to the general goods price level P—the long-term relative price P''/P should be proportional to the per capita income (p''): = P''/P, and it applies $p''(t)$ = by + $b'dp''/dt$; b and b'—whereby b' is a parameter for lowering the emission cap—are positive parameters, t is the time index: thus, the long-term relative price is $p''\#$ = by, if the per capita income y is constant for simplification; you can also read the equation like this: $dp''/dt - p''/(b'y) = -b/b$. This is important because in a regionally or nationally isolated certificate market, the relative price would be higher in OECD countries with high per capita incomes than in countries with lower per capita incomes. Accordingly, the integration of certificate markets into a world market results in the relative prices of certificates falling in the industrialized countries (with higher per capita income) and rising in the developing and emerging countries (with lower per capita incomes), provided that the parameter b is not significantly lower in the Global North than in the Global South.

SIMULATIONS: ESTIMATING THE ADVANTAGE OF A GLOBALLY INTEGRATED CO_2 CERTIFICATE TRADING SYSTEM

Qi and Weng (2016) have examined how certificate prices would have developed by 2030 if there were to be a major international integration of the certificate systems of important countries: their finding is that the certificate prices for the US, the EU and China would be lower than if the countries only had isolated national certificate systems; in some other G20 countries, the CO_2 certificate price would be higher in the case of integration than in the case of a national certificate trading system. The analysis, using the so-called Calculable General Equilibrium Model, is carried out for the case of the integration of certificate systems on the one hand; on the other hand, calculations are also made in the model for the case that national certificate trading systems would continue to coexist without integration. The simulation results show what can be expected against the background of theoretical considerations: there is a global reduction in the cost to global society of achieving climate protection and thus in the longer term also for achieving climate neutrality.

According to the authors' calculations, in the case of an integration the global market price for certificates would be \$30 per metric ton of CO_2, which is significantly lower than \$45 per metric ton of CO_2 in the US, \$41 per metric ton of CO_2 in the EU and \$37 per metric ton of CO_2 in China—but higher than \$8 per metric ton of CO_2 in the case of India and \$4 per metric ton of CO_2 in the case of Russia, each with nationally organized certificates markets. Countries such as India and Russia would thus be able to sell emission rights to the US, the EU and China in an integrated world certificate market, which will lead to a decline in the production of CO_2-intensive and emission-intensive goods in India and Russia; on the other hand, the production of emissions-intensive goods in the US, the EU and China could expand more in an integrated certificate system than in nationally independent certificate trading systems. The sale of certificates abroad results in positive revenue effects for companies or households and therefore also positive impulses for investment and consumption; the world income effect is clearly positive—according to the analysis of Qi and Weng.

This means—and these are additional considerations—in turn that for the macroeconomic money market certificate trading possibly leads to liquidity absorption in the money market, which has an effect on the overall economic price level. The positive real income effect is important here, because higher income means a higher demand for money from companies and households. It is also important that the average price level of goods falls. The latter effect results from the fact that a falling certificate price in the leading OECD countries will lead to lower price levels in various sectors of these countries and thus to a drop in the overall price level. As a lower price level reduces demand for money from companies and households, while a positive real income effect increases demand for money from households, the overall effect on aggregate demand for money could be broadly neutral. However, more detailed investigations are necessary here.

The Possibility of Reducing the CO_2-Related Cost Burden for Industry

One can therefore look at individual industrialized countries (plus China) and the global economy under the assumption that national certificate trading systems exist in isolation, which means international price differences for CO_2 certificates. Or one assumes an integrated global CO_2 certificate trading system (which would entail only one single world market price, as with oil). The differences are enormous with regard to the total burden on companies in the Western industrial countries, Japan, the Republic of Korea and China. If, for example, the certificate invoice for a steel company in 2020 is €100 million for one year, this is a considerable amount, which initially leads to an asymmetrical advantage for steel suppliers from countries without a CO_2 certificate market, namely artificially strengthening their international competitiveness. This makes it all the more important that all G20 countries and other countries have certificate markets (or introduce equivalent CO_2 taxes). If the certificate markets of all G20 countries are integrated, the average CO_2 certificate price in industrialized countries and China will fall by about one-third. This is of course very important for industry in EU countries such as Germany, France, Italy, Spain, the Netherlands, Belgium, Poland as well as non-EU countries such as the UK, and for employment in local industry. Thus, there are important arguments in favor of EU countries, China and other countries advocating for a G20-wide integrated certificate market, starting around 2030.

Assuming that 40 billion tons of CO_2 are traded by the G20 countries mentioned here and the difference in the "G20/global average price" in the case of an integrated trading systems is $37 per metric ton of CO_2—compared to $32 per metric ton of CO_2 otherwise (the price mentioned is then a weighted average of the G20 countries considered)—a global savings effect for companies and households of $200 billion results in just one year. In the 20 years between 2030 and 2050, there would therefore be accumulated savings effects of $4000 billion, which would roughly correspond to Germany's GDP in 2030 and represent around 3 percent of world income. If the price difference for CO_2 certificates in the case of the integration of trading systems would be $10 instead of $5, compared to a world economy with unconnected trading systems, the world economy could save about $8000 billion through an integration of the trading systems by 2030 in the years following such an integration of markets, that is, 6 percent of world income, or almost 0.25 percent of the world gross domestic product per year in the period 2030–2050—in relation to every citizen on Earth, this corresponds to an income gain of more than $1000 over the period 2030–2050. In reality, the profits from integrated certificate trading systems could be even greater than initially quantified here, since the assumption of QI/WENG that all the G20 countries considered have certificate trading systems is not correct.

Moreover, there is a special role for development aid policy when countries in the Global South—such as South Africa, Nigeria or Indonesia—introduce emissions trading and then integrate their trading systems into a combined G20+ system. It would therefore be appropriate for the richer OECD countries and also China to pay countries in the south of the world economy adjustment transfers for about a decade so that the transition to a higher global certificate price (from the perspective of the countries in the Global South, there is a rise in the certificate price) can be cushioned. These transfers to developing countries would have to be in addition to existing development aid payments. A special channel for North-South technology transfer for CO_2-light technologies for a transitional period is also worth considering. The burden on the national budgets of OECD countries is relatively low, and the benefits for both sides are considerable. After all, the industrialized countries benefit from lower certificate prices than usual. The developing countries receive a technological modernization impulse and transfers from the Global North, which could be used, for example, for higher expenditure on education and infrastructure projects.

Even the transition to national certificate trading systems generally brings very considerable economic and ecological advantages for the G20+ countries under consideration compared with the previous situation without CO_2 pricing (or with CO_2 taxes). The welfare gains for the global economy by 2050 would probably be $10,000 billion or more. It would therefore be a huge error if the countries of the world—at least the G20 countries—could not achieve an integration of their respective certificate trading systems. However, in an initial step, those G20 countries, which do not yet have any CO_2 certificate trading systems, would first have to be persuaded to introduce such a system by 2030, as Fig. 23.7 also shows.

The degree of coverage—for example, 45 percent of emissions as in the EU, 65 percent as in the Republic of Korea or 85 percent as in California—should be determined with ambition. The certificate systems should start by 2025 in a trial phase in the G20+ countries that do not yet have

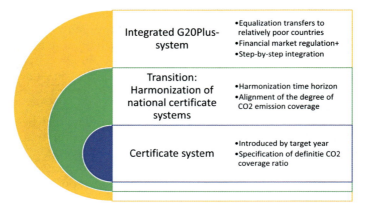

Fig. 23.7 Steps toward an integrated G20+ certificate system. (Source: Own representation)

certificate systems. One conceivable scenario would be to harmonize the certificate systems within five years; the degree of coverage would certainly have to be largely harmonized. This will be followed by the installation of an integrated G20+ system—from around 2030. Not to be forgotten is the need to adequately regulate financial markets, including CO_2 certificate markets, also with a view to financial market stability.

While these proposals would seem to suggest a utopian scenario, one has to be aware that while the steps toward an integrated G20+ certificate system must be discussed and carefully planned and implemented, the benefits of the proposed system are nevertheless so enormous that scientific and public pressure in a critical minimum number of countries is indeed likely to provide an impetus to move toward just such a proposed system. A functioning and integrated G20+ certificate system would be a global cooperation approach that would bring enormous global benefits both for the global economy and for the environment, and ultimately for sustainable prosperity, climate protection and political stability.

As far as energy, industry, transport and housing are concerned, all these areas can be included in the certificate trading system; in the case of agriculture, the livestock sector in particular, which causes the largest proportion of CO_2 emissions in agriculture, should also be included. A farmer who has to buy a quantity x of emissions certificates per year per cow or head of cattle will have an incentive to change their selection of feed toward less methane-heavy feed, and of course the relatively high quantity of certificates necessary for dairy herds/beef cattle will make the keeping of poultry, pigs or even fish more attractive. As beef prices rise relatively worldwide, demand for beef will decline. As a result, agriculture will have significantly reduced CO_2 emissions after a few years and can then proudly contribute to climate neutrality. It would make sense to initially facilitate the integration of agriculture into the certificate trade with a relatively low certificate price.

Concerning the market price for CO_2 certificates in the EU, California, Republic of Korea and China, the question of whether there are negative external effects of CO_2 emissions will have to be addressed (this question can of course be asked for all countries). Then one would first have to internalize these negative external effects via a sectoral Pigou tax. If there are such national and international negative external effects (e.g., coal-fired power generation damages the image of nearby resorts, which depresses the turnover in the local tourism industry), then the production of the companies concerned—without a Pigou tax—is too high and the demand for CO_2 certificates is artificially inflated. This leads to a higher CO_2 price than in the case of internalization, that is, with a Pigou tax in order to increase the production costs of the companies concerned—providing an incentive to reduce production. The increased certificate price reduces the volume of profitable production through higher production costs in all sectors, which is of course a distortion. This is not desirable.

Findings on Cost-Benefit Analysis at CPB

In the Netherlands, the CPB research institute presented a study on the cost-benefit analysis of CO_2 reduction, one of the cases considered being a 60 percent reduction in CO_2 emissions in the EU by 2050; another simulation case examines an 80 percent CO_2 reduction, which allows compliance with the 2-degree target. Some aspects of innovation are also considered. It is important to distinguish between the market price of CO_2 certificates and what the authors of the study (CPB/PBL, 2016) call "efficient prices". An efficient price also reflects the external effects of emission reductions in the emissions trading sector energy and industry. For 2015, in the 60 percent reduction by 2050 scenario, the efficient certificate price is set at €48 per metric ton of CO_2, while the market price was €5; however, the market price had reached a good €25 per metric ton by mid-2019. For an emissions reduction of 60 percent by 2050, the authors estimate a price of €80 per metric ton CO_2 in 2030 and €160 per metric ton of CO_2 in 2050, with €200–1000 per metric ton of CO_2 for an 80 percent reduction. The stronger the innovation progress in CO_2-light technologies is, the more likely it is that the order of magnitude of the price for 2050 will arrive at around €200 per metric ton; with low innovation dynamics, the expected efficient certificate price will be significantly higher.

The CPB document unfortunately contains no indications of a figure to represent the marginal damage of one metric ton of CO_2—that is, the CO_2 damage costs—which could amount to €180 per metric ton of CO_2 in the EU (the figure €180 per metric ton comes from the German Environment Agency). In the case of compliance with the 2-degree limit, that is, an 80 percent reduction in CO_2 emissions by 2050, the order of magnitude is €60–300 for 2015. Not quite convincing is the way in which the study extrapolates the expected CO_2 price in 2050 back to earlier years, namely by applying the so-called Hotelling rule. This does not really make sense when it comes to process innovations over time, which mean that the costs of resource extraction over time decrease. However, this is very important for the EU and the G20 countries, especially in the transition process until 2050, as climate-friendly innovations are particularly promoted in many countries.

At the end of the day, it can be said that the issues in almost all important areas can be analyzed scientifically when it comes to achieving climate neutrality by 2050. It is obvious that the Netherlands has a special interest in this because strong global warming is likely to confront the country, which is partly below sea level, with serious flood risk. Of course, it can be assumed that the Dutch government will also limit the risk of such floods by investing in the protection of coastal dam works by the sea. It should be very useful to include analyses from the Netherlands in particular in the G20+ analyses. The economic and ecological analyses of many research institutes and researchers from the Netherlands can be regarded as particularly valuable in the climate field.

Even in the Netherlands, which is advanced in the area of wind and solar energy, there are further opportunities for expansion. This holds even more for many other countries which, despite good climatic conditions, still make insufficient use of these two types of renewable energy or indeed hydroelectric power plants, bioenergy and geothermal power plants. In 2017, the global use of renewable energies increased by 5 percent compared to the previous year, with hydropower accounting for 65 percent, wind for 18 percent, bioenergy for 8 percent, solar for 7 percent and geothermal energy for the remaining share. All these forms of energy production can expand in absolute terms, with wind, bioenergy and solar energy likely to account for significantly higher shares in the longer term.

NEW APPROACHES AND A CRITICAL SUM OF INDIVIDUAL MEASURES ESSENTIAL

While new approaches are being developed in the transport sector—with a focus on electromobility—in many countries around the world, there is still a great deal of work to be done in the real estate sector, which in terms of value could represent around 40 percent of the capital stock of OECD countries. The very innovative passive house approaches existing in some EU countries should become an important issue worldwide. Especially in Europe, China, Japan, the Republic of Korea, the US and other G20 countries, it should become standard for new buildings to be passive in the medium term; developments in the pioneering country in this field, namely Austria, should be given special attention. However, cost-effective and affordable building and climate friendliness need not be mutually exclusive, as climate neutrality should be a global project for all people. In the Netherlands you can find many successful examples of solid, inexpensive yet environmentally friendly construction. If cheaper meant low quality, nobody would really be helped in the long run, especially when it comes to sustainability. The fact that national and regional building standards—regulations—prevent the diffusion of environmentally friendly building innovations in the EU, that is, the spread of good projects and new building approaches, cannot be stressed often enough. This is actually an EU scandal and also an undermining of the EU's Internal Market, which cannot deliver its advantages here because of political barriers between EU member states. This is a big issue when it comes to climate change, and the EU, and the individual EU member countries, should finally take a serious look at these aspects, especially as part of the innovation dynamics in Austria in terms of passive homes is due to EU-funded projects. More contradiction in EU policy is hardly possible, than to fund innovations which cannot be disseminated across the EU.

Broadband Internet access via more infrastructure investments should be rapidly implemented in Germany and the other EU countries (in the Netherlands it has already been largely implemented), across the board; in practice this may mean 99 percent coverage of a given area. Otherwise autonomous driving cannot be realized. If autonomous driving becomes standard, the private vehicle fleet in OECD countries is likely to shrink significantly. If you can get the car you want in just a few minutes via an app on your smartphone—sometimes a small car for a short trip in the city, sometimes a larger one because you want to go on holiday with your family—then you no longer need to own your own car. Driving a car could become a digital service that can be subscribed to from various providers. This in turn would make another significant contribution to reducing CO_2 emissions.

With the real interest rates for the state being (foreseeably) very low in the decade after 2019, it will certainly be possible to finance such large infrastructure and additional research programs in the Eurozone (with research more clearly anchored than before in climate and environmentally friendly innovation projects). Individual Eurozone countries could take the initiative here with regard to networked infrastructure projects. For Germany, one can imagine a figure of around €350 billion over a decade, with around one-tenth of that figure reserved for more continuing vocational training, so that the income gap between skilled and unskilled workers does not widen too sharply in the wake of global climate policy (one could wait to see whether new railway tracks, for example, will be laid in the Black Forest region—where the last "new" construction of a kilometer of railway is dated 1912—St. Blasien still has no railway connection, or in important holiday regions of eastern Germany).

Similar infrastructure programs should also be designed and implemented by other EU and G20 countries. The expansion of railway systems would make economic and ecological sense for many countries, but it is important to keep an eye on costs and prices while improving quality. If the G20+ countries do not come up with comprehensive, improved climate policies based on efficient concepts, many regions of the Earth could become effectively inhabitable by 2050. In many regions, global warming means even more heat plus, on top of that, poorer air quality, but also massive migration pressures. If a stable world economy is to be maintained, climate change must be taken very seriously as a strategic problem yet at the same time accepted as a positive innovation challenge. To date, this has hardly been the case in G20 countries beyond some good individual projects and some clever new approaches in certain companies, states and even by millions of individuals. That fiscal policy should not only consider fiscal policy in narrow economic terms, but also reflect a structural expansive fiscal policy in the area of climate policy for a decade or more is expressly advocated here.

Monetary policy in the Eurozone should gradually raise the interest rate to reasonable nominal values within a decade. The unusual combination of structural expansionary fiscal policy and a gradually less expansionary monetary policy could be an approach to normalizing the situation on financial markets by 2030. It goes without saying that even with counter-cyclical fiscal policy, more emphasis should be placed on sustainability projects than has been in the past. Thus far, few approaches have been visible in the OECD countries; the OECD could also approach the issue with a view to G20 countries such as Brazil, India and China via the OECD Development Center. As far as tax policy is concerned, it is generally advisable to follow Denmark and the Netherlands, which take in about 4 percent of national income in the form of environmental taxes. Germany, France, Italy, Spain, Poland and many other EU countries could raise their own environmental taxes accordingly, while at the same time ensuring more sustainable growth through reductions of the income and corporate tax rates.

If environmental taxes are gradually increased in these countries, and at the same time income tax rates lowered, this should increase the acceptance among the electorate of a more sustainability-oriented tax policy or a committed climate policy. Finally, the state can also provide an impetus through regulatory requirements for insurance companies, for example, by requiring insurers to invest at least 10 percent of their assets in sustainability-certified or climate protection-certified investments that have a credit rating of at least A. This could also deepen the market for "green bonds". At the same time, it makes little sense—as can be seen in the US, for example—for property owners in areas at high risk of flooding to obtain property insurance at particularly low rates. In all OECD and G20+ countries, it would make sense to ensure that the market signals for the pricing of climate risks are strengthened and not virtually obscured by intervention by the state in the market. The wealthy OECD countries should be able to counter long-term flood risks with dam reinforcement measures and new construction standards for buildings and infrastructure. Poorer countries should be given targeted assistance by the better off OECD countries for a transitional period and also granted access to novel flood protection technologies under certain conditions. In the end, climate neutrality will not be achievable without associated costs—how else could a major historical structural change of the world economy be achieved—but with timely and sensible decisions, one can probably overcome such challenges, at least if one keeps in mind the focus on efficiency on the one hand and the connection to an appropriate social policy on the other.

The fact that research results and simulation studies contain a certain margin of uncertainty—as always in science (which has nevertheless brought enormous progress in medicine, production, transport, energy, the information and communication technology sector and so on)—does not mean that politicians have a carte blanche to spread ideological tales that the problem of global warming is non-existent or not urgent. One particularly stupid argument is occasionally heard or read according to which science—despite the many, many empirical analyses and simulation studies—cannot make any meaningful predictions at all: that those who present simulation results and consider them to be relevant to reality simply stand for presumption to hold some piece of knowledge which is in essence unknowable (in Germany, certain elements of the right-wing and populist AfD holds this position, which can be considered peculiar against the background of modern empirical research). This is nonsense, but it must nevertheless be pointed out in analysis results from empirical studies or simulation studies that there is indeed a certain margin of error in forecast values. Despite such "problems" in science, NASA has managed to bring US astronauts to the moon; and for example, Italian, Scandinavian, US, British, German, Korean, Russian, French and Japanese engineers have managed to build great cars and trucks; similar successes can be seen in Russia, the US, India, Japan, the EU and China, which are permanently active in the field of space exploration, medicine, ICT and so on. The US, Russia, China, the EU, Japan and many other countries rely on the research results of science in many fields, usually for good reason. With fundamental knowledge—even if not 100 percent proven—one can still certainly make very good progress in innovation and production.

In this context, the Fridays for Future movement is, from a scientist's point of view, an important possible ally in increasing the public understanding that scientific research is an indispensable pillar in tackling future problems. Scientific analysis is rarely important for wider society in the form of a single journal paper or piece of work by an individual scientist. In essence, it is more important how the scientific consensus develops and changes course in a particular discipline; this does not mean that outsiders or heterodox positions in individual research fields cannot also be very well positioned or argued. But confusing ideological claims to power with science is not progress. In addition to science, climate neutrality also needs other pillars. It is desirable to bring a large body of people into a large tent to tackle the climate neutrality project and to strive to provide understandable explanations for the public debate—it is one of the tasks of science and politics.

Four Final Points

We must set about creating a reasonable incentive for private households in Europe and indeed worldwide to do more—specifically to reduce emissions:

- The state should require insurance companies above a certain size to offer "conditional building insurance rates" to private households (and companies) for 30 years depending on the expected global CO_2 emission level. In principle, it should be that a significant reduction (Case A) in global CO_2 emissions by 2050 would result in lower premiums to be paid over three decades than would be the case for a relatively weaker reduction of global emissions (Case B) by 2050; for example, a low discount factor of 1 percent for future payments—useful at the current low global interest rate—would result in a substantial difference in the present value of insurance payments over 30 years in Case B when compared to Case A. If we assume that the difference is €10,000, this is an indirect incentive for individuals to pursue more climate protection policy. Whether Case A or rather Case B should be regarded as the more relevant should be determined on the basis of a standardized G20+ indicator value for climate protection.
- The problem with private CO_2 reduction activities is that each individual is only responsible for a small share in global emissions, and it is not clear whether other economic entities around the world are similarly committed to CO_2 reduction measures (if there are enough individuals committed to reducing CO_2 worldwide, one ends up in the desired Case A). Here, the Internet can also help with a view to a global private initiative for climate protection, since all 7.7 billion inhabitants around the world could actually connect to a global pro-climate network via the Internet. It does not really have to be a single group or network, since one could also form a "network of networks" or groups. The prospect of Case A will also reduce the pres-

sure to increase rents, as landlords will pass on insurance costs to renters; Case B, on the other hand, will contribute to rent increases.
- The establishment of a Pro-Global Climate group is therefore worth considering. In the case of private households, measures that fall outside the emissions trading system would be particularly important. The sub-groups at local, regional and national levels would each have to obtain certification from an institution (e.g., a relevant foundation) for their actions, as otherwise it would not be possible to rely on the provision of private climate protection services using the honor system alone. Large telecom network operators could get involved in such a campaign. Scientists would have to make CO_2 reduction calculators available—some of them exist on the Internet under the heading of a "Carbon Footprint Calculator" (which are often not really differentiated in terms of the types of activities which it is possible to record)—which should function according to a globally accepted methodology.
- As for green government bonds to finance climate-friendly activities, government could increase the popularity of such bonds by guaranteeing for this type of bond a minimum redemption value of 50 percent of the issue price at any time during the bond term (usually 30 years). For this guarantee to be credible, the government should in turn collateralize such bonds with government assets amounting to at least one-third of the issue value.

These are just four possible practical elements to support the world on the path toward climate neutrality. Here, too, one can see that there are many and varied ways to step out of the comfort zone of traditional economic policy approaches. A climate policy for all can indeed work in certain circumstances. However, it would not be wise to simply wait for traditional policy actors to begin to act on an innovative and vigorous basis.

In the end, the consideration—which was discussed in the very first chapter—remains, namely, that G20+ diplomacy is particularly and enormously important for achieving climate neutrality. The economic and climate policies of the G20+ countries will not be able to make a reasonable contribution to climate neutrality if they fail to put meaningful cooperation between them on a reliable footing. There is no lack of economic advice on how to shape sustainability and climate protection policy—see, for example, Sachs (2015) and Welfens et al. (2017).

What is not yet available are conceptual approaches for an efficient networking of the G20+ with the aim of developing a cleverly networked climate protection policy. The Fridays for Future movement is likely to be an important global actor creating pressure for more political reason and an energetic, well-thought-out climate protection policy. The commitment of young people in many areas is very welcome; channeling their energy and creativity into a rational global climate protection policy is an enormous task—there is no reason for pessimism.

G20 CO_2 Certificates and a Corona Vaccination Program as a Dual Strategy

The new report of the Intergovernmental Panel on Climate Change (IPCC, 2021) with its worsening estimates of the climate-related challenges to be expected by 2030 and the extreme weather events of summer 2021 in North America, Europe and Asia are drawing more attention than ever to the question of how climate protection and ultimately climate neutrality can be achieved efficiently by 2050. A secondary question concerns the role which leading economies of the G20 could play here. The options proposed within offer an innovative approach that allows the goal of climate neutrality to be achieved at minimal cost, while also emphasizing several sub-points which are crucial as the basis for success. In the current context of the Coronavirus pandemic, it will be essential to motivate the critically important G20 countries of the Global South to first introduce national, and later internationally integrated, CO_2 certificate systems with special incentives—including the prospect of more local vaccine production. This idea of a two-pronged strategy is new.

First of all, the strategic approach to climate protection: according to the UN 2015 Paris Climate Agreement, a good 190 countries are called upon to each make their respective contributions in order to achieve climate neutrality. In terms of the sheer number of countries involved, this is certainly a very complicated undertaking. With regard to the problem of the hole in the ozone layer and the fight against hydro- and chlorofluorocarbons, a spearhead group of twenty-four countries plus the EU successfully led the critical negotiations to conclude the Montreal Agreement of 1987. Subsequently, all UN countries came on board. Therefore, in terms of the climate neutrality task, it would be appropriate to set up CO_2 certificate trading as a G20 project first. The G20 alone, after all, already stands for almost 80 percent of global CO_2 emissions.

If all of the G20 countries could be persuaded to create a national emissions trading system and, in a second step, to integrate them across borders, the result would essentially be a globally uniform CO_2 price with enormous trading profits or global real income gains. On the other hand, it will not be possible to harmonize national CO_2 tax rates internationally—it would be politically illusory.

It is easy to see how large the potential trading gains could be, for example, if the existing regional and national CO_2 allowance trading systems were integrated as envisaged here by taking the CO_2 trading systems of the EU, California and China as an example. Thus far, the EU has covered the energy and industry sectors, which accounted for about 45 percent of the EU's CO_2 emissions in 2019, while the Californian emissions trading system covered about 80 percent of California's CO_2 emissions. Meanwhile, China's allowance trading scheme—in place since 16 July 2021 and covering only the energy sector—stands for circa 40 percent of national CO_2 emissions.

The EU's Emissions Trading System leads to climate neutrality first through the politically determined annual reduction target for CO_2 emissions for the EU as a whole; and similar processes occur in California and China in terms of their own trading systems. In the EU, it would be wise to avoid setting too low an annual reduction target prior to 2030. Otherwise—a situation which is already clearly foreseeable—a shock increase in the reduction rate will have to be applied in the future (i.e., post-2030) if climate neutrality is to be achieved by 2050.

The price of a metric ton of CO_2 in mid-2021 was a good €50/ton in the EU, €18 in California and €7 in China. An integration of the three certificate markets would likely bring a "world market price" of about €35/ton and at the same time would result in massively increased global innovation dynamics. If the three countries agreed on a common quantitative CO_2 reduction target of, for example, 4 percent per year, this would reduce costs for industry in the EU and result in more production, jobs, real income and tax revenues than would be the case without internationally integrated certificate trading systems.

Compared to the initial situation in mid-2021, EU companies would naturally purchase certificates from California or from Californian companies, but also from companies in China. The CO_2 avoidance costs per ton are obviously significantly lower in California than in the EU, so that an increase in climate protection innovation dynamics and thus a US CO_2 reduction in California (and the US as a whole) makes a lot of sense. For climate protection, the geographical distribution of CO_2 savings is irrelevant. It is the global trade in CO_2 certificates that ensures that the most innovative companies in the G20 group at any given time achieve the politically prescribed CO_2 reductions.

Of course, there would be enormously increased CO_2 savings effects in the US and China compared to the initial situation in the middle of 2021: above all, however, there would be an induced high-level of climate-friendly innovation dynamics. The more dramatic the climate problem is, and the greater the North-South income differences, the more important it is to make use of minimum-cost CO_2 certificate trading worldwide. Those who widely renounce such a trade in certificate will ultimately be responsible for billions of dollars in global income losses and millions more poor and hungry people particularly in the Global South.

It would certainly be wise to integrate national CO_2 allowance trading systems in a gradual fashion. Ideally, a first step would be for all participating countries to have certificate trading with a CO_2 coverage rate of around 80 percent, as is already the case in California. With regard to Europe, it stands to reason that the European Commission is also planning medium-term CO_2 certificate trading under the heading of the European Green Deal, which will include the real estate and transport sectors. From 2026 on, the European Commission wants to include fuel supply in the mobility and real estate sectors in CO_2 certificate trading, whereby a CO_2 tax rate will still apply in Germany in 2021. This burden is to be transferred to EU Emissions Trading System in the medium term; quite sensibly, if only the commercial real estate sector is included here—sparing the private sector the high CO_2 price fluctuation.

Among the G20 countries, the hardest to win over for a CO_2 certificate trading system is probably India with its coal-intensive economy: which also features many state-owned coal mines and power plants. India's government argues that it has a historical right to emit as much CO_2 in total over the present and the near future via energy combustion as, for example, the US has done for its own benefit in its circa 200-year history of industrial development. Such an egocentric view of India cannot be regarded as reasonable from the G20's perspective.

However, the US, Japan and the EU could offer India a compensation payment in order to make the swift transition to CO_2 certificate trading more palatable for the country. Since India is also the fifth-largest global user of solar power, the US, Japan and the EU could open their own markets more broadly to Indian exporters of solar plants, provided that India first starts the same certificate trading that China has already introduced. That the Biden administration in the US should learn from California's success in CO_2 mitigation at the national level is desirable: that should be a key part of the transatlantic debate.

Incidentally, it cannot be ruled out that major philanthropic foundations will link up with private companies to fund the global disclosure of important climate protection-related patents. What Tesla founder Elon Musk has done with his patents—in the interest of expanding electromobility—is also quite conceivable in sub-sectors of the renewable energy sector or green hydrogen technologies.

The West will have to ask itself whether it should not also buy up important corona vaccine patents at the G7 level, thus quickly enabling more license-based production of coronavirus vaccines in ASEAN and other leading countries particularly in the Global South, for example; this would then also overcome the resistance to CO_2 pricing via certificate trading in important G20 countries such as Indonesia or Brazil. Overcoming pandemics and advancing climate policy can be achieved in parallel.

References

CPB/PBL. (2016). *Valuation of CO_2 Emissions in CBA: Implications of the Scenario Study Welfare, Prosperity and the Human Environment, Netherlands Bureau of Economic Policy Analysis (CPB) and Netherlands Environmental Assessment Agency (PBL)*, The Hague.

De Haas, R., & Popov, A. (2019). *Finance and Carbon Emissions* (ECB Working Paper Series, No 2318). European Central Bank: Frankfurt am Main. https://www.ecb.europa.eu/pub/pdf/scpwps/ecb.wp2318~44719344e8.en.pdf

Dechezleprêtre, A., Glachant, M., Haščič, I., Johnstone, N., & Ménière, Y. (2011). Invention and Transfer of Climate Change-Mitigation Technologies: A Global Analysis. *Review of Environmental Economics and Policy, 5*(1), 109–130. https://doi.org/10.1093/reep/req023

Federal Ministry for the Environment, Nature Conservation and Nuclear Safety. (2019). G20 – The Group of Twenty. Retrieved 6 September, 2019, from https://www.bmu.de/en/topics/europe-international-sustainability-digitalisation/international-environmental-policy/g7-and-g20/g20/

Fridays for Future. (2019, August 5–9). *Summer Meeting in Lausanne Europe (SMiLE)*. Retrieved 6 September, 2019, from https://smileforfuture.eu/

German Environment Agency. (2013, August). Schätzung der Umweltkosten in den Bereichen Energie und Verkehr – Empfehlungen des Umweltbundesamtes [transl. PJJW: An Estimation of the Environmental Costs in the Areas of Energy and Transport, Recommendations of the Germany Environment Agency]. Retrieved 6 September, 2019, from https://www.umweltbundesamt.de/sites/default/files/medien/378/publikationen/hgp_umweltkosten_0.pdf

Glachant, M., Dechezleprêtre, A., Fankhauser, S., Stoever, J., & Touboul, S. (2020). *Invention and Global Diffusion of Technologies for Climate Change Adaptation: A Patent Analysis*. The World Bank. https://openknowledge.worldbank.org/handle/10986/33883

Hennicke, P., & Welfens, P. J. J. (2012). *Energiewende nach Fukushima: Deutscher Sonderweg oder weltweites Vorbild?* [transl. Energy Transition After Fukushima: A Special Path for Germany or a Worldwide Role Model]. oekom Verlag.

ICAP. (2021). *Emissions Trading Worldwide: Status Report 2021*. International Carbon Action Partnership.

IPCC. (2021). Climate Change 2021: The Physical Science Basis, contribution of Working Group I to the Sixth Assessment Report of the Intergovernmental Panel on Climate Change. In V. Masson-Delmotte, P. Zhai, A. Pirani, S. L. Connors, C. Péan, S. Berger, N. Caud, Y. Chen, L. Goldfarb, M. I. Gomis, M. Huang, K. Leitzell, E. Lonnoy, J.B.R. Matthews, T. K. Maycock, T. Waterfield, O. Yelekçi, R. Yu, & B. Zhou (Eds.). Cambridge University Press. In Print (Approved version dated 7 August 2021). https://www.ipcc.ch/report/ar6/wg1/downloads/report/IPCC_AR6_WGI_Full_Report.pdf

LBBW. (2019). *Chancen und Risiken der CO_2-Regulatorik für Industrieunternehmen* [transl. PJJW: Opportunities and Risks of CO2 Regulation for Industrial Companies]. Landesbank für Baden-Württemberg (LBBW). https://www.lbbw.de/konzern/medien-center/presseinfos/2019/20190730_lbbw_blickpunkt_chancen_und_risiken_der_co2-regulatorik_fuer_industrieunternehmen_9ugstcqtp_m.pdf. Accessed 15 Aug 2019.

Liedtke, C., & Welfens, M. J. (2008). *Mut zur Nachhaltigkeit. Von Wissen zum Handeln, Didaktische Module* [transl. PJJW: The Courage for Sustainability. From Knowledge to Action, Didactic Modules]. Wuppertal Institute Forum for Responsibility, WI, ASKO-EUROPA Foundation.

Niti Aayog (2015). *Report on India's Renewable Energy Roadmap 2030, Toward Accelerated Renewable Electricity Deployment*, National Institute for Transforming India (NITI Aayog), Government of India, New Delhi.

Probst, B., Touboul, S., Glachant, M., & Dechezleprêtre, A (2021). Global Trends in the Innovation and Diffusion of Climate Change Mitigation Technologies. In *Review: Nature Portfolio, Research Square*. https://doi.org/10.21203/rs.3.rs-266803/v1

Qi, T., & Weng, Y. (2016). Economic Impacts of an International Carbon Market in Achieving the INDC Targets. *Energy, 109*, 886–893. https://doi.org/10.1016/j.energy.2016.05.081

Sachs, J. (2015). *The Age of Sustainable Development*. Columbia University Press.

Stern, N. (2006). *The Stern Review on the Economics of Climate Change*. Commissioned by Her Majesty's Government of the United Kingdom.

The Economist. (2018, August 2). India Shows How Hard it Is to Move Beyond Fossil Fuels – A Renewable-Energy Revolution Is Neither Imminent Nor Pain-Free. *The Economist* online edition https://www.economist.com/briefing/2018/08/02/india-shows-how-hard-it-is-to-move-beyond-fossil-fuels

Tietenberg, T. (2010). Cap-and-Trade: The Evolution of an Economic Idea. *Agricultural and Resource Economics Review, 39*(3), 359–367. https://doi.org/10.22004/ag.econ.95836

UNEP. (2018, November). *Emissions Gap Report 2018, United Nations Environment Programme*. United Nations Environment Programme, Nairobi. https://www.unenvironment.org/resources/emissions-gap-report-2018

UNEP and Climate and Clean Air Coalition. (2021). *Global Methane Assessment: Benefits and Costs of Mitigating Methane Emissions*. United Nations Environment Programme.

Vorländer, H. (2019). *Demokratie* (3rd ed.). Munich.

Welfens, P. J. J. (2020a). Macroeconomic and Health Care Aspects of the Coronavirus Epidemic: EU, US and Global Perspectives. *International Economics and Economic Policy, 17*, 295–362. https://doi.org/10.1007/s10368-020-00465-3

Welfens, P. J. J. (2020b). *Corona Weltrezession – Epidemiedruck und globale Erneuerungs-Perspektiven* [transl. PJJW: Corona World Recession – Pandemic Pressure and Perspectives for Renewal]. Springer.

Welfens, P. J. J., & Celebi, K. (2020). CO_2 *Allowance Price Dynamics and Stock Markets in EU Countries: Empirical Findings and Global CO_2-Perspectives* (EIIW Discussion Paper No. 267) https://uni-w.de/ndf2l

Welfens, P. J. J., Bleischwitz, R., & Geng, Y. (2017). Resource Efficiency, Circular Economy and Sustainability Dynamics in China and OECD Countries. *International Economics and Economic Policy, 14*(3), 377–382. https://doi.org/10.1007/s10368-017-0388-0

Appendix 1: Climate Policy Information on California

Table A1.1 Comparison of ETS: EU and California

California ETS	EU ETS
Coverage ca. 85 percent of California's total GHG emissions (<500 firms)	*Coverage ca. 40 percent of EU28 (plus Norway, Iceland and Liechtenstein) total GHG emissions (ca. 11,000 firms)*
GHGs covered: CO_2, CH_4, N_2O, SF_6, HFCs, PFCs, NF_3 and other fluorinated GHGs Sectors: Large industrial facilities (including cement, glass, hydrogen, iron and steel, lead, lime manufacturing, nitric acid, petroleum and natural gas systems, petroleum refining, pulp and paper manufacturing, including cogeneration facilities co-owned/operated at any of these facilities), electricity generation, electricity imports, other stationary combustion, and CO_2 suppliers, suppliers of natural gas, suppliers of reformulated blend stock for oxygenate blending and distillate fuel oil, suppliers of liquid petroleum gas in California and suppliers of liquefied natural gas.	GHGs covered: CO_2, N_2O, PFC from aluminum production Sectors: Energy-intensive industries, including power stations and other combustion plants, with ≥20 MW thermal rated input (except hazardous or municipal waste installations), oil refineries, coke ovens, iron and steel, cement clinker, glass, lime, bricks, ceramics, pulp, paper and board, aluminum, petrochemicals, ammonia, nitric, adipic, glyoxal and glyoxylic acid production, CO_2 capture, transport in pipelines and geological storage of CO_2.

(*continued*)

Table A1.1 (continued)

California ETS	EU ETS
Coverage ca. 85 percent of California's total GHG emissions (<500 firms)	*Coverage ca. 40 percent of EU28 (plus Norway, Iceland and Liechtenstein) total GHG emissions (ca. 11,000 firms)*
	Aviation: The aviation activities within the initial scope of the EU ETS included all flights from or to an aerodrome situated in the territory of a member state to which the Treaty applies, with some exceptions. Since 2012, only applicable to flights within EEA.

Source: Own representation based on the following sources; for California: ICAP (2019), USA—California Cap-and-Trade Program, https://icapcarbonaction.com/en/?option=com_etsmap&task=export&format=pdf&layout=list&systems[]=45 for EU ETS: European Commission (2016), The EU Emissions Trading System, Factsheet https://ec.europa.eu/clima/sites/clima/files/factsheet_ets_en.pdf and ICAP (2019), EU Emissions Trading System, https://icapcarbonaction.com/en/?option=com_etsmap&task=export&format=pdf&layout=list&systems%5B%5D=43

CALIFORNIAN CAP-AND-TRADE SYSTEM

(from www.C2ES.org: Center for Climate and Energy Solutions; Courtesy, Center for Climate and Energy Solutions; 2019)

California cap-and-trade program, launched in 2013, is one of a suite of major policies the state is using to lower its greenhouse gas emissions. California's program is the fourth largest in the world, following the cap-and-trade programs of the European Union, the Republic of Korea and the Chinese province of Guangdong. In addition to driving emission cuts in one of the world's largest economies, California's program provides critical experience in creating and managing an economy-wide cap-and-trade system.

California's emissions trading system is expected to reduce greenhouse gas emissions from regulated entities by more than 16 percent between 2013 and 2020, and by an additional 40 percent by 2030. It is a central component of the state's broader strategy to reduce total greenhouse gas emissions to 1990 levels by 2020 and 40 percent below 1990 levels by 2030.

The cap-and-trade rule applies to large electric power plants, large industrial plants and fuel distributors (e.g., natural gas and petroleum). Around

450 businesses responsible for about 85 percent of California's total greenhouse gas emissions must comply. California has linked its program with similar programs in the Canadian provinces of Ontario and Quebec, meaning that businesses in one jurisdiction can use emission allowances (or offsets) issued by one of the others for compliance. This broadens the number of businesses under the cap, leading to additional economic efficiencies. The following [see Fig. A1.1] shows greenhouse gas emissions (CO_2 equivalents) in percentage composition of total emissions by sector, where transport, industry and the energy sector are to the fore.

CALIFORNIA CAP-AND-TRADE DETAILS

California's program represents the first multi-sector cap-and-trade program in North America. Building on lessons from the northeast Regional Greenhouse Gas Initiative (RGGI) and the European Union Emission

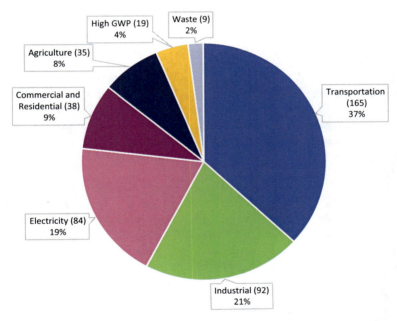

Fig. A1.1 California emissions by sector in 2015. (Source: Greenhouse Gas Inventory Data (CARB, 2015); Courtesy: Center for Climate and Energy Solutions www.C2ES.org)

Trading Scheme (EU ETS), the California program blends proven market elements with its own policy innovations.

The California Air Resources Board (CARB) implements and enforces the program. The cap-and-trade rules first applied to electric power plants and industrial plants that emit 25,000 tons of carbon dioxide equivalent per year or more. Beginning in 2015, the program was extended to fuel distributors meeting the 25,000-metric ton threshold. The program's overall greenhouse gas emission cap declines by 3 percent annually from 2015 through 2020 and faster (details still to be determined) from 2021 through 2030.

Emission allowances are distributed by a mix of free allocation and quarterly auctions. The portion of emissions covered by free allowances varies by industry and by how efficient each facility is relative to industry benchmarks. These policy elements, and other relevant details of California's cap-and-trade program, are summarized in Table A1.2. Figure A1.2 shows in green the maximum emissions volumes for California (the red line indicates a business-as-usual scenario, without policy interventions).

CALIFORNIA'S OVERALL CLIMATE CHANGE PROGRAM

California's cap-and-trade program is only one element of its broader climate change initiative, as authorized in the California Global Warming Solutions Act of 2006 (AB 32) and the 2016 extension bill SB 32. AB 32 sets a statewide carbon limit for 2020 while SB 32 sets a statewide limit for 2030. AB 32 seeks to slow climate change through a comprehensive program reducing greenhouse gas emissions from virtually all sources statewide.

AB 32 and other state laws also require a variety of actions aimed at reducing the state's impact on the climate, like a Renewable Portfolio Standard, a Low Carbon Fuel Standard and a variety of land use and energy efficiency standards and incentives. California's cap-and-trade program acts as a backstop to ensure its overall greenhouse gas target is met, regardless of the performance of these complementary measures. Figure A1.3 shows the programs CARB is implementing to achieve the goals of AB 32 and the projected impact of each. For more information on actions taken by CARB in response to AB 32, visit the AB 32 Scoping Plan page, with the latest information from CARB about how the state is achieving its greenhouse gas reduction goals.

Table A1.2 California cap-and-trade details

Issue	Details and discussion
Status of regulation	
Legal status	California Air Resources Board (CARB) adopted final regulations on 20 October 2011. The regulation has been amended periodically since then. The legislature authorized an extension of the program through 2030 in 2017.
Regulation coverage	
Threshold of coverage	Sources that emit at least 25,000 metric tons CO_2e/year are subject to regulation, including importers of electricity to the state.
Gases covered	The six gases covered by the Kyoto Protocol (CO_2, CH_4, N_2O, HFCs, PFCs, SF_6), plus NF_3 and other fluorinated greenhouse gases.
Sectors covered: Phase 1 (2013–2014)	Electricity generation, including imports. Industrial sources.
Sectors covered: Phase 2 (2015 onward)	Includes sectors covered in Phase 1, plus: Distributors of petroleum. Distributors of natural gas.
Point of regulation	Electricity generators (within California). Electricity importers. Industrial facility operators. Fuel distributors.
Allowance allocation	
Distribution method	Free allocation for electric utilities, industrial facilities and natural gas utilities (investor-owned utilities must sell free allowances and redistribute funds to customers). Free allocation to utilities declines over time. Other allowances must be purchased at auction or via trade.
Allocation methodology	Industry: Based on output and sector-specific emissions intensity benchmark that rewards efficient facilities. Electricity: Based on long-term procurement plans. Natural gas: Based on 2011 sales.
Auction	Quarterly, single round, sealed bid, uniform price. Price minimum: Began at $10 in 2012 and increases 5 percent annually over inflation. Price maximum: Additional allowances are available for sale when prices reach an upper threshold, set at $40 in 2012, increasing 5 percent annually over inflation. Beginning in 2021 a hard price ceiling will be set, and an unlimited supply of allowances will be available at this price. Investor-owned utilities must consign their free allowances to be sold at auction; must use proceeds for ratepayer benefit. Additional information, including auction results, can be found here.

(*continued*)

Table A1.2 (continued)

Issue	Details and discussion
Emission targets/ allowance budget	162.8 MMT in 2013 (electricity and industry). 394.5 MMT in 2015 (includes all covered sectors). 334.2 MMT in 2020. 200.5 MMT in 2030. (See Fig. A1.2 below).
Compliance flexibility	
Banking	A participating entity may bank allowances for future use, and these allowances will not expire. However, regulated entities are subject to holding limits, restricting the maximum number of allowances that an entity may bank at any time. The holding limit quantity is based on a multiple of the entity's annual allowance budget.
Borrowing	Borrowing of allowances from future years is not allowed.
Offsets: quantity	Allowed for 8 percent of total compliance obligation through 2020; 4 percent between 2021 and 2025; 6 percent between 2026 and 2030. Beginning in 2021 at least half the offsets used for compliance must come from projects that directly benefit California.
Offsets: protocols	Offsets must comply with CARB-approved protocols. Protocols currently exist for forestry (including urban forestry), dairy digesters, ozone depleting substances projects, mine methane capture and rice cultivation. Offset projects may be located anywhere in the US. All offset projects developed under a CARB Compliance Offset Protocol must be listed with an ARB-approved Offset Project Registry.
Strategic reserve	A percentage of allowances is held in a strategic reserve by CARB in three tiers with different prices: $40, $45, $50 in 2013, rising 5 percent annually over inflation. The strategic reserve will help constrain compliance costs by adding supply to the market when prices would otherwise be above the tiers.
Compliance period	Three-year compliance periods (following two-year Phase 1), with a partial surrender obligation due each year.
Emissions reporting and verification	
Reporting	Covered entities must report annually (as required since 2008).
Registration	Covered entities and other participants must register with CARB to participate in allowance auctions.
Verification	Reported emissions must be verified by a third party.
Compliance and enforcement	
Annual obligation	Entities must provide allowances and/or offsets for 30 percent of their previous year's emissions each year.
Compliance period obligation	At the end of every multi-year compliance period, entities must provide allowances and/or offsets for the balance of emissions from the entire compliance period.
Noncompliance	If a deadline is missed or there is a shortfall, four allowances must be surrendered for every metric ton not covered in time.

(*continued*)

Table A1.2 (continued)

Issue	Details and discussion
Trading and enforcement	The regulation expressly prohibits any trading involving a manipulative device, a corner of or an attempt to corner the market, fraud, attempted fraud, or false or inaccurate reports. Violations of the regulations can result in civil or criminal penalties. Perjury statutes apply. The program includes mechanisms to monitor for and prevent market manipulation.
Linking	
Direct linkages	California's program is directly linked with similar programs in Québec (as of 1 January 2014) and Ontario (as of 1 January 2018). Offsets and allowances can be traded across jurisdictions. The linked jurisdictions hold joint auctions together.
Indirect linkages	California has a memorandum of understanding with the Mexican state of Chiapas and the Brazilian state of Acre to develop sector-based offsets from projects that reduce emissions from deforestation and land degradation (REDD). A working group submitted recommendations for REDD protocols, though no REDD compliance protocols have been approved by CARB. Washington state's Clean Air Rule accepts allowances from out-of-state programs for a facility's compliance obligation. Washington's Department of Ecology is working to identify which carbon market(s)'s allowances would be eligible, and California is one possibility. If out-of-state buyers entered the market for California allowances, it could affect prices for California entities through an indirect linkage.

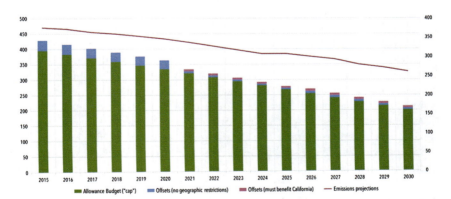

Fig. A1.2 California emission cap and business-as-usual forecasts. (Source: 2020 Business-as-Usual (BAU) Emissions Projection 2014 Edition (CARB, 2017); Courtesy: Center for Climate and Energy Solutions www.C2ES.org)

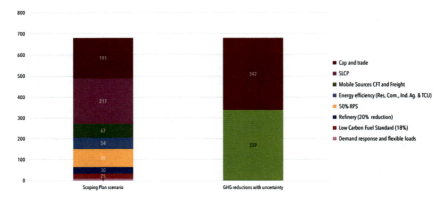

Fig. A1.3 Projected reductions (in MMT CO_2e) caused by AB 32 measures by 2020 and share of total. (Source: California Greenhouse Gas Emission Inventory Program (CARB, 2017); Courtesy, Center for Climate and Energy Solutions www.C2ES.org)

Auction Revenue

Although a significant number of emission allowances are freely allocated in California's program, many are also sold at auction. The first year of auctions generated more than $525 million in revenue for the state. The state anticipates annual auction revenue to rise over time. A pair of 2012 laws established guidelines on how this annual revenue is disbursed. The two laws do not identify specific programs that would benefit from the revenue, but they provide a framework for how the state invests cap-and-trade revenue into local projects.

The first law, AB 1532, requires that the auction revenue be spent for environmental purposes, with an emphasis on improving air quality. The second, SB 535, requires that at least 25 percent of the revenue be spent on programs that benefit disadvantaged communities, which tend to suffer disproportionately from air pollution. The California Environmental Protection Agency identifies disadvantaged communities for investment opportunities, while the state's Department of Finance oversees the expenditures of this revenue to mitigate direct health impacts of climate change. AB 398, which Gov. Jerry Brown signed on 25 July 2017, further clarifies the priorities for investments as:

- Reducing air toxic and criteria air pollutants
- Promoting low- and zero-carbon transportation
- Sustainable agriculture
- Healthy forests and urban greening
- Reducing short-lived climate pollutants
- Promoting climate adaptation and resilience
- Supporting climate and clean energy research

Appendix 2: CO_2 Emissions in a Macro Model of the Closed Economy: World Economy

A simple, medium-term new macro model of the world economy (a closed economy) is useful for a consideration of the problem of CO_2 emission effects and necessary climate protection research expenditures. Considered on the right side of the equals sign (i.e., as part of aggregate demand) in a modified expenditure equation for the real gross domestic product Y (Eq. A2.1) or in the goods market equilibrium condition are consumption C, corporate investment $[b(ßY/K - r)(1-v''P'/P)]$, real research expenditure for climate protection $R'(P'/P)$, where P' is the CO_2 certificate price and P is the goods price level and G is government consumption; R' is an exogenous research expenditure parameter in the system. The macroeconomic production function is $Y = (1-H'P'/P)K^ß(AL)^{(1-ß)}$, where K is real capital, A is knowledge and L is labor; $0<ß<1$; where $H'>0$ and $0<H'P'/P$ hold, and the term H'P'/P represents a loss factor due to climate change and related problems—ultimately reflecting corresponding floods and extreme weather events. The marginal product of capital is thus ßY/K, and the investment function uses a positive parameter b (and the difference between the marginal product of capital and the real interest rate r) and a climate protection investment b'v''P'/P (b'>0 is a company parameter, v'' a positive policy parameter), which represents a subsidy surcharge by the state (with v''>0) proportional to the real CO_2 certificate price.

© The Author(s), under exclusive license to Springer Nature Switzerland AG 2022
P. J.J. Welfens, *Global Climate Change Policy*, Sustainable Development Goals Series,
https://doi.org/10.1007/978-3-030-94594-7

Research expenditures for climate protection amount to R'(P'/P), whereby R' in the simplest case can be regarded as a government research subsidy amount.

$$Y = c(1-\tau)(1-vP'/P)Y + \left[b(\beta Y/K - r) + b'v''(P'/P)\right] + R'(P'/P) + G \qquad (A2.1)$$

The slope in the Y-(P'/P-diagram) results from Eq. (A2.1). From this equilibrium condition, the equilibrium line of the goods market can—for a constant r—be represented in Y-(P'/P)-diagram. The differentiation of the above equation gives the slope of the ISP' curve. The next equilibrium condition shows nominal money supply M = nominal money demand—for the situation of an expected inflation rate of 0 (parameters V' and h are each positive). The effective price level is the goods price level plus a surcharge factor for the amount of the CO_2 emission certificate price. The certificate market is implicitly determined in equilibrium by Eq. (A2.3), whereby the relative price P'/P depends positively on Y and negatively on the effective research expenditure R'(P'/P):

$$M = P(1+V'P')Y/(hr) \qquad (A2.2)$$

$$P'/P = n'Y - n''(1 = R'(P'/P)) \qquad (A2.3)$$

The variables Y, r and P' (or P'/P) are endogenous here; multipliers for this simple medium-term model are to be considered:

dY/dM, dY/dG, dY/dR', dY/dτ
dr/dM, dr/dG, dr/dR', dr/dτ
dP'/dM, dP'/dG, dP'/dR', dY/dτ

It should also be noted that investment subsidies increase the income tax rate, as tax revenues must be sufficient in order to finance government consumption and real investment subsidies. The welfare effects could be represented by a function H(Y, P'/P), whereby the partial derivation in relation to P'/P is positive, since a high P'/P price relation means a low level of CO_2 emissions and ultimately amounts to a quasi-increased consumption risk (in the case of more floods and extreme weather events). In fact, an extended stochastic macro model could be developed and implemented empirically.

A long-term growth model—as an endogenous growth model—would be necessary to complement the long-term analysis here. However, one can already refer to comprehensive new modeling in this regard—see Bretschger (2019).

Appendix 3: World Heat Map, July 2019 (University of California at Berkeley)

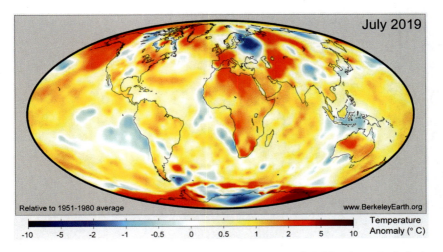

Fig. A3.1 World Heat Map, July 2019 (University of California at Berkeley). (Source: Rohde (2019). World Heat Map, July 2019. Retrieved from https://twitter.com/RARohde/status/1162011232095920128. Robert Rohde, Lead Scientist at BerkeleyEarth.org)

Appendix 4: Sustainable Development Goals

The United Nations has adopted a series of Sustainable Development Goals (see overview in Fig. A4.1), which are often addressed individually in the political sphere. From an analytical point of view, however, this is not really convincing, as some of the objectives are obviously linked in terms of content. For example, as has been shown, the issue of climate protection policy is indirectly linked to the task of limiting greater inequality. There is a need for more extensive research on this issue.

Fig. A4.1 Overview of the UN Sustainable Development Goals. *Note: The content of this publication has not been approved by the United Nations and does not reflect the views of the United Nations or its officials or member states.* (Source: United Nations Sustainable Development Goals. Communication Materials. Retrieved 01/11/2021 from the website of the United Nations Sustainable Development Goals https://www.un.org/sustainabledevelopment/)

Appendix 5: Composition of the "German Coal Commission" (Chairpersons and Other Members of the Commission for Growth, Structural Change and Jobs)

Four Chairpersons

Brandenburg's former head of government Matthias Platzeck, former head of the Chancellor's Office Ronald Pofalla (DB Rail Board Member), Professor Barbara Praetorius and Saxony's former Prime Minister Stanislaw Tillich.

Further Members

Prof. Dr. h.c. Jutta Allmendinger, President of the Social Science Research Center Berlin
Antje Grothus, Buirer Citizens' Initiative for Buir and Coordinator of Coal Policy NRW at the Climate Alliance Germany
Gerda Hasselfeldt, President of the German Red Cross (DRK e.V.)
Christine Herntier, Mayor of Spremberg, spokesperson for the Brandenburg municipalities of the Lausitzrunde
Martin Kaiser, Managing Director Greenpeace
Steffen Kampeter, Chief Executive of the Federation of German Employers' Associations (BDA—Bundesvereinigung der deutschen Arbeitgeberverbände)

Stefan Kapferer, Chairman of the Executive Board of the Federal Association of Energy and Water Management (Bundesverband der Energie- und Wasserwirtschaft e.V.)

Prof. Dieter Kempf, President of the Federation of German Industries (Bundesverband der deutschen Industrie e.V.)

Stefan Körzell, Member of the Executive Board of the German Confederation of Trade Unions (Deutschen Gewerkschaftsbundes)

Michael Kreuzberg, District Administrator of the Rhein-Erft District

Dr. Felix Matthes, Research Coordinator Energy and Climate Policy, Öko-Institut e.V.

Claudia Nemat, Member of the Board of Management of Deutsche Telekom AG

Prof. Dr. Kai Niebert, Head of the Chair of Didactics of Natural Sciences and Sustainability Researchers at the University of Zurich and Visiting Professor at the Sustainability Faculty of Leuphana University Lüneburg

Prof. Dr. Annekatrin Niebuhr, Professor of Labour Market and Regional Research at the Christian-Albrechts-Universität zu Kiel and Research Associate at IAB Nord

Reiner Priggen, Chairman of the Board of the Regional Association for Renewable Energies for North Rhine-Westphalia (Landesverband Erneuerbare Energie NRW e.V.)

Katherina Reiche, Managing Director of the Association of Municipal Enterprises (Verband kommunaler Unternehmen e.V.)

Gunda Röstel, Managing Director of Stadtentwässerung Dresden GmbH and authorized signatory at Gelsenwasser AG

Andreas Scheidt, Member of the Federal Executive Committee of the trade union ver.di

Prof. Dr. Hans Joachim Schellnhuber, Director, Potsdam Institute for Climate Impact Research (Potsdam Institut für Klimaforschung PIK)

Dr. Eric Schweitzer, President of the Association of German Chambers of Industry and Commerce (Deutscher Industrie- und Handelskammertag e.V.)

Michael Vassiliadis, Chairman of the Mining, Chemical and Energy Industries Union (Industriegewerkschaft Bergbau, Chemie, Energie)

Prof. Dr. Ralf B. Wehrspohn, Director of the Fraunhofer Institute for Microstructures of Materials and Systems IMWS

Hubert Weiger, Chairman of the German Association for the Environment and Nature Conservation (BUND e.V.)

Hannelore Wodtke, Chairperson of the Green Future Welzow Voter Group

1.1.1 Members of the German Bundestag Who Participate in the Meetings of the Commission as Persons with the Right to Speak but Without the Right to Vote

Andreas G. Lämmel, MdB
Dr. Andreas Lenz, MdB
Dr. Matthias Miersch, MdB

Appendix 6: Members of the Ethics Commission for a Safe Energy Supply

After the Fukushima nuclear power plant accident in Japan in 2011, the German federal government set up a commission on the question of the possible phasing-out of nuclear energy production in Germany with 17 members. The following list was drawn up from information on the website of the federal government (https://www.bundesregierung.de/breg-de/suche/schnell-und-gruendlich-arbeiten-335528 last accessed on 10.09.19 and Wikipedia last accessed on 10.09.19). The Commission was led by two persons, namely:

- Klaus Töpfer (CDU), former German Federal Environment Minister and former Executive Director of the United Nations Environment Programme (UNEP)
- Matthias Kleiner, President of the DFG (German Research Foundation)

Other Members of the Commission

- Ulrich Beck, former sociology professor at the Ludwig-Maximilian-University Munich

- Klaus von Dohnanyi (SPD), former Federal Education Minister
- Ulrich Fischer, Bishop of the Protestant Regional Church in Baden
- Alois Glück (CSU), President of the Central Committee of German Catholics
- Jörg Hacker, President of the German Academy of Sciences Leopoldina
- Jürgen Hambrecht, Chairman of the Board of Executive Directors of BASF
- Volker Hauff (SPD), former Federal Minister for Research and Technology
- Walter Hirche (FDP), President of the German UNESCO Commission
- Reinhard Hüttl, Chairman of the Board of the German Research Centre for Geosciences Potsdam and President of the German Academy of Science and Engineering
- Weyma Lübbe, philosopher, member of the German Ethics Council
- Reinhard Marx, Archbishop of Munich and Freising
- Lucia Reisch, economist, professor at Copenhagen Business School, member of the Council for Sustainable Development (RNE)
- Ortwin Renn, risk researcher, sociology professor at the University of Stuttgart, Chairman of the Sustainability Advisory Board of Baden-Württemberg
- Miranda Schreurs, political scientist, Director of the Environmental Policy Research Center at Freie Universität Berlin
- Michael Vassiliadis (SPD), Chairman of the German Mining, Chemical and Energy Workers' Union (IG Bergbau, Chemie, Energie)

The composition of this commission, too, shows a number of personalities and groups represented whose presence in such a forum cannot easily be denied given the senior dignitaries and authority figures which make up the commission (beyond reproach for most people)—this is, in effect, a substitute parliament—but that cannot be the purpose of a democracy. Politicians may argue that they wanted to include a wide range of social and lobby groups, but in fact such mega-commissions—without a focus on expertise in the matter under consideration, namely energy and nuclear, but with a focus on influential groups in society such as religious representatives—illustrate a quasi-authoritarian approach; the recommendations of the commission are virtually beyond reproach. The public debate on a very important issue, namely the phasing-out of nuclear power, which was actually necessary, was sidelined into commission talks. Such an approach is detrimental to democracy. One can understand to some extent that the federal government wanted to avoid a fractious public debate by establishing such a mega-commission for reasons of convenience, but this approach is not compatible with the model of Western democracy. The name "Ethics Committee for a Secure Energy Supply" sounds particularly devout—dissuading normal citizen and even members of parliament from commenting on the issue of the nuclear phase-out as it was shrouded in a veil of high-brow philosophy and ethics.

Appendix 7: The G20+ in 2019

Table A7.1 The G20+ in numbers, 2019 (Mt = megatons)

Country	Emissions MtCO2	Population	CO2 per capita in kg	GDP PPP, in billions (constant 2017 Intl. $)	Share of World CO2 Emissions in %
Argentina	178.9395	44,938,712	3,981.856	991.52	0.49%
Australia	411.0157	25,365,745	16,203.573	1,254.48	1.13%
Austria	68.4951	8,879,920	7,713.482	495.80	0.19%
Belgium	99.7089	11,502,704	8,668.301	594.30	0.27%
Brazil	465.7158	211,049,527	2,206.666	3,092.22	1.28%
Bulgaria	42.0065	6,975,761	6,021.780	161.78	0.12%
Canada	576.6505	37,593,384	15,339.149	1,831.55	1.58%
China	10174.6811	1,397,715,000	7,279.511	22,492.45	27.92%
Croatia	17.8822	4,065,253	4,398.791	116.89	0.05%
Cyprus	7.3157	1,198,575	6,103.665	35.48	0.02%
Czechia	101.0098	10,671,870	9,465.052	434.32	0.28%
Denmark	32.0755	5,814,422	5,516.541	335.36	0.09%
Estonia	13.8884	1,326,898	10,466.818	48.87	0.04%
Finland	41.6526	5,521,606	7,543.566	268.61	0.11%
France	323.7471	67,055,854	4,828.021	3,082.30	0.89%
Germany	701.9551	83,092,962	8,447.829	4,457.05	1.93%
Greece	67.184	10,717,169	6,268.820	325.44	0.18%
Hungary	49.101	9,771,141	5,025.104	317.91	0.13%
India	2616.4488	1,366,417,754	1,914.823	9,155.08	7.18%
Indonesia	617.5126	270,625,568	2,281.797	3,196.68	1.69%
Ireland	37.1177	4,934,040	7,522.781	427.04	0.10%
Italy	337.0862	60,302,093	5,589.959	2,549.66	0.93%
Japan	1106.6644	126,264,931	8,764.622	5,244.86	3.04%
Latvia	8.2623	1,913,822	4,317.173	59.07	0.02%
Lithuania	13.4834	2,794,137	4,825.604	103.56	0.04%
Luxembourg	9.7849	620,001	15,782.071	70.64	0.03%
Malta	1.5538	504,062	3,082.557	21.90	0.00%
Mexico	438.4976	127,575,529	3,437.161	2,513.41	1.20%
Netherlands	154.8266	17,344,874	8,926.361	982.22	0.42%
Nigeria	140.0265	200,963,599	696.775	1,032.05	0.38%
Poland	322.6265	37,965,475	8,497.892	1,257.44	0.89%
Portugal	48.5978	10,286,263	4,724.534	357.90	0.13%
Romania	75.0841	19,366,221	3,877.065	578.53	0.21%
Russian Federation	1678.3668	144,406,261	11,622.535	3,956.04	4.61%
Saudi Arabia	582.1496	34,268,528	16,987.879	1,609.32	1.60%
Slovakia	33.3148	5,454,147	6,108.160	173.79	0.09%
Slovenia	13.6964	2,088,385	6,558.369	81.25	0.04%
South Africa	478.6081	58,558,267	8,173.194	730.91	1.31%
South Korea	611.2632	51,709,098	11,821.192	2,208.96	1.68%
Spain	252.6832	47,133,521	5,361.008	1,923.33	0.69%
Sweden	42.7666	10,278,887	4,160.626	539.38	0.12%

Table A7.1 (continued)

Country	Emissions MtCO2	Population	CO2 per capita in kg	GDP PPP, in billions (constant 2017 Intl. $)	Share of World CO2 Emissions in %
Turkey	405.1264	83,429,615	4,855.906	2,352.64	1.11%
UK	369.8784	66,836,327	5,534.092	3,111.52	1.02%
US	5284.6967	328,239,523	16,100.123	20,524.95	14.50%
Sum	29,053	5,023,537,431	Ø 5,783	105,098	
World	36,441	7,673,656,872		129,624	
EU27/World	**8.00%**	**5.83%**		**15.27%**	
G20/World	**79.34%**	**62.85%**		**80.28%**	
G20+/World	**79.73%**	**65.46%**		**81.08%**	

Source: Own representation of data available from the World Bank, World Development Indicators

Appendix 8: An Optimum Emission Reduction

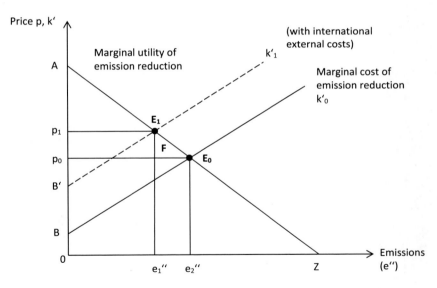

Fig. A8.1 Optimum emission reduction. (Source: Own representation)

In a stylized model, one can determine the optimal emission level (e''), whereby a national perspective alone leads to a high emission quantity e_2''; if one additionally considers on the cost side the international marginal external costs—the "additional costs" abroad for people living there, ignored by private providers on markets in the country under consideration—then the optimal market solution will lie at a reduced emission quantity e_1''; the equilibrium point is E_1 and not, as initially, E_0. The market price level (i.e., the certificate price) is p_1.

Appendix 9: Greenhouse Gas Emission Statistics: Emissions Register

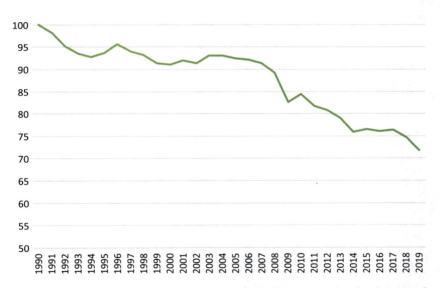

Fig. A9.1 Total greenhouse gas emissions (including international aviation and indirect CO_2, excluding LULUCF) trend, EU-28, 1990–2019 (Index 1990 = 100). (Source: Own representation based on data from https://ec.europa.eu/eurostat/web/environment/data/database

© The Author(s), under exclusive license to Springer Nature Switzerland AG 2022
P. J.J. Welfens, *Global Climate Change Policy*, Sustainable Development Goals Series,
https://doi.org/10.1007/978-3-030-94594-7

Table A9.1 Total greenhouse gas emissions (including international aviation and indirect CO_2, excluding LULUCF), by country, 1990–2017 (million tons CO_2 equivalents)

	1990	1995	2000	2005	2010	2015	2017	Share in EU-28[a]
EU-28	5722.9	5397.8	5287.2	5362.0	4 917.5	4 470.3	4 483.1	100.0%
Belgium	149.7	157.6	154.5	148.9	137.1	121.6	119.4	2.7%
Bulgaria	102.6	75.5	59.8	64.5	61.1	62.2	62.1	1.4%
Czechia	199.8	158.7	151.1	149.5	141.7	129.5	130.5	2.9%
Denmark	72.1	80.1	73.2	68.8	65.5	50.8	50.8	1.1%
Germany	1263.2	1 138.1	1064.7	1016.5	967.0	931.8	936.0	20.9%
Estonia	40.5	20.3	17.4	19.3	21.3	18.3	21.1	0.5%
Ireland	56.5	60.3	70.3	72.0	63.4	61.7	63.8	1.4%
Greece	105.6	111.8	128.9	138.9	121.0	98.2	98.9	2.2%
Spain	293.3	335.3	397.1	452.6	370.1	351.8	357.3	8.0%
France	556.6	553.8	567.0	570.7	528.0	477.3	482.0	10.8%
Croatia	32.4	23.2	26.1	30.3	28.4	24.6	25.5	0.6%
Italy	522.1	538.3	562.1	589.2	514.7	443.7	439.0	9.8%
Cyprus	6.4	7.9	9.2	10.2	10.3	9.1	10.0	0.2%
Latvia	26.5	13.0	10.6	11.6	12.7	11.6	11.8	0.3%
Lithuania	48.6	22.5	19.6	23.0	20.9	20.5	20.7	0.5%
Luxembourg	13.1	10.7	10.6	14.3	13.4	11.6	11.9	0.3%
Hungary	94.2	75.9	73.9	76.2	65.7	61.3	64.5	1.4%
Malta	2.3	3.0	3.1	3.2	3.2	2.5	2.6	0.1%
Netherlands	226.4	239.3	229.8	225.8	224.1	207.5	205.8	4.6%
Austria	79.6	80.9	82.1	94.5	86.8	81.0	84.5	1.9%
Poland	475.0	445.7	396.3	404.3	413.1	392.3	416.3	9.3%
Portugal	60.8	70.8	84.3	88.1	71.7	71.1	74.6	1.7%
Romania	248.9	187.8	143.6	151.7	124.4	117.2	114.8	2.6%
Slovenia	18.7	18.8	19.1	20.6	19.7	16.9	17.5	0.4%
Slovakia	73.4	53.3	49.2	51.3	46.4	41.8	43.5	1.0%
Finland	72.3	72.8	71.3	71.2	77.4	57.2	57.5	1.3%
Sweden	72.7	74.7	70.4	68.6	66.4	55.7	55.5	1.2%
United Kingdom	809.9	767.6	741.9	726.2	642.1	54 1.5	505.4	11.3%
Iceland	3.8	3.7	4.4	4.4	5.2	5.4	5.9	0.1%
Lichtenstein	0.2	0.2	0.2	0.3	0.2	0.2	0.2	0.0%
Norway	51.9	51.8	55.7	56.3	56.8	56.1	54.4	1.2%
Switzerland	56.7	56.1	57.2	58.3	58.5	52.9	52.6	1.2%
Turkey	219.8	248.4	300.5	340.6	404.6	483.4	537.4	12.0%

[a] Share in EU-28 total in year 2017

Source: Eurostat (env_air_gge), European Environment Agency https://ec.europa.eu/eurostat/statistics-explained/index.php/Greenhouse_gas_emission_statistics#Trends_in_greenhouse_gas_emissions

APPENDIX 9: GREENHOUSE GAS EMISSION STATISTICS: EMISSIONS REGISTER   457

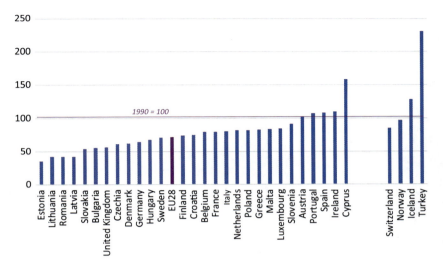

Fig. A9.2 Total greenhouse gas emissions (including international aviation and indirect CO_2, excluding LULUCF), by country, 2019 (index 1990 = 100). (Source: Own representation based on data from https://ec.europa.eu/eurostat/web/environment/data/database)

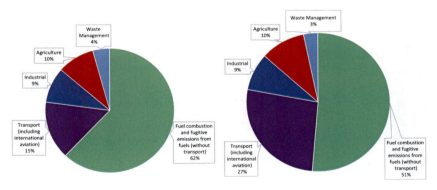

Fig. A9.3 Greenhouse gas emissions by sector, EU28, 1990 and 2019 (percentage of total emissions). (Source: Own representation based on data from https://ec.europa.eu/eurostat/web/environment/data/database)

Appendix 10: Germany—A Model for Climate Change Policy?

In its 2019 Special Report, the German Council of Economic Experts posed the question of how to proceed in terms of climate policy. The main alternatives are as follows:

- An expansion of the existing EU certificate trading system (ETS)
- The introduction of a new EU allowance trading system for sectors not yet covered by the ETS
- The introduction of a CO_2 tax in sectors not yet covered by the ETS
- Differentiated regulatory approaches for sectors not yet covered by the ETS

Looking at the starting situation in 2019, these four existing alternatives can be viewed from many different angles: for example, with regard to cost efficiency, administrative feasibility, the timeliness of political feasibility, planning security for the actors involved, European connectivity as well as other points that are represented in the white fields of Table A10.1. In the view of the Council, there are a number of points in favor of introducing a CO_2 tax in the short term, including the possibility of coordinating the introduction of such a tax with other countries, the low administrative costs involved, the short-term feasibility and the additional tax revenue generated. This can be seen in the way that CO_2 taxes would first be introduced pragmatically in sectors outside the 45 percent or so of

© The Author(s), under exclusive license to Springer Nature Switzerland AG 2022
P. J.J. Welfens, *Global Climate Change Policy*, Sustainable Development Goals Series,
https://doi.org/10.1007/978-3-030-94594-7

Table A10.1 An evaluation of different carbon pricing options

	The integration of additional sectors in the EU ETS	A separate ETS for non-EU ETS sectors	CO2 tax for non-EU ETS sectors	For information purposes: Regulatory law
Achievement of 2021-2030 targets under EU Effort Sharing Regulation	No more national targets necessary	When retaining the path for certificate issuance	Regular readjustment necessary	Challenging, small-scale readjustment necessary
Cost efficiency	Cross-sector and EU-wide	Within system framework	Within system framework	Low
Administrative feasibility	Medium effort (monitoring)	Medium effort (monitoring)	Relatively little effort	Medium effort (enforcement necessary)
Timely political feasibility	Medium term, EU negotiations	Short to medium term	Short term	Short term
Revenue for redistribution	Additional revenue	Additional revenue	Additional revenue	No additional revenue
Reaction to changes in the economic environment	Endogenous reaction	Endogenous reaction	Readjustment difficult	Readjustment difficult
Planning security for agents	Price corridor possible at the expense of target achievement	Price corridor possible at the expense of target achievement	Fixed price path only without readjustments	Dependent on design
European integrability	A common/joint EU instrument	Connection possible	Coordinated tax rates possible	Low

■ = Option largely meets criterion, ■ = Neutral, ■ = Option unlikely to meet criterion

Source: German Council of Economic Experts (2019), Setting out for a new climate policy, July 2019, p. 62

emissions covered by the EU Emissions Trading System; in the longer term, there would then be a transition toward the expansion of the EU Emissions Trading System. However, the view of the Council cannot be considered as entirely appropriate either, if the following aspects are taken into account:

- Once CO_2 taxes have been introduced, politicians will be extremely reluctant to abolish them. Many parliamentarians believe that the abolition of any tax (or taxes) creates budget gaps for the state and generally gives rise to demands for the abolition of further taxes: from the point of view of the members of parliament, the political distribution mass is decreasing, which threatens to limit their own popularity. With a view to a parallel introduction of CO_2 taxes in EU countries, there is a risk that similar policy perspectives will make a desirable medium-term transition to an extended emissions trading system very difficult in the longer term. The incentives to reduce CO_2 emissions provided by CO_2 taxes can hardly be deployed in a targeted manner; when compared with an emissions trading system, control efficiency is generally inferior in the longer term.

- The benefits of a direct extension of the EU Emissions Trading System—or even of an additional emissions trading scheme—are very good in terms of cost efficiency (when considering an ETS extension to other sectors) or at least good. California has achieved very broad coverage with an 85 percent share of emissions in its emissions trading system (California plus Quebec). That level of coverage by emissions trading should therefore also be possible in the EU, and a target of up to 90 percent is conceivable.
- In the medium and long term, every type of certificate trading system should be merged with the certificate trading systems of other countries; that is, initially the EU ETS with that of the Republic of Korea and China plus Japan (where there is a trading system for Tokyo and certain other prefectures) plus California with provinces in Canada. In view of the important aspect of global connectivity—which the German Council of Economic Experts does not reflect upon—an expansion of the EU Emissions Trading System or the establishment of a new emissions trading system for additional sectors is clearly superior to a CO_2 tax.
- Of course, in the end about 15–20 percent of value added or production would probably be left over where emissions trading cannot be introduced. In this case, a targeted sector-specific CO_2 tax as a method of pricing CO_2 emissions makes sense.
- If Germany or the EU is to set an international example, then a broad emissions trading system would be an important signal for many other countries, especially India and Japan.

From the EU's point of view, it would be obvious to advocate for an emissions trading system or coupled, that is, internationally integrated, certificates trading systems within the framework of trade negotiations and agreements and vis-à-vis major trading partners. Japan, which only has a certificate trading system covering Tokyo and Saitama prefectures, should be asked to expand its emissions trading system—at the latest when the EU countries expand their ETS. The integration of EU-Japan trading systems would, in a next step, be mutually beneficial. The (marginal) costs of emission reduction will then probably fall for both sides, and further integration with other countries with emission certificate trading systems would, of course, also make sense.

There is, by the way, a paradoxical reason as to why fleet caps for emission values could be useful in the transformation to climate neutrality:

- Such a limit or cap creates pressure to transition to a critically high proportion of hybrid and electric vehicles—up to affecting a changed, pro e-mobility lobby position of large car companies. If the large automobile manufacturers in Germany and France no longer take a stand against electric mobility, but rather come out clearly in favor of e-mobility, then this should make it easier for politicians to direct the system toward much more climate protection.
- Since there are economies of scale of a static and dynamic nature in automotive engineering—also in the case of electric cars—there will be a kind of self-acceleration of electric car expansion after a certain period of high shares of electric cars in the total number of automobiles produced. Significantly cheaper and more environmentally friendly batteries are likely to be part of the expansion of electric vehicles. One can now also build batteries with less rare metals and minerals than before.

In China, the US, Japan and the Republic of Korea, similar arguments can be formulated with a view to the automotive industry, whereby the US has at least one important innovative automotive company in the form of the pioneering company Tesla. It is remarkable that Tesla boss Elon Musk voluntarily discloses his patents in the field of electric mobility so that electric cars can assert themselves worldwide much more quickly. The innovation dynamics that market economies offer to a large extent under certain conditions can be a key to sustainability and climate change policy.

As already mentioned, the present study offers an added value, since it considers the temporary increase in income inequality while measures aimed at reducing this increase in income inequality are also proposed. Moreover, options for global reforestation will be discussed as well as possibilities for geoengineering to cool the Earth's atmosphere. Finally, aspects relating to the modernization of international organizations in the direction of climate protection are also considered here; see, for example, the example of the EBRD, which is based in London and which is responsible for post-Socialist countries in particular in the area of international public financing.

Bibliography

Agrawal, D. R., & Fox, W. F. (2017). Taxes in an e-commerce Generation. *International Tax and Public Finance, 24*(5), 903–926. https://doi.org/10.1007/s10797-016-9422-3

Akimoto, K., Tehrani, B., Sano, F., Oda, J., Kainuma, M., Masui, T., & Oshiro, K. (2015). *MILES (Modelling and Informing Low Emissions Strategies) Project—Japan Policy Paper: A Joint Analysis of Japan's INDC.* Research Institute of Innovative Technology for the Earth (RITE) and National Institute for Environmental Studies. Retrieved September 1, 2019, from https://www-iam.nies.go.jp/aim/publications/report/2015/miles_japan.pdf.

Antholis, W. C. (2009, July 18). *India and Climate Change.* Op-ed for the Brookings Institution. Retrieved September 6, 2021, from https://www.brookings.edu/opinions/india-and-climate-change/

Arimura, T. (2018). *The Potential of Carbon Market Linkage Between Japan and China, Carbon Market Cooperation in Northeast Asia.* Asia Society Policy Institute.

Aswathy, V. N., Boucher, O., Quaas, M., Neimeier, U., Muri, H., Mülmenstädt, J., & Quaas, J. (2015). Climate Extremes in Multi-model Simulations of Stratospheric Aerosol and Marine Cloud Brightening Climate Engineering. *Atmospheric Chemistry and Physics, 15,* 9593–9610. https://doi.org/10.5194/acp-15-9593-2015

Bastin, J. F., Finegold, Y., Garcia, C., Mollicone, D., Rezende, M., Routh, D., Zohner, C. M., & Crowther, T. W. (2019). The Global Tree Restoration

Potential. *Science,* *365*(6448), 76–79. https://doi.org/10.1126/science.aax0848

BCG/Prognos. (2018, January). *Klimapfade für Deutschland [Climate Paths for Germany]*. Study for the Federation of German Industries. Retrieved September 6, 2019, from https://www.prognos.com/uploads/tx_atwpubdb/20180118_BDI_Studie_Klimapfade_fuer_Deutschland_01.pdf

Bell, A., Chetty, R., Javarel, X., Petkova, N., & Van Reenan, J. (2019). Do Tax Cuts Produce More Einsteins? The Impacts of Financial Incentives Versus Exposure to Innovation on the Supply of Inventors, Joseph A. Schumpeter Lecture 2017. *Journal of the European Economic Association, 17*(3), 651–677. https://doi.org/10.1093/jeea/jvz013

Borenstein, S., Bushnell, J., Wolak, F., & Zaragoza-Watkins, M. (2019). Expecting the Unexpected: Emissions Uncertainty and Environmental Market Design. *American Economic Review, 109*(11), 3953–3977. https://doi.org/10.1257/aer.20161218

Bovenberg, L. A., & Goulder, L. H. (2001). Neutralizing the Adverse Industry Impacts of CO_2 Abatement Policies: What Does It Cost? In C. Carraro & G. E. Metcalf (Eds.), *Behavioral and Distributional Effects of Environmental Policy* (pp. 45–85). University of Chicago Press.

Bretschger, L. (2019). *Malthus in the Light of Climate Change* (CER-ETH – Center of Economic Research at ETH Zurich Working Paper 19/320).

Burmeister, J., & Peterson, S. (2017). *National Climate Policies in Times of the European Union Emission Trading System (EU ETS)* (Kiel Working Paper No. 2052, Institute for World Economics).

Burtraw, D., & Palmer, K. L. (2008). Compensation Rules for Climate Policy in the Electricity Sector. *Journal of Policy Analysis and Management, 27*(4), 819–847. https://doi.org/10.1002/pam.20378

Bushnell, J. B., Chong, H., & Mansur, E. T. (2013). Profiting from Regulation: Evidence from the European Carbon Market. *American Economic Journal: Economic Policy, 5*, 78–106. https://doi.org/10.1257/pol.5.4.78

Coady D. et al. (2015). *How Large Are Global Energy Subsidies?* (IMF Working Paper). International Monetary Fund: Washington, DC.

Coady, D. et al. (2019). *Global Fossil Fuel Subsidies Remain Large: An Update Based on Country-Level Estimates* (IMF Working Paper). International Monetary Fund: Washington, DC.

Cogan, J. F., Taylor, J. B., Wieland, V., & Wolters, M. H. (2013). Fiscal Consolidation Strategy. *Journal of Economic Dynamics and Control, 37*(2), 404–421. https://doi.org/10.1016/j.jedc.2012.10.004

Committee on Climate Change. (2019). *Reducing UK Emissions – 2019 Progress Report to Parliament*. London. Retrieved September 2, 2019, from https://www.theccc.org.uk/publication/reducing-uk-emissions-2019-progress-report-to-parliament/

CPB/PBL. (2016). *Valuation of CO_2 Emissions in CBA: Implications of the Scenario Study Welfare, Prosperity and the Human Environment, Netherlands Bureau of Economic Policy Analysis (CPB) and Netherlands Environmental Assessment Agency (PBL)*. The Hague.

Dachs, B. (2017). *Techno-Globalization as the Engine of the Catching-Up Process in the Austrian Innovation System* (EIIW Discussion Paper No. 222). https://uni-w.de/n3s70

Dachs, B. (2019). Techno-Globalisierung als Motor des Aufholprozesses in österreichischen Innovationssystem [transl. PJJW: Technoglobalization as a Driver of Catching-Up in the Austrian Innovation System]. In P. J. J. Welfens (Ed.), *EU-Strukturwandel, Leitmärkte und Technoglobalisierung*. De Gruyter.

Dachs, B., & Budde, B. (2019). Fallstudie Nachhaltiges Bauen und Lead Markets in Österreich. In Welfens, P. J. J. (Ed.), *EU-Strukturwandel, Leitmärkte und Techno-Globalisierung* [transl. PJJW: A Case Study in Sustainable Building and Lead Markets in Austria. In Welfens, P.J.J. (Ed.), *EU Structural Change, Lead Markets and Technoglobalisation*]. De Gruyter.

Daly, H. (2019, March 19). Growthism: Its Ecological, Economic and Ethical Limits. *Real-World Economic Review* (87), 9–22. http://www.paecon.net/PAEReview/issue87/Daly87.pdf

Dasgupta, S., Laplante, B., Wang, H., & Wheeler, D. (2002). Confronting the Environmental Kuznets Curve. *The Journal of Economic Perspectives, 16*(1), 147–116. https://doi.org/10.1257/0895330027157

De Bruyn, S., Schep, E., & Cherif, S. (2016). *Calculation of Additional Profits of Sectors and Firms from the EU ETS*. Report 7.H44, CE DELFT – Committed to the Environment, Delft.

De Haas, R., & Popov, A. (2019). *Finance and Carbon Emissions* (ECB Working Paper Series, No. 2318). European Central Bank: Frankfurt am Main https://www.ecb.europa.eu/pub/pdf/scpwps/ecb.wp2318~44719344e8.en.pdf

Dechezleprêtre, A., Glachant, M., Haščič, I., Johnstone, N., & Ménière, Y. (2011). Invention and Transfer of Climate Change-Mitigation Technologies: A Global Analysis. *Review of Environmental Economics and Policy, 5*(1), 109–130. https://doi.org/10.1093/reep/req023

Den Butter, F. A. G., & Verbruggen, H. (1994). Measuring the Trade-Off between Economic Growth and a Clean Environment. *Environmental and Resource Economics, 4*(2), 187–208. https://doi.org/10.1007/BF00692203

Drews, S., Antal, M., & Van Den Bergh, J. C. J. M. (2018). Challenges in Assessing Public Opinion on Economic Growth Versus Environment: Considering European and US Data. *Ecological Economics, 146*, 265–272. https://doi.org/10.1016/j.ecolecon.2017.11.006

Du, H. (2017). *Mapping Carbon Emissions Embodied in Inter-Regional Trade of China*. Presentation at the EIIW in Wuppertal at 8th of November 2017.

Dunlap, R. E., & York, R. (2008). The Globalization of Environmental Concern and the Limits of the Postmaterialist Values Explanation: Evidence from Four Multinational Surveys. *The Sociological Quarterly, 49*(3), 529–563. https://doi.org/10.1111/j.1533-8525.2008.00127.x

EBRD. (2017). *Sustainability Report*. European Bank for Reconstruction and Development.

ECOPLAN/SIGMAPLAN. (2007). *Auswirkungen der Klimaänderung auf die Schweizer Volkswirtschaft (nationale Einflüsse)*.[transl. PJJW: Effects of Climate Change on the Swiss Economy (National Influences)]. Commissioned by the Swiss Federal Offices of the Environment (FOEN/BAFU) and Energy (SFOE/BFE). http://webarchiv.ethz.ch/vwl/down/v-schubert/oekonomie1/Artikel/Ecoplan2007.pdf

Erdem, D. (2015). *Foreign Direct Investments, Innovation Dynamics and Energy Efficiency*. Verlag Dr. Kovač.

ETH Zurich/Crowther Lab. (2019, July 4). *How Trees Could Save the Climate*. Press release. Retrieved September 6, 2021, from https://ethz.ch/en/news-and-events/eth-news/news/2019/07/how-trees-could-save-the-climate.html

EUROSTAT. (2021). *Greenhouse Gas Emission Statistics – Emission Inventories*. Retrieved March 15, 2021, from https://ec.europa.eu/eurostat/statistics-explained/index.php/Greenhouse_gas_emission_statistics

Fankhauser, S., Gennaioli, C., & Collins, M. (2015). The Political Economy of Passing Climate Change Legislation: Evidence from a Survey. *Global Environmental Change, 35*, 52–61. https://doi.org/10.1016/j.gloenvcha.2015.08.008

Fankhauser, S., Gennaioli, C., & Collins, M. (2016). Do International Factors Influence the Passage of Climate Change Legislation? *Climate Policy, 16*(3), 318–331. https://doi.org/10.1080/14693062.2014.1000814

Federal Environment Agency. (2018). *Konsum 4.0: Wie Digitalisierung den Konsum verändert* [transl. PJJW: Consumption 4.0: How Digitalization Is Changing Consumption]. Federal Environment Agency. https://www.umweltbundesamt.de/sites/default/files/medien/1410/publikationen/fach-broschuere_konsum_4.0_barrierefrei_190322.pdf

Federal Government of Germany (2007, June 7). *Breakthrough on Climate Protection*. G8 Summit Heiligendamm. Retrieved September 6, 2021, from http://www.g-8.de/Content/EN/Artikel/__g8-summit/2007-06-07-g8-klimaschutz__en.html

Federal Ministry for the Environment, Nature Conservation and Nuclear Safety. (2018). *Klimaschutz in Zahlen – Fakten, Trends und Impulse deutscherKlimapolitik* [Climate Protection in Numbers – Facts, Trends and Impulses of German Climate Policy], Issue 2018, Federal Ministry for the Environment, Nature Conservation and Nuclear Safety: Berlin. https://www.bmu.de/fileadmin/Daten_BMU/Pools/Broschueren/klimaschutz_in_zahlen_2018_bf.pdf

Federal Ministry for the Environment, Nature Conservation and Nuclear Safety. (2019). *G20 – The Group of Twenty*. Retrieved 6 September, 2019, from https://www.bmu.de/en/topics/europe-international-sustainability-digitalisation/international-environmental-policy/g7-and-g20/g20/

Federal Office for the Environment. (2018). *Switzerland's Climate Policy – Implementation of the Paris Convention*. Environment Information 2018, Federal Office for the Environment, Swiss Confederation, FOEN.

Federal Office for the Environment. (2020). *Emissionen von Treibhausgasen nach revidiertem CO2-Gesetz und Kyoto-Protokoll, 2.Verpflichtungsperiode (2013–2020)* [tranls. PJJW: *Emissions of Greenhouse Gases According to the Revised CO2-Law and Kyoto Protocol, 2. Implementation Period (2013–2020)*]. Federal Office for the Environment, Swiss Confederation, FOEN.

Flauger, J., & Stratmann, K. (2011, March 24). Die wahren Kosten der Kernkraft [tranls. PJJW: The True Costs of Nuclear Power]. *Handelsblatt* (p. 1). Handelsblatt Media Group: Düsseldorf.

Fouarge, D., Schils, T., & De Grip, A. (2013). Why Do Low-Educated Workers Invest Less in Further Training? *Applied Economics, 45*(18), 2587–2601.

Franzen, A., & Vogl, D. (2013). Acquiescence and the Willingness to Pay for Environmental Protection: A Comparison of the ISSP, WVS, and EVS. *Social Science Quarterly, 94*(3), 637–659. https://doi.org/10.1111/j.1540-6237.2012.00903.x

Fridays for Future. (2019, August 5–9). *Summer Meeting in Lausanne Europe (SMiLE)*. Retrieved 6 September, 2019, from https://smileforfuture.eu/

German Advisory Council on Global Change. (2019). *Towards Our Common Digital Future*. WBGU: Berlin. Retrieved September 6, 2021, from https://issuu.com/wbgu/docs/wbgu_hg2019_en?fr=sM2QyYzU1OTI4OA

German Advisory Council on the Environment. (2019). *Demokratisch regieren in ökologischen Grenzen – Zur Legitimation von Umweltpolitik* [transl. PJJW: Democratic Government Within Environmental Limits – On the Legitimation of Environmental Policy]. Special Report June 2019, Berlin.

German Council of Economic Experts. (2016, November). *Time for Reforms*. Annual Report 2016/17, Berlin https://www.sachverstaendigenrat-wirtschaft.de/en/publications/annual-reports/previous-annual-reports/annual-report-201617.html

German Council of Economic Experts. (2019). *Setting Out for a New Climate Policy*. Special Report, July 2019: Berlin. Retrieved 1 September, 2019, from https://www.sachverstaendigenrat-wirtschaft.de/fileadmin/dateiablage/gutachten/sg2019/sg_2019_en.pdf

German Environment Agency. (2013, August). *Schätzung der Umweltkosten in den Bereichen Energie und Verkehr – Empfehlungen des Umweltbundesamtes* [transl. PJJW: An Estimation of the Environmental Costs in the Areas of Energy and Transport, Recommendations of the Germany Environment Agency]. Retrieved 6 September, 2019, from https://www.umweltbundesamt.de/sites/default/files/medien/378/publikationen/hgp_umweltkosten_0.pdf

Glachant, M., Dechezlepêtre, A., Fankhauser, S., Stoever, J., & Touboul, S. (2020). *Invention and Global Diffusion of Technologies for Climate Change Adaptation: A Patent Analysis*. The World Bank. https://openknowledge.worldbank.org/handle/10986/33883

Goolsbee, A. (2000). In a World Without Borders: The Impact of Taxes on Internet Commerce. *Quarterly Journal of Economics, 115*(2), 561–576. https://www.jstor.org/stable/2587003

Goulder, L. H., & Hafstead, M. A. C. (2013). *Tax Reform and Environmental Policy: Options for Recycling Revenue from a Tax on Carbon dioxide* (Discussion Paper RFF DP 13-31). Resources for the Future: Washington, DC.

Goulder, L. H., Hafstead, M. A. C., & Dworsky, M. (2010). Impacts of alternative Emissions Allowance Allocation Methods Under a Federal Cap-and-trade Program. *Journal of Environmental Economics and Management, 60*(3), 161–181. https://doi.org/10.1016/j.jeem.2010.06.002

Grossman, G. M., & Krueger, A. B. (1995). Economic Growth and the Environment. *Quarterly Journal of Economics, 110*, 353–377. https://doi.org/10.2307/2118443

Häring, N. (2019, April 28). Experten-Kommission hält Klimarettung aus der Portokasse für möglich [transl. PJJW: Expert Commission Considers Climate Rescue from Petty Cash Possible], *Handelsblatt Online Edition*. Retrieved 17 July, 2019, from https://www.handelsblatt.com/politik/deutschland/umweltpolitik-experten-kommission-haelt-klimarettung-aus-der-portokasse-fuer-moeglich/24260878.html?ticket=ST-10234801-U7otBXQIoXKfZMeEqHWN-ap3

Hebbink, G., et al. (2018). *The price of transition: An analysis of the economic implications of carbon taxing* (DNB Occasional Studies 1608). Netherlands Central Bank, Research Department.

Hennicke, P., & Welfens, P. J. J. (2012). *Energiewende nach Fukushima: Deutscher Sonderweg oder weltweites Vorbild?* [transl. PJJW: Energy Turnaround after Fukushima: A Special Path for Germany or a Worldwide Role Model?]. oekom Verlag.

Hsu, A., & Weinfurter, A. (2018, September 24). All Climate Politics Is Local. *Foreign Affairs*. Online Edition https://www.foreignaffairs.com/articles/united-states/2018-09-24/all-climate-politics-local

I4CE/ENERDATA. (2015, November). *Exploring the EU ETS Beyond 2020*. COPEC Research Program: The Coordination of EU Policies on Energy and CO2 with the EU ETS by 2030, A First Assessment of the EU Commission's Proposal for Phase IV of the EU ETS (2021–2030). Institute for Climate Economics/Enerdata.

ICAP. (2018). *Emissions Trading Worldwide: Status Report 2018*. International Carbon Action Partnership. https://icapcarbonaction.com/en/?option=com_attach&task=download&id=547

ICAP. (2021). *Emissions Trading Worldwide: Status Report 2021*. International Carbon Action Partnership.

IMF. (2019, May). *Fiscal Policies for Paris Climate Strategies – From Principle to Practice* (IMF Policy Paper). International Monetary Fund: Washington, DC. https://www.imf.org/~/media/Files/Publications/PP/2019/PPEA 2019010.ashx

Inglehart, R. (1971). The Silent Revolution in Europe: Intergenerational Change in Post-industrial Societies. *American Political Science Review, 65*, 991–1017. https://doi.org/10.2307/1953494

Inglehart, R. (1997). *Modernization and Postmodernization: Cultural, Economic and Political Change in 43 Societies*. Princeton University Press.

IPCC. (2021). In V. Masson-Delmotte, P. Zhai, A. Pirani, S. L. Connors, C. Péan, S. Berger, N. Caud, Y. Chen, L. Goldfarb, M. I. Gomis, M. Huang, K. Leitzell, E. Lonnoy, J. B. R. Matthews, T. K. Maycock, T. Waterfield, O. Yelekçi, R. Yu, & B. Zhou (Eds.), *Climate Change 2021: The Physical Science Basis, Contribution of Working Group I to the Sixth Assessment Report of the Intergovernmental Panel on Climate Change*. Cambridge University Press. In Print (Approved version dated 7 August 2021) https://www.ipcc.ch/report/ar6/wg1/downloads/report/IPCC_AR6_WGI_Full_Report.pdf

IRENA. (2021). *Renewable Capacity Statistics 2021*. International Renewable Energy Agency, IRENA.

Jakob, M., Flachsland, C., Steckel, J. C., & Urpelainen, J. (2020). Actors, Objectives, Context: A Framework of the Political Economy of Energy and Climate Policy Applied to India, Indonesia, and Vietnam. *Energy Research & Social Science, 70*. https://doi.org/10.1016/j.erss.2020.101775

Jaumotte, F., Lall, S., & Papageorgiou, C. (2008). *Rising Income Inequality: Technology, or Trade and Financial Globalization* (IMF Working Paper WP/08/185). International Monetary Fund: Washington, DC.

Jones, R., & Basu, S. (2002). Taxation of Electronic Commerce: A Developing Problem. *International Review of Law, Computers & Technology, 16*(1), 35–51. https://doi.org/10.1080/13600860220136093

Jorgenson, D. W., & Wilcoxen, P. J. (1993). Reducing US Carbon Emissions: An Econometric General Equilibrium Assessment. *Resource and Energy Economics, 15*(1), 7–25. https://doi.org/10.1016/0928-7655(93)90016-N

Jungmittag, A. (2017). *Techno-Globalization* (EIIW Discussion Paper No. 221). https://uni-w.de/0wdse

Kade, C. (2008, August 31). Merkel Backs Climate Deal Based on Population. *Reuters.com*. Retrieved September 6, 2021, from https://www.reuters.com/article/uk-japan-germany-kyoto-idUKT26940120070831

Kearney, I. (2018, September 13). *The Macroeconomic Effects of a Carbon Tax in the Netherlands*. Retrieved 31 August, 2019, from https://www.dnb.nl/media/ac2prbq0/appendix3-macroeconomic-scenarios.pdf

Keohane, R., & Victor, D. (2010, January). *The Regime Complex for Climate Change*. The Harvard Project on International Climate Agreements, Harvard Kennedy School (Discussion Paper 10-33). Retrieved September 6, 2019, from https://www.belfercenter.org/sites/default/files/legacy/files/Keohane_Victor_Final_2.pdf

Kim, E. S. (2014). Imagining Future Korean Carbon Markets: Coproduction of Carbon Markets, Product Markets and the Government. *Journal of Environmental Policy & Planning, 16*, 459–477. https://doi.org/10.1080/1523908X.2013.865510

Kohlstadt, M. (2019, August 12). Grüne fordern mehr Tempo bei Ausbau der E-Bus-Flotte in NRW [transl. PJJW: Greens demand a faster expansion of the E-Bus fleet in NRW], *Westdeutsche Allgemeine Zeitung*. WAZ Online Edition. Retrieved 29 March, 2021, from https://www.waz.de/politik/landespolitik/gruene-fordern-mehr-tempo-bei-ausbau-der-e-bus-flotte-in-nrw-id226746875.html

Korus, A. (2019). Erneuerbare Energien und Leitmärkte in der EU und Deutschland [transl. PJJW: Renewable Energies and Lead Markets in the EU and Germany]. In Welfens, P.J.J. (Ed.), *EU-Strukturwandel, Leitmärkte und Techno-Globalisierung* [transl. PJJW: EUStructural Change, Lead Markets and Technoglobalisation]. De Gruyter.

Kozluk, T., & Zipperer, V. (2014). Environmental Policies and Productivity Growth – A Critical Review of Empirical Findings. *OECD Journal: Economic Studies, 1*, 155–185. https://doi.org/10.1787/eco_studies-2014-5jz2drqml75j

Latif, M. (2007). *Bringen wir das Klima aus dem Takt? Hintergründe und Prognosen*. [transl. PJJW: Are We Destabilizing the Climate? Background and Prognoses]. Forum for Responsibility. Fischer Taschenbuch

LBBW. (2019). Chancen und Risiken der CO2-Regulatorik für Industrieunternehmen [transl. PJJW: Opportunities and Risks of CO_2 Regulation for Industrial Companies], Landesbankfür Baden-Württemberg (LBBW), Stuttgart. https://www.lbbw.de/konzern/medien-center/pressein-fos/2019/20190730_lbbw_blickpunkt_chancen_und_risiken_der_co2-regulatorik_fuer_industrieunternehmen_9ugstcqtp_m.pdf. Last accessed 15 Aug 2019.

Lenton, T. M., & Vaughan, N. E. (2009). The Radiative Forcing Potential of Different Climate Geoengineering Options. *Atmospheric Chemistry and Physics Discussions, 9*, 2559–2608.

Lesch, H., & Zaun, H. (2008). *Die kürzeste Geschichte allen Lebens* [transl. PJJW: The Shortest History of Life]. Piper: Munich.

Liedtke, C., & Welfens, M. J. (2008). *Mut zur Nachhaltigkeit. Von Wissen zum Handeln, Didaktische Module* [transl. PJJW: The Courage for Sustainability. From Knowledge to Action, Didactic Modules]. Wuppertal Institute Forum for Responsibility, WI, ASKO-EUROPA Foundation.

Menges, R., & Untiedt, G. (2016). *Ökostromförderung in Schleswig-Holstein: Empirische Analyse der regionalen Verteilungswirkungen der EEG-Zahlungsströme* [transl. PJJW: Green Power Promotion in Schleswig-Holstein: An Empirical Analysis of the Regional Distribution Effects of EEG Cash Flows], Study on Behalf of KSH-Gesellschaft für Energie- und Klimaschutz Schleswig-Holstein GmbH, Kiel, GEFRA.

Moore, F., & Diaz, D. B. (2015). Temperature Impacts on Economic Growth Warrant Stringent Mitigation Policy. *Nature Climate Change, 5,* 127–131. https://www.nature.com/articles/nclimate2481

NITI Aayog. (2015). *Report on India's Renewable Energy Roadmap 2030*, Toward Accelerated Renewable Electricity Deployment, National Institute for Transforming India (NITI Aayog), Government of India, New Delhi.

Nordhaus, W. D. (2017). Revisiting the Social Cost of Carbon. *PNAS February 14, 114*(7), 1518–1523. https://doi.org/10.1073/pnas.1609244114

Oates, W. E., & Portney, P. R. (2003). Chapter 8: The Political Economy of Environmental Policy. In K. G. Mäler & J. R. Vincent (Eds.), *Handbook of Environmental Economics – Environmental Degradation and Institutional Responses* (Vol. Vol. 1, pp. 325–354). North-Holland. https://www.sciencedirect.com/science/article/pii/S1574009903010131?via%3Dihub

OECD. (2017, October). *OECD Economic Survey: United Kingdom.* Retrieved 15 October, 2021, from https://www.oecd-ilibrary.org/docserver/eco_surveys-gbr-2017-en.pdf?expires=1635959459&id=id&accname=ocid177160&checksum=0C3FFFC40D106393388A2D2CE7D01B66

OECD. (2018). *Effective Carbon Rates 2018, Pricing Carbon Emissions Through Taxes and Emissions Trading.* Organisation for Economic Cooperation and Development.

Olivier, J. G. J., & Peters, J. A. H. W. (2018). *Trends in Global CO2 and Total Greenhouse Gas Emissions: 2018 Report.* PBL Netherlands Environmental Assessment Agency.

Parra, P. Y., Hare, B., Fuentes Hutfilter, U., & Roming, N. (2019, July). *Evaluating the Significance of Australia's Global Fossil Fuel Carbon Footprint.* Report Prepared by Climate Analytics for the Australian Conservation Foundation (ACF).

Parry, I., Shang, B., Wingender, P., Vernon, N., & Narasimhan, T. (2016). *Climate Mitigation in China: Which Policies Are Most Effective?* (IMF Working Paper WP/16/148). International Monetary Fund: Washington, DC.

Pennekamp, J. (2019, June 27). Regierungsberater: Mehr Macht für das Umweltministerium, Veto-Recht für Umweltministerium und Generationenrat [transl. PJJW: Government Advisor: More Power for the Environment Ministry,

Veto Right for Environment Ministry and Generation Council]. *Frankfurter Allgemeine Zeitung*, FAZ Online Edition https://www.faz.net/aktuell/wirtschaft/regierungsberater-mehr-macht-fuer-das-umweltministerium-16257225.html

Peters, G. P., Minx, J. C., Weber, C. L., & Edenhofer, O. (2011). Growth in Emission Transfers Via International Trade from 1990 to 2008. *Proceedings of the National Academy of the Sciences of the United States of America, 108*(21), 8903–8908. https://doi.org/10.1073/pnas.1006388108

Pittel, K., & Henning, H.M. (2019, July 12). Klimapolitik: Energiewende erfolgreich steuern, Was uns die Energiewende wirklich kosten wird [transl. PJJW: Climate Policy: Successfully Managing the Energy System Transformation, What the Energy System Transformation Will Really Cost Us]. *Frankfurter Allgemeine Zeitung*, FAZ Online Edition. Retrieved July 22, 2019, from https://www.faz.net/aktuell/wirtschaft/klimapolitik-energiewende-erfolgreich-steuern-16280130.html

Probst, B., Touboul, S., Glachant, M., & Dechezleprêtre, A (2021). Global Trends in the Innovation and Diffusion of Climate Change Mitigation Technologies. *Review: Nature Portfolio, Research Square*. https://doi.org/10.21203/rs.3.rs-266803/v1.

Qi, T., & Weng, Y. (2016). Economic Impacts of An International Carbon Market in Achieving the INDC Targets. *Energy, 109*, 886–893. https://doi.org/10.1016/j.energy.2016.05.081

Rehse, D., Riordan, R., Rottke, N., & Zietz, J. (2019). The Effects of Uncertainty on Market Liquidity: Evidence from Hurricane Sandy. *Journal of Financial Economics, 134*(2), 318–332. https://doi.org/10.1016/j.jfineco.2019.04.006

Research Services of the Bundestag. (2018a, May). Maßnahmen zur Minderung von Emissionen in der Schifffahrt – Alternative Kraftstoffe und Antriebe, Sachstand [transl. PJJW: Measures to Reduce Emissions from Shipping, Alternative Fuels and Propulsion Systems, State of Play], German Bundestag, WD 8-3000-032/18.

Research Services of the Bundestag. (2018b, April). *Die CO2-Abgabe in der Schweiz, Frankreich und Großbritannien Mögliche Modelle einer CO2-Abgabe für Deutschland* [transl. PJJW: The CO_2 Tax in Switzerland, France and the UK, Possible Models of a CO2 Tax for Germany]. German Bundestag, WD 8-3000-027/18.

Roeger, W., & Welfens, P.J.J. (2021). *Foreign Direct Investment and Innovations: Transmission Dynamics of Persistent Demand and Technology Shocks in a Macro Model* (EIIW Discussion Paper No. 300). https://uni-w.de/g9xs2

Royal Society. (2009, September). *Geoengineering the Climate – Science, Governance and Uncertainty*. The Royal Society, RS Policy Document 10/09, London.

Sachs, J. (2015). *The Age of Sustainable Development*. Columbia University Press.

Sauga, M. (2019, July 20). *Unheilige Allianz* [transl. PJJW: An Unholy Alliance]. *DER SPIEGEL*, No. 30.

Smale, R., Hartley, M., Hepburn, C., Ward, J., & Grubb, M. (2006). The Impact of CO_2 Emissions Trading on Firm Profits and Market Prices. *Climate Policy*, 6, 31–48. https://doi.org/10.1080/14693062.2006.9685587

Spash, C. L., & Smith, T. (2019, March 19). Of Ecosystems and Economies: Re-connecting Economics with Reality. *Real-World Economics Review* (87), 212–229. http://www.paecon.net/PAEReview/issue87/SpashSmith87.pdf.

Stern, N. (2006, October). *The Stern Review on the Economics of Climate Change*, Commissioned by Her Majesty's Government of the United Kingdom.

Takeda, S., Arimura, T., & Sugino, M. (2015, March). *Labor Market Distortions and Welfare-Decreasing International Emissions Trading* (WINPEC Working Paper Series No. E1422). www.waseda.jp/fpse/winpec/assets/uploads/2015/06/No.E1422Takeda_Arimura_Sugino.pdf

The Economist. (2018, August 2). India Shows How Hard It Is to Move Beyond Fossil Fuels – A Renewable-Energy Revolution Is Neither Imminent Nor Pain-free. *The Economist* online edition https://www.economist.com/briefing/2018/08/02/india-shows-how-hard-it-is-to-move-beyond-fossil-fuels

Tietenberg, T. (2010). Cap-and-Trade: The Evolution of an Economic Idea. *Agricultural and Resource Economics Review*, 39(3), 359–367. https://doi.org/10.22004/ag.econ.95836

Transport & Environment and Trade Justice Network. (2017, November). *Can Trade and Investment Policy Support Ambitious Climate Action?* https://www.transportenvironment.org/sites/te/files/publications/2017_11_trade_and_climate_report_final.pdf

Udalov, V. (2019). *Behavioural Economics of Climate Change – New Empirical Perspectives*. SpringerBriefs in Climate Studies.

Udalov, V., Perret, J. K., & Vasseur, V. (2017). Environmental Motivations behind Individual's Energy Efficiency Investments and Daily Energy Saving Behaviour: Evidence from Germany, the Netherlands and Belgium. *International Economics and Economic Policy*, 14(3), 481–499. https://doi.org/10.1007/s10368-017-0381-7

Udalov, V., & Welfens, P. J. J. (2021). Digital and Competing Information Sources: Impact on Environmental Concern und Prospects for Cooperation. *International Economics and Economic Policy*, 18, 631–660. https://doi.org/10.1007/s10368-021-00503-8

UNEP. (2018, November). *Emissions Gap Report 2018, United Nations Environment Programme*. United Nations Environment Programme, Nairobi. https://www.unenvironment.org/resources/emissions-gap-report-2018

UNEP and Climate and Clean Air Coalition. (2021). *Global Methane Assessment: Benefits and Costs of Mitigating Methane Emissions*. United Nations Environment Programme.

Vorländer, H. (2019). *Demokratie* (3rd ed.). Munich.
Walz, R. (2015). Green Industrial Policy. In Mazzucato, M., Cimoli, M., Dosi, G., Stiglitz, J., Landesmann, M., Pianta, M., Walz, R. & Page, T. (Forum), Which Industrial Policy Does Europe Need? *Intereconomics, 50*(3), 120–155. https://doi.org/10.1007/s10272-015-0535-1
Wegener Center. (2017, October). *Das Treibhausgas-Budget für Österreich* [transl. PJJW: The Greenhouse Gas Budget for Austria]. University of Graz.
Weimann, J. (2019). Der Ausstieg aus der Kohle: alternativlos oder verantwortungslos? [transl. PJJW: The Exit from Coal: No Alternative or Irresponsible?]. *Perspektiven der Wirtschaftspolitik., 20*(1), 14–22. https://www.degruyter.com/downloadpdf/j/pwp.2019.20.issue-1/pwp-2019-0011/pwp-2019-0011.pdf
Welfens, P. J. J. (2011, March 24). Atomstrom ist extrem teuer [transl. PJJW: Nuclear Power Is Extremely Expensive]. *Handelsblatt* (p. 38).
Welfens, P. J. J. (2019). *The Global Trump – Structural US Populism and Economic Conflicts with Europe and Asia*. Palgrave Macmillan.
Welfens, P. J. J. (2020a). Macroeconomic and health care aspects of the coronavirus epidemic: EU, US and global perspectives. *International Economics and Economic Policy, 17*, 295–362. https://doi.org/10.1007/s10368-020-00465-3
Welfens, P. J. J. (2020b). *Corona Weltrezession – Epidemiedruck und globale Erneuerungs-Perspektiven* [transl. PJJW: Corona World Recession – Pandemic Pressure and Perspectives for Renewal]. Springer.
Welfens, P. J. J. (2020c). Trump's Trade Policy, BREXIT, Corona Dynamics, EU Crisis and Declining Multilateralism. *International Economics and Economic Policy, 17*, 563–634. https://doi.org/10.1007/s10368-020-00479-x
Welfens, P. J. J., & Bahlmann, J. (2021). *Environmental Policy Stringency and Foreign Direct Investment: New Insights from a Gravity Model Approach. EIIW Discussion Paper No., 294*. https://uni-w.de/4y04u
Welfens, P. J. J., Bleischwitz, R., & Geng, Y. (2017). Resource efficiency, circular economy and sustainability dynamics in China and OECD countries. *International Economics and Economic Policy, 14*(3), 377–382. https://doi.org/10.1007/s10368-017-0388-0
Welfens, P. J. J., & Celebi, K. (2020). *CO2 Allowance Price Dynamics and Stock Markets in EU Countries: Empirical Findings and Global CO2-Perspectives* (EIIW Discussion Paper No. 267). https://uni-w.de/ndf2l
Welfens, P. J. J., & Debes, C. (2018). *Global Sustainability 2017: Results of the EIIW-vita Sustainability Indicator* (EIIW Discussion Paper No. 231). https://uni-w.de/0o0hg
Welfens, P. J. J., & Lutz, C. (2012). Green ICT dynamics: key issues and findings for Germany. *Mineral Economics, 24*(2), 155–163. https://doi.org/10.1007/s13563-012-0017-x

Welfens, P. J. J., Perret, J. K., Yushkova, E., & Irawan, T. (2015). *Towards Global Sustainability: Issues, New Indicators and Economic Policy.* Springer.

Welfens, P. J. J., Yu, N., Hanrahan, D., & Geng, Y. (2017). The ETS in China and Europe: dynamics, policy options and global sustainability perspectives. *International Economics and Economic Policy, 14*(3), 517–535. https://doi.org/10.1007/s10368-017-0392-4

Welfens, P. J. J., Yu, N., Hanrahan, D., Schmülling, B., & Fechtner, H. (2018). *Electrical Bus Mobility in the EU and China: Technological, Ecological and Economic Policy Perspectives* (EIIW Discussion Paper No. 255). https://uni-w.de/0nfih

White House. (2021a, January 27). *FACT SHEET: President Biden Takes Executive Actions to Tackle the Climate Crisis at Home and Abroad, Create Jobs, and Restore Scientific Integrity Across Federal Government.* White House Briefing Room, Statements and Releases. Retrieved 26 April, 2021, from https://www.whitehouse.gov/briefing-room/statements-releases/2021/01/27/fact-sheet-president-biden-takes-executive-actions-to-tackle-the-climate-crisis-at-home-and-abroad-create-jobs-and-restore-scientific-integrity-across-federal-government/

White House. (2021b, April 22). *FACT SHEET: President Biden Sets 2030 Greenhouse Gas Pollution Reduction Target Aimed at Creating Good-Paying Union Jobs and Securing U.S. Leadership on Clean Energy Technologies.* White House Briefing Room, Statements and Releases. Retrieved April 26, 2021, from https://www.whitehouse.gov/briefing-room/statements-releases/2021/04/22/fact-sheet-president-biden-sets-2030-greenhouse-gas_emission_statistics-digitalisation/international-environmental-policy/g7-and-g20/g20/_and_climate_report_final.pdf-pollution-reduction-target-aimed-at-creating-good-paying-union-jobs-and-securing-u-s-leadership-on-clean-energy-technologies/

World Bank. (2019, April). *World Bank Climate Change Overview.* Updated April 2019, Retrieved 15 September, 2019, from https://www.worldbank.org/en/topic/climatechange/overview

WTO. (1999). *Trade and Environment, Special Studies 4.* World Trade Organization. https://www.wto.org/english/tratop_e/envir_e/environment.pdf

WTO/UNEP. (2019). *Making Trade Work for the Environment, Prosperity and Resilience.* World Trade Organization.

Index[1]

A

Afforestation, 128, 137, 183, 263, 349, 373
Africa, 144, 244, 298, 398
African Development Bank, 244
Agriculture, 35, 72, 78, 96, 115, 151, 158, 175, 202, 209, 271, 379, 392, 401, 408, 431
Albedo effect, 152, 183
Algeria, 224, 225
Amazon, 155, 203, 330, 353
Antarctica, 77, 80, 89, 153, 169
Arctic, 77, 80, 144, 152, 153, 169
Argentina, 108, 140, 203, 227, 230, 283, 306, 307, 390
ASEAN, 51, 62, 220, 242, 243, 308, 387, 420
Asia, vii, 31, 38, 47, 49, 51, 58, 62, 63, 85, 118–120, 138, 144, 145, 150, 162, 175, 179, 189, 195, 226, 238, 240, 243, 244, 260, 263, 275, 294, 298, 301, 349, 364, 395–398, 417
Asian Development Bank, 243, 244, 260, 396
Asian Infrastructure Investment Bank, 244, 260
Australasia, 398
Australia, 24, 78, 88, 119, 134, 138, 175, 224, 225, 227, 283, 297, 301, 302, 306, 390
Austria, 37, 59, 83, 146, 187, 211, 217, 274, 281, 296, 383, 411
Authoritarian, 34, 42, 297, 400, 446
Automotive, 63, 119, 202, 365, 368, 374, 462
Azevêdo, Roberto, 19

---

[1] Note: Page numbers followed by 'n' refer to notes.

B

Bank for International Settlements (BIS), 62, 123
Benin, 319
Biden Administration, v, vi, ix, 32, 54, 55, 379, 419
Biden, Joe, v, vi, ix, 32, 33, 54–58, 264, 276, 335, 345, 350, 379, 419
Bloomberg, Michael, 264
Bolsonaro, Jair, 90, 109, 170, 216, 307, 330, 331
Brazil, vi, x, 4, 5, 8, 20, 28, 44, 51, 60, 71, 83, 89, 109, 119, 134, 135, 138, 151, 170, 203, 216, 224, 226, 230, 283, 294, 295, 299, 301, 306, 307, 330, 341, 379, 382, 390, 413, 420
Brexit, v, 32, 35, 39, 53, 90, 144, 173, 177, 308, 344, 349, 385, 396

C

California, vii, ix, 4, 8, 14, 16, 22, 26, 39, 40, 44, 58, 76, 86, 91–95, 97, 99, 101, 102, 106, 107, 116, 117, 123, 128, 130–132, 147, 158, 171, 173, 202, 215, 216, 249–252, 260, 262, 264, 272, 281, 282, 284, 301, 333, 337, 345, 364, 368, 375, 376, 378, 379, 383, 384, 395, 403, 407, 409, 418, 419, 423–431, 437, 461
Cameron, David, 35
Canada, vii, 19, 20, 44, 61, 70, 76, 91, 95, 97, 109, 117, 134, 138, 173, 224–227, 264, 275, 282, 283, 306, 325, 341, 355, 378, 381, 395, 461
Cap-and-trade, 376, 424–426, 430
Carbon Border Adjustment Tax, 58, 59
Carbon leakage, 40, 58, 163, 164, 185
Chavez, Hugo, 156
Chile, 227, 230, 282, 307
China, vi, vii, xi, 4, 5, 8, 14, 17, 19, 22, 24, 26–28, 32, 38, 40, 44, 50, 51, 58, 60, 61, 63, 71–73, 76, 83, 86, 89, 91–95, 97, 99, 106, 108, 117, 119, 120, 123, 129, 134, 138, 140, 147, 150, 151, 158, 164, 168, 170, 171, 174, 176–181, 185, 212, 216, 224–227, 230, 231, 235–237, 242, 243, 251, 258, 260, 262, 281–283, 285, 294, 297, 298, 300, 306, 307, 309, 312, 315–318, 320, 322–326, 328, 333, 337, 345, 355, 359, 363, 366, 368, 375, 380–382, 384, 385, 392, 395, 403–405, 407, 409, 411, 413, 414, 418, 419, 461, 462
Climate
   change, vi, viii, ix, 3, 4, 6, 9, 11–13, 28, 34–36, 47, 49, 52, 56, 57, 59–62, 64, 78, 94, 95, 110, 129, 138, 144, 148, 150, 152, 162, 169, 170, 176, 177, 189, 190, 193, 214, 223, 244, 246, 252, 284, 285, 291, 312, 331, 365, 380, 411, 412, 426, 430, 433, 462
   neutrality, vii, x, 3, 4, 6–10, 14, 16, 19, 20, 22, 28–30, 33, 36, 37, 39, 44–46, 49, 52–54, 60–65, 72–74, 78, 84, 94, 97, 98, 107, 109–111, 118, 123, 149, 202, 247, 259–265, 284, 296, 299–301, 303, 336, 337, 342, 369, 372, 374, 375, 379, 380, 382, 386, 390, 394, 400, 401, 403, 404, 408, 410, 411, 413, 414, 416–418, 461

INDEX 479

policy, v–ix, 3–9, 11, 12, 16, 26, 27, 31, 34, 38, 39, 42, 43, 46, 48–50, 52–54, 59, 60, 65, 72–74, 85, 88, 90, 99, 107, 113, 114, 124, 125, 134, 138, 144–150, 152, 153, 155, 156, 162–165, 171, 181–183, 185–187, 189, 194, 200–204, 207, 214, 215, 233, 240, 243, 250, 252, 261, 263, 272, 273, 284, 286, 292, 294, 301, 309, 311, 312, 342, 343, 345, 346, 350, 364, 372, 374, 375, 380, 394, 401–404, 412, 413, 416, 420, 459, 460

protection, v–x, 4–6, 8–14, 17–21, 26–49, 51–54, 69–71, 73, 74, 76–78, 80, 83–85, 87–90, 94–99, 101, 102, 104, 106, 107, 109–111, 113–118, 124, 128–130, 134, 138, 140, 144–148, 152, 163–166, 170, 175, 176, 179, 181–183, 185, 186, 189, 191–195, 199–204, 207, 212, 214–216, 220, 223, 224, 228, 234, 236–247, 249–252, 254, 259–265, 271, 272, 275, 279, 280, 285, 291–295, 300–303, 305, 307–309, 324, 325, 331, 334–336, 342, 343, 345, 346, 349, 351, 354, 356, 359, 363, 368, 371, 372, 375, 379, 382, 383, 385, 387, 388, 390–395, 397–402, 404, 408, 413, 415–418, 420, 433, 434, 439, 462

protection policy, v, 4, 5, 8, 9, 11–13, 17–20, 26–49, 52–54, 74, 84, 87, 89, 96, 106, 107, 109, 110, 114, 115, 117, 118, 128, 130, 134, 140, 147, 152, 175, 189, 191, 193–195, 220, 236–240, 242, 244, 245, 250, 251, 254, 260, 262, 265, 275, 291, 301, 303, 305, 307, 308, 331, 342, 356, 379, 382, 385, 392, 394, 395, 398–402, 415–417, 439

CO_2, vi–ix, xi, 3, 4, 6–8, 10, 12, 14, 16–26, 28–31, 33, 37–41, 43–49, 52, 53, 58, 59, 61, 69–72, 74–78, 80–99, 101–108, 110, 113–117, 121–124, 128–134, 137, 138, 143–152, 156–158, 162–164, 166–177, 179, 181, 183, 185–187, 191, 193, 199, 201, 202, 205, 207–220, 223–225, 233–235, 237–239, 241–243, 246, 247, 249–252, 254, 257–265, 267–269, 271–275, 279–286, 292, 294, 295, 298–303, 305, 307, 330, 333, 334, 336, 337, 341–346, 354, 355, 359, 372–380, 382–409, 412, 415–420, 423, 425, 427, 433–435, 455–457, 459–461

certificate price, 16, 17, 39, 43, 71, 82, 92, 95, 99, 105, 116, 129–133, 146, 172–175, 200, 210, 212, 218, 249–251, 261, 262, 267, 279, 293, 333, 336, 345, 355, 374, 383, 384, 389, 402–409, 433, 434, 454

certificate trading, 6–8, 12, 16, 17, 39, 47, 74, 78, 85–87, 91, 95, 107, 110, 116, 122–124, 130, 151, 185, 199, 203, 210, 258, 272, 279, 334, 373–376, 378, 379, 395, 396, 404–405, 407, 417, 419

concentration, 21, 80, 87, 171

CO_2 (*cont.*)
  emissions, vii–ix, 3, 4, 7, 8, 10, 16, 17, 20, 22–26, 28–31, 33, 37–40, 43, 52, 61, 69, 71, 72, 77, 78, 80–82, 84–87, 89–94, 96–99, 101, 102, 104–107, 113–115, 121, 128–134, 137, 138, 143, 144, 146–148, 150–152, 156–158, 162–164, 166, 168, 170–172, 174–177, 179, 182, 183, 187, 191, 193, 201, 202, 208, 209, 212, 215–217, 223, 225, 233–235, 237–239, 241, 243, 246, 247, 249, 250, 252, 257, 261–263, 271–274, 280, 281, 292–295, 298, 300, 301, 303, 305, 330, 337, 341, 342, 344, 345, 354, 359, 372, 374–376, 378, 380, 382, 386, 389, 390, 392, 395, 401, 403, 408–410, 412, 415, 417, 418, 434, 460, 461
  reduction, vi, viii, xi, 6, 18, 38, 43, 46, 49, 53, 69, 72, 75, 78, 88, 91, 94, 95, 97, 101, 105, 108, 116, 117, 128–133, 138, 146, 151, 185, 209–211, 218, 239, 251, 253, 261, 263, 264, 273, 286, 300, 345, 374, 378, 382, 383, 389, 392, 394, 403, 409, 415, 416, 418
  tax, vii, ix, 3, 6, 7, 14, 17, 19, 30, 48, 54, 71, 75, 81, 86, 87, 92, 95, 96, 101, 102, 115–117, 124, 128–133, 145, 146, 149, 151, 152, 175, 181, 185, 186, 193, 202, 209–211, 216–220, 239, 241, 242, 247, 257, 258, 272, 275, 279–281, 292, 293, 295, 302, 336, 342–346, 354, 373, 374, 380, 383–398, 403, 406, 407, 418, 419, 459–461

Coal, 18, 19, 36, 37, 41, 43, 46, 75, 81, 88, 91, 99, 103, 104, 106–108, 110, 121, 140, 143, 144, 150, 151, 163, 168, 178, 181, 190, 224, 225, 227, 233, 265, 294, 297, 301–303, 309, 330, 341, 342, 396, 398–400, 409, 419
Collective good, 10, 70, 87, 176, 190, 375
Coronavirus
  pandemic, vi, 35, 39, 46, 60, 115, 148, 277, 346, 417
  recession, 393
  recovery, 33, 378
  shock, vi, 60, 388
Costa Rica, 319, 320

D

Deforestation, 134, 295, 429
Democracy, 11, 34, 36, 42, 47, 303, 391, 394, 395, 397, 400, 446, 447
Denmark, 19, 37, 187, 193, 282, 346, 413
Desertec, 297, 298
Digital, v, vii, 16, 32, 33, 63, 83, 189, 194, 226, 292, 299, 324, 326, 346, 351–353, 388, 391, 396–398, 412
  digitalization, 32, 150, 351, 352, 392

E

Earth, 7, 20, 21, 36, 41, 46, 56, 69, 76, 80, 84, 87, 166–168, 171, 177, 205, 212, 299, 403, 406, 412, 462
EBRD, *see* European Bank for Reconstruction and Development

INDEX 481

Economy, vi, ix, xi, 5, 6, 9, 13, 14, 16–20, 22, 27–29, 33, 34, 36, 39, 42–46, 49, 53, 55, 59, 61, 64, 65, 70, 73, 75, 83, 86, 88, 89, 92, 93, 97, 101, 102, 106, 110, 113, 114, 116, 118, 123, 128, 130, 132, 133, 138, 144, 146, 151, 152, 156, 157, 166, 168–170, 175, 176, 179, 215, 217, 219, 220, 223, 225, 226, 233, 234, 244, 246, 252, 261–264, 268, 294, 298, 299, 303, 305, 307, 309, 312, 314, 341, 342, 345, 346, 351, 352, 365, 368, 372, 378, 380, 381, 385, 387, 390, 391, 396, 402, 405–408, 412, 413, 419, 424, 433

Egypt, 119, 224, 225

Electric cars, 115, 185, 207, 236, 244, 343, 364–368, 462

Electricity, 10, 14, 33, 43, 54, 57, 75, 77, 78, 96, 103, 106, 107, 119, 121, 124, 138, 140, 156, 157, 203, 207, 208, 212, 213, 224–228, 230–234, 246, 247, 253, 263, 267, 272, 274, 275, 281, 294, 297, 298, 346, 351, 359, 362, 364, 366, 368, 390, 398–400, 423, 427, 428

El Niño, 21, 90

Emissions
certificate trading, xi, 3, 8, 12, 14–18, 22, 29, 30, 39–41, 44, 45, 51, 75, 76, 82, 85–88, 91, 92, 94, 97, 99, 101, 105–107, 113, 115, 117, 118, 122, 123, 128–133, 138, 149, 151, 158, 173, 174, 185, 193, 199–203, 212, 216, 217, 239, 241, 249–251, 253, 258, 259, 264, 267, 272, 292, 293, 335, 337, 342, 354–356, 374–376, 378, 382, 384, 385, 390, 391, 395, 396, 403–408, 418–420, 459, 461

Emissions Trading System (ETS), vii–ix, 3, 9, 22, 26, 28, 29, 35, 58–61, 78, 81, 98, 101, 103, 105, 106, 109, 122, 128, 173, 174, 214, 249–254, 260, 265, 268, 282, 325, 333–337, 354–356, 373, 374, 376, 382, 384, 386, 389, 391, 392, 394, 395, 401, 403, 415, 417, 418, 423–424, 426, 459–461

Energy sector, vii, 14, 16, 17, 33, 40, 41, 44, 55, 77, 86, 88, 91, 99, 101, 103, 104, 106, 108, 110, 115, 137, 158, 199, 201, 213, 223, 225, 241, 246, 249, 254, 265, 267, 268, 271, 308, 375, 392, 395, 418, 420, 425

Environmental Protection Agency, 163, 190, 430

Estonia, 346

Ethiopia, 319

ETS, *see* Emissions Trading System

EU27, *see* European Union

Europe, v, vii, 6, 9, 14, 17, 21, 30–33, 38, 41, 45, 48, 49, 51, 53, 60, 61, 63, 81–83, 85, 87, 88, 97, 99, 107, 113, 118, 120, 128, 132, 140, 144–147, 150–153, 155, 161–163, 168, 169, 172, 175, 176, 179, 181, 182, 189, 195, 217, 219, 226, 230, 233, 234, 237, 238, 240, 243, 245, 251, 260, 263–265, 268, 274–276, 279, 281, 286, 291, 294, 298, 300, 301, 303, 312, 325, 329, 331, 343–345, 349, 350, 359, 363–369, 373, 374, 377, 393, 394, 398, 411, 415, 417, 419, 459

482 INDEX

European Bank for Reconstruction and Development (EBRD), 243, 244, 462
European Central Bank, 42, 269
European Commission, vi, 27, 59, 128, 149, 168, 199, 202, 245, 254, 268, 308, 325, 345, 349, 374, 386, 419, 424
European Council, 97, 122, 128, 219, 346, 366
European Economic Area, 59, 85, 220
European Green Deal, 419
European Institute for International Economic Relations (EIIW), xi, 48, 50, 50n1, 90, 311–331, 373
European Investment Bank, 311, 329
European Parliament, 12, 49, 90, 107, 122, 145, 147–150, 182, 199, 239, 342
European Systemic Risk Board, 269, 383
European Union, vi–ix, xi, 4, 7, 8, 12, 14–20, 22, 25, 26, 28–32, 35–41, 43–46, 48–51, 54, 58–64, 72, 75, 76, 78, 81–87, 89–110, 113–118, 120–123, 128–134, 138, 143, 145–147, 149, 151, 156, 158, 163, 165, 168–176, 178, 181, 182, 185, 187, 199–204, 207, 209–212, 214–216, 218–220, 223, 226, 227, 239, 241, 243–247, 249–254, 258–260, 262–265, 267, 268, 274, 275, 279, 281–284, 292, 293, 295, 298–300, 307–309, 311, 323–326, 333–337, 341–346, 349, 350, 354–356, 359, 362–364, 366, 372–379, 381, 383–390, 392, 395–407, 409–414, 417–419, 423–424, 426, 455, 459–461
Eurozone, vi, 42, 92, 116, 199, 220, 252, 281, 293, 329, 330, 334, 346, 378, 388, 412
Extinction, 154, 277

F
Fiji, vi
Financial markets, 7, 8, 15, 19, 20, 62, 74, 95, 103, 110, 122, 123, 200, 201, 251, 252, 269, 305, 330, 336, 355, 356, 385, 391, 403, 407, 413
Finland, 119, 194, 282
Fiscal policy, viii, 21, 345, 388, 412, 413
Flooding, x, 18, 69, 77, 91, 114, 144, 145, 176, 261, 300, 413
Fossil fuels, 14, 17, 19, 37, 69, 70, 81, 121, 143, 144, 152, 156, 171, 181, 208, 211, 212, 223, 292, 303, 308, 341, 371, 399
France, vi, 4, 5, 7, 19, 23, 33, 38, 59, 71, 72, 78, 83, 109, 119, 122, 162, 165, 176, 189, 192–194, 199, 212, 213, 217, 218, 223, 225–227, 231, 243, 258, 259, 280, 282, 283, 296, 301, 306, 315, 323, 329, 330, 334, 337, 344, 347, 378, 381, 383, 406, 413, 462
Fridays for Future, vii, viii, 4, 7, 11, 12, 30, 49, 52, 54, 83, 97, 150, 153, 157, 177, 181–184, 237, 243, 301, 303, 342, 346, 367, 388, 391, 393, 394, 414, 416
Fukushima, 50, 139, 214, 233, 235, 236, 300, 445

G
G7, 48, 60, 70, 296, 301, 305, 335, 346, 378, 420
G20, vi, x, 3–6, 8–10, 14, 16, 17, 19, 20, 26, 27, 29, 30, 37, 39, 44–49, 52, 54, 58–61, 63, 70–74, 78, 85, 86, 88, 89, 92, 97, 99, 108–111, 113, 123, 133, 147,

INDEX 483

149, 156, 158, 168, 174, 187, 195, 203, 207, 219, 230, 242, 258, 260, 264, 274, 283, 295, 296, 299–302, 305–309, 318–319, 326, 335, 337, 341–343, 346, 349, 354, 355, 371, 372, 374, 375, 378, 379, 381, 382, 384, 386, 387, 390, 392, 395, 396, 398–401, 403, 404, 406–408, 410–413, 415–420, 449, 450

G20+, x, 8, 17, 20, 29, 30, 44, 52, 54, 74, 97, 99, 108–110, 113, 123, 203, 355, 382, 386, 387, 392, 403, 407, 408, 410, 412, 413, 415, 416, 449, 450

Gas, 19, 22, 23, 26, 33, 38, 57, 58, 61, 69, 71, 80, 81, 88, 91, 98, 99, 107, 108, 137, 138, 143, 144, 146, 157, 164, 168, 170, 176, 178, 181, 207, 208, 212, 214, 224, 225, 275, 276, 298, 301–303, 324, 330, 364, 368, 379, 387, 423–427

Geoengineering, 19, 45, 117, 118, 128, 183, 242, 462

German Coal Commission, 15, 41–43, 89, 104, 107, 252, 400, 441–443

Germany, v, vi, ix, xi, 4, 5, 9, 15, 17, 19, 21, 23, 28, 30, 34, 35, 38, 39, 41–43, 45, 46, 48, 49, 50n1, 54, 59, 63, 71, 72, 81–83, 87, 88, 93–96, 103, 104, 106, 107, 109, 110, 113, 114, 116–122, 128, 134–140, 143, 145–151, 155, 161, 162, 165, 171, 175, 177, 181, 182, 187, 189, 190, 192–194, 199, 207, 212–215, 217, 219, 223, 224, 226, 227, 231–236, 238–243, 246, 247, 249, 252, 254, 258, 259, 265, 271–274, 277, 279, 281, 283, 284, 286, 292–294, 296, 297, 302, 306, 314, 319, 320, 322, 323, 325, 326, 329, 330, 337, 342–344, 346, 347, 350, 354, 359–369, 371, 372, 378, 380, 381, 383, 385, 388, 390, 393, 399, 400, 406, 411–414, 419, 441, 445, 459–462

Global
 north, 28, 40, 48, 60, 73, 92, 133, 170, 230, 379, 381, 382, 404, 407, 419
 south, 28, 34, 40, 47, 60, 73, 92, 133, 162, 170, 191, 285, 379, 381, 382, 404, 406, 407, 417, 419, 420
 temperature, 21, 82, 169
 warming, v, vi, viii–x, 4, 6, 9, 11–13, 18, 21, 22, 34, 35, 46, 47, 49, 70–73, 76–78, 80, 81, 87, 89, 91, 99, 109, 110, 113, 114, 123, 139, 143–145, 147, 148, 151–153, 156–158, 162, 163, 165, 168–170, 176, 177, 179, 181, 183, 189, 191, 194, 205, 206, 212, 236, 237, 240, 249, 301, 312, 313, 342, 380, 381, 410, 412, 414

Globalization, 27, 34, 47, 59, 150, 192, 234, 238, 243, 285, 307, 324, 392

Gramegna, Pierre, 330

Great Recession, 105, 268

Greece, 165, 312

Green bonds, vi, 311, 329, 330, 372, 413

Greenhouse gas, v, viii, 22–26, 76, 77, 80, 81, 91, 118, 137, 158, 177, 183, 214, 246, 312, 423, 424, 426, 427, 455–457

Greenland, x, 18, 77, 144, 153

Group of Twenty, *see* G20

Growth, viii, ix, 7, 14, 18, 21, 25, 33, 38, 41, 42, 49, 53, 62, 63, 65, 80, 89, 94, 108, 110, 118, 119, 134, 140, 148, 150, 156, 161, 165, 166, 171, 202, 211, 232, 233, 249, 251, 257, 258, 260, 261, 284, 285, 295, 299, 300, 307, 308, 312, 323, 324, 330, 335, 342, 346, 352, 379, 381, 388, 390, 399, 403, 413, 435

H
Hawaii, 21
High income countries, 62

I
Iceland, 220, 282, 319, 423
ICT, *see* Information and Communication Technology
Income, 93, 102, 166, 187, 192–195, 239, 261, 268, 279, 285, 291, 350–352, 355, 378, 412, 413, 419
  dampening, ix, 219, 258, 261
  distribution, 3, 9, 257, 392
  inequality, 9, 28, 84, 191, 238, 239, 242, 392, 396, 462
  loss, 43, 144, 169
  national, viii, 61, 146, 355, 399, 413
  per capita, 60, 64, 82, 88, 132, 147, 179, 191, 262, 285, 296, 306, 352, 386, 404, 406
  real, 132, 145, 150, 176, 203, 219, 234, 257, 279, 355, 405, 417, 418
  tax, ix, 25, 38, 218, 257, 259, 350, 413, 434
  world, 10, 17, 73, 97, 132, 133, 139, 144, 147, 174, 179, 215, 261, 262, 292, 329, 344, 379, 387, 403, 405, 406, 419
India, vi, 4, 5, 8, 17, 19, 24, 26, 28, 38, 44, 51, 58, 60, 61, 63, 71, 73, 80, 88, 89, 93, 94, 104, 108, 119, 133, 138, 147, 151, 168, 212, 224, 226, 227, 235, 258, 262, 283, 297, 298, 306, 309, 318, 326, 375, 379, 382, 384, 390, 392, 395, 396, 398–401, 405, 413, 414, 419, 461
Indonesia, vi, 4, 8, 28, 44, 60, 71, 89, 108, 224, 225, 227, 283, 300, 306, 382, 390, 407, 420
Industrialization, 31, 69, 76, 78, 80, 91, 134, 143, 144, 148, 152, 161, 177, 181, 212, 298, 341, 342, 393
Industry, viii, ix, 8, 9, 16, 35, 40, 41, 63, 64, 75, 91, 96, 101–104, 106, 108, 115, 119, 121, 137, 157, 158, 161, 165, 176, 199, 201, 210, 225, 228, 235, 241, 249, 254, 265, 267, 271, 272, 275, 276, 285, 295, 318, 354, 364, 365, 368, 373–375, 384, 389, 392, 395, 399, 405–409, 418, 425, 426, 428, 462
Inequality, vii, xi, 3, 34, 37, 63, 64, 74, 78, 84, 117, 149, 187, 189, 191–194, 239, 242, 342, 343, 391, 439
Information and Communication Technology (ICT), 63, 124, 192, 324, 353, 414
Infrastructure, 33, 37, 42, 47, 58, 64, 73, 157, 243, 263, 334, 347, 359, 362–364, 366, 372, 388, 407, 411–413
Innovation, vi, viii–x, 3, 4, 6, 7, 9, 15, 19–21, 25–27, 29, 36, 39–41, 47, 48, 50–52, 55, 58, 60–63, 65,

71, 75, 95, 97, 116, 118, 121,
122, 129–131, 138, 145, 149,
152, 156, 165–167, 171, 172,
175, 186, 187, 191, 194, 200,
201, 208, 210, 211, 213, 216,
218, 238, 242, 244, 253, 258,
262, 263, 274, 275, 280, 281,
283, 284, 295, 299–300, 313,
314, 324–326, 333, 334, 341,
344, 345, 349, 350, 365, 374,
376, 378–381, 383–398, 401,
409, 411, 412, 414, 418,
419, 462
  dynamics, 3, 4, 6, 9, 20, 21, 25–27,
29, 36, 41, 48, 50, 62, 63, 95,
117, 122, 130, 156, 165, 166,
191, 211, 218, 258, 263, 313,
324, 325, 341, 349, 350, 385,
389, 394, 409, 411, 418,
419, 462
  green, ix, 22, 27, 186, 187, 194,
201, 211, 281, 349, 380, 381
Intergovernmental Panel on Climate
Change (IPCC), vi, 5, 52, 76, 85,
165, 205, 417
International cooperation, x, 9, 11,
29, 31, 32, 34, 38, 39, 49,
52–54, 65, 70, 72, 74, 110, 121,
149, 152, 170, 174, 190, 215,
216, 220, 238, 263, 296, 300,
303, 308, 333, 346, 349, 386,
387, 394, 395
International Monetary Fund (IMF),
21, 62, 140, 260, 282, 336
International Telecommunications
Union (ITU), 354
Internet, v, 5, 7, 13, 32, 37, 47, 48,
52, 110, 165, 167, 181, 203,
207, 234, 253, 263, 275, 286,
292, 299, 351, 353, 386, 388,
394–396, 398, 411, 415, 416
IPCC, *see* Intergovernmental Panel on
Climate Change

Iran, 216, 224–226
Iraq, 224, 226
Ireland, 194, 195, 219, 282
Italy, vi, 4, 23, 38, 44, 59, 63, 71, 90,
109, 119, 155, 165, 192–194,
213, 226, 258, 259, 281, 283,
306, 323, 346, 361, 378, 381,
406, 413

J

Japan, vi, 4, 5, 8, 10, 14, 19, 22, 23,
33, 38, 40, 44, 61, 63, 74, 76,
89, 91, 93–95, 97, 102, 106,
109, 117, 119, 120, 123, 138,
139, 147, 151, 154, 157, 162,
168, 174, 178, 194, 199, 212,
226, 230, 233, 236, 237, 259,
260, 262, 264, 282, 283, 294,
296, 297, 299, 300, 306–309,
320, 354–356, 362, 371, 372,
378, 381, 385, 395, 396, 406,
411, 414, 419, 445, 461, 462
Johnson, Boris, v, 24, 122

K

Kuwait, 224, 226
Kyoto Agreement, 144, 217, 382

L

Labor
  skilled, 58, 63, 84, 117, 164, 187,
191–195, 219, 237, 238, 242,
343, 344, 396, 412
  unskilled, 84, 117, 164, 187, 192,
193, 239, 242, 259, 343, 345,
396, 412
Latin America, x, 21, 134–137, 155,
175, 227, 240, 301, 398
Latvia, 346
Lindner, Christian, 182

Liquefied natural gas, 297
Low-income countries, 44
Luxembourg, 329, 330

M

Macron, Emmanuel, 231, 280, 301
Maduro, Nicolas, 156
May, Theresa, 53, 122, 272
Mercosur, 62, 203, 220, 243, 295, 307, 308, 387
Merkel, Angela, 148, 265, 365, 400
Methane, 76, 91, 144, 148, 151, 152, 157, 191, 202, 212, 373, 379, 380, 408, 428
Mexico, vi, 4, 8, 28, 29, 109, 119, 216, 224, 226, 282, 283, 306, 328, 329, 390
Mobility, 10, 77, 96, 116, 120, 124, 157, 207, 212, 224, 297, 354, 363, 366–368, 387, 388, 419, 462
   electromobility, v, ix, 78, 119, 179, 207, 236, 281, 343, 364–367, 387, 411, 420, 462
Modi, Narendra, 399
Monetary policy, 412
Multilateralism, 19, 34, 45, 51, 52, 215, 238, 395
Musk, Elon, 349, 368, 420, 462

N

NASA, *see* National Aeronautics and Space Administration
National Aeronautics and Space Administration, x, 34, 79, 152, 153, 230
NATO, 114, 224, 301
Nepal, 319, 320
Netherlands, 18, 24, 37, 38, 59, 83, 114, 119, 194, 203, 219, 225, 231, 257, 259, 296, 330, 343, 344, 346, 361, 366, 372, 381, 406, 409–411, 413
New Zealand, 14, 76, 119, 282, 403
Nigeria, 8, 10, 29, 44, 54, 97, 99, 109, 113, 224, 226, 355, 406
North America, 31, 38, 49, 85, 99, 120, 157, 162, 168, 173, 175, 185, 189, 195, 226, 238, 240, 281, 300, 349, 417, 425
Norway, 20, 133, 194, 220, 224–226, 282, 303, 319, 322, 330, 331, 423
Nuclear
   power, v, 10, 33, 139, 233–236, 243, 400
   power plant, 10, 33, 108, 119, 120, 139, 223, 231, 233, 235, 236, 298, 300, 390, 400, 445

O

Obama administration, 14, 163, 264
Obama, Barack, 14, 162, 163, 171, 264
OECD, *see* Organisation for Economic Co-operation and Development
Oil, 9, 16, 18, 19, 30, 57, 81, 88, 99, 107, 109, 143–145, 156, 157, 164, 168, 176, 178, 181, 206–208, 224–226, 246, 276, 295, 297, 298, 301–303, 330, 402, 405, 423
One Belt One Road Initiative, 177
Ontario, vii, 281, 345, 395, 403, 425, 429
OPEC, *see* Organization of the Petroleum Exporting Countries
Organisation for Economic Co-operation and Development (OECD), v–vii, 3, 25–27, 33, 36, 60, 63, 71, 77, 85, 86, 114, 117, 120, 130, 150, 178, 194, 195, 204, 216, 220, 235, 242, 259,

260, 275, 282, 283, 295, 302, 309, 313, 314, 319–322, 324, 328, 335, 350, 380–382, 389, 390, 392, 394, 395, 404, 405, 407, 411, 413
Organization of the Petroleum Exporting Countries (OPEC), 9, 89, 178, 298, 306
Ozone layer, 84, 89, 379, 417

P

Paraguay, 307, 319, 320
Paris Climate Agreement, vi, 3, 8, 29, 31, 45, 49, 55, 56, 70, 143, 156, 170–171, 190, 208, 215, 217, 237, 264, 301, 309, 312, 325, 386, 387, 417
Passive housing, 274, 275, 411
Patagonia, 227
Permafrost, 157, 212
Poland, 194, 227, 366, 406, 413
Pollution, 25, 27, 55, 57, 58, 75, 101, 131, 151, 172, 173, 277, 352, 430
Popper, Karl, 35, 42
Populism, 32, 34, 39, 387
Portugal, 165, 277, 282, 312
Protectionism, 13, 34, 39, 110, 164, 297, 307, 349

Q

Qatar, 224, 225
Quebec, 95, 102, 260, 281, 325, 345, 395, 403, 425, 461

R

Railway, 88, 354, 359–363, 398, 412
Real estate, 124, 139, 190, 192, 204, 219, 252, 261, 269, 272, 273, 337, 354, 373, 374, 379, 401, 411, 419
Redistribution, vii, 9, 41, 85, 231–233, 250, 268, 396, 403
Reforestation, xi, 45, 134, 148, 299, 462
Refugees, 13, 34, 40, 48, 73, 91, 145, 148, 156, 162, 169, 300
Regional Greenhouse Gas Initiative (RGGI), 22, 425
Regulation, 149, 252, 276, 413, 459
Renewable energies, v, 10, 14, 33, 44, 50, 54, 57, 61, 75, 77, 88, 90, 103–105, 108–111, 118–121, 138, 140, 150, 157, 171, 179, 203, 212, 213, 223, 225, 226, 228, 229, 231–236, 247, 254, 263, 274, 275, 281, 294, 298, 299, 302, 309, 311–313, 322, 341, 351, 359, 362, 364, 368, 390, 399, 410, 420
  bioenergy, 119, 410
  geothermal, 44, 108, 119, 212, 223, 226, 410
  hydropower, 20, 109, 139, 155, 212, 410
  solar, 19, 44, 61, 76, 77, 103, 104, 108, 109, 119, 121, 140, 168, 179, 183, 204, 205, 213, 223, 226, 228, 230, 231, 234, 235, 274, 275, 294, 297–299, 309, 326, 341, 342, 399, 410, 419
  wind, 19, 44, 57, 61, 80, 90, 99, 103, 104, 108–110, 118–121, 139, 140, 150, 153, 213, 223, 224, 226–228, 230–232, 234, 235, 294, 309, 326, 341, 342, 364, 399, 410
Republic of Korea, 8, 14, 44, 61, 76, 97, 106, 109, 117, 119, 123, 130, 158, 168, 199, 216, 251, 259, 260, 264, 268, 296, 297, 300, 337, 395, 396, 403, 406, 407, 409, 411, 424, 461, 462

Republic of the Congo, 319
Research and development (R&D), ix, 22, 26, 27, 65, 88, 122, 167, 193, 211, 324, 334, 380, 381, 394
Rosatom, 400
Russia, vi, 4, 5, 8, 17, 19, 33, 38, 44, 51, 58, 61, 71, 72, 83, 93, 94, 108, 120, 134, 138, 157, 170, 171, 216, 224–227, 230, 231, 262, 283, 295, 297, 305–307, 359, 382, 384, 390, 392, 400, 405, 414

S

Saudi Arabia, 44, 89, 109, 224–226, 283, 298, 306
Schmidt, Helmut, 393
Schumpeter, Joseph, 63, 295, 313, 380
Sea level, x, 18, 21, 69, 145, 154, 162, 169, 410
Slovakia, 194
Slovenia, 346
Social market economy, 46, 50, 54, 63, 341–347
South Africa, vi, 8, 26, 28, 44, 71, 108, 151, 224, 227, 230, 282, 283, 306, 390, 406
South America, 90, 120, 226, 227
Spain, vi, 44, 59, 83, 108, 116, 165, 194, 213, 281, 312, 362, 406, 413
Steel, 75, 86, 121, 191, 267, 341, 375, 406, 423
Stock market, 18, 251, 252, 381
Structural change, viii, 7, 14, 21, 27, 52, 70, 84, 107, 109, 115, 133, 163, 164, 170, 175, 189, 238, 263, 297, 325, 326, 342–344, 413

Subsidies, ix, 10, 17, 26, 37, 58, 69, 70, 88, 101, 103, 104, 109, 139, 156, 213, 214, 233–236, 243, 292, 293, 306, 308, 366, 371, 390, 434
Sustainability, v, vii, xi, 7, 10, 12, 17, 27, 29, 38, 48, 50, 51, 54, 62, 77, 89, 90, 123, 124, 179, 244, 251, 263, 292, 295, 311–313, 319, 320, 323, 324, 326, 329, 330, 347, 349, 353, 354, 411, 413, 416, 462
Sustainable Development Goals, 439, 440
Sweden, ix, 23, 31, 86, 96, 146, 151, 170, 178, 181, 210, 217, 247, 279, 280, 282, 330, 342, 345, 366, 381, 384
Swiss Central Bank, 330
Switzerland, ix, 14, 17, 22, 23, 40, 54, 76, 81–83, 85–87, 146, 151, 152, 170, 178, 187, 193, 217, 220, 234, 259, 272, 280, 282, 296, 342, 345, 346, 354, 360–362, 368, 383, 384, 386, 403

T

Tajikistan, 319
Tesla, 349, 368, 420, 462
Thunberg, Greta, 11, 12, 31, 49, 107, 153, 177, 181, 182, 237, 393
Tourism, 122, 409
Trade, ix, 3, 5–7, 14, 15, 22–27, 31, 39, 40, 43, 47, 51, 59, 61, 65, 94, 99, 102, 110, 114, 115, 122, 131, 145, 149, 155, 157, 163, 164, 171, 173–176, 185, 193, 203, 210, 216, 230, 231, 258–260, 263, 267, 281, 284, 293–297, 299, 307, 308, 325,

335, 336, 343, 344, 355, 356, 372, 375, 381, 382, 385, 387, 390, 395, 399, 408, 418, 419, 427, 442, 461
Transatlantic Banking Crisis, 43, 47, 74, 95, 122, 172, 306, 329
Transport, xi, 11, 35, 36, 46, 115, 120, 122, 124, 137, 145, 155, 157, 158, 167, 175, 177, 185, 203, 209, 210, 212, 214, 233, 240, 244–245, 247, 271, 272, 275, 276, 281, 284, 297, 354, 359–365, 367, 368, 373, 383, 388, 392, 401, 408, 411, 414, 419, 423, 425
Trinidad and Tobago, 319, 326
Trump administration, 17, 34, 54, 163, 190, 312
Trump, Donald, viii–xi, 13, 17, 18, 32, 34, 45, 54, 60, 70, 88, 89, 91, 122, 150, 156, 163, 169, 170, 176, 177, 190, 215, 224, 237, 264, 294, 296, 297, 301, 307, 312, 325, 335, 345, 350, 372, 392, 393
Tunisia, 298, 319
Turkey, 4, 8, 71, 108, 119, 227, 283, 306, 390
Turkmenistan, 224, 225

U

Ukraine, 58, 227, 319
UN, *see* United Nations
United Arab Emirates, 19, 118, 224, 226
United Kingdom, v, vi, 4, 5, 19, 23, 24, 32, 33, 35, 38, 53, 59–62, 71, 72, 83, 90, 109, 119, 121, 122, 144, 145, 152, 161, 162, 165, 172, 177, 182, 193–195, 199, 212, 215, 217–219, 225–227, 231, 243, 252, 253, 264, 272, 282, 283, 291, 301, 306, 308, 315, 323, 344, 349, 350, 378, 381, 385, 396, 399, 406
United Nations (UN), vi, viii, xi, 4, 8, 28–31, 33, 37, 45, 52, 63, 70–72, 74, 76, 80, 84, 85, 133, 143, 144, 155, 167, 168, 171, 176, 190, 205, 217, 293, 300, 302, 309, 312, 325, 349, 379, 393, 417, 439, 440, 445
United States (US), v–ix, xi, 4, 5, 8, 13, 14, 16–20, 22, 23, 27, 32, 33, 38, 40, 44–46, 49, 51–61, 64, 70–73, 83, 86, 88, 89, 91–94, 99, 102, 108, 116, 119, 120, 122, 123, 132–134, 138, 140, 145, 147, 149–152, 156, 157, 161–164, 167–171, 173–176, 179, 187, 190, 192–194, 210, 212, 213, 215, 224–227, 230, 231, 234–238, 243, 245, 250, 252, 257–260, 262–264, 268, 269, 275, 276, 282–284, 294, 297, 300, 301, 305–307, 309, 311, 312, 323, 325, 326, 329, 335, 345, 349, 350, 355, 365, 368, 371, 372, 375, 376, 378, 379, 381, 383, 385, 391–393, 395, 404, 405, 411, 413, 414, 418, 419, 462
Uruguay, 307
US, *see* United States

V

Venezuela, x, 155, 156, 224, 226, 307
Vita Foundation, 50n1
von der Leyen, Ursula, 122, 199, 333, 345, 374
von Hayek, Friedrich, 35

W

Weather, 21, 73, 80, 157, 206
   extreme events, 19, 64, 69, 90, 91, 124, 139, 144, 145, 148, 158, 162, 176, 182, 223, 252, 261, 269, 379, 380, 393, 417, 433, 434

Welfare
   effects, 35, 355, 434
   gain, 355, 407
   loss, 40

West, vii, 32, 35, 43, 47, 60, 89, 170, 179, 297, 299, 301, 302, 331, 346, 378, 387, 395, 398, 399, 420

World Bank, 21, 24, 29, 48, 50, 61, 73, 108, 117, 243–245, 283, 300, 306, 311–313, 329, 380

World Meteorological Organization (WMO), 21, 76

World Trade Organization (WTO), 19, 59, 86, 114, 145, 293, 335, 375

World Values Survey, 89, 284, 351

Printed in the United States
by Baker & Taylor Publisher Services